Sports and Freedom

SPORTS AND HISTORY

Peter Levine and Steven Tischler, General Editors

Sports and Freedom: The Rise of Big-Time College Athletics
Ronald A. Smith

SPORTS AND FREEDOM

The Rise of Big-Time College Athletics

RONALD A. SMITH

NEW YORK   OXFORD
OXFORD UNIVERSITY PRESS

Oxford University Press

Oxford   New York   Toronto
Delhi   Bombay   Calcutta   Madras   Karachi
Petaling Jaya   Singapore   Hong Kong   Tokyo
Nairobi   Dar es Salaam   Cape Town
Melbourne   Auckland

and associated companies in
Berlin   Ibadan

Copyright © 1988 by Ronald A. Smith

First published in 1988 by Oxford University Press, Inc.,
200 Madison Avenue, New York, New York 10016

First issued as an Oxford University Press paperback, 1990

Oxford is a registered trademark of Oxford University Press

Library of Congress Cataloging-in-Publication Data
Smith, Ronald A. (Ronald Austin), 1936–
Sports and freedom.
(Sports and history)
Includes bibliographical references and index.
1. College sports—United States—History.   2. College sports—
England—History.   3. Yale University—Athletics—History.
4. Harvard University—Athletics—History.   I. Title.   II. Series.
GV351.S6   1988   796'.07'1173   88–17855
ISBN 0-19-505314-1
ISBN 0-19-506582-4 (pbk.)

Portions of this book appeared previously in Ronald A. Smith, "Pre-
ludes to the NCAA: Early Failures of Faculty Intercollegiate Athletic
Control," *Research Quarterly* LIV (Dec. 1983) : 372–82. Reprinted
by permission of the American Alliance for Health, Physical Education, Recreation and Dance, 1900 Association Drive, Reston, VA 22091.

The author also thanks the Meckler Corporation for permission to reprint portions of his article "The Rise of College Baseball," which appeared in *Baseball History* I (Spring 1986) : 23–41, and Frank Cass
Publishers for permission to reprint portions of his article, "The Historic Amateur-Professional Dilemma in College Sport," which appeared in *The British Journal of Sports History* II (Dec. 1985) : 221–31.

2 4 6 8 9 7 5 3 1

Printed in the United States of America
on acid-free paper

To two winners:
Daniel and Penelope

PREFACE

GROWING UP ON a dairy farm in southern Wisconsin seems far removed from writing a history of intercollegiate athletics, which began in America with two eastern institutions, Harvard and Yale. Yet, the same dairy farm allowed me to first get good at several sports, honing individual skills which could eventually be incorporated into popular team sports. I could pitch against a concrete milkhouse wall, shoot baskets in a homemade arena on a wooden barn floor, and throw and kick footballs on a large, green lawn. I was fortunate to have had parents who not only valued education but who appreciated athletic skill development. What if, with bat in hand, I was late swinging at an older brother's fastball and drilled a foul ball through a window of the house or missed helping with the milking because I was more interested in attempting to hit fifteen straight free throws?

Shooting a basketball or throwing a baseball did not get me into Northwestern University, but it helped. Northwestern, like Yale and Harvard before it, wanted to excel in a variety of activities, academic and non-academic. Intercollegiate athletics, which have traditionally given greater visibility to educational institutions than any other activity, were important to Northwestern. It was every bit as vital to Northwestern to compete in the highly visible Big Ten Conference as it was to me to compete at an intercollegiate level.

Who can say how much influence intercollegiate athletics had on the development of colleges or universities such as Northwestern University or on the growth of individual academic departments such as a history department? What there can be no doubt about is that nearly every important institution of higher education in

America has at some point in its history emphasized big-time intercollegiate athletics. Many have continued to do so for well over a century. It was first true at Harvard, Yale, and Princeton, who for the first six decades of intercollegiate competition were dominant athletically. Later, institutions which generally are believed to be academic leaders, such as Columbia and Cornell, Chicago and Michigan, California and Stanford, all were at times dominant in phases of big-time intercollegiate athletics.

Well before television and prior to the radio, earlier than the invention of the airplane or the automobile, and before the development of the telephone and the electric light, possibly a million spectators watched an intercollegiate spectacle, a boat race between Harvard and Oxford universities. At the time, 1869, there were professional coaches, rigid training regimens, and eligibility controversies, and there were college faculties who questioned the worth of intercollegiate athletics. Before the NCAA was founded out of the football crisis in 1905, the first concrete stadium in America had been constructed on a college campus, colleges were granting "scholarships" for athletic competence, and part-time athletic coaches were being paid more than full-time professors at some of America's most prestigious institutions of higher learning.

Big-time college athletics are not an anomaly in America despite their apparent contradiction to the higher-education goals of the creation and transmission of knowledge. American colleges were born to a system of local autonomy and freedom to develop unencumbered by national or regional standards. Colleges were not created by either a national church or a national government as occurred in some European countries. American colleges were created by a wide variety of churches, private individuals, and local and state governments. For a century and more after the American Revolution, a multitude of institutions of higher education were created in relative freedom. They were allowed to exist and grow or to wither and die on their own merits. Athletics eventually came to be an important part of the success equation.

As colleges multiplied in the nineteenth century, there was a need for institutional visibility to attract both students and a supportive public. Winning in athletics gave that visibility in a physical form. The physical nature of the individual and of American society appeared to be a desired quality in the age of Darwin. It was also important for the image of America as a world power. Athletic victories gave an image of virility to institutions of higher learning—something evidently needed to garner public and private support in the later years of the nineteenth and into the twentieth century.

This volume has an East Coast flavor. Harvard and Yale more than any other two colleges gave form to intercollegiate athletics. They and other eastern institutions were the first to form intercollegiate teams. Eastern colleges brought forth both commercialized and professionalized athletics. They began the practice of paying professional coaches to turn out winners. They inaugurated the huge, permanent stadiums. The eastern colleges set the standards for each of the sports, including the playing rules. The rest of the nation's colleges inevitably looked eastward for athletic leadership— and continued to do so even after athletics were no longer dominated by eastern schools.

The narrative of this book has been organized both around the four major sports in the first half-century of intercollegiate athletics and around specific topics which influenced all the college sports. Thus, after an overview of the background of intercollegiate athletics, there is a focus upon crew, baseball, football, and track and field development. It is followed by five significant influences on the growth of college sports: changing patterns of institutional athletic control, specifically student and faculty; early failure to bring about inter-institutional control; the impact of the professional coach on big-time athletics; the false concept of amateurism in college athletics; and the need to develop eligibility rules. This is followed by a chapter on the creation of the NCAA after a national controversy erupted over brutality and questionable ethics in football. The book closes with historical insights into two issues of special significance to intercollegiate athletics. The first concerns the question of freedom—freedom of the institution to deal with intercollegiate athletics and the freedom of the individual athlete relative to the institution. The second issue concerns the relationship between the early history of college athletics and the development of college sports through the twentieth century.

Several themes emerge from the narrative. First, the fundamental nature of college sport was revealed in the nineteenth century. From the first contest, intercollegiate sport has been a commercial enterprise, and professionalism followed closely on its heels. The process of rationalizing athletics to create efficiency and victories was well developed before the NCAA was created. In other words the push for excellence and winning had evolved at an extremely early time. The stage for imitating Harvard and Yale was set in the nineteenth century.

A second theme is centered on a powerful American belief in freedom, an ideology which was clearly evident at the time of the American Revolution. Athletics on the American college campus began as an aspect of students freeing themselves from a rigid and staid curriculum and a suffocating college life dictated by the institution's faculty. There was and continued to be a friction between the student's desire for freedom and the faculty's desire for control and authority. The interplay between freedom and authority continued as intercollegiate athletics intensified and became the dominating feature of college life. The tension was never fully resolved, but by the early twentieth century students had essentially lost the freedom to control athletics. Institutional control came to replace student control in the form of faculty athletic committees, governing board mandates, alumni interference, and coach dictates. Freedom was always an issue, and its parameters kept changing. It is a thread which weaves its way through this entire volume.

There is no question that the freedom to participate in intercollegiate athletics has led at times to excesses. Through the years American intercollegiate athletics have been held in contempt for prostituting higher education. They have also been honored in an almost fundamentalist religious fervor. There are those who condemn the present collegiate athletic scene and look to the past as both an athletic Valhalla and a utopia of athletic amateurism when "sports were played for sports' sake." A study of intercollegiate sport will probably show that it has had both a negative and a positive effect and that there was no period in which athletics were free from problems or possessed the virtues sometimes attributed to them. For the cynic as well as the romantic, the advice of England's Lord Chesterfield over two centuries ago might well be heeded: "Speak of Moderns without contempt, and of the Ancients without idolatry; judge them all by their merits; but not by their ages. . . ."[1]

A third theme is that of a continual influence of British sport and especially the colleges of Oxford and Cambridge universities. The nineteenth-century Oxbridge universities were the early model for the Americans. If the rest of America copied Harvard and Yale, the two leading colleges looked across the sea for their inspiration. American colleges were generally about a generation behind Oxford and Cambridge in adopting the various intercollegiate sports.

Harvard and Yale and other colleges accepted British conventions such as written rules and the ideal of amateurism. Because of cultural differences such as less class distinction and a greater emphasis upon freedom of opportunity, the American intercollegiate athletic system differed from that of Oxford and Cambridge. Intercollegiate athletics would not be limited to a few eastern elite colleges, nor would the British system of amateurism be maintained, except in name only. The professional model with a strong commercial base resulted. Those who protested ended up losing the cause and, just as significant, losing contests.

There has been no attempt to deal with two important nineteenth- and twentieth-century questions in sports and in the larger society—the questions of gender and of race. There is no mention of women's intercollegiate athletics, although women in both coeducational and women's colleges were involved in sport, and by the turn of the century women had been introduced to intercollegiate competition. Development of women's intercollegiate athletics deserves a monograph of its own. Black participation in college sports is principally a twentieth-century phenomenon, although the first black all-American football player, William H. Lewis, played at Amherst and Harvard in the early 1890s. The problem of "Jim Crowism" could have been included, but it would be more appropriate to approach it more thoroughly in a second volume on twentieth-century college athletics.

I wish to acknowledge several individuals and a number of institutions for their aid in researching and writing this volume. The Department of Exercise and Sport Science at Penn State University has contributed greatly in allowing me to take two sabbaticals on which I have searched numerous libraries and archival collections. Among the college and university libraries are: Brown, Bucknell, Cambridge, Columbia, Cornell, Dartmouth, Dickinson, Drake, Harvard, Manhattan, North Carolina at Chapel Hill, Oxford, Pennsylvania, Penn State, Princeton, Rutgers, Swarthmore, United States Military Academy at West Point, United States Naval Academy at Annapolis, Wesleyan, William and Mary, Wisconsin, and Yale. Other libraries searched were the British Library of London, Free Library of Philadelphia, Library of Congress, National Collegiate Athletic Association in Mission, Kansas, New York Public Library, Oxford City Library of England, and the State Historical Society of Wisconsin. I want to thank several individuals whose insights or commentary have helped me along the way. Among those are Bruce

Bennett, Jack Berryman, Dick Crepeau, Maureen Devlin, Marvin Eyler, Roger Geiger, Steve Hardy, Jay Helman, Guy Lewis, John Lucas, Randy Roberts, Alan Sack, and David Voigt. Two earlier academic mentors should be mentioned, Gerald Kenyon and Karl Stoedefalke. I was fortunate to have Rachel Toor as editor and Stephanie Sakson-Ford for her critical eye as copy editor. No one has been more helpful than my wife and friend, Susan Fernald Smith.

University Park, Pennsylvania   R.A.S.
February 1988

CONTENTS

CHAPTER I

The English Background
of Early American College Sport   3

CHAPTER II

Sport, the Extracurriculum,
and the Idea of Freedom   13

CHAPTER III

The First Intercollegiate Sport:
Crew and the Commercial Spirit   26

CHAPTER IV

Crew: Internationalism, Expansion,
and the Yale-Harvard Pullout   38

CHAPTER V

The Rise of College Baseball   52

CHAPTER VI

From the Burial of Football
to the Acceptance of Rugby   67

CHAPTER VII

The Americanization of Rugby Football:
Mass Plays, Brutality, and Masculinity   83

CHAPTER VIII

College Track: From the Paper Chase
to Olympic Gold   *99*

CHAPTER IX

Student Control and Faculty Resistance   *118*

CHAPTER X

The Early Failure of Faculty
Inter-Institutional Control   *134*

CHAPTER XI

The Rise of the Professional Coach   *147*

CHAPTER XII

Amateur College Sport: An Untenable Concept
in a Free and Open Society   *165*

CHAPTER XIII

Eligibility Rules in a Laissez-Faire
Collegiate Scene   *175*

CHAPTER XIV

Brutality, Ethics, and the
Creation of the NCAA   *191*

CHAPTER XV

The Swarthmore Case:
An Addendum on Freedom   *209*

EPILOGUE

A Twentieth-Century Meaning
of American College Athletics   *213*

Appendix   219

Notes   221

Index   277

Illustrations follow page 146

Sports and Freedom

I

The English Background of Early American Collegiate Sport

THE SUPERINTENDENT OF the Boston, Concord, and Montreal Railroad, James Elkins, was enjoying the company of Yale College's James Whiton, a junior and member of the Yale Boat Club in 1852. They might well have been discussing whether the underground railroad would be suppressed by the Fugitive Slave Act passed two years before and whether the attempt to prevent blacks in southern states from achieving their freedom northward would be successful. Elkins, though, was likely more interested in the freedom to pursue his own dream—a profitable above-ground line which would increase his passenger traffic as the railway passed from Boston to Montreal through the vacation lands of New Hampshire. The impending north-south confrontation was likely far from the minds of the young man from Yale, who was to become the first recipient of a Ph.D. in America, and the striving magnate in America's dominating nineteenth-century enterprise. While superintendent Elkins thought of the smooth water of the Winnipesaukee River as it entered New Hampshire's largest lake by the same name, he suggested to Yale's Whiton: "If you will get up a regatta on the Lake between Yale and Harvard, I will pay all the bills."[1]

The eight-day, all-expenses-paid trip was consummated with a Harvard victory over Yale in America's first intercollegiate contest.

The commercial venture in college athletics was highly successful for the collegians. The excursion train planned by Elkins didn't reach expectations, yet several hundred or possibly even a thousand spectators were on hand, many of them observing the race from the train. Some even got to see General Franklin Pierce, a native of New Hampshire, as he campaigned as the successful Democratic candidate for the presidency.[2] The serenity of that "perfect summer day, cloudless, moderately warm, with a light zephyr from the northwest," August 3, 1852, was not always repeated in American college sport.[3] The freedom to pursue what appeared to be a pleasurable and innocent pastime sometimes led to rancor as the strong competitive element in American society dominated the commercially stimulated collegiate contests.

Intercollegiate sport, after that first meet, grew up with the emerging industrial America. Colleges and their sports took on many of the features of the larger America and its capitalistic rush for wealth, power, recognition, and influence. In the years between 1852 and the initial meeting of the National Collegiate Athletic Association in 1905, the basis for the highly commercial and professional sports in colleges was established. Huge crowds in enormous stadiums with large gate receipts, highly paid coaches in control of recruited athletes receiving handsome financial rewards, and the media telling the story and promoting the events were all in evidence. There were also those who regretted that Yale and Harvard had given commercialized sport to American colleges and had been the leaders of the most highly visible part of the non-academic aspect of colleges into the twentieth century.

All of that, however, is ahead of the story. Intercollegiate athletics did not just happen when a railroad magnate approached a Yale rower about a meet with Harvard. There was a tradition of sport being played on college campuses for over a century before the first intercollegiate contest. In England, the country upon which America patterned its colleges and its sporting activities, there was a much longer tradition of sport dating back to the period before American colonization. Even in intercollegiate athletics, Oxford and Cambridge predated Harvard and Yale by a quarter-century.

The Oxford-Cambridge Collegiate Connection

England was the first modern sporting nation, and students at its two principal universities followed the pattern. At Oxford, formed in 1167, and Cambridge, founded four decades later, much of the participation in sport reflected the elite nature of the student body. Boating, cricket, horse racing, hunting, and tennis were all participated in during the sixteenth, seventeenth, and eighteenth centuries, as well as bowling on the green, boxing, bull-baiting, cock-fighting, cudgel-playing (fighting with sticks), fishing, fives (handball), football, and swimming.

These sports were not particularly well organized, and they often drew the scorn of university officials. Swimming in the Thames at Oxford or in the River Cam at Cambridge was popular. An injunction forbidding entering any pool or river in the county of Cambridge was issued at Cambridge University in 1571. The enforcement must have been short-lived, for twenty years later a similar prohibition was issued.[4] Over a century later, two students raised a subscription to build a bathing pool outside of Cambridge. When George Byron, the eventual great poet and satirist, entered Trinity College at Cambridge in 1805 as Lord Byron, he enjoyed gambling, boxing, cricket, and swimming. On many mornings, Byron "was to be seen riding on his grey horse . . . wearing a white hat and a silky grey cloak, out of town to bathe."[5] Rank had its privileges.

The privileged set at Cambridge and Oxford played the elite game of tennis before King James I popularized it and before Jamestown was settled in America. In the early 1600s, an Oxford student described an aspect of student life and his place in the University. "The two marks of his seniority," he wrote, are "the bare velvet of his gowne, and his proficiency at tennis, where when he can play a set, he is a Fresh-man no more."[6] Though tennis was somewhat popular, there is strong evidence that hunting and equestrian activities of aristocrats were valued most by the collegians up to the early 1800s.

Hunting was prized among British gentlemen and among their collegiate sons. It was so popular in the 1500s that one college of Oxford found it necessary to ban the keeping of hunting dogs, ferrets, hawks, and hares within the grounds.[7] One student did little, according to his own account, other than fox hunting, stealing deer, hunting hares, going to dancing school, and wenching—never studying.[8] Another student who stole deer from land near Oxford, land owned by the king, was later taken to court and imprisoned.[9] Fox hunting with hounds was possibly the favorite pastime. Even in the early 1800s, when sports such as cricket and boating were becoming highly popular, a Cambridge student wrote that: "The passion for hunting . . . is so high at Cambridge, that no weather, distance, or other convenience, is a stop to its indulgence."[10] An aristocratic student at Oxford asked rhetorically: "How can a young man of rank and fortune spend the day better, when not reading, than following a pack of fox-hounds?"[11] Besides that, he argued, educated clergymen and scholars were often sportsmen themselves and could influence younger men to look "more kindly to their Latin and Greek," the basic educational fare at both Oxford and Cambridge.[12]

Had fox-hunting been conducive to intercollegiate competition, it would likely have been the first because of its great popularity. That honor, however, goes to a team sport of the 1820s, cricket, followed closely by rowing. Cricket had been a favorite in England for over a century.[13] Like most sports participated in by Cambridge and Oxford students, the British boys of the "Great Public Schools," the elite preparatory schools such as Eton, Harrow, Westminster, and Winchester, partook of a variety of sports including cricket. Eton had played Westminster in a cricket match as early as 1788, and Harrow and Eton first competed in the early 1800s.[14] In 1805, Eton and Harrow elevens first competed at the Marylebone Cricket Club, the arbiter of cricket rules since 1787. Young Lord Byron was one of the participants at Marylebone's Lord's Ground only weeks before matriculating at Cambridge University.[15] The desire for inter-institutional matches of the elite public schools eventually reached the two great universities. Charles Wordsworth, a nephew of William Wordsworth, the British poet laureate, attended Oxford following a cricket and rowing career at Harrow. Wordsworth knew a number of university men at Cambridge, where his father headed a college. Like the Eton and Harrow public school boys, Wordsworth arranged an Oxford-Cambridge cricket match at Lord's Ground in London in 1827.[16] Intercollegiate athletics were born.

Two years after the first intercollegiate cricket match, the two institutions rowed the first of their races. Until the early 1800s, rowing at Oxford was generally done by professional watermen. In this two-century-old tradition, an undergraduate or a don (professor) would sit in the stern and enjoy the calm of the Thames River while the watermen provided the power. In 1805, some undergraduates borrowed a six-oared boat and a tradition was born.[17] In a decade, at the time Napoleon met his military end against the English and others at Waterloo, Oxford students began the tradition of bumping races. Various boats would start out at intervals, and if one of the trailing boats would catch the one in front by bumping it, the contest was over. Generally, bets, such as who would pay for the meal and ale at the inn downstream, would lead to rigorous matches.[18] As one satirical Oxford man wrote at that time:

> All shall be there, the Idles and the Sot,
> Those who can row, can steer, can leap, or not;
> The dull when sober, and the brave in drink,
> Those who do all but reason, read, or think;
> Whose brain in wine, as skiffs in water float—
> Gods of the cloth, or heroes of the boat.[19]

By the time students from Oxford's Christ College challenged and lost an eight-oar race for £200 stakes to a hand-picked London crew in 1828,[20] students at most colleges of Cambridge had formed crews. They had their own races similar to those at Oxford. It was natural, then, that Charles Wordsworth of Oxford University, who came from Cambridge and who had initiated the Oxford-Cambridge cricket match two years before, should be the stimulus for the first crew meet. Wordsworth, who previously rowed at Harrow, had discussed the possibility of a race with Charles Merivale of Cambridge.[21] When a challenge arrived from Cambridge, Oxford soon accepted, and a race at Henley was agreed to.

Henley, a small town on the Thames about twenty-three miles east of Oxford on the way to London, hosted the first intercollegiate crew meet in 1829 before a gigantic crowd of some 20,000 spectators. The curious assemblage, ranging from the beautiful and fashionable to the "humbler cottager" and the "vulgar," may have been increased because of the rumor spread by *The Sporting Magazine* that the race would be for £500 a side bet, a significant sum of money.[22] Betting ran high as the Oxford crew of eight wearing black hats and matching handkerchiefs readied its 972-pound, 45-foot boat for the challenge of the Cambridge crew, dressed in white with pink handkerchiefs.[23]

Waiting at the starting line, the Oxford crew members were likely hoping that the four lengthy rows of 46 miles to Henley and back in the two weeks prior to the race would help them in the mid-June contest. The race started at 7:15 p.m. when the two sister universities began their 2¼-mile race against the current. Oxford led early, but going around a curve in the river its boat cut off the Cambridge eight, causing the oars of one boat to lock with the other. The two crews agreed to start again. This time Oxford led the entire distance, beating Cambridge by two lengths in a time of about 14 minutes.[24] The fans went wild cheering the nearby favorites from Oxford. "Never," wrote a London correspondent, "shall I forget the shout that arose among the hills. . . ."[25]

The excitement and business generated in this meet probably stimulated Henley to host an annual regatta for all amateur boatsmen after Oxford and Cambridge moved their annual boat race to London. By the time Cambridge and Oxford established their annual four-mile race on the Thames from Putney to Mortlake in the 1840s, both Yale and Harvard had rowing clubs, the first organized sports clubs in American colleges. The early influence of Oxford and Cambridge was clearly seen in American college sport.

Colonial American Colleges: Sport and the Reaction

Yale and Harvard led American colleges into organized intercollegiate athletics in the mid-nineteenth century, but sport existed in colleges even before the Revolutionary War officially separated the colonies from the British. In 1734, when only three colleges existed in America, students at Harvard were playing at least two popular sports. It may be surprising to some that over a century before Abner Doubleday was supposed to have invented baseball at Cooperstown, New York, in 1839, Harvard freshmen played both baseball and football and were required by custom to provide "the rest of the scholars with bats, balls, and foot-balls." This requirement was one of twenty-two written rules foisted on Harvard freshmen which included upper classmen's demands to remove hats when approaching seniors, to run errands for them, and to never "mingo" against the college walls or go into the fellows' privy.[26] That sport was part of the freshmen's initiation rites and an integral mechanism for hazing and fagging the newcomers will be seen later.

In the South, some similarity to the elite sports in British colleges was seen at the College of William and Mary in Virginia in the mid-1700s. The fact that the colonial college in Williamsburg was staffed principally with Oxford University-trained ministers, rather than a more sporting group of Englishmen, may have resulted in less sporting activity at William and Mary than one might have expected.[27] The planters' sons who attended this sole southern college had a tradition of attending horse races, betting on cock-fights, and hunting numerous wild game including foxes.[28] The fondness of horse racing and betting at the College of William and Mary was so strong and so much at cross purposes with the goals of the institution that college officials banned students from keeping horses, making races, or betting on those made by others. They furthermore ordered that no students should "presume to appear playing or Betting at ye Billiards or other gaming Tables, or be any way concern'd in keeping fighting Cocks under Pain of ye like severe Animadversion or Punishment."[29]

The negative response to sport by eighteenth-century American college authorities, such as William and Mary officials, was stronger than that found at either Oxford or Cambridge. The antipathy to sport appears natural, for most of America's nine pre-revolutionary colleges were products of either the Protestant Reformation or the evangelical religious fervor of the eighteenth-century Great Awakening. "Dreading to leave an illiterate Ministry to the Churches," Harvard was created in 1636, six years after the Puritans arrived in Massachusetts.[30] William and Mary was founded in 1692 to provide Church of England clergymen for the Virginia Crown colony. Yale was formed in 1707 in part to counteract the liberal tendency in religion occurring at Harvard. Of the six remaining pre-revolutionary colleges chartered after 1745, only King's College (Columbia) and the College of Philadelphia (University of Pennsylvania) were non-sectarian. The College of New Jersey (Princeton), Dartmouth, the College of Rhode Island (Brown), and Queen's College (Rutgers) were, in order, Presbyterian, Congregationalist, Baptist, and Dutch Reformed—all founded by ministers with a revivalist impulse from the Great Awakening.[31] Religion was not their entire focus, but it was a primary function, casting a pious cover over the activities of colonial colleges. The sporting undergraduate who partook of a variety of outdoor activities in England, at Cambridge and especially Oxford, was not as apparent in American colleges.

College authorities in addition to those at William and Mary responded to sport on colonial campuses in several ways. Most colleges supported physical activity at times but generally restricted sport. Two decades after Harvard's founding, the 1655 Laws of Harvard College allowed for some free time but commanded that "noe undergraduate upon any pretense of recreation . . . shall be absent from his studyes [for] he shall studiously redeeme his time. . . ."[32] By the early eighteenth century, however, the governing body of Harvard purchased an orchard and assigned it as a "place of recreation & exercise for the scholars."[33] Yet, not long after, Harvard had rules prohibiting hunting, fishing, or skating without permission of Harvard officials.[34] The liberty to recreate did not mean the license to do so at the whim of the student. And that was true at other colonial colleges as well.

The pre-revolutionary Laws of Yale College lend support to the theme that American college officials looked unkindly on various sports. "If any Scholar," the document stated, "shall play at Hand-Ball, or Foot-Ball, or Bowls in the College-yard, or throw any Thing against the College, by which Glass may be endangered . . . he shall be punished six pence."[35] At about the same time, the president of newly opened Dartmouth College cried out against activities which were "puerile, such as playing with balls, bowls, and other ways of diversions."[36] At the College of Philadelphia, the trustees believed that the honor and reputation of the institution was at stake and thus banned a number of activities including gaming and the playing of "ball or use of any kind of diversion within the walls of the building."[37] Not far away, Princeton students were hunting game off campus. On campus they were playing townball, a form of baseball, and handball, as well as field hockey, then called shinny or bandy. Only a few years after the Yorktown defeat of the British, the Princeton faculty banned shinny as "low and unbecoming gentlemen and scholars."[38] Most colleges forbade students to leave the college grounds without permission for recreation or any other diversion. At King's College in New York City, one student was caught swimming or bathing off campus and was punished by being confined to his room, where he was commanded to translate Latin for a week.[39] Cruel and unusual punishments were not uncommon in colonial America.

Despite the dampening effect on sport of religious orthodoxy and the belief that college authorities should act on behalf of students' parents, the rapid growth of colleges gave rise to the competitive spirit among institutions of higher learning. The religiously motivated rivalry and the freedom to pursue different religious and educational aims would eventually lead colleges to use the publicity value of sport to promote growth, both financial and enrollment. The competitive nature was there almost from the beginning. College sport competition for institutional purposes, however, would await a post-Civil War change when attitudes toward sport became more relaxed.

The Collegiate Way and College Sport

Religious fervor restrained the growth of college sport, but some aspects of the nature of college religious and social life created the climate in which college sport could eventually grow. The particular life on the college campus became known as the "collegiate way." English-educated Henry Dunster introduced the Cambridge University classical curriculum to Harvard in 1640, the essence of which lasted for the next two centuries and was repeated by other American colleges. Not only was the structure of educational instruction patterned after the English but the form of collegiate living, the collegiate way, was borrowed from the English. As in England, most American colleges were founded in rural settings, not in urban areas as were the great European medieval universities in Paris, Vienna, Cologne, and Padua. Planting colleges in rural areas, with some notable exceptions such as New York City's King's College and to a lesser extent Williamsburg's William and Mary, had placed colleges outside the supposed seductiveness of unvirtuous cities. The collegiate way would be developed in rustic America.

Once colleges were located in "character-building" pastoral environments, there was a need to provide student housing. Dormitories were built, serving to gather students under one roof where, it was believed, with proper supervision by college authorities, the young men could expand religiously, intellectually, and socially. The communal dining hall, the commons, served the same function. That the dormitories created a milieu for rebellion as well as for higher purposes, and that the commons often produced food riots as well as sustenance, shows that the results of the collegiate way were not always those proposed by college presidents and faculties.[40]

College officials believed that with students rooming and boarding in the college edifice, their paternalistic and religious leadership would help mold the character of the future learned clergy as well as private and public officials. The emphasis upon moral and religious education was a major part of the collegiate way. To college authorities, religious growth was more important than intellectual development. Mandatory chapel as often as fourteen times a week added another dimension to the collegiate residential orientation. If sports could have been shown to have character-building values, as they were generally believed to have in the latter nineteenth century, they would have fit well into that part of American higher education which was non-intellectual, often anti-intellectual. Athletics would eventually be sanctioned by college authorities but not before freedom-loving students organized them as a reaction to the classical curriculum and what they deemed to be the negative aspects of the collegiate way.

II

Sport, the Extracurriculum, and the Idea of Freedom

FOOTBALL WAS PLAYED every fair fall day at Dartmouth College in the mid-1830s. Ex-president S. C. Bartlett recalled his earlier freshman playing days at the New Hampshire institution. He remembered a senior who used "stupendous boots he had made on purpose with soles fully a half inch thick." Bartlett, nearly six decades after the event, could still see the hulking upperclassman as he stood "on the extreme edge of a dense, surging mass of struggles, the foot-ball far out of sight in the centre, but the boots going like a horizontal trip-hammer" in one of those glorious class battles.[1] It appeared at least as important to incapacitate the lowly "frosh" as it was to score the next goal. Though seniors often participated, the annual freshman-sophomore class battle was probably the most bitterly fought contest. The Dartmouth faculty, more interested in piety and the classics, was nevertheless concerned about the confrontation between the lower two classes.[2]

There was a remarkable change in college life between the 1830s, when a faculty was concerned about interclass rivalries, and the 1890s, when an ex-president wrote a history of athletics at Dartmouth. In the middle decades of the nineteenth century the college extracurriculum became highly developed at Dartmouth and elsewhere, and sport came to dominate the extracurriculum while challenging the curriculum for importance on the college campus. In that time, an American ideology based upon the rhetoric of the

13

American Revolution played a role in this transformation of college life.

College Paternalism and Collegiate Rebellions

For a country conceived in "liberty and the pursuit of happiness," the American college was extremely slow in changing its attitude of strict paternalism. The practice of granting college officials parental authority ("in loco parentis") over young men was rich in the possibilities for rebellion. Not only did college authorities take the "in loco parentis" authority seriously, they actuated a control much harsher than most parental discipline.[3] Colleges in the early nineteenth century were still dominated by the clergy, who more often believed in the depravity of man than in the goodness of mankind.

It is likely that the overriding sacred values of the college faculties came into conflict with the strong post-revolutionary secular values of some students. Faculties prohibited numerous activities, including drinking, smoking, dancing, card playing, vain or idle sports, and absences from campus without permission. They demanded regular chapel attendance, often twice daily at about 6 a.m. and 5 p.m. In addition, there were regular room checks and compulsory study hours. An inflexible curriculum at many colleges emphasizing Greek and Latin recitation likely bored some students beyond endurance.[4] Faculties met regularly in an attempt to enforce the myriad of rules and regulations found in the College Laws. They kept busy doling out penalties which included fines, private and public admonitions, suspensions, rustications (suspensions to be served under specific individuals or locations), being dropped a grade in school, and finally expulsions.[5] One logical result was campus rebellions.

At no time in American history were campus riots more common than in the period following the Revolutionary War until the mid-nineteenth century.[6] Nearly every college history records the defiant acts of students as they rejected the overbearing paternalism. It appears that students made sport, certainly games, in a rejection of their highly restricted lives. They would harass tutors, who often lived in the dormitories, by placing animals in their desks, depositing "sulphuretted hydrogen" in their rooms, or rolling red-hot cannonballs through their doors. Students might provoke professors by stamping their feet in recitation rooms, lighting fire to a professor's rug, or setting off gunpowder in the classroom.

College presidents were sometimes taunted while crossing the campus, had their beer, wine, or brandy stolen, or found rocks and sticks thrown through their residence windows. Disturbances in compulsory chapel were probably the most common—throwing hymnals, carving graffiti in the pews, releasing turkeys in the chapel prior to prayers, making animal noises during the prayer, or even cutting a Bible open and inserting a deck of cards.[7]

More serious crimes such as stabbing a tutor, stoning the president, or burning down the college occurred with enough regularity to lead one to consider why a select group of students, less than 1 percent of the available young men in America,[8] would attempt to destroy both the college and the authorities. Was it, as a number of college religious leaders believed, because man was naturally depraved? If so, stricter rules, more effectively enforced, might have been the answer. Or was it due to the young people's desire to be free and independent, without being externally controlled in most actions? If the latter was the case, and evidence points in this direction, greater concern for students' rights and responsibilities could possibly have led to more positive results.

College authorities, though, continued their attitudes of "in loco parentis" through the end of the eighteenth century and even increased their repressive paternalism in the early years of the nineteenth century.[9] College students, nevertheless, began to form their own activities to meet the vacuum created by a sterile curriculum and inadequate social, intellectual, aesthetic, and physical life. The college extracurriculum was born out of student necessity, or as one Amherst college man said, the customs of the students "have served to vary the monotony, and relieve the dryness of college duties."[10]

The Extracurriculum Fills a Void

The status quo curricular and religious policies of most college officials were challenged when students created their own college institutions. The extracurriculum began, not surprisingly, in the domain of intellect more than in social and physical concerns, which eventually came to dominate. Literary societies, sometimes called debating clubs, were formed at Yale, Princeton, and Harvard shortly before the Revolutionary War. They were probably an outgrowth of the intellectual ferment of the European Enlightenment combined with the political awakening in the American college.

The societies, generally two competing groups in each college, spread westward to nearly all colleges.[11] The contrast of a freer and more open debate of a literary society to the sterile intellectual exercise of memorized recitations in the classroom can well be imagined. Questions were raised by these societies in the first half of the nineteenth century that would not have been approached in the classroom: Ought the study of modern languages be substituted for the ancient? Are the abilities of the sexes equal? Can liberty exist without laws? Is the science of geology reconcilable with the first two chapters of Genesis? Would socialism improve the conditions of mankind? Debate topics ranged from slavery and prohibition of alcohol to duelling and the value of Sir Walter Scott's Waverly novels. As the societies purchased books on topics as varied as current fiction and modern science, their libraries grew to challenge and often surpass the college library in both quantity and usefulness.[12]

There was never 100 percent backing of the literary societies by college authorities, but there was certainly more faculty support for the debating clubs than there was later for either fraternities or athletics clubs.[13] Princeton and Dartmouth serve as examples in the 1820s. The Princeton faculty attempted to dictate when the literary societies could meet, recommending to the trustees that holding meetings during study hours should be prohibited.[14] The Dartmouth faculty feared that the multiplication of literary societies was "dividing the attention and consuming the time of students."[15] Yet, literary societies prospered well before athletics were organized on college campuses, giving students a model for the creation of other aspects of the extracurriculum.

By the 1830s and '40s, literary societies began to lose some of the extracurricular impact as smaller organizations, fraternities, began to take their place, especially in eastern colleges.[16] Fraternities, which began with the Phi Beta Kappa society at William and Mary in 1776, were basically social rather than literary. The "pursuit of happiness" of a small campus community coincided well with the national charge of Thomas Jefferson in that same year. It may not have been coincidental that the writer of the Declaration of Independence was a graduate of William and Mary. It is not surprising that college students, who looked favorably upon American freedom, sought a liberating influence in their own lives.[17] While Phi Beta Kappa became an academic honorary fraternity by 1840, a myriad of national and local social fraternities soon came into existence.

There were mixed feelings about the value of fraternities. College authorities saw some advantages in them: they did help to house students and free institutional resources for other purposes while liberating faculties from some of their supervisory duties. Yet there was the fear that fraternities, most of which were secret organizations, might lead to conspiracies against authority.[18] To the students Greek-letter societies filled a social vacuum that had been created by monotonous recitation periods sandwiched between twice-a-day prayers at chapel. College officials had done too little to reform college life and the curriculum, so students had fashioned their own collegiate reform. College was becoming a social experience shaped by the students rather than by the curriculum or the faculty. And the extracurriculum kept expanding.

Students contributed to collegiate regeneration in other ways in the early to mid-nineteenth century.[19] With the beginning of student government, the principles of republican government resulting from national independence were acted out in some colleges after the Revolution. The influence of student governance within the "in loco parentis" college confines was not, however, effective or permanent. Political clubs were started at a variety of schools, but political movements in American colleges lacked the strong revolutionary element found in European universities. Students had greater success in journalistic endeavors, as literary magazines, generally monthly publications, began to appear. Being elected editor of a school magazine was nearly as prestigious as being the class orator. Musical societies also appeared in the extracurriculum in the postrevolutionary era, in the form of choirs, orchestras, and bands. The large number of social, intellectual, political, and aesthetic associations on college campuses does not mean that the religious concerns of the colonial college were completely forgotten. Religious groups, such as missionary societies, praying circles, and gatherings dedicated to improving morals, were found on most campuses and were highly active. Interest groups dedicated to saving souls were part of the extracurriculum. Others were more intent on doing something for the body.

Classes, Class Battles, and the Sporting Spirit

Extracurricular activities were often organized, as was the curriculum, around the class as the primary unit. Students began together as the freshman class, remained intact the next four years through commencement, and were recognized by their class for a lifetime. College classes were small, intimate groups from the time of the Revolution until well after the Civil War. There was only about one college graduate for every 1,000 population at the time of the Revolution. In the peak colonial enrollment year of 1775, only 152 students graduated from the nine colonial colleges, and there were a meager 3,000 living alumni in all the original states.[20] Even as late as 1850, the average number of students in a specific class of nineteen New England colleges was less than forty students, and it was much lower in the Midwest and the South. Harvard class size at mid-century was about 150; Yale was somewhat smaller.[21] The tightly knit class in the early years of the extracurriculum was most apparent in sport, where class battles became significant occasions.

Before sport-oriented class battles became common, following the Revolutionary War, a tradition of upperclassmen's persecution of the lowly freshmen was developed. Taking the lead of European universities, American college students both hazed and fagged freshmen. Harvard had created the custom of fagging freshmen from an early time. Fagging, or personal servitude which was often humiliating, included doing errands for upperclassmen such as heating water for tea, carrying in wood for the fire, or removing ashes. Fagging in the eighteenth century was institutionalized as the faculty included some of the fagging customs in the "Freshmen Laws."[22] Hazing of freshmen was similar, but rather than making a servant out of the freshman, it consisted of an entire class, usually the sophomores, tyrannizing the freshman class or individuals in it. Included among hundreds of affronts to individual dignity, sophomores would throw a blanket over a frosh's head and blow tobacco smoke under it until he became sick; replace bedding sheets with burrs and sticks; hold a college novice under cold water for long periods of time; cut off the freshman's hair and brand the body with indelible ink; gag and bind a lowly frosh and place him in a cemetery; or place salt and water—or molasses—on the freshmen's seats.[23] The hazing of freshmen at chapel was not only an affront to those who favored the religious life of a college, but confrontations at chapel may have led to what became known as rushes, class battles, and eventually sport rushes.

Students daily sat according to class at chapel and left the same way at the close of prayers. The desire to leave chapel quickly following services sometimes led to the freshmen being crowded or rushed from the rear. The sophomores might attempt to run over the freshmen once out of the building, and this rush could easily lead to a fight. Decades later, the chapel rush was still popular among colleges, "a sort of safety-valve, when all the ill-feeling between classes is let off in a harmless way."[24] Whether the term "rushes," which became synonymous with class battles, came from chapel confrontations is not known, but it is clear from colonial times through the nineteenth century that rushes became popular and formalized in sport.

The sophomore-freshman hazing in sport became institutionalized in the early fall "rush." Annually, on the first Monday of the fall term in the late 1700s, Harvard sophomores would challenge individuals of the freshman class to wrestling matches. If the sophomores should by some chance be defeated by being thrown down, then the juniors would challenge. If the juniors lost, then the seniors would take on the freshmen. "It was a kind of initiatory process for newcomers," a member of the Harvard class of 1805 stated.[25] The tradition of rushes or class battles, though not necessarily wrestling, was found on most nineteenth-century college campuses.

The cane rush, however, was similar to the wrestling battles. A common practice of upperclassmen was to carry canes on campus and to disallow freshmen to do so. Freshmen would, nevertheless, challenge the custom by sporting a cane or canes. This meant an immediate challenge, and often a cane rush would result. The object, of course, was for the sophomores to wrestle the canes away from the upstarts and then to destroy the wooded symbols of power. If the freshmen remained in possession of the majority of canes, they won the right to carry canes for the remainder of the year.[26] By the latter half of the century, cane rushes were institutionalized with rules, and some were even sanctioned by college officials. Controlled fights, it seemed, were superior to those illegal and uncontrolled class battles of an earlier period.[27] Whether wrestling individuals or grappling over canes, the scenes must have looked similar. Another form of freshman-sophomore conflict, though, gained increasing attention on a number of campuses—the football rush.

The Popularity of the Football Rush

The football rush was the principal ritualized freshman-sophomore war well before football became the dominant intercollegiate sport by the 1890s. The nature of early football lent itself effectively to the desire for hazing and class fights. Football, a soccer-type game, provided the sophomores an opportunity not only to win a game but to beat or kick the freshmen into submission. The annual game between the youngest two classes may have first been played at Harvard in the early 1800s, and it was contested on the first Monday of the fall term. "Bloody Monday is the traditional time to haze freshmen" said a nineteenth-century Harvard man, "because there is always a faculty meeting—no protection for the frosh."[28] A freshman in the 1820s described the mêlée as "a furious contest with those enemies, the Sophs, at kicking and shins."[29] Playing on the famous pie-shaped field at Harvard, the Sophomores, who enjoyed listening to the "low murmurings of some annihilated Frosh upon the Delta," invariably won the game.[30] This was logical according to John L. Sibley, longtime librarian, who had been at Harvard since 1821 and had seen many Bloody Mondays.

> The Sophomores of course know each other & consequently know who are the Freshmen. The Freshmen of course know but few of their classmates & cannot well distinguish them from the Sophomores. The different classes come together, the ball is thrown down among them & the object of each class is to kick the other & bark their shins as much as possible.[31]

One can imagine the scene of 50 or 100 young men opposing each other flailing away at shins (hacking) or at the ball, which was generally an animal bladder encased in leather or a leather bag filled with leaves or rags. "The great annual battle between the Sophs and the Fresh came off at the beginning of the term," a Harvard sophomore wrote at mid-century. "We 'licked' them 'all hollow,' of course. The Freshman class," he said, "have to furnish balls, and it costs them about $30 a year."[32]

The importance of the football battles to the students should not be underestimated. A class poem in the 1840s shows something of the significance.

> The Delta can tell of the deeds we've done,
> The fierce fought fields we've lost and won

> The shins we've cracked
> And noses we've whacked,
> The eyes we've blacked, and all in fun.[33]

A decade later, a Harvard sophomore caught the animated scene upon the Delta:

> The parties rushed from this side to that, now battling desperately contend for every foot, I might add with every foot, then as the ball flew yards over the heads to one side or the other running at full speed to gain it first, it gives one an idea of a real battle with its charges, retreating and desperate rallies.[34]

Once the contest was won, the sophomores might join hands and form a double column, and rush across the Delta knocking over all who did not flee. With a sophomore victory, the hazing of the Bloody Monday rush was complete, and the new school year could begin.[35]

This type of activity was repeated at other colleges. Often it was a freshman-sophomore battle such as that which occurred at Yale after an 1850s sophomore challenge to freshmen:

> Come!
> And, like sacrifices in their trim,
> To the fire-eyed maid of smoky war,
> All hot and bleeding will we offer you.[36]

But at other times the juniors would join the freshmen in a contest against the seniors and sophomores. Still others would just gather together and divide up in somewhat equal sides during late afternoons in the fall.[37] At Dartmouth, a freshman reported that some of his classmates had "the insolent audacity to kick the Seniors" when they battled at football. That was far different than two generations before when college rules prohibited "puerile [diversions] such as playing with balls."[38]

College Sport as Community Ritual

Rushes continued as ritualistic encounters well into the 1900s, more than a half-century after intercollegiate sport appeared on the scene.[39] Those battles on the playing field apparently filled a need for community—not just separate class unity but occasions for the entire student body to take part in an intense experience. Those who reminisced about their nineteenth-century college life often cited their campus sport activities. A student at Trinity College, now Duke University, described the popular game of bandy or field hockey in North Carolina prior to the Civil War.

Imagine thirty or forty athletes, from sixteen to twenty-five years of age, half on one side, and half on the other, with big clubs bent around at the lower end, stretched out facing each other on the campus—watchful, ready to spring as the leader says "High Buck" or "Low Doe," and as the big hard ball is thrown up or down, see them rush up to it with uplifted clubs, and strike right and left crying "Shin on your side," and see them jump into the air to avoid a savage blow, and the ball is knocked whirling, and all rush for it, and sticks fly, and hands are hurt, and limbs are bruised, and heads are struck, and still the excited, panting players rush after the ball to gain the victory. It was exciting, it was fun and the weak timid boy was not in it.[40]

Working together in a struggle, as in war, provided a sense of belonging to something larger than themselves. A Dartmouth graduate of 1845, writing a generation later, remembered the importance of his football contests. "And now I cross the commons," he said, "famous for football in the olden times. . . . What fierce, sanguinary, raiment-rending contests we did have. To this day I bear the marks of one desperate battle."[41]

It is not surprising that team sports rather than individual sports met the need for community. In the pre-intercollegiate athletic era, the sports which brought students together in rituals of community were football, mass wrestling, bandy, cricket, and baseball—all team sports. It did not occur with the more individualized sports, all of which were participated in before intercollegiate athletics were popularized: boxing, fencing, fishing, fives (handball), hare and hound running (cross country), hunting, ice skating, marbles, nine pins (bowling), quoits (similar to horse shoes), riding horses, sailing, and swimming. Once intercollegiate sports developed after the mid-nineteenth century, the team sports remained focal points for students and eventually public support—crew, baseball, and football at first, and basketball by the twentieth century.

One of the values of team sports on a college campus, in the pre-intercollegiate era as well as later, was their tendency to draw the student body together in dynamic, yet symbolic activities. If the extracurriculum of sport existed for no other reason, it would have served a most useful purpose. Even a rigidly religious faculty could likely see that it was less harmful, and maybe even beneficial, to allow a certain degree of indecorous physical mayhem on campus than to try to subdue it completely. The class battles did not die out until the twentieth century. While they contributed to a sense of community, the development of intercollegiate athletics began to replace them. As class size rose in the latter nineteenth century, the need for community became even more important, and athletics played an increasingly vital role in creating it.

The Ideas of Freedom and Equal Rights and the Rise of Sport

Once created, students were covetous of their extracurriculum. Literary societies did much to free students to pursue affairs of the intellect and to ponder current questions not found in the rather staid curriculum. Intellectual freedom appeared to be a concern of college students from the time of the revolutionary era. Fraternities were to social life what literary societies had been to intellect and reasoning. Students had, without faculty sanction, ushered in a new social system in American colleges by the mid-nineteenth century. Fraternities offered a social escape from the monotony of class recitations and daily prayers at chapel. A degree of social freedom was prized by students across America. In a like manner, athletics spoke for freedom of the body as literary societies had done for intellect and fraternities had done for social life.

The ideological beliefs of freedom and equal rights emerging from the revolutionary period help to explain both the numerous student rebellions from the revolutionary period into the nineteenth century, as well as the student creation of an independent extracurriculum in the late 1700s and early 1800s.[42] An authority of Princeton complained in 1785 that freedom and equality undermined discipline by stripping away the "submissive forms of politeness" existing in European colleges.[43] "Nothing but riot and confusion!" wrote an undergraduate in an 1800 rebellion at Brown, "No regard paid to superiors. Indeed Sir, the spirit of '75 was displayed in its brightest colors."[44] Within the decade, the president of Vermont bemoaned the condition of student protests which he said were the result of "erroneous notions of liberty and equality, from the spirit of revolutions in the minds of men."[45] But a Harvard student of the period argued that "passive obedience" should be given up for "manly independence."[46] One of the rioters of the Princeton rebellion of 1807 agreed with his peer from Cambridge: "The faculty affirm that we had no right to form ourselves into a combination," he wrote home. "It is astonishing to me that any set of men should be so weak as to make such an observation in a country the fundamental principle of whose government is liberty of action."[47] The extracurriculum and the student rebellions appear to have gained much of their strength from the freedom-equality ideology growing out of the revolutionary period.

As most college leaders and faculty were clergymen, it was only natural that they witnessed the post-revolutionary period with some despair. Nationally, the church-state relationship of the colonial period was being torn asunder, while the religiosity of students dropped rapidly until after 1800. Those clergymen who had favored American independence, and most did, began to question the degree of independence students desired. There were many college leaders who, like their Federalist counterparts in state and federal government, feared that the freedoms and equal rights attained through the American Revolution were going to lead to anarchy following the lead of the French Revolution of the 1790s. These leaders blamed campus unrest upon the extreme notions emanating from the French Jacobins as well as the spread of anarchy, deism, atheism, and anti-Federalist thought.[48]

College authorities attempted to halt the liberating tendencies of the students with an "increasingly repressive paternalism" after 1800.[49] Passage of stricter college laws, intensification of "in loco parentis," promotion of evangelical awakenings in the student body, and replacement of liberal classroom texts, such as Jean Jacques Rousseau's *The Social Contract* and Thomas Paine's *The Age of Reason,* were all signs that college faculties and presidents were attempting to strengthen obedience and submission and to weaken liberality.

Yet, while college students were treated like irresponsible children by college authorities, young men in their own domain of the extracurriculum used what they believed was an inalienable right to structure an intellectual, social, aesthetic, and physical world of their own. "The spirit of liberty was contagious," an historian has stated, and the college authorities were unable to successfully immunize their students against it.[50] The extracurriculum, which began with literary societies and the freeing of the intellect, was by mid-nineteenth century transformed into the life-blood of student social and physical life in the leading colleges in America. Athletics were soon to bring the students of various colleges together in displays of excellence and competition that faculty saw only rarely in the classroom. It all began with rowing competitions.

III

The First Intercollegiate Sport: Crew and the Commercial Spirit

MORE THAN A DECADE after Oxford and Cambridge engaged in their first intercollegiate crew meet, seven members of the junior class at Yale purchased a four-oared boat in New York City. That 1843 purchase established a tradition in rowing. There was no hint of the commercial spirit which was soon to grip college crew. The expense for the year's rowing was $7.19 for each rower.[1] In reality it was more a social activity than a competitive one. Even after three additional boats were purchased by Yale students, a four-oared, an eight-oared, and a log canoe, the first challenge race did not occur until the summer of 1844. The dug-out canoe owners challenged the students with the eight-oared, lapstreak gig to a four-mile race to a lighthouse.

That was the year in which Harvard sophomores organized a crew club and purchased an eight-oared boat, the *Oneida*. They, too, found the activity more social than athletic. Drinking was often involved. Charles W. Eliot, a Harvard student in the late 1840s and early 1850s, and later longtime president of the college, reminisced that the wide lapstreak boats were used to row into Boston in spring and fall, not so much for exercise as to transport students to drinking establishments. The floors of the boats were used, he said, to bring home "members of the crew who did not propose to return sober from an evening in Boston."[2] Competition in more than drinking, though, did play a part.[3] Three years after the club was established, the Harvard crew competed in a race.

The challenge to the Harvard club by a crew from Boston was a logical progression. Two decades earlier, not only Boston but Eastern cities from New York and Philadelphia in the north to Baltimore, Charleston, and Savannah in the south had boat clubs.[4] In New York, the leading sporting city in the nation from early in the nineteenth century, rowing matches predated the American Revolution by a score of years. Competitive rowing, however, grew most rapidly after the War of 1812 as professional watermen plied their trade in rowing contests. By the mid-1820s, an estimated 20,000 to 50,000 spectators viewed an English versus American four-mile crew race in New York harbor. The victory satisfied American nationalistic desires and likely contributed to an increased interest in rowing.

By the decade of the 1830s, the establishment of rowing clubs by more socially prominent citizens helped rowing to become a socially acceptable sport. These clubs, much like those of the collegians that followed them, were at first possibly greater displays of fashion than of competition. Intracity regattas and a few intercity matches of the more amateur-like social clubs occurred in New York and other coastal cities as did the races of the professional watermen.[5] Rowing, with the exception of thoroughbred racing and harness racing, gained more attention than any other sport in the 1830s.[6] Thus, when the Harvard club accepted the challenge and somewhat surprisingly beat a Boston crew in 1846,[7] the leading American college was not only reflecting the participation of English college crews but that of the competing urban rowing clubs in America.

The Commercialization of the Yale-Harvard Meet of 1852

Nearly ten years after a group of Yale students formed a rowing club, Yale met Harvard in the first American intercollegiate contest, a boat race in New Hampshire. A New York newspaper predicted that intercollegiate sport would "make little stir in a busy world."[8] The offer by a railroad superintendent to transport and house the crews of the two most prestigious colleges at a vacation spot over a hundred miles from the Cambridge campus and nearly twice that distance from New Haven was the beginning of commercialized college sport in America. The railroad official believed that there was enough interest in colleges and in an athletic contest to produce a profit in his commercial venture even after paying all expenses for an eight-day trip for the Harvard and Yale crews.⁹ Businessmen, in addition to the rail superintendent James Elkins, saw the commercial possibilities in the race. The quiet summer resort at Center Harbor on Lake Winnipesaukee became "full of life and excitement" and added revenues to the local hotel and the steamer on the lake during late July when the crews arrived.¹⁰ It is likely, though, that the forty-one Harvard and Yale students who participated did not consider it part of the commercial spirit of the nineteenth century. To them, as one said later, it was merely a "jolly lark."¹¹

The extreme organizational effort and competitiveness which came to dominate intercollegiate athletics from an early point was not apparent in the first meet. It was not that the Harvard and Yale crews did not want to win—they did. What was missing in the first contest was the careful preparation and prolonged training that soon found their way into the contests. The businesses did far more to commercialize the event than the colleges did to professionalize and rationalize it. There were no professional coaches, no abstentions from drinking and smoking, and no regimented training schedules. Those would exist by the next decade.

The Harvard and Yale students experienced a week of social life and enjoyable sport. Arriving on a Friday, the three crews from Yale and the one from Harvard practiced the next day among vacationers lounging on house boats on the lake and under snowy sails tacking across the bay. On Sunday, they of course observed the Sabbath, strictly kept by most mid-nineteenth-century Americans of their social status. When Monday came, the day before the meet, the crews practiced again in their large and heavy-keeled boats, which one person likened to whale boats. The Yale men were concerned enough with their diet to abstain from pastries.¹² The Harvard men appeared to be less careful. On the day of the meet, there were actually two races, one in the morning, a practice race of one and a half miles to give an idea of boat speeds, and the two-mile contest in the afternoon.¹³ The Harvard crew won the morning race in about seven and a half minutes. Returning to the wharf, the friends of the Harvard rowers, one crew member recalled, "immediately seized us and took us to their rooms, where we were regaled with ale, mineral water, and brandy." They then ate a hearty meal, and "after a little rest and a cigar," returned to the wharf, and were taken to the starting line for the 4 o'clock start of the official race.[14]

While the training was not severe, the race was hard fought. Harvard's rowers, decked out in red, white, and blue, lined up against the two eight-oared Yale boats (the four-oared boat was withheld). There was near-silence among the estimated one thousand spectators as they watched the three crews, framed by the Red Hills in the background, ready themselves to race toward the harbor. The Harvard boat, *Oneida*, shot out to a quick one-length lead, leaving Yale's white and blue clad Shawmut crew and the red and white shirted Undine men behind. The silhouette of the Harvard crew showed their "firm lips" and determined will. Despite having to row over a floating board at one point, the Harvard men left the Yale boats behind by four and eight lengths. The judges' boat was passed after 10 minutes to the cheers of the crowd and the sounds of the Concord Mechanics Brass Band. The winners were then presented with a handsome pair of black, silver-tipped, walnut oars as prize, as General Franklin Pierce, the Democratic presidential candidate, looked on.[15]

The week was not concluded with the contest. The plans were to host another race on the other side of Lake Winnipesaukee at Wolfeboro, the site of one of the finest summer hotels in America.[16] That contest was never completed, because of inclement weather. The crews, however, did set their oars and row a bit for the gratification of the townspeople and visitors. The prize for the scheduled race, a silver ornamented boat hook, was awarded to the second-place Yale crew of the earlier race.[17] That act of sportsmanship was much less likely to occur in another decade. An informal invitation from Lake officials was given for a return of the two institutions the next year, one that was never filled. Had the profits been greater for the sponsoring railroad, there would have been a greater likelihood of a rematch.

The Early Regattas

Yale and Harvard were not the only two colleges involved in rowing, for students at Brown, in Providence, Rhode Island, had purchased a boat in 1848. Yet Brown rowers remained relatively inactive until the late 1850s.[18] Students at the University of Pennsylvania organized a University Barge Club in 1854, four years before the famous Schuylkill Navy was formed in Philadelphia.

When the Club soon admitted graduates and non-students, undergraduates lost interest. Nearly two decades elapsed before Pennsylvania began to row competitively.[19] Trinity College students in Hartford began rowing on the Connecticut River in the mid-1850s and were involved in the earliest college association of rowers in 1858, but rowing never prospered in the early years.[20] In the mid-1850s, Dartmouth and Amherst men also began tenuous boating experiences on the Connecticut River in New Hampshire and Massachusetts, as did Bowdoin in Maine and Union College in upstate New York.[21] Columbia students began to row on the Harlem River in the late 1850s, but were not serious about competition until the 1870s.[22] Wesleyan, a small Methodist college in Connecticut, also began rowing in the late 1850s and had five boat clubs by 1860.[23]

Increased rowing matches in the mid-1850s among several colleges may have been stimulated by the second Harvard-Yale meet in Springfield, Massachusetts, during the summer of 1855. Yale had challenged Harvard to another race. At the time, Yale had about ten boats in its somewhat organized navy, while Harvard had six boat clubs, but was lacking organization even more than Yale. The hundred students involved at Harvard were likely more interested in the appearance of their colorful rowing jackets, which they displayed each evening on the river, than in muscular competition.[24] Nevertheless more concern was shown regarding the outcome of the race than in 1852. Men from Harvard, it was reported, believed that the Yale crews were stimulated to purchase new boats and invigorate their practice for the second contest. Yale, on the other hand, had cause to be upset when Harvard chose a graduate of two years to be coxswain—the same position he had held for the winning crew three years before.[25]

The commercial atmosphere created in 1852 by a rail line was not as apparent at the 1855 race. Springfield business men were pleased that the Connecticut River running through their city was chosen for the three-mile row. To show their appreciation, Springfield citizens supplied an elegant set of colors for the winning crew.[26] Within a few years communities would vie for the honor of hosting the big regattas by offering financial rewards to the competing crews. In this meet, won again by Harvard, no evidence was found to show that the Harvard and three Yale crews had either their travel expenses or lodging paid by commercial concerns.

The annual intercollegiate race between Harvard and Yale or a regatta among several colleges was only a few years away. After the second Harvard-Yale meet, each institution participated in local non-collegiate regattas.[27] There was considerable interest in these regattas. A Harvard man reported that students lost $1700 betting on a defeated Harvard crew, an amount equivalent to a professor's yearly salary.[28] One of the professors, a minister, attempted to make a religious point about the race fought and lost. The day after the contest at the morning chapel service, students were requested to sing:

> There is a battle to be fought,
>   an upward race to run,
> A crown of glory to be sought,
>   A victory to be won.
> O, faint not, Christian! for thy sighs
>   Are heard before his throne.
> The race must come before the prize,
>   The cross before the crown

This inkling of Muscular Christianity of pious Reverend Ward was recast again at afternoon chapel as he read the moralistic verse:

> But oars alone can ne'er prevail
>   to reach the distant coast;
> The breath of Heaven must swell the sail,
>   or all the toil is lost.[29]

Those in the audience who had just been defeated and were out large sums of money may have learned that success in athletics and in religion was difficult to achieve. They would, however, continue their quest, at least in sports, in both betting and racing.

Harvard and Yale competed in separate non-collegiate regattas in 1858; Yale crews were double winners in the New London Regatta, and Harvard beat an Irish longshoremen's crew in a Boston regatta. At this time the distinction between amateur and professional was not as important as it was two decades later. The winning Harvard crew members included two who were graduate students, Alexander Agassiz, later a noted Harvard professor, and Charles W. Eliot, Harvard president from 1869–1909. They and the other four members received the $100 first prize. Because of a deal they had struck with the Irish professionals prior to the race, they gave $25 of their winnings to add to the $50 prize of the second-place crew. The remaining $75 was enough to pay for their new six-oared boat.[30]

Harvard, that same year, proposed a college boat club congress and an annual intercollegiate regatta, an imitation of the annual English regatta of Cambridge and Oxford. Students from Brown and Trinity colleges, in addition to Yale and Harvard, agreed to meet annually beginning that year. Springfield was accepted as the site, although citizens of Worcester, Massachusetts, suggested competing on Lake Quinsigamond. Crews from the four colleges arrived early to practice on the Connecticut River. Yale even purchased a four-oared boat "expressly to beat Harvard at Springfield."[31] Unfortunately, six days before the event was to take place, a member of the Yale crew, George Dunham, stroke of the four-oared boat, was accidentally drowned when the single scull he was rowing capsized after colliding with another boat. The 1858 regatta was canceled.[32]

The following year Brown and Yale sent one crew each while Harvard contributed two crews to the regatta held this time at Lake Quinsigamond. The commercial spirit which had been seen before was apparent. Hotels were filled, and all the beds in houses were taken. The Boston and Worcester Railroad ran special trains to the event with tickets priced at twenty-five cents, while omnibuses, stages, carriages, hacks, and wagons were rented for the short journey from Worcester to the lake. Wooden bleachers for several thousand spectators to observe the festivities were erected for those who were willing to pay fifty cents, half a day's wage for an average laborer. The city of Worcester provided the traditional set of flags for the winning crew, and a band was hired to entertain the crowd, estimated at 15,000 or 20,000.[33] Some newspapers took great cognizance of the event: the *New York Herald* replaced the news of the ending of the French-Austrian War in Italy with a three-column front-page spread of the regatta. The Yale crew in its quest for victory was becoming more intense in its training by "running faster, eating more and rawer food" in a hope that it would "not all be in vain."[34] Yale, nevertheless, lost another race to Harvard, this time claiming unsuccessfully a foul. The lumbering 350-pound Brown boat, which was obviously not designed for racing, came in last.[35]

The first College Union Regatta was followed the next day by a meet sponsored by the city of Worcester, which put up a $100 first prize and a $75 second prize for six-oared boats. This time only Harvard and Yale competed. Yale, for the first time, conquered its rival in a close match attended by some 10,000 spectators. "After all our reverses, after continual ridicule and derision both at home and abroad," wrote a Yale student, they had found themselves "in less than twenty minutes the victors of that world-known Harvard crew." Yale students and graduates, he said, actually walked into the lake to greet the victorious crew.[36] Upon its defeat by Yale, Harvard crew members suggested a third race for money, staking $1,000 on Harvard to $500 on Yale. Nothing came of the talk, but as one writer for the *New York Clipper* offered: "Small beginnings lead to great results, and trivial rivalries lead to the most energetic competitions."[37] The enthusiasm would expand.

Less than a year before the firing upon Fort Sumter and while some Americans were discussing whether a victory by Abraham Lincoln in the 1860 election would cause the South to withdraw from the Union, Yale and Harvard expanded their own competitive battles. Not only would they continue the regular crew race at Lake Quinsigamond, where Brown also rowed, but they introduced the annual freshman and sophomore crew races. The festivities expanded beyond crew to include a Harvard Glee Club concert, a Harvard-Yale chess match, and exhibitions by the great billiard professional Michael Phelan. A "scientific" gymnastic display by students under the guidance of the gymnasium directors at Yale and Harvard, Charley Ottignon and "Professor" Molyneux, was followed by a sparring session by the two gymnasium leaders. A freshman billiard match between Harvard and Yale, begun the year before, remained as a feature. Harvard continued its dominance over Yale as it won each of the contests except the chess match, which ended in a draw.[38] Students, possibly as many as half of each student body, had come to take part in the festive atmosphere. Partying, celebrating, and betting began to create disturbances in the city of Worcester. It may have been the unruly behavior which prompted the Yale Board of Trustees to ban future regattas during term time. As Harvard's term ended about two weeks before Yale's, the Harvard crew was unwilling to give up its vacation time to continue the regatta. Thus college policy and Harvard crew desires, rather than the onset of the Civil War, produced a cessation of the annual regatta.[39]

It seems clear that within less than a decade, several factors not commonly attributed to early intercollegiate athletics had crept into their contests. The prestige obtained from winning, the honor brought to the college, and the interest of the public in the physical prowess of the educational elites were all in existence. In addition, the value of sponsoring the contests for commercial gain and the concern for the outcome by bettors contributed to the growth. There was even a charge that Harvard threw the second 1859 race with Yale.[40] It was more likely that when money was on the line, such as that of the City Regatta sponsored by Worcester, the crews tried harder. Yale cut 64 seconds off its pace of the previous day in vying for the $100 prize, while Harvard was two seconds faster than its previous pace.

Though commercialization predated professionalism in college sports, both occurred early as the spirit of winning quickly replaced any thought that participation in friendly competition was the principal end of college athletics.[41] The crew meet held in the midst of America's greatest armed conflict indicates that the two leading colleges increased their efforts to do what was necessary to win, that is, to make victory a rational or logical process. Improved training methods, better facilities, and the professional coach entered the scene.

Professionalism: The Coach and "Scientific" Training

Yale had a four-year delay before it put a united effort into its desire to beat Harvard. Shortly after the start of the Civil War, Yale undergrads raised $1,000 for the erection of a new boat house. Alumni showed some concern by contributing $150. With the help of two college professors and the college treasurer, the boat club borrowed the remaining $2,000 to construct a 90' x 55' boat house, built during the summer that the Confederates invaded the North near Gettysburg.[42] The construction of a boat house, as a single action, would not have been overly significant. But, combined with a change in the organization of the Yale navy, a rational method of raising money, and a system of physical training, it was symbolic of changes in an effort to beat the best, Harvard. Yale crew members reorganized their navy by having membership in the boat clubs extended through all four classes rather than having class teams as in the past. This change, Yale believed, would "bring the navy to the highest perfection possible."[43] To raise money the crew asked the faculty to allow it to put on an exhibition in the gymnasium. The faculty, acting "in loco parentis," allowed the exhibition after its appointed censors accepted the program.[44]

Achieving excellence in crew or any sport required more than facilities, financing, and organization. It called for some type of older leadership in the form of coaching and training. After the Yale crew challenged Harvard to another race in 1864, it decided to hire a professional to train the men for the contest. William Wood, a New York City gymnastic and physical education instructor, became the first professional trainer for an American college team. The 1864 Yale crew under Wood, it was claimed, put in the most severe training experienced in colleges in that early time. The regimen in the four weeks before the Harvard meet consisted of rising at 6:00 a.m. and running and walking three to five miles before breakfast in heavy flannels. Later in the morning they would row four miles at racing speed and do the same in the afternoon. They also worked out on weights in the gymnasium.[45] Under its professional trainer, Yale bested Harvard by more than 40 seconds at Lake Quinsigamond. For a moment that summer Yale's feat seemed far more important to those associated with it than did reports of General Sherman approaching Atlanta and General Grant pressuring the Confederates around Richmond and Petersburg.[46] Its importance as an athletic event was certainly greater than was the first Harvard-Yale baseball game played in conjunction with the regatta.

The crew training, based on what was considered to be the best methods of the day, differed significantly from that of a decade before. A Harvard crew member in 1852 remarked that "they had not rowed much for fear of blistering their hands."[47] Charles Eliot in 1858 took the advice of his fiancée to "row just as hard as I comfortably can, and not a bit harder."[48] That attitude, however, would not be successful after the first couple years of beating Yale. By the end of the decade Harvard's training intensified and consisted of walking, running, and gymnasium work, including tossing of twelve-pound cannon balls, as well as regular rowing in the morning and afternoon. The Harvard diet, which may have been a detriment rather than a help, included rare beef and mutton, stale bread, oatmeal gruel, only small quantities of milk and water, and no fruit or vegetables.[49] Both the Harvard and Yale training methods by the 1860s attempted to reduce the flesh to the bare minimum producing the hungry look, and, they thought, better performances. By the 1864 meet, both crews were working harder, and Yale had added the discipline which often comes with hiring a coach or trainer.

With success, Yale kept William Wood as professional trainer the next year. As a result of good leadership from the Yale captain, Wilbur Bacon, whose arms were larger than heavyweight champion "Benicia Boy" Hennan's,[50] and the help of a professional, Yale won again in 1865. Harvard's captain that year, William Blaikie, was probably more valuable for the future of Harvard rowing than a professional trainer would have been. Blaikie, who later wrote the multi-edition treatise *How to Get Strong and How to Stay So*, decided that Harvard must get help to again win the rowing crown. Blaikie visited the Oxford University crew to learn the English rowing technique, returning to teach it to his Harvard crew. Harvard's series of five victories was in great part attributable to acquiring English rowing methods. Though Blaikie was not considered a professional coach because he had graduated from Harvard and was therefore an alumnus coach, he acted in much the same capacity. He was instrumental in achieving a more sane training procedure at Harvard than had previously existed. He opposed the policy of overheating, by wearing flannel garments, to lose weight, a training method copied from professional boxers. In fact, he believed that reducing to mere flesh was harmful, and thus did away with the near absence of fluids. He also opposed the old idea which eliminated fruits and vegetables, and instead allowed crew members to eat nearly anything they enjoyed.[51] Training for the annual summer race by the 1870s was carried out through the entire school year, with indoor rowing machines used in cold weather.

The Harvard-Yale saga continued to dominate rowing concerns through the 1860s. Crowds, possibly as large as 25,000, came to see the meets. The students attending the Lake Quinsigamond meets would often become disorderly with demonic yelling, obscene songs, and drunken sprees which, according to one reporter, was a "grand bacchanalian carnival." On one occasion it resulted in chinaware thrown through hotel windows, carpets ripped up, furniture destroyed, and doors battered down. Police arrested more than a score of young people, who were both jailed and fined.[52] The Yale faculty was concerned about the "gross immoralities" attending the races and voted to cooperate with the Harvard faculty to suppress the annual event, but with no success.[53]

Greater antagonism between the crews was also evident. Competition for the prestigious championship flags and gold medals worth $50 each to winning crew members may have contributed to the hostilities.[54] As evidence of the competitive turmoil, one might turn to the 1869 meet. That year, Harvard sent its best crew to race against Oxford in London, but nevertheless defeated Yale in a close contest. The loss so angered one Yale crewman that he drove his oar through the bottom of his defeated boat.[55] The following year, Yale finished ahead of Harvard, but a collision and foul at the turning stake gave the victory to Harvard in a highly controversial contest.[56] As a result athletic relations between the two schools were severed, and a new era in rowing was ushered in. Harvard and Yale would be involved in the commercially successful regattas, but the two institutions would not dominate athletically in rowing as they had done before. Their prestige, though, would give them leverage to influence the expansion of intercollegiate regattas for the next generation and into the twentieth century.

IV

Crew: Internationalism, Expansion, and the Yale-Harvard Pullout

HARVARD'S DOMINANCE of crew as the first two decades of intercollegiate contests came to a close led its crew members to consider challenging the supposed supremacy of England's Oxford and Cambridge universities. The natural rivalry between the English and the Americans had been most marked by two major wars, the American Revolution and the War of 1812, but it also had been spurred on by the Civil War in which England had given aid to the Confederacy. Americans had sporadically contested the English in boating, boxing, cricket, horse racing, running, and yachting in non-collegiate contests in the decades before the Civil War. Americans may not have liked the English, but they did look up to them and their culture. Sport was an important part of that culture, and Americans had a desire to see how they would stand up in competition. If American colleges were to challenge the best of England, it was logical that Harvard should lead the way. It was the oldest, wealthiest, and most prestigious American college, and in America's first intercollegiate sport, crew, it was the best.

The Harvard-Oxford Boat Race of 1869

Less than six months before the 1869 Harvard-Oxford crew meet, Charles Sumner, a leading senator and chairman of the Senate Foreign Relations Committee, spoke to the Senate condemning the British and the proposed joint Anglo-American treaty, the Johnson-Clarendon Convention. The intent of the proposed agreement was to end outstanding disputes between the two countries. Central to the controversy was the claim by Sumner that the proposal lacked two basic provisions. First, England refused to admit its wrong-doing in providing naval vessels to the Confederacy, such as the *Alabama*, during the Civil War. Second, there was no provision for a large reparation to be paid by England to America for the damages done by the *Alabama* and other ships. Sumner's speech in Congress, which noted "a deep-seated sense of enormous wrong" leaving "heart-burning and rancor," set off a furor which lasted for months.[1]

Sumner's claim that British intervention on the side of the Confederacy caused a doubling in the length of the war, which cost over $4 billion, led others to demand $2 billion in reparations from the British. In Congress, after defeating the Johnson-Clarendon Treaty 54 to 1, Senator Zachariah Chandler of Michigan demanded that Great Britain cede Canada to America as punishment "for her national sins."[2] Leading newspapers followed suit.[3] A prominent weekly periodical in America asked, Is there a "war party" in the United States as a result of the Alabama Claims? The English *Pall Mall* wrote of the "fruitlessness of further negotiations, and the necessity of being prepared for war."[4] This backdrop of the August 1869 crew meet on the Thames in London was one of agitation and national-istic pride. While calmer voices eventually prevailed and any po-tential for war was averted, it added to the attention focused on the boat race. Wrote one American in a lighter vein well before the race: "If we are beaten, we must include the damages to our feel-ings in the Alabama Claims. . . ."[5]

Two years earlier, before the Alabama Claims became a major in-ternational incident, Harvard had attempted to send its eight-oared crew to a Paris Exposition, but only seven crew members were will-ing to make the journey. They intended to row against both Cam-bridge and Oxford at that time. The next year, Harvard sent a chal-lenge to Oxford for a meet in boats without coxswains. As Oxford rowed with a coxswain, it would not accept the offer.[6] After a failed attempt by Oxford in 1868 to schedule a match for the next year, Harvard, in April 1869, a week before Sumner made his outrageous demand on England, challenged Oxford to a four-oared race with coxswains. It was to be held in August on the four-and-a-quarter-

mile race course familiar to Londoners from Putney to Mortlake on
the River Thames. Oxford and Cambridge had rowed this course
since 1845, with Oxford dominating in the 1860s.[7] Cambridge University
was also invited as a courtesy by Harvard, but the American
crew was most interested in competing against the best, Oxford.

After Harvard raised several thousand dollars through private
theatricals given by Harvard students and gifts from alumni and
friends of Harvard, the crew sailed for England.[8] Arriving over a
month before the contest, they took careful precautions in an attempt to secure victory. First the rowers brought their own cook,
fearing both unfamiliar food and the possibility of drugging. Second, they purchased a double allowance of food and drink in the
period shortly before the race, one being bought in secret as they
feared that gamblers might attempt to make sure of their bets on
the race. In addition, the crew party included their graduate advisor, William Blaikie, and their New York boat builder. The crew
took two boats with them, but Elliott, the builder, also brought a
model and all the ribs necessary to construct a new boat which he
believed might be necessary for the best rowing on the Thames. Not
only did he build one in England which was ready five days before
the contest but three other builders from England were asked to
construct their best, and they borrowed another to test out. Harvard
had seven boats from which to choose—finally deciding upon Elliott's new one.[9] This rational approach to winning seemed almost
irrational. Indeed, the *Manchester Guardian* suggested that Harvard's practicing with three different boats on one day shortly before the race was not a practical thing to do.[10]

The Harvard crew, without a professional coach and with an
American-built boat, felt satisfied with its training prior to the race.
One of the largest crowds ever to watch an athletic contest in person massed along the Thames. An estimated 750,000 or possibly over
a million people were policed along the shore by eight hundred of
London's best, and another forty police patrolled in river boats,
twenty times the number used in the annual Oxford-Cambridge
crew meet.[11] The scene, which was already crowded in the morning
for the late-afternoon contest, was a true nineteenth-century hap-
pening. Many of the elite of English society were there, including
the Prince of Wales, the newly elected Prime Minister, William
Gladstone, novelists Charles Dickens and Charles Reade, the Count
de Paris, philosopher John Stuart Mill, and the "Swedish Nightin-
gale" Jenny Lind, who was nearing the end of her extraordinary

singing career. She may have even been humming to the band's playing of "Yankee Doodle" and "God Save the Queen" as the crews readied themselves and umpire Thomas Hughes looked on. Hughes, a Member of Parliament and author of the highly popular *Tom Brown's School Days* (1857) and *Tom Brown at Oxford* (1861), was an athlete and had a brother on both the Oxford crew and the cricket team in the 1840s. The stature of Hughes, who combined brains, brawn, social prestige, and political power, added to the occasion.[12]

"Are you ready?" William Blaikie, the starter, cried out. "No," replied the huge—for that time—190-pound captain of the Oxford four-oared boat. After a moment's delay the race began. Harvard, rowing at a rapid 46 strokes per minute, broke to an early lead against the Oxford crew, all of whom began their rowing years before at the upper-class Eton Public School.[13] Shortly after the mile mark, Harvard expanded its lead to a length and a half, enough to legally cut in front of the Oxford boat and in so doing shorten one of the curves in the river. If Harvard had taken its opponent's water, it would have put an extra burden on the heavily favored English crew. Harvard coxswain Burnham, at the request of the Harvard captain, refused to do this as they considered it ungentlemanly, what was then called "jockeyism." Crew advisor William Blaikie, more in tune with the American practice of gamesmanship, which emphasized using the rules to one's advantage, had previously suggested taking Oxford's water if the opportunity arose. Harvard's fatal mistake of sportsmanship that day, according to Blaikie, may have caused it to lose the race.[14] Oxford drew even to Harvard by the half-way mark and won by about three lengths.

The meet was much more than a race between an English and an American educational institution. It was symbolic of the world's most industrialized and powerful nation, Great Britain, and its increasingly muscle-flexing offspring. The meet's significance as a symbol of American nationalism was evident in the use of the Atlantic cable, laid in 1866, to give almost immediate results to the United States. Because of the cable's expense, rare were events given more than a few words, but journalists giving accounts leading up to the race and the meet itself made liberal use of the new medium.[15] The boat race was used by the English to justify their culture, their education, and their manliness. Americans did the same, and would likely have attributed a victory to their way of life. The crew, for instance, was concerned that the British press know that it used its own training methods, its own style of stroke, and a boat made by an American builder.[16] The Oxford-Harvard meet had been one of those rare non-military occasions in which national pride had been exhibited on a massive scale.

The Gala College Rowing Association Regattas, 1871–1876

Harvard did not return to the victorious hundred-gun salute planned by New York City,[17] but it continued to be the leader of American rowing. Harvard and Yale crews would likely have continued their dual meets had not a serious incident occurred in the 1870 race. At the Lake Quinsigamond course site, Harvard was leading by a narrow margin at the turning stake when the Yale boat collided with it, breaking the rudder. Yale, rowing for the first time with sliding seats, easily reached the finish line before Harvard's hobbled shell limped home. Harvard cried foul. After a lengthy evening meeting of judges, Harvard was ruled the victor. Yale crew members, distraught over its constant losing, claimed that the rudder broke on the turning stake, not from their shell.[18] The pride of the Yale crew was so bruised that it refused to row Harvard again unless a straightaway course was agreed upon. The correspondence between the two crews during the ensuing winter and spring was as strained as the diplomacy surrounding the English-American Alabama Claims. When Yale failed to agree to Harvard's terms for another meet, Harvard called for delegates from all rowing colleges to attend a convention for the establishment of a straight-away college regatta. "If Yale refuses to take part in the annual regatta of American colleges," a communique from Harvard to Yale read, "Harvard insists on the right of the challenged party to name the time and place of the race, and Yale can only row for the championship a race similar to the one in which she was last year defeated."[19] The arrogance shown by Harvard and the expression of Yale's wounded pride resulted in broken athletic relations for a short period.

The pride of Harvard and the intransigence of Yale led to the democratizing of crew through the Rowing Association of American Colleges. This was certainly not the intent of Harvard when it organized the regatta, but it was clearly the result. Had Harvard ever considered the possibility of losing its favored position among boating colleges, it almost surely would never have suggested a regatta open to all colleges. At the original meeting in Springfield in April 1871, Harvard hosted delegates from Brown, Bowdoin, and the Massachusetts Agricultural College of Amherst. Yale, strangely, was "unofficially" present. A regatta committee was appointed immediately, and three colleges agreed to row at the three-mile straight-away Springfield site. Harvard, Brown, and the "Farmer Boys" from the Massachusetts Agricultural College initiated half a dozen years of the greatest college athletic spectacle in nineteenth-century America, with the possible exception of the New York City Thanksgiving Day football games of the 1890s.

The Association meeting became a noteworthy athletic festival probably because of the outcome of the first regatta. The betting odds greatly favored Harvard, the masters of intercollegiate rowing, with light support for the crew from Brown. Almost no mention was made of the Massachusetts Aggies except to confuse them with Amherst College. Most believed that the six solid silver cups worth about $800 and the set of colors would be won by the Harvard six-oared crew.[20] Yet, the "Farmers' College" crew of "hay-seeds" from the hills, five sons of Massachusetts farmers and a Portland, Maine, resident, beat Harvard by fourteen lengths and Brown by twenty lengths. The natural strength of the farm boys and the ten days of coaching by a professional rower, Josh Ward, combined to defeat the Brahmins from Boston. Chiding the Aggie crew on whether the farm boys had gotten "the hay-seed out of their eyes" may have given a strong impetus to best their social superiors from Harvard.[21] The victory did more than give advertising and recognition to the Massachusetts land grant institution of 150 students; it gave real hope to other colleges that they might win honor by beating Harvard at its own game. A New York journalist warned future Harvard athletes to be wary of the "knight who rides into the list with a wisp of hay on his shield. . . ."[22] It was an important concern for elite eastern institutions well into the twentieth century.

Harvard did not immediately withdraw from a losing proposition which it had initiated. In fact, Yale joined the Association the next year, giving the regatta additional prestige. Brown dropped out, but Bowdoin, Williams, and Amherst entered crews. The Massachusetts Aggies were unable to repeat as champions, as the upstart Amherst College crew under its professional coach, John Biglin, beat Harvard. The 15,000 spectators were again making the college crew regatta a spectacle of note.[23] The defeat of Harvard for the second time and the last-place finish of Yale gave added incentive to smaller colleges to enter the fray.

The regatta in 1873 saw Columbia, Cornell, Dartmouth, Trinity, and Wesleyan join the other hopefuls in search of prestige brought to the event by Harvard and Yale. Eleven colleges, eight of which had professional coaches, crowded the starting line on the Connecticut River in Springfield.[24] This time, Harvard and Yale had outstanding crews, even without professional coaches, and battled each other for the entire three-mile race. As Harvard passed what it believed was the finish line, the crew ceased rowing. The so-called "diagonal finish line" race went to Yale, which was on the short side of the incorrectly placed finish line. Confusion and rancor reigned among the crews and the 25,000 or 30,000 spectators.[25] Dissatisfaction over the Springfield site, its water crowded with eleven crews, led the Association to change the location of the next year's regatta.

The decision to hold the meet at one of the most elite summer resorts, horse racing centers, and gambling scenes in America, at Saratoga Lake, New York, was not taken lightly by the Association. While most of the student delegates to the early 1874 regatta convention favored Saratoga, Dartmouth and especially Amherst believed that to choose the site dominated by ex-boxer, gambler, and New York politician John Morrissey was offensive to their probity and piety. The head of the high-class Saratoga Rowing Association attempted to bring the collegians to Saratoga Lake, offering inducements to the crews to come to his site. With or without inducements, it was one of the best accommodations in America for rowing, including a shore which offered excellent observation of the race and water which could accommodate twenty crews if necessary. Following a lengthy discussion and a letter read by the governor of New York indicating that Saratoga would be an hospitable site, the Rowing Association voted 9 to 3 to accept Saratoga, but with the provision that no gifts or prizes would be accepted from any organization.[26] The crews, which previously had felt little restraint in accepting financial favors and expensive prizes, were probably attempting to dissociate themselves from any taint connected to holding their meet at the "home of Morrissey."

With the high cost of sponsoring a team sport such as crew without gate receipts, some small colleges were forced to withdraw for financial reasons. Yet the opportunity and desire to defeat Harvard and Yale kept some smaller institutions in the annual fray. Princeton, which was not one of the lesser colleges, finally joined the Regatta Association for the first time in 1875. The expense of sending Princeton varsity and freshman crews to Saratoga their first year was $765, for which students subscribed $415 and alumni the remainder.[27] The cost to Cornell was over $2,000 to train and compete at Saratoga Lake. Harvard, possibly the biggest spender, needed $2,000 to $3,000 each year to support its crews.[28] While a large, relatively wealthy college such as Harvard had difficulty raising sufficient money to finance its crew, it was much more difficult for a small college such as Amherst or Wesleyan to do so. The specter of indebtedness was an annual affair. Nevertheless, no greater opportunity, curricular or extracurricular, was presented to a college for notoriety and prestige than to win the annual regatta. A Cornell student wrote, prior to the 1874 regatta, that if the Cornell crew was to enter the race it must be financed so that it was well equipped and trained. "We can hardly expect to compete with Harvard or Yale on equal terms," he wrote, yet "if they go, we want them prepared to *win* the race. . . ."[29]

Nine colleges vied for honors in 1874, but the focus during the race was on Harvard and Yale. It was unfortunate for the harmony of the race that the two esteemed institutions were placed near each other at the starting line. Referee William Wood said that early in the race "the disposition of Yale to encroach upon Harvard" was clearly apparent. Wood, the first professional trainer at Yale two decades before, charged that it "really appeared as if Yale had tried to carry away Harvard's rudder, but missed it." Later in the race Yale veered toward the Harvard boat and fouled it. Wood, who was directly following the action in a steam boat, commented officially that "it seemed as if Yale, finding that all her efforts would not carry her beyond Harvard, chose to foul Harvard." He declared that "it cannot be supposed that I should be prejudiced against Yale, when I prepared for victory the first crew with whom Yale beat Harvard, and had charge of the other Yale crews afterward."[30] Immediately following the race, which Yale dropped out of and Harvard was slowed to a third-place finish, Yale men offered two bets of $5,000 and $2,000 that it could beat Harvard in a two-boat challenge race. Captain Robert Cook issued the challenge after he had hurled unsportsmanlike comments at Harvard during the race. Harvard replied curtly: "After the conduct of the Yale University Crew, not only during, but also at the conclusion of the race just completed, the Harvard University Crew refuses to entertain any challenge whatever from the Yale University Crew."[31]

Negative attention was paid to Yale and Harvard, but excitement generated around the winner, Columbia, was unsurpassed in the press. The *New York World*, probably with some home-town boosterism, carried eleven full columns of news of the race covering all but one column of the front page. The regatta completely dominated news of the Indian wars in Oklahoma, Texas, and Wyoming.[32] Upon returning to New York City in a palace car, the most stylish of Pullman's railroad cars, the Columbia crew was given a parade up Fifth Avenue to the gates of the college. President Barnard gave a stirring tribute to the team. "I congratulate you most heartily upon the splendid victory you have won, and the luster you have shed upon the name of Columbia College," he pronounced before an excited crowd. "I thank you for the Faculty of the College, for the manifest service you have done to this institution. . . . I am convinced," he uttered unashamedly, "that in one day or in one summer, you have done more to make Columbia College known than all your predecessors have done since the foundation of the college by this, your great triumph." The president continued his deference to the crew by noting that the telegraph had carried the name of Columbia to Hong Kong and Calcutta as well as to the banks of the Seine and the Thames. He concluded his geography and advertising lesson to the crew and other listeners when he said: "I assure you in the name of the Faculty and the Board of Trustees, whom I represent, that whatever you ask in the future you will be likely to receive."[33] The crew heard those words and soon the basement of the library at Columbia contained a rowing tank for year-round training. In the late 1890s, when Columbia moved to its present site, another rowing tank was built in the basement of the library. It is still there and in use, though the library holdings have been moved. One might say that at Columbia, athletics had become closely associated with learning.

Following the Columbia victory, a record number of thirteen colleges entered the 1875 extravaganza at Saratoga Lake. The sponsoring Saratoga Rowing Association, helping with college expenses, agreed to provide a number of services free of charge. These included transportation for all crews and boats to Saratoga and return, a boat house and raft at Saratoga Lake for each crew, stage coach transportation while at the lake, regular delivery of mail, steamboats for the referee and judges, tickets to the grandstand, expensive prizes for the winners, and entertainment climaxing in a grand ball to conclude the festivities. In addition, comfortable quarters and good board were provided at $10 a week per man, while the entire three-mile racing course was to be bouyed for lanes.[34] Evidently the College Rowing Association accepted the generous offer, though it had rejected that kind of commercialism the year before. Financial support may have contributed to Bowdoin, Hamilton, and Union colleges sending crews for the first time, while Amherst and Brown rejoined the competition. The thirteen crews and approximately 30,000 spectators participated in the most prominent of the first generation of college regattas.

Cornell, founded less than a decade before, was to take center stage in 1875. Its first boat club had been formed only six years before. This was followed by a stream of activity after England's Thomas Hughes visited Cornell in 1870 and offered a silver cup to be competed for by Cornell College crews on Cayuga Lake. The famed author of *Tom Brown's Schooldays* stimulated rowing, and by the next year, a hundred students had formed a University Boat Association with active support from Cornell's president, Andrew D. White. White, who had rowed at Yale as an undergraduate in the early 1850s, saw the value of crew for the men of Cornell and for the institution's prestige. Showing his concern, White presented a new six-oared boat to the Cornell crew in 1873 when it first competed at the college regatta. Even Ezra Cornell, the founder, contributed to the crew, though not before exclaiming that "if the boys wanted to work and exercise themselves, he had plenty of stone on his farm that needed moving."[35]

Cornell was prepared in two more years to contest for the championship. The "boat load of mechanics from Ithaca" had no professional coach in 1875 because of Association rules, but its captain, J. N. Ostrom, was ready for the challenge of training the crew and determining scientifically the most rational method of defeating the opposition. Ostrom first determined that his crew should not train according to the old professional coaches' methods, which included losing weight by exercising in heavy flannel clothes. At Cornell, Ostrom noted, the earlier professional coach "used to have us bundle up in flannel suits and then take a walk at the top of our speed, for about seven miles ending with a smart run. We were then obliged," Ostrom told President White, "to huddle into a small room, close all the doors and windows and stay there until we were nearly suffocated with heat." This method, he believed, led to a skin-and-bones look while creating a tremendous thirst and skin boils, as the men were forbidden to drink sufficient liquids for their needs. Rather, Ostrom would have his crew eat a balanced diet including a liberal amount of liquids while the meat would be cooked to individual tastes rather than raw as before. Racing over a three-mile course twice daily brought his crew to a fine fitness level. While at Saratoga Lake, Ostrom determined the quality and speed of each competing crew by borrowing a large telescope from a Cornell professor. Observing the crews during each practice, Ostrom was sure Cornell would win the contest.[36]

Cornell indeed won both the varsity race and the freshman contest. Celebrations erupted. "The University chimes are ringing, flags flying and cannons firing," President White proudly telegraphed his crew.[37] He wrote in his diary, "Everybody in estatics here. No end of demonstrations and joy."[38] At the contest, New York State Senator Wagner ordered a special palace car for the crew's return to Ithaca, while Commodore Vanderbilt provided another drawing-room car for their pleasure. When the victors reached Ithaca, individuals at the crowded station lifted the crew members onto a float, proceeded through Main Street, ascended the steep hill to Cornell University, and entered through a huge triumphal arch constructed of evergreens for the occasion.[39] Cornell could consider itself at the summit of the collegiate athletic world. It had arrived within a decade of its origin and competed successfully with Harvard and Yale at their own game.

The Yale-Harvard Pullout

The success of the newer and less prestigious institutions reached its zenith in 1875, but it also led to the collapse of the intercollegiate regatta. Both Yale and Harvard chafed over their annual failures at the regatta and considered withdrawing from it. Yale at least won once, but Harvard, many of its supporters believed, "cannot honorably leave until she has won a race."[40] Yale's sixth-place finish in 1875 after coming in last the previous year caused the crew to discuss withdrawal with Harvard. Wrote one observer who appears to have been accurate in his appraisal: The two "aristocratic colleges are not disposed to struggle and be beaten by the younger, more vigorous, and less exclusive universities. . . ."[41] Walter Camp, the most prominent man in intercollegiate athletics in the nineteenth century, conceded some years later that "it really was not thoroughly palatable to be defeated annually by some of the smaller colleges."[42] Not only were they beaten on the water but also at the ballot. No Yale or Harvard man had been elected to any office of the Intercollegiate Rowing Association for several years.[43] Snubbed at the polls and beaten at their own game, the two elite schools withdrew into their own shell and rowed each other. Harvard did it with a greater appearance of style as it voted to compete in the next regatta before withdrawing.

The decisions of Yale and then Harvard to withdraw led them to go back to the dual meet structure where each crew could come in no worse than second. In truth, though, Harvard and Yale, even in the large regattas, were primarily interested in beating the other, while the public appeared to be concerned about the overall winner. What mattered to the two leading colleges in the 1870s, as it did over a century later, was whether they could win "The Game." A Yale partisan expressed the view clearly: "I don't care if Yale comes in last, if she only beats Harvard."[44] When Yale and Harvard departed from the regatta, they copied the Oxford-Cambridge format and began rowing in eight-oared shells with coxswain rather than the six-oared boats used in the regatta. With their disengagement from the lesser institutions, the notoriety and advertising value gained by the smaller colleges was lost.

In the meantime the intercollegiate regatta died. Even with Harvard competing as a lame-duck appearance in 1876, fewer spectators arrived at Lake Saratoga. Only six colleges participated as Harvard trailed the repeat champion Cornell crew to the finish line. The Saratoga Regatta, celebrated just two weeks after the centennial of American independence, was a scene of "utter apathy among the public."[45] The regatta folded, and despite the interest rekindled in the annual Harvard-Yale meet, intercollegiate crew never again regained the national prominence that it held in the mid-1870s.

The question of the withdrawal of Harvard and Yale creates an important issue regarding egalitarianism in America. Would it be possible for two socially elite institutions to remove themselves from less prestigious colleges and retain their position in a society which professed equalitarian beliefs? Could Harvard and Yale, as Oxford and Cambridge succeeded in doing in class-conscious England, remain leaders in a society which lacked the strict class barriers so obvious in England? Even Harvard students understood the question and the dilemma it presented. "'To leave now, when both have been beaten fairly, and one badly, would cause no end of dissatisfaction and abuse," wrote a Harvard newspaper editor. "It is all very well to say that we are both above popular preju-

dice . . . 'adi profanum vulgus' " he continued, "but in this democratic country, no one college, or pair of colleges, can afford to
affect an aristocratic contempt for the opinion of the many."[46] A
Harvard alumnus noted, "It is idle talk, to say we, the aristocrats,
prefer to race each other, and not compete with farmers and mechanics," but, he said, "we must take our choice: either go with the
tide, or lose our prominent position among colleges."[47] In the long
run, that observation was correct, for the elite institutions of the
east could not stay above the fray in crew or any other intercollegiate sport while remaining in a prominent position athletically in
the eyes of the public. Egalitarianism was too strong a current in
America to dismiss. In the short run, however, Harvard and Yale
were successful in their decision to abandon their losing efforts in
the intercollegiate regatta and return to dual meets.

Crew in the Post-Saratoga Period

While enthusiasm for crew diminished in American colleges, it remained in at least four colleges, Harvard, Yale, Columbia, and Cornell. Columbia and especially Cornell were snubbed by the aloof
duo. When Cornell challenged both Harvard and Yale to a meet,
Harvard gave a courteous rejection while Yale replied: "Your chal
lenge is received and refused."[48] A Harvard editor disdained the
"bell-ringing, machinery oiling" academic majors at Cornell.[49] Meanwhile Columbia sent its 1878 crew to the famed Henley Regatta and
won the Visitor's Challenge Cup over three Oxford and Cambridge
college crews, becoming the first foreign crew to win a Henley trophy.[50] Columbia was similarly snubbed by the men from Harvard
and Yale, though some meets between Harvard and Columbia were
held. Cornell also traveled to Henley to try to beat the English in
1881 but was not as successful as Columbia had been three years before. It seemed that a trip to England was one solution to rejection
at home. Finally, after two decades of Harvard and Yale rejecting
most of the other college offers to row, Harvard agreed to row against
both Cornell and Columbia, in addition to Pennsylvania—but only
after Harvard and Yale had broken relations over a series of disagree-
ments in all major sports.[51] It was a chance for four of the top intercollegiate crews to contest once again for supremacy. Cornell, chaf-
ing from the previous years of rebuff, beat Harvard by three seconds
over a four-mile course, with Penn and Columbia trailing far behind.
Cornell was even more excited the following year, 1897, when

Yale reopened relations with Harvard and a race between the three resulted. For the first time in twenty-two years, the Cornell crew was given the opportunity to compete with its social betters whom it had defeated in 1875, and to prove that it was not athletically inferior. Shortly before the race the Yale coach, Robert Cook, agreed with Harvard's coach that "both Harvard and Yale will defeat Cornell. . . ."[52] Cornell's coach, the famed Charles Courtney, knew the importance of the contest to Cornell. "Boys, do you know what this means?" he asked his crew just before the race. "It means that you're Cornell or you're nothing."[53] Defeat would mean, he believed, an end to Cornell's fight for recognition. A number of the throng of about 15,000 probably felt the same way. Among that group were 4,000 people who bought $2 to $15 tickets on about fifty open cars of an observation train. They saw what many believed was an unexpected win by the outsider Cornell. "Victory," a newspaper reported, "means equality, freedom, [and] assured position" for Cornell.[54] But it didn't. A Yale professor commented on the situation more accurately. "In the future," he said, "let us play with people in our class."[55]

When Cornell beat Harvard and Yale again the next year, the two losers returned once more to their dual meets, leaving Cornell to row in the Intercollegiate Rowing Association Regatta which Columbia, Penn, and Cornell had founded in 1895.[56] Harvard and Yale continued throughout the next century to hold their joint meetings as Oxford and Cambridge did in England. The Harvard-Yale meet, however, never meant to America what the Oxford-Cambridge contest meant to England. Harvard historian Albert B. Hart was correct when he wrote at the time: "There is no 'Oxford and Cambridge of America.' "[57] Harvard and Yale athletics had not waned by 1900, but crew had already taken a less prominent place than either baseball or football at most American colleges.

V

The Rise of College Baseball

"Whoever wants to know the heart and mind of America," wrote Jacques Barzun at mid-twentieth century, "had better learn baseball, the rules and realities of the game."[1] Barzun's aphorism was particularly true when applied to the heart of the collegiate extracurriculum in the nineteenth century. Baseball was the dominant sport of the 1800s in most American colleges, as it was in all of America until well into the twentieth century. Cricket, on the other hand, was played rather widely by collegians before intercollegiate competition began in the mid-nineteenth century. Though England gave America nearly all of its sports, cricket, the "national pastime" of England in the nineteenth century, never became popular in American society. Baseball, described by Mark Twain as the "very symbol, the outward and visible expression, of the drive and push and rush and struggle of the raging, tearing, booming nineteenth century,"[2] became the landed symbol of intercollegiate pride that crew had become for a select group of eastern colleges. Baseball also showed that the freedom of students to pursue intercollegiate athletics led to commercialism and professionalism. That process challenged the concept of amateurism which Americans had borrowed from the British.

The First Intercollegiate Baseball Game:
Amherst vs. Williams

Seven years after the first intercollegiate crew meet, two other New England colleges, Amherst and Williams, met and inaugurated baseball. Baseball, unlike crew, had been played by American collegians for well over a century before intercollegiate play began. By the 1840s and '50s, many forms of baseball were played, but two particular styles had developed from the English game known as rounders. In New England, baseball was called the New England or the Connecticut or Massachusetts game. It was characterized by a rectangular field, rather than a diamond, by a particularly short distance from home plate to first base, and by calling any batted ball a "fair" ball. One out retired the side, and generally the winning team was the first one to score 100 runs, while batsmen and runners were put out when they were literally hit with a thrown ball. In contrast, the New York game, developed with the written rules of the New York Knickerbocker team, was spreading in popularity in the 1850s. The Knickerbockers did away with "soaking" the runner to put him out, and developed the rule of three outs per side. Eventually, a nine-inning game replaced 21 runs in determining the length of a game. They played the game on the recognizable diamond shaped field with bases 90 feet apart.[3] There was no clear choice of baseball styles, New England or New York, until after a group of New York clubs banded together to form the National Association of Base Ball Players (NABBP) in 1858.[4] The NABBP modified the Knickerbocker rules, and within a few years the New York game became the American game.

In colleges the transition to the New York game began in the 1850s. Harvard students formed their Lawrence Base Ball Club in 1858, half a year after the NABBP adopted its rules. The Harvard men, playing on Monday and Thursday afternoons, determined that only the NABBP rules would be used. The baseball club, like the early boat clubs at Harvard, was a social club with membership dues of one dollar, and, like other amateur clubs of its time, fined members for non-attendance at games (10 cents) and for missing meetings (3 cents).[5] Farther to the south, Princeton was changing from the old Connecticut game to the New York game in 1858, when three New Yorkers entered Princeton as freshmen. The Nassau Baseball Club soon adopted the NABBP rules. The Princeton club had fines for ungentlemanly behavior: 10 cents for profane language, 5 cents for disputing an umpire or disobeying the captain, and 3 cents for giving an audible expression on a doubtful play before the umpire made his decision.[6] Many colleges were playing baseball in addition to Amherst and Williams, both of which still enjoyed the New England variety of baseball.

Like the Harvard-Yale crew meet in 1852, the inaugural Amherst-Williams baseball game was a product of the nineteenth-century technological revolution. Until 1859, one could not take a train to Williamstown in northwestern Massachusetts, the site of Williams, but had to travel through the Berkshire Mountains by stage coach. In that year, however, the Troy and Boston Railroad was completed, connecting Williamstown with the rest of the state.[7] The Amherst senior class president brought up the question of challenging Williams College to a game of Massachusetts baseball. Perhaps Williams' newly acquired accessibility by rail stimulated this action. The student body, at the conclusion of morning prayers, passed the motion for a challenge match. Following a meeting with Williams delegates and further mail negotiations, the rules were agreed upon. Each team would use its own ball, which could be batted in any direction as in cricket, and they decided that the team which garnered 65 runs would be victor. A major question in baseball at the time was also settled by negotiations. It was traditional to consider a batter out if either the ball was caught on the fly or on the first bounce. Even the NABBP was debating the issue in 1859. It was considered more "mannish" to catch the ball on the fly, and the two schools decided to do the masculine thing.[8]

The two colleges were invited to Pittsfield at the end of June with teams of seventeen players. The Williams players were dressed alike and wore belts marked "Williams." A large contingent including Professor John Bascom watched. Amherst players lacked uniforms and had only blue ribbons pinned to their shirts. The game started at 11:00 in the morning, first batting with the light two-ounce, seven-inch circumference ball of Williams and then with the small two-and-a-half ounce, six-inch ball produced by Amherst. A total of over 100 runs were scored as Amherst won easily, 73-32.[9]

One outstanding feature of the 3½ hour game, which would be more significant as college sport developed, was the key position of the Amherst captain, J. T. Claflin. Claflin was undoubtedly a strong leader on the field, as he was later as a college president. As captain, he had both the offense and defense highly organized, in what a newspaper described as "perfect military discipline."[10] Williams players, however, threw the ball, "each where he pleased" while on defense and ran with uncontrolled passion on the bases. The Amherst men, though, played with few mental errors in the field and on the bases "ran only at the word of their captain," generally preventing them from getting "soaked" with the ball between bases.[11] Williams professor Bascom, who later became president of the University of Wisconsin, contrasted the disciplined play of Amherst with that of his favorites. Williams players showed "alertness and skill [with] moderate practice," the professor of rhetoric and oratory said, while the Amherst players had "taken the game from the region of sport and carried it into the region of exact and laborious discipline."[12] Amherst had found the key to success in competitive athletics. Americans would refine the process as it moved from the dominating captain to the commanding coach as the methods of rationalized sport progressed. Amherst discovered early that the vigorous use of freedom of opportunity to develop its physical skills to a high level brought recognition through winning.

Amherst students back at the campus soon learned of the decisive win and almost immediately ascended College Hill to celebrate. The chapel bell was rung, a large bonfire was lit, and charged yelling arose while fireworks were set off in jubilation. The gala occasion continued the following day as the momentary heroes returned, driven in a triumphal coach-and-four proceeding to the college. Speeches were made and responded to by the players as Amherst showed the esprit de corps for which college athletics became known.[13]

The Civil War Stimulus and the Harvard Tour

Large numbers of colleges did not immediately turn to baseball. Amherst played a second match with Williams on the Fourth of July to begin the decade of the 1860s. The beginning of the Civil War, however, probably delayed the move toward intercollegiate competition. Nevertheless, colleges such as Bowdoin in Maine, Middlebury in Vermont, Dartmouth in New Hampshire, Brown in Rhode Island, Trinity in Connecticut, Hamilton in New York, Princeton in New Jersey, and Kenyon in Ohio had baseball teams before the firing upon Fort Sumter.[14]

The immediate effect of the Civil War was to slow the growth of baseball, but the long-term consequences were to give the "national pastime" a surge of growth. Soldiers, North and South, played the game, often being introduced to New York style of baseball for the first time. At one camp, an estimated 40,000 military spectators observed a Christmas Day 1862 game between two picked nines of their comrades.[15] When soldiers were home on furlough or were mustered out of the army, they brought with them a keen interest in continuing their game. Harvard organized its first baseball club during the Civil War. A Civil War volunteer, home on leave, played in the first game against Williams, which was part of the occasion of the Harvard-Yale regatta of the summer of 1865.[16] Williams, which beat Harvard that day, traveled to Princeton in November of the same year for the first intersectional college baseball game. The aftermath of the Civil War must have seemed far from the minds of the two teams as the Williams players, after their loss, were treated grandly to a dinner consisting of turkey, duck, snipe, ham, beef, chicken, oysters, plum pudding, mince, apple, and custard pie, ice cream, fruit, and assorted cakes and candies.[17]

The Civil War had given impetus to all kinds of sport, and the rapid growth of baseball immediately following the conflict was apparent. There was hardly a college in America that did not organize a team and begin playing intercollegiate baseball in the years immediately following Appomatox. Within two years of the collapse of the Confederacy, baseball teams were formed at the University of Virginia and the University of Georgia.[18] Similarly they were found as far west as the Platteville Normal School in Wisconsin and the University of Kansas, both having formed teams within a year of their establishment as educational institutions.[19]

The matriculation of returning Civil War veterans may have contributed to the rapid development of baseball for several reasons. The first is that the experience with baseball during the war gave them a good knowledge of the game. Then, too, their war involvement may have contributed to their organizational skills, obviously needed for student controlled teams. There is also the probability that the more mature ex-soldiers had a greater zest for life, including the on-campus extracurriculum, and were more aggressive and less fearful in demanding from the faculty and president dynamic sports programs than were younger, less experienced undergraduates.[20]

The athletic extracurriculum, unlike the literary one, was looked upon by many faculty as questionable if not outright damaging to the mental and moral outcomes of college life. But strong-willed students, such as war veterans, were generally successful in a quest for some collective freedom from college authorities. There was always a delicate balance between moving from freedom toward anarchy on the part of students and the tendency to move from authority toward totalitarianism on the part of the faculty. Civil War veterans were more likely to resist faculty authority than were seventeen-year-olds.

Harvard, the leading American college, might serve as an example of the post-Civil War influence in baseball. In the fall of 1865, half a year after Robert E. Lee's surrender, Harvard traveled to New York City to meet the famed Brooklyn Atlantics of the NABBP, losing 58-22. The next spring the team again visited the New York area, losing four games to some of the premier non-collegiate baseball clubs. At home, or at least in Boston, Harvard was attracting as many as 10,000 spectators when it played the Lowells of Boston in a three-game series.[21] Harvard also began competing against its arch-rival Yale in 1868 as part of the Lake Quinsigamond Regatta at Worcester, as well as beginning its series against Princeton. This was the start of competition among the so-called "Big Three." By 1869, Harvard had a seventeen-game schedule in the spring in addition to seven games the previous fall.[22]

The year 1869 was a significant one for Harvard baseball and for organized baseball in general. In that year the first all-salaried baseball team, the Cincinnati Red Stockings, made its coast-to-coast, nearly 12,000-mile tour, not losing a single game of its total of fifty-eight. Harvard contributed one to the Cincinnati total, losing 30-11. The Crimson ended its season with a 12-5 record, beating the three colleges it played. The club took a journey of nearly two weeks throughout New York State and to Philadelphia, where it beat the Athletics, a pro team.[23] The extended trip, though, was moderate relative to the following year.

Archie Bush was elected captain to lead the 1870 Harvard baseball team. Bush, a Civil War captain before attending Harvard, led the Crimson on a twenty-five game western tour from early July to the middle of August. The trip was originally planned to take the team to San Francisco as Cincinnati had done the year before, but was modified to take the club only as far west as St. Louis, Chicago, and Milwaukee. Despite liberal terms of the newly founded Union Pacific Railroad, the expense was too great to reach California. Playing such well-known teams as the Troy Haymakers, Philadelphia Athletics, Washington Olympics, Cleveland Forest Cities, and the Chicago White Stockings, the Harvard team showed that collegians could compete successfully with those who played for pay.[24]

The Cincinnati game was probably the most outstanding of the trip. Cincinnati had only recently lost its first game since 1868. Harvard built up a lead in the early and middle innings after Bush had smashed a hit off the head of Asa Brainard, the Cincinnati pitcher. Going into the last inning Harvard led 17-12. With two outs and a ground ball to third, the fielder chose to throw home rather than make the easy play to first. The throw was late, and Cincinnati went on to take the game.[25] Bush did not let this great disappointment last long, for shortly Harvard was on its way to Chicago to challenge the White Stockings. Bush, the regular catcher, became a relief pitcher in that game and used his "change of pace" to good effect in shutting down a late rally and defeating the professionals.[26]

The Harvard trip and the leadership of Bush was worthy of note and was possibly as important to baseball as the Harvard-Oxford boat race of 1869 was to crew. The 17-8 record on the forty-three day western trip involved losses only to professional teams. In fact, Bush, who also captained the team in 1871, never lost to an amateur club, college or otherwise.[27] The position of authority which Harvard commanded educationally was transferred to the intercollegiate athletic scene, giving other colleges the needed precedent to expand their own programs, especially in baseball. Larger schedules, more intersectional games, and a greater number of contests against professional teams were the result.

The College Baseball Association, 1879–1887

Baseball continued to be the dominating sport on most college campuses, only challenged by rowing in select eastern colleges. Harvard was probably the dominant school in that decade, though it was never again to have a forty-four-game schedule, twenty-six during the term, as it had during the school year of 1870. The faculty made sure of that as it began first by enacting legislation limiting games to Saturdays and holidays and later easing a bit by limiting the number of games to four which could be played on other days.[28] At other colleges, faculties began to set limits on their baseball teams' activities: restricting the number of away games and controlling non-athlete attendance at these games, while controlling practice time and the areas where practice could be held.[29] The freedom of students to participate was being jeopardized, but only after a degree of liberty from an earlier stringent period had been relaxed to allow intercollegiate athletics to grow.

The students took their game very seriously, and, of course, that was what concerned many faculty members. It was not just a game—winning mattered as much to the collegians as it did to the professionals. There was never really that much difference between amateurs and professionals in terms of conducting a contest anyway. The best of the colleges competed often and sometimes successfully with the teams of the first major league, the National Association of Professional Base Ball Players (NAPBBP), formed in 1871. Harvard, for example, played the Boston Red Stockings, the best NAPBBP team, twenty times and won two games in the novice league's five-year existence. Yale played nearly twice as many games against pros from 1865–75 as it did against colleges.[30] When the National League was formed in 1876, colleges continued to challenge the pros, winning now and then. College students were nevertheless more interested in beating fellow collegians. Thus, the first college baseball league was a logical progression in the late 1870s.

Controversies surrounding several major college baseball teams in 1879 led to the development of the American College Base Ball Association. The three major issues which arose were all an outcome of the overwhelming desire of collegians to win. The first dealt with the question of the number of championship games. By the end of the 1870s a group of eastern colleges, consisting of Amherst, Brown, Dartmouth, Harvard, Princeton, and Yale, were playing regular home and away series of games. The team with the best record in this informal arrangement would claim the championship. The number of games scheduled and played by each college was not clearly stated, nor was it clear if the number of games won or the number of series between teams won was the determining factor. This led to claims and counterclaims during and following the 1879 season. In addition, there were two questionable issues of eligibility which contributed to the boiling of tempers.

Harvard, which had won the mythical championship in 1878, lost an early season game in 1879 to Brown by the embarrassing score of 21-5. A week later Harvard was beaten by Yale. Humbled and humiliated, the Harvard captain prevailed upon two former Harvard players of the class of 1876, Harold Ernst and James Tyng, who had pitched and caught with uncommon success for the Crimson the past several years. Ernst at the time was in his last year of medical school at Harvard, while Tyng was in the Harvard Law School. These four- and five-year veterans agreed to help Harvard in its quest for continued glory. The other colleges were angry. A writer for a Princeton paper was incensed: "It is a blot on the fair name of Harvard that she descends to such tricks to obtain the championship. . . ."[31] But, as no written eligibility rules existed among the schools, the two Harvard alums continued to participate.

Brown University, though, met that challenge with college baseball's premier pitcher, Lee Richmond. When Harvard was beaten by Brown, 6-2, in a return game, the Harvard student newspaper said that Richmond "surpasses any college athlete, combining skillful pitching, heavy batting, excellent base-running, and at the same time splendid executive judgment in the management of his Nine."[32] It was an accurate appraisal. Richmond led his team to the college championship when Brown beat Yale 3-2 in what must have been one of the great college games of the nineteenth century. Brown was leading by one run in the last inning as Yale had the bases loaded with two outs. Richmond recounted the situation:

> The game literally turned on one ball pitched[,] for the next batter waited till he had two strikes and eight balls. [It took nine balls for a walk.] The grandstand was as still as death. Numbers of fellows had gone behind the grandstand unable to watch the game. When the last ball was struck at and caught by the catcher—well—I can't tell you my feelings. I remember having professor Lincoln shake my hand, and wondering if the other fellows found it as uncomfortable to be hoisted up on shoulders as I did.[33]

Brown won the championship, but Richmond was also a professional by the time the Yale game had been played.

About a week before the championship game, Richmond had received a telegram from the manager of the Worcester, Massachusetts, professional team asking Richmond: "Will you pitch in Worcester tomorrow pay you well." Three days later when Manager Frank Bancroft telegraphed Richmond again that he could pitch against the Chicago White Stockings with Cap Anson, the best-known nineteenth-century ball player, and Abner Dalrymple, the National League leading hitter of 1878, Richmond accepted. Richmond and his college catcher, Bill Winslow, took the forty-four mile train ride to Worcester to do battle against the best of the pros. The left-hander threw a no-hitter in his professional debut.[34]

The fact that Richmond played professionally as well as at Brown and the fact that alumni were allowed on student teams created a crisis in college baseball. The *Harvard Advocate* recognized the problem and called for an official college league. "If college base ball is to preserve its present reputation for fairness and good feeling," the paper cautioned in its own biased way, "the line must be sharply drawn between professional and amateur players."[35] It chose not to include any reference to Harvard playing graduate students. Princeton did not forget, and when a Springfield, Massachusetts, conference of the six colleges was called for in December 1879, the issues of graduate and professional participation were major agenda items. The students representing baseball interests argued for over two hours whether Brown's Richmond and Winslow should be eligible. They finally agreed to prevent future professional players from participating but would not make it ex post facto. Yale, in a huff, shortly thereafter walked out of the conference, but it did so only after attacking the Ernst-Tyng question of playing alumni and members of professional schools. Yale withdrew a motion which would have prevented professional school students from participating and substituted a motion to prevent any student from playing more than five years. This was defeated, though Yale got a pledge from Harvard not to play either Ernst or Tyng.[36] The acrimonious meeting ended after each college, with the exception of Yale, agreed to play a two-game, home and away series with each of the other five colleges. Yale said maybe, but when a later appeal to prevent the Brown professionals from playing failed, Yale withdrew for a year from the conference.[37]

The Baseball Association was as unstable as the student-controlled collegiate regattas of the 1870s. There was public interest in major games such as the Harvard-Yale game of 1880, which 2,500 spectators including President Rutherford B. Hayes attended. That number at the gate was considerably more than most National League games at that time, when 1,000 or fewer spectators were common.[38] Dartmouth, however, drew poorly at the gate, and the travel distance to the New Hampshire college was a real concern. After Dartmouth defeated Harvard 11-10 in 1882, Harvard asked the conference to expel Dartmouth because games drew no crowds and were uninteresting. The Dartmouth question, symbolizing the unamicable relations among the colleges, was solved by a conference vote. Yale, according to a Dartmouth source, stood by Dartmouth, asserting that Dartmouth afforded it better games than Harvard. Princeton, with a hatred of Yale, was allied this time with Harvard. Amherst, it was claimed, deserted Dartmouth at a critical point, and Harvard carried the motion.[39] With Dartmouth out, Williams College was voted in, but that arrangement lasted only until 1887 when the Big Three voted to count the Amherst, Brown, and Williams contests as practice games, not championship contests. The elite Big Three joined with Columbia to form a league of their own, while Amherst, Brown, Dartmouth, and Williams formed a separate one.[40] While the first baseball league disbanded, one central question, unique to any of the intercollegiate sports, remained.

The Summer Baseball Question

When Lee Richmond played for money in 1879 while remaining eligible for college ball, he was the first important collegiate player to do so. He left a controversial legacy for college baseball that has never been adequately solved. The question which he raised, and which was modified in future years, was whether a college player could have the freedom to earn money playing baseball during the summer and remain eligible for his amateur college team. The concern was not so much whether collegians could play on major league teams, as Richmond had done, but to be paid to play on "non-professional" local and city baseball teams and, more importantly, on resort teams which entertained vacationers.

The 1880s were years of prosperity in America, and baseball prospered as the Great American Game. The rail system was well established and carried summer vacationers to eastern shore resorts and mountain hotels. Baseball played at resorts was a logical result. To fill the teams, resort owners looked for players who were both physically and socially skilled, acceptable to well-to-do patrons. Collegians from the prestigious eastern institutions were avidly sought. To obtain the players, the hotel owners would offer room and board and an allowance of five or ten dollars or more per week. Some players, usually pitchers, were paid by the game. Still others were paid subscriptions made up by patrons who appreciated good performances.

By the end of the 1880s the summer baseball earnings were a concern for the colleges, for they affected not only the eligibility for baseball teams but for other teams. A Harvard football player's eligibility was challenged by the Harvard Athletic Committee because he, along with seven Princeton men, had played on the Cape

May, New Jersey, nine, receiving board and a $25-per-month al-
lowance. When the Yale football captain was contacted, he indicated that this was a common occurrence and did not challenge
the Harvard man's football eligibility.[41] Another Harvard baseball
player, Dudley Dean, traveled with Albert Spalding's professional
baseball tour of England and was paid £4 a week plus expenses.
The same year, a star Princeton running back, Knowlton "Snake"
Ames, had received money for playing baseball near Chicago.
Though Ames produced a notorized statement that he was not a
professional athlete, there was good evidence that he indeed was
paid to play baseball.[42] All three individuals retained their football and baseball eligibility, though there was more concern about
Ames because he received specific sums for special games. A
Princeton professor rationalized Ames' action by stating that the
money received by Ames on one occasion did not constitute professionalism, for, he said, professionalism was the practice of taking
money habitually.[43]

Habitual or not, by the 1890s and into the 1900s, summer baseball for pay was one of several charged issues in intercollegiate
sport, possibly next in intensity to brutality in football. The question
of brutality in football was eventually solved, but payment during
summers to college baseball players remained unresolved. Walter
Camp, Yale's athletic advisor and the person generally regarded as
the "Father" of American football, deplored the situation. "Ten
years ago," Camp wrote in the early 1890s, "had some thrifty specu-
lator approached a college athlete with a suggestion that he display
himself as an attraction at some resort, for which act he should
receive a certain sum of money to be called expenses, he would
have been met with a very rigorous point-blank refusal."[44] Not so
by the 1890s. By then summer baseball had created a mild crisis.
The University of Pennsylvania faculty in 1896 ruled as ineligible
all but two members of the baseball team, because they had played
summer ball for pay.[45] Brown University was apparently more
lenient in allowing its paid athletes to continue in varsity baseball.
This led the amateur crusader, Caspar Whitney of *Harper's Weekly*,
to exclaim: "A day of reckoning is coming for Brown, now the only
institution which persists in harboring the 'summer nine' players.[46]
Whitney, who favored the elitist British attitude of looking negatively both at professionalism in sport and at manual labor as a way
of making a living, was wrong in his prediction. Brown was only

one of many colleges whose players earned money through baseball, and a day of reckoning never arrived. An attempt, however, was made.

Brown University officials, in their desire to find answers to vexing problems in intercollegiate athletics, called for a conference in 1898 in order to reach a uniform set of rules among colleges.[47] Faculty, alumni, and students from eastern institutions—today's Ivy League minus Yale—sent representatives to Providence to discuss athletic problems, including the summer baseball issue. Summer baseball was only one of the issues of professionalism and commercialism in college sport that the conference explored. The conference struck a committee on rules which met and condemned the practice of athletes playing for money at any time, specifically during the summer. Yet the multitude of rules devised by the committee to eliminate what it considered to be athletic evils were never ratified by the individual colleges and were thus not collectively put into effect. Summer baseball continued.

The case of Walter Clarkson at Harvard may be helpful in clarifying a larger question which summer baseball illustrated; a question of whether it was acceptable among the educated and more socially elite in America to earn a living by playing baseball or any other sport. Walter Clarkson was born to well-to-do parents in Cambridge, Massachusetts, in a baseball-playing family. Two older brothers played in the major leagues. One, John Clarkson, was a future Hall of Famer. Walter Clarkson entered Harvard, not in the liberal arts college but in the much less prestigious Scientific School. It was common in turn-of-the-century American colleges to harbor athletes in the scientific curricula or as special students, but this was probably not the case with Clarkson, who eventually became a lawyer. Clarkson was apparently keenly interested in pursuing his baseball career, leading Harvard to five career wins without a loss to Yale and playing baseball all summer.

From the beginning of his career at Harvard, Clarkson was held under suspicion for playing summer baseball.[48] And for good reason, for in 1901 he had evidently pitched under an assumed name at a summer hotel. Yale, which had not beaten Harvard in their season's series since 1898, became much concerned after losing to Clarkson in 1901 and 1902. The next year, a friend of Yale's athletic advisor, Walter Camp, did a private investigation of Clarkson's summer baseball and reported that the "purity in athletics" at Harvard was much less than claimed. Clarkson, he said, had earned

$15 per game at North Attleboro, Massachusetts, but that everyone there "gave Clarkson their word of honor that it would never be known outside."[49] Not being able to get affidavits that Clarkson had been paid, Clarkson again pitched for Harvard in its win over Yale.

The next year, Clarkson was eligible for his fourth varsity season at Harvard. During the season, he signed a contract with the New York Yankees[50] of the American League, a quarter-century after Lee Richmond turned professional while continuing to play for Brown University. Because Clarkson wanted to complete the baseball season at Harvard, he had a verbal agreement that he would not begin pitching for New York until Harvard's last game with Yale.

The conscientious Harvard Athletic Committee was in a dilemma. It might not be legal to declare him ineligible, yet Harvard had a reputation of fair play and sportsmanship to uphold. Furthermore if the Athletic Committee banned him, he would be made a "martyr" in the eyes of the students and the Athletic Committee would appear to be anti-Harvard. The Committee decided to send a faculty member to discuss the matter with the dean of the Columbia Law School, who was on Columbia's Athletic Committee. The law professor believed that Clarkson was legally eligible if he had not received any money at that time.[51] The Harvard Athletic Committee questioned him and discovered that Clarkson had accepted a large bonus when he signed. The Committee, thereupon, declared him not eligible.[52]

The Clarkson dilemma at Harvard is a recurring theme in college athletics. In a society that had no entrenched upper class as found in England, could America hope to have the same amateur ideals in sport as those espoused by England's aristocratic-led sporting elite? Whereas it would have been almost unthinkable for an Oxford or Cambridge undergraduate to turn professional in association football or cricket, it was much more socially acceptable for Walter Clarkson, or for Lee Richmond a generation before, to do so. Despite the statement of a Harvard professor that "a gentleman has something better to be than a professional athlete,"[53] it was not below the dignity of Clarkson to earn money during the summers from his baseball skills, nor was it socially unacceptable for a college-educated individual to accept payment for sport participation as a means of livelihood. Yet, paradoxically, there was pressure for American colleges to appear to the outside world as if they had accepted the English amateur code. Walter Camp, the best-known figure in college athletics, stated for public consumption that "a gentleman [athlete] does not sell himself," while he himself became wealthy from his own writings on amateur sport.[54] What ensued was a public condemnation of professional practices, while the practice of summer baseball for pay continued. The intercollegiate sport scene was not ready in the early 1900s to take the advice of the president of Clark University, G. Stanley Hall. The noted psychologist wanted to eliminate the rampant hypocrisy occurring in college baseball. "I'm not only saying that it is right for a man to play summer ball for money," Hall said in a sermon, "but I'm going further than that. . . . He is failing in his duty to himself and to the world if he does not take advantage of it and use it to the best of his ability."[55] Many of the players would have undoubtedly agreed.

College baseball was the most important college sport after football at the time the National Collegiate Athletic Association was founded in 1905. It would later decline in stature. Baseball had been dominated by the professionals since the 1870s and continued that role through the twentieth century. Yet certain college baseball games often outdrew the professional games, and some of the innovations in baseball, such as the invention of the catcher's face mask and chest protector, came from the colleges. The summer baseball question continued to be debated annually well into the twentieth century, but it was never resolved. Eventually as baseball faded from its onetime position of primacy on the intercollegiate scene, it became less of a heated issue. Baseball had made its mark on the American college, but no sport came to rule the extracurriculum as did football.

VI

From the Burial of Football
to the Acceptance of Rugby

WELL BEFORE HARVARD AND YALE lifted an oar together or Amherst
and Williams faced each other with bat and ball, collegians were
playing football on the various campuses. College football, an outgrowth of upperclassmen's hazing and initiation rites imposed upon
freshmen, was a well-established ritual on most college campuses
when intercollegiate crew and baseball arose in the 1850s. Thomas
Wentworth Higginson, a writer of some renown, reminisced about
Harvard in the days before intercollegiate rivalries: "I can recall,"
wrote Higginson of the 1840s, "the feeling of exhilaration as one
drew near to the 'Delta,' on some autumn evening, while the game
was in progress,—the joyous shouts, the thud of the ball, the sweet
smell of crushed grass . . . [and] the magnificent 'rush.' It seemed
a game for men and giants. . . ."[1] But there weren't all shouts of
joy, for the nature of the game led to its extinction on several campuses. The kicking game, as one contemporary described it, was
played with a degree of "violence & brutality."[2] Football died by
the hand of the faculty and was buried on more than one campus.
It was, though, reborn in another form and was elevated, god-like,
by the latter 1800s, and on Thanksgiving Day even worshipped.

The Burial of Freshman-Sophomore Inter-Class Football

The social and academic life of the mid-nineteenth-century collegian was centered around his academic class. This was seen no

67

more clearly than in the annual class battles on the campus grounds. Wrote a Yale freshman and sophomore about the football class battle in the early 1850s:

> There were yellings and shoutings and wiping of noses,
> Where the hue of the lily has changed to the rose's,
> There were tearing of shirts, and ripping of stitches,
> and breaches of peace, and pieces of britches.[3]

At Harvard the annual "Bloody Monday" contest on the first day of each fall term became such a ferocious meeting of the college new-comers and the cocky sophomores that the faculty banned the annual battle in 1860. The sophomores were specifically warned that dis-obedience of the faculty injunction regarding football or other forms of hazing would lead to immediate expulsion.[4]

Harvard sophomores showed their abhorrence of the faculty edict by conducting an elaborate funeral and burial of football. The new freshmen, 136 strong, looked on as a procession marched slowly through town, led by a pair of mourners performing on muffled drums. Behind them were four spade bearers, and six pall bearers carrying a six-foot coffin on their shoulders. The rest of the sopho-more class, wearing torn shirts and trousers reminiscent of past battles, followed in full ranks. The freshmen could only look on as the class of 1863 moved toward the scene of previous battles, where football was to be put to rest. Wearing crepe on their left legs, the second-year students reached the Delta, formed a circle, and passed the coffin around, beholding the remains of past games. The grave was dug. "Dearly Beloved:—We have met together," the eulogy began. Sighs, groans, and lamentations filled the evening air. The freshmen listened as the elegy continued: "Exult, ye freshmen, and clap your hands! The wise men who make big laws around a little table have stretched out their arms to encircle you, and for this once, at least, your eyes and 'noses' are protected, you are shielded behind the aegis of Minerva," the Roman goddess of wisdom and war.[5] When the last shovelful of earth had encased the bier contain-ing the leather-covered bladder, boisterous cheers of class loyalty were given. One loud groan expressed their collective feeling to-ward the faculty who had tried to destroy an important part of the community of students.

The faculty's "in loco parentis" and desire for order won out momentarily over the freedom of students to conduct their own activities. Nevertheless, the students' love of their games and of the extracurriculum was too great to be denied for long. This was true not only at Harvard. The faculty banned football for periods at a number of schools, including Brown, Williams, Yale, and West Point. At the U.S. Military Academy in 1850, Philip A. Sheridan was punished for kicking a "football in the vicinity of the barracks."[6] Cadet Sheridan was apparently not damaged permanently by the reprimand, for a little more than a decade later he commanded a Civil War cavalry unit.

Broken window panes were probably the major concerns at West Point, but broken bones brought about faculty opposition at other institutions. Yet the soccer-type football game continued to be played, banned or not. At Marietta College in Ohio, the breakage of windows helped diminish the game, giving a boost to the playing of marbles.[7] At Wisconsin's Beloit College, football was played from time to time, and on one occasion two collarbones were broken within a period of one hour, indicating the rough nature of the game.[8] Broken bones or cracked windows did not prevent football from becoming the fourth intercollegiate sport in America, following crew, baseball, and cricket.

Rutgers vs. Princeton: A Football First

Football, with its "bleeding hands, scarred limbs, and clogged breath," wrote a Rutgers student journalist a few months before intercollegiate football began, "prove no obstacle in this rugged path to glory."[9] Rutgers students, like most other collegians, were playing their part in the frosh-soph ritual battles. William Leggett, one member of the bloodied freshman class which lost to the sophomores, 3 goals to 2, became an integral part of the development of intercollegiate football.

Leggett, who captained the victorious Rutgers team over Princeton in the fall of 1869, was probably the outstanding scholar and athlete of his class. Before graduating, he was a prize winner in Latin, mathematics, and declamations; was president of the student newspaper and of his class; and was director of the baseball club, captain and stroke of the crew, and captain of the football team.[10] The Hudson, New York, native invited the Princeton football team to a three-game series, the first and last to be played at Rutgers.

William S. Gummere, Leggett's counterpart at Princeton, had been chosen captain at the time the Rutgers challenge was accepted. Gummere was an important player on the Princeton baseball team, one that had defeated Rutgers in their first intercollegiate game by the embarrassing score of 40–2 three years earlier. Gummere led his team and a small number of partisans on a train ride to New Brunswick on Saturday morning, November 6, 1869. The day was auspicious for both the captains and the future of intercollegiate sport. Leggett, a future distinguished Dutch Reformed clergyman, and Gummere, destined to be chief justice of the New Jersey Supreme Court, drew up common rules from the two disparate campus customs. In the process they launched American colleges into what would become their dominating sport.[11]

The rather casual nature of this first intercollegiate football contest can be seen in its preliminaries. Arriving in New Brunswick at mid-morning, the athletes and student followers were met by a contingent of Rutgers' faithfuls. They strolled around town for several hours, playing billiards and eating, before arriving at the athletic grounds at about 3 o'clock that afternoon. There were no uniforms for the players. The footballers, twenty-five on each team, removed their hats and coats in readiness for the contest. The Rutgers men did wear red scarves or turbans around their heads, not unlike the handkerchiefs first worn by the Harvard crew the decade before.[12] There was an amicable agreement on the rules as Princeton's Gummere agreed to nearly all the Rutgers customs, despite the effect the rules could have on the game's outcome.

Both sets of rules were similar to association football, the game Americans called soccer. In neither case could players run with the ball or throw it, although it could be batted with hands or fists. Princeton, though, gave up a fundamental part of its game known as the free kick, whereby a player could catch the ball in the air or on first bounce and kick it without hindrance.[13] In short, the game allowed for twenty-five players on a side who could kick or bat the round, inflated rubber ball toward goals eight paces wide. No tripping or holding of players was allowed on the large 360′ x 225′ field. The first team to score six goals was to be the victor.[14]

As the players lined up to await the kick-off, or mount, as it was called, there was an obvious difference in the body size of Princeton men and those of Rutgers. According to one account, the Princeton men "were almost without exception tall and muscular," while most of the Rutgers players were "small and light."[15] Another writer said that Princeton "sent her chosen twenty-four men, and one Goliath, to combat our twenty-five striplings."[16] Even with Princeton's J. E. "Big Mike" Michael ready to break up the massing of Rutgers players around the ball, it is not likely that either team averaged more than about 150 pounds and 5'8" in height, which was greater than average for college students at the time.[17]

With Rutgers winning the toss and choosing the wind behind them, Captain Gummere of Princeton decided to kick off. Though it was probably not a reflection of the intelligence of Princeton men or of Gummere's judgement as a future lawyer, it was not a wise decision to mount the ball into the wind. Rutgers received the ball and after a brief struggle drove it between the goal posts for the first score. The hometown crowd cheered its momentary heroes. Princeton made a contest of it by scoring the next goal, as "headlong running, wild shouting, and frantic kicking" continued.[18] Midway through the contest, the most memorable event occurred as the spectators seated on top of a wooden fence were catapulted to the ground along with the fence as Princeton's Big Mike and a Rutgers man collided into the barrier. It is obvious that the game meant something more than a pleasant pastime to the two teams. After Princeton tied the score at four, Rutgers tallied the final two goals, winning the first intercollegiate football game 6–4.[19]

While there were no eligibility rules for this unpolished football game, there well could have been an eligibility incident had the Rutgers faculty wished to create it. Only the day before the game, William McKee, a freshman on the team, had been reported to the faculty for unexcused absences during the week.[20] Unlike latter-day faculties which often punished wrongdoing by withholding athletic privileges, it chose only to note the absences. The next week, after the Rutgers win, the absences of McKee were recorded as "excused."[21] The world will never know if the Rutgers victory had any influence on the faculty decision. The faculty at a later time might also have reacted to the academic deficiencies of four other Rutgers players, three of whom were failing algebra and one who was defeated at geometry.[22] The three who were failing freshman algebra were a possible sign for the future that freshman ineligibility for athletics might have some academic merit.

The faculties of the two institutions may have been concerned about the effect that football was having on arousing interest in athletics rather than on academic affairs, but there is no strong evidence that the faculties banned future contests in 1869. A week following the first game, Rutgers students traveled to Princeton for the second of three scheduled contests. Playing under Princeton rules, which allowed fair catches and free kicks, Rutgers was beaten soundly. Princeton had developed a strategy of close, direct kicks to advance the ball, and they won eight goals to none.[23] The third game was never played, due possibly to a college administrative decision, but it is more likely that there was no consensus among the players of the two institutions regarding the rules to be used for that game.[24]

The two contests started a rivalry on the football field that was to last for more than a century. Princeton was not again to lose to Rutgers for nearly seven decades, and when Rutgers began to win regularly in the 1970s, Princeton refused to play against its neighbor. The rivalry started out in a most cordial manner, though it did not end that way. On the evening of the first game, Rutgers hosted a banquet featuring roasted game birds, impromptu speeches, and the singing of college songs.[25] As the Rutgers student newspaper reported: "Our guests went home, in high good spirits, but thirsting to beat us next time, if they can."[26] After the second contest at Princeton, the Nassau men hosted a fine supper featuring "practical gastronomy, . . . speeches and songs" before the evening train bore the Rutgers men home. "If we must be beaten," wrote one Rutgers scribe, "we are glad to have such conquerors."[27] The era of good feelings following athletic contests was short-lived in the male world of sport. Shortly, the desire to win, as in crew and baseball, left little room to socialize with the losers following hard-fought contests.

The Short Life of Association Football

The first three years of the 1870s saw several other colleges entering the intercollegiate football scene or at least forming teams. The year after the Rutgers-Princeton matches, Columbia formed a team and lost its only contest to Rutgers, 6–3. Meanwhile, Rutgers and Princeton continued their rivalry, as Princeton was victorious.[28] Increased interest on other campuses became apparent. At Ithaca, New York, Thomas Hughes, the famed English author of *Tom Brown's Schooldays*, visited Cornell and played football with the students. Within a short time the Cornell Football Association was founded to promote the game.[29] The University of Pennsylvania organized a team in 1871 and played an intraschool contest at the Philadelphia Cricket Club that year. At about the same time, Princeton formed its Football Association.[30] Harvard, too, renewed the "Old Boston" game after a decade of little football activity following the banishment of the annual frosh-soph battle. Accompanying the revival was the organization of the Harvard College Foot Ball Club.[31] Soon after, at Yale, where football had died at the hands of the faculty a dozen years before, students joined the rush to football that was gaining momentum. Ironically, the student who revived football was David Schaff, who had learned the rugby-style game while attending Kornthal School in Germany at which English boys were present. Schaff promoted a junior-senior class game of association football rather than rugby. Following the game, Schaff was elected president of the Yale Football Association.[32]

The fall of 1872 saw the codification of football at three important colleges: Harvard, Yale, and Princeton. The leadership of these three institutions, especially Harvard and Yale, would determine the direction football, and other college sports, would take in the future. At Princeton and Yale, similar written rules for football were drawn up within a year of each other. They resembled soccer rules. Harvard, however, playing the Boston game, drafted rules which allowed for fewer players on a side, but, more important, permitted any player to catch or pick up the ball. The player could even run with the ball, but, strangely, only if he were pursued by an opponent. Though the rule appears bizarre, it worked well. It succeeded, said one Harvard player, because the pursuer of the ball carrier always called out when he stopped chasing, and "if the runner did not at once also stop, the cry was taken up by the whole pack of opponents."[33] The acceptance of a British upper-class attitude of "playing the game" under the spirit of the rules, with "a taboo for unfair play," led to little tendency to cheat.[34] The opportunity to run with the ball was a key to the development of a non-soccer-type game in America.[35]

Competition grew in the soccer game, however, as only Harvard played with its rules, which were more amenable to rugby than to soccer. The Yale-Columbia game in the fall of 1872 is significant, for it was Yale's first intercollegiate football match. The Yale victory was the beginning of what would become the most successful college football program, in terms of victories, in the first century of college football. By the next year, a western school, Michigan, challenged Cornell to a football game which would have been played in Cleveland, half-way between the two institutions. The Cornell faculty took issue with the plan when Cornell students petitioned it, unanimously defeating the request.[36] Cornell President Andrew D. White, who had earlier that year given the Cornell crew a rowing shell in hopes of winning the intercollegiate regatta, also refused to sanction the contest. White's reply to Michigan is a classic: "I will not permit 30 men to travel four hundred miles merely to agitate a bag of wind."[37] Enough interest was being generated in association football for the Yale Football Association to call for a convention to determine whether a league should be formed to play under a uniform code of rules. Invitations were sent to Columbia, Harvard, Princeton, and Rutgers, though not Cornell and Michigan, for a mid-October 1873 meeting in New York City.[38] Though Columbia and Harvard were absent, Princeton, Rutgers, and Yale decided to draw up common rules, although they chose not to create a league schedule. The new rules were almost identical to the Yale rules for soccer.[39]

The absence of Harvard from the 1873 convention was a key to the history of college football, for the Harvard College Foot Ball Club chose to remain with its independent rules. This was done despite the pressure for intercollegiate competition already in existence in crew, baseball, cricket, and track and field. "Harvard stands entirely distinct by herself in the game of football," wrote Harvard Captain Henry Grant in declining the convention invitation. In recognizing Harvard's lack of common rules with the other colleges and the unlikelihood of convincing the others of the value of Harvard's game, Grant replied to Yale rather abruptly:

> We cannot but recognize in your game much but brute force, weight, and especially 'shin' element. Our game depends upon running, dodging, and position playing,—i.e., kicking across field into another's hands. We are perfectly aware of our position in regard to other colleges. I assure you we gave the matter a fair discussion last spring. We even went so far as to practice and try the Yale game. We gave it up at once as hopeless.[40]

Harvard understood well that it was making a choice between participating in intercollegiate football or retaining the game it loved to play. Soccer, however, was soon to be rejected in favor of Harvard's eventual choice of rugby football.

Harvard and the Game of Rugby

Harvard's action in rejecting the Yale-sponsored agreement to play under soccer rules drastically changed the history of American football. While Yale, Princeton, Columbia, and Rutgers, and evidently other schools, agreed to common soccer rules, Harvard went its own way. This eventually led to a series of matches with McGill University of Montreal. The captain of the McGill rugby team, David Rodger, sent a letter to Captain Grant of Harvard, proposing two games, one to be played at Harvard under rugby rules in the spring of 1874 and a return game in the fall at McGill with Harvard rules. Harvard indicated that it would be pleased to compete but felt sure that the Harvard faculty would not allow the team to travel to Montreal during the term. McGill then agreed to play both matches at Cambridge. The McGill ruggers arrived for a May 14, 1874, game to be played with Harvard's Boston game rules, which would be followed by a rugby game the following day. A fifty-cent admission charge was levied to provide for the entertainment of the visitors. Beginning at about 4:00 on a Thursday afternoon, about five hundred fans, including a group of Yale athletes who wanted to see the comparative games, watched the proceedings.[41] Harvard kicked off and in five minutes scored a goal. The primitive goal marker was a rope strung about 4 feet high the entire length of the end zone. It took only a total of twenty-two minutes for Harvard to easily defeat McGill, 3–0. This was not unexpected, for the Canadians had neither practiced with the Harvard rules nor used a round rubber ball before.[42] The eleven McGill players outshone the Harvards in only one category—their neat uniforms. McGill dressed in traditional English rugby suits of red and black striped shirts, caps, and stockings, and white pants. Harvard had to contend with a traditional crew-like magenta handkerchiefs tied around their heads, and somewhat similar but raggedy white undershirts and dark pants.[43]

The first rugby match participated in by an American college occurred the following day. This Canadian gift to American intercollegiate sport was played with ten players on a side and an oval ball. Players took sight of the $2.50 goal posts constructed for the game as they played three thirty-minute periods. Not a goal was kicked from the field. Not a ball was touched down over the goal line. But it was exciting, and the Harvard players who tied the McGill team decided that they liked the new game. "The rugby game is in much better favor," wrote a student journalist, "than the somewhat sleepy game played by our men."[44] There was not only a good feeling about the Canadian game but a pleasant feeling existed between the two schools. Following the second game, the teams enjoyed the hefty admissions proceeds by going to a banquet in Boston for the evening where the champagne flowed freely.[45]

American football, rugby-style, was ready to spring from its Harvard genesis.

Harvard, that spring, attempted to draw up acceptable rules with Yale, but failed, and returned to schedule another match with McGill. For some reason, the Harvard team was given permission by the faculty to leave Cambridge, missing three days of class in the fall of 1874 to travel northward for a game at the prestigious Montreal Cricket Club. Harvard, playing before about 1500 fans, won three goals to none. They were entertained royally at a dinner following the game and even saw a fox hunt the next day.[46]

As enjoyable as the association was with McGill, Harvard had Yale much more on its mind. While attempting unsuccessfully to get Yale to agree to its new rugby game, Harvard scheduled a game with nearby Tufts College in June 1875. But the Harvard men, more interested in their spring baseball team and rowing, gave little attention to the Tufts game. "Our Elevens are not in practice every day, as our Nines are," the student newspaper reported.[47] And while the Harvard freshman baseball victory over Yale was much more newsworthy, the Tufts team defeated Harvard 1–0 in the first solely American college rugby game. If Harvard did not play the part of a football powerhouse in its loss, for the first time it looked the part. The players' new uniforms consisted of white shirts, crimson trimmed pants, and crimson stockings.[48] As for Tufts College, it was soon forgotten as the first victor of American rugby football as Yale came on the scene.

That fall, after Harvard again rejected an offer to join the association of soccer-playing colleges, Yale and Harvard agreed to a game with "concessionary" rules. They were possibly called concessionary to save face for Yale, as the rules were essentially those of rugby. The editor of the *Yale Record* knew that Yale "should not have given so much to Harvard."[49] Yet Yale needed Harvard more than Harvard needed Yale. At that time, Yale had announced that its crew had withdrawn from the Intercollegiate Regatta Association after having done so poorly against what it considered lesser colleges. It was attempting to convince Harvard that it should immediately withdraw and go to a dual meet rowing competition. Yale wanted the Harvard competition for prestige purposes, and agreed to play using Harvard's own rules.

The Harvard-Yale game was the pivotal point in the downfall of soccer and the rise of rugby in America. Yale secured the game, but lost its first rugby match, while an interested group of Princeton players attended to observe the contest.[50] Yale, wearing blue shirts and yellow caps, was overwhelmingly defeated, four goals and four touchdowns to nothing, but, more important for Yale, it was able to compete against its more prestigious neighbor. The Princeton men returned home to discuss the two types of games, and for the next year, Princeton was torn between the game its students favored and the rugby game which Harvard and Yale adopted. "We stand to lose much," the *Nassau Literary Magazine* of Princeton stated, "and gain little by a change."[51] But Princeton either had to change or lose out in competition with both Harvard and Yale.

Princeton, always the last school mentioned in the Harvard, Yale, Princeton trilogy, chose to join the two more prestigious colleges. In the fall of 1876, the Princeton Football Association, after a close vote to adopt rugby rules, sent an invitation to Harvard, Yale, and Columbia for a joint meeting to adopt standard rugby rules and to form an Intercollegiate Football Association.[52] All four colleges met in Springfield, Massachusetts, generally agreed to the English rugby rules and formed a new league.

Yale, while deciding to play rugby against the other members, did not join the student-run Intercollegiate Football Association. The new league chose to compete with fifteen players on a team rather than eleven which Yale favored. Yale recalled its play against Eton, an English public school, three years earlier in which elevens competed in the soccer-type game. The Yale Football Association favored this number, if for no other reason than that they had believed that the faculty would look more favorably on allowing eleven students to leave campus for away games than a larger number.[53] Yale also favored a scoring system which allowed scores only for kicking goals, either during actual play or after a ball was touched down across the goal line. The Association, however, voted to count four touchdowns equal to one kicked goal.[54] What Yale was doing by being the only negative vote in forming the league was attempting to preserve its policy of independence in athletics, something it was more prone to do for the next generation than were its chief competitors.

A significant decision of the Intercollegiate Football Association was to provide for a championship game on Thanksgiving Day, a resolution which began a tradition of a century and more. The idea was to have the two leading teams of the previous year be scheduled for the Thanksgiving Day game.[55] Yale and Princeton were chosen for the championship game scheduled for Hoboken, New

Jersey. Although the rules were agreed upon only four days before, Yale requested that the game be played with eleven on a side and that goals alone be counted in scoring. Princeton agreed. Yale scored two goals and shut out Princeton. The first goal was kicked following the controversial run of a Yale freshman, Walter Camp. Camp, who only a decade later would be called the "father of American football,"[56] got the ball out of a scrum and proceeded on a long run. Just as he was being tackled, he tossed the ball to a teammate, who ran for a touchdown. Princeton protested, claiming the pass was forward and therefore illegal. The referee ended the dispute with a coin toss, which Yale called correctly. The touchdown was allowed, and Yale promptly kicked a goal, giving it the lead and, indeed, college football's first championship.[57]

The Development of the Thanksgiving Day Game

No other feature of nineteenth-century college athletics became as prominent as the Thanksgiving Day Game. Its only rival was the annual rowing regatta from 1871 to its death after 1875, when first Yale and then Harvard withdrew. In football, with Harvard and Yale involved in the championship competition, it was almost assured of success. When the leading city in America, New York, became the site of the annual contest, and the social elites made it the start of the winter social season, the Thanksgiving Day Game became the premier athletic event in colleges by the mid-to-late 1880s.

Though Harvard's involvement in the Football Association was crucial to the league and to the Thanksgiving Day Game, it was Yale and Princeton who dominated athletically from the beginning. The first contest between Princeton and Yale at the St. George's Cricket Grounds in Hoboken was won by Yale and attended by one thousand spectators, as a few New Yorkers crossed the Hudson to view the proceedings. Princeton and Yale became the perennial contestants, with few exceptions, for the next two decades of its existence, as Harvard failed to defeat Yale from 1876 to 1890. After the initial Yale victory, there was only one goal scored by either team for the next five Thanksgiving Day Games, with Princeton winning one goal to nothing in 1878. For the next three years the championship remained with Princeton, as Yale was unable to defeat the Princeton team. In that time the game was moved from Hoboken to New York City's Polo Grounds, and attendance increased dramatically. By 1883, about 15,000 fans came to watch the game as Yale and Princeton competed for their eighth straight championship.[58]

The Thanksgiving Day Game had combined the educationally elite colleges on the athletic field with the social elite in the stands. The "gilded age" in American history was seen no more clearly than at the football stadium. This was especially true by the 1890s, when as many as 40,000 viewed the Thanksgiving Day classic. Even as early as the late 1870s, when the contest was held at St. George's Cricket Club in Hoboken, and a large crowd was seven thousand, a number of clergymen, judges, and political dignitaries began attending the game. Carriages drawn by as many as four horses lined up along the cricket grounds as the canvas-jacket-clad football players performed for individual and college prestige.[59]

Beginning in 1880 and through most of the decade, the Thanksgiving Day Game carved a deeper fashionable status at New York City's Polo Grounds. Many of the 10,000 cheering spectators in 1881 yelled themselves hoarse with the "Rah-rah-rah-rah" yell of Yale and the memorable skyrocket "Hurrah, hurrah, sizz, boom, ah" of the Princeton partisans. Yale players averaging almost 170 pounds were dressed in canvas jackets, corduroy pants, and blue stockings and caps. The Princeton men wore their customary orange and black shirts, white flannel pants, and black stockings and caps, as the wearing of helmets was a thing of the future.[60]

These two teams played the noted "block game" in 1882 in which Princeton early on had decided to play a conservative running game with little passing between players, as was usual in rugby football. An orange-striped player would get the ball and run directly into the line. Not once did a Princeton runner pass the ball to a teammate or kick the ball to Yale. Because there were no rules for gaining a certain number of yards in a specific number of tries or downs, Princeton, after obtaining the ball, kept it for the entire first half. Yale played a similar game in the second half. There was only one kick, made by Yale's Walter Camp, during the entire scoreless contest and no long or exciting runs. Wrote an Englishman after watching America's version of his beloved game: "I was woefully disappointed."[61] Another Englishman suggested a remedy after calling the block game "an unmitigated evil." In a widely reprinted letter, he suggested "allowing a team only four scrimmages, the ball then to change opponents."[62] A rule change similar to this was soon adopted.

The streak of seven straight Thanksgiving Day games between Yale and Princeton was broken in 1883 when Harvard unsuccessfully contested the men from New Haven. Only twice were Princeton and Yale not the game's players in the two decades that important Thanksgiving Day games were held in New York City. After a disputed 1884 game in Gotham and the refusal of Princeton's president to allow a New York game, the Yale-Princeton game reverted for two years to the college sites. Yale, however, chose to play Wesleyan, the newest member of the Intercollegiate Football Association, in New York City. Wesleyan cooperated, losing 61–0.[63]

Two years later Harvard again played Yale before the largest crowd ever to assemble at the Polo Grounds up to that time. A goodly number of the fashionable crowd of 23,000 were "perched high in gayly decked drags and looking resplendent in beautiful winter costumes."[64] These "shining lights of the social world" included most of the student bodies of the two colleges as well as students from the other three Association colleges. After the Yale victory of 1887, the two thousand or so students from the Intercollegiate Football Association—Harvard, Yale, Princeton, Columbia, and Wesleyan—partied in New York City night spots, raising as much raucous cheering at the theaters as at the game.[65] That was the last Thanksgiving appearance in New York City for the Harvard team, as it withdrew from the Intercollegiate Football Association following the defeat at the hands of both Princeton and Yale in 1889. As one contemporary noted about Harvard: "They must lead or they will not remain."[66]

Yale and Princeton, though, continued the tradition for the next six years, the glory years of the Thanksgiving Day Game. Huge crowds averaging over 30,000 spectators attended, with over 40,000 seeing the 1893 Princeton 6–0 win over Yale, a throng which flew in the face of the 1893 banking crisis and depression. The game was preceded by a four-hour parade up Fifth Avenue to Harlem and then to Manhattan Field. The coach and fours were decorated with flags and blankets of the school colors, and the streets were lined with those who wanted a close look at both the society's best and the collegiate warriors on the way to the big game. Many of the prominent attended the games, from multi-millionaires, such as Cornelius Vanderbilt, and state governors, to playwrights and social leaders, such as Mrs. William Whitney and Mrs. Douglas Stewart. Sitting in box seats costing the enormous sum of $5, ten times the cost of attending a major league baseball game, the elegant Mrs.

Stewart "might have poised as the goddess of Yale," wearing a "Yale gown, real university style, with trimmings of blue." Mrs. Whitney in her conspicuous box seat showed the New York social world her "cafe au lait broadcloth, with garnet and sable trimmings, made a la Russian and royally fitted."[67] Thorstein Veblen, writing at about the time, would have looked despairingly at the New York City Thanksgiving Day sporting scene, attacking the leisure class and its dry rot of conspicuous consumption and pecuniary emulation.[68]

Few then would have agreed with Veblen's *The Theory of the Leisure Class* as the Thanksgiving Day phenomenon spread across the nation. As the *New York Herald* editorialized in 1893, "Thanksgiving Day is no longer a solemn festival to God for mercies given. It is a holiday granted by the State and the nation to see a game of football."[69] From New England to the Gulf to the Pacific coast, most colleges had begun playing football by the early 1890s, and many participated in an annual Thanksgiving Day Game. The Catholic college of Georgetown, the private University of Chicago, the state University of Missouri, and the national Naval Academy of Annapolis each had a Thanksgiving Day Game by the 1890s.[70] Said President Warfield of Lafayette College in Pennsylvania: "The Thanksgiving game in football for a big time team brings in revenue greater than the total expenditure of the trustees supporting 25 professors and educating 300 men."[71] There may have been little exaggeration to his words. In 1894, Harvard's football team took in $42,000, most of it at two games, one with Yale and the other on Thanksgiving Day with Penn.[72] Yale and Princeton took in even more money at their New York City Thanksgiving Day Game in the 1890s. Even the University of Chicago, less than a decade old, had played the first major indoor football game against Michigan on Thanksgiving Day in 1896, with gate receipts of almost $11,000 at the Chicago Coliseum. That was more than triple the income of its football team for the entire season the previous year.[73]

As college football teams searched for money, it was only logical that Thanksgiving Day became a commercial day for colleges. There is little question that smaller, less prestigious colleges followed where Yale, Princeton, and Harvard led. By the mid-1890s, it was estimated that 5,000 football games, involving 120,000 athletes, were played on Thanksgiving Day.[74] Many of those games, of course, involved athletic clubs and high schools, but the traditional game had spread to all parts of America. It was at this time that the

Princeton-Yale game was terminated in New York City. While the Thanksgiving Day games continued, the high point had been reached by the mid-1890s. When the greatest crisis in intercollegiate football occurred in 1905, one of the first football excesses to be terminated at a number of schools was the commercialized Thanksgiving Day Game played in large cities.[75] Colleges by then had begun building their own large stadiums. The commercialization and mass mayhem which often accompanied the Thanksgiving Day Game could be better controlled on the college campus than in a large city such as New York.

VII

The Americanization of Rugby Football: Mass Plays, Brutality, and Masculinity

THE RUGBY GAME, first introduced by McGill to Harvard, became the dominant American college sport by the 1890s. The vast benefits which were believed to accrue to colleges from the growth of football were not without cost. The positive values of developing an image of virility in what was often looked upon as effete college education and increasing the visibility of collegiate life had a reverse side. The negative involved the whole question of academic integrity and the place of organized sport in institutions which were formed to further moral and intellectual qualities. Football, more than any other sport, received the credit and took the brunt of criticism given to college sport. To many it was a cancer because of its brutal side and unethical play; to others it was valued for its promotion of character, virility, and esprit de corps. Football began to represent college sport, and no individual came to represent college sport more than Walter Camp.

Walter Camp, Father of American Football

For the historian, who sees some kind of balance between the major forces in history and the influence of prominent individuals, Walter Camp is a prime example of how powerful men helped give direction to American college sport during the period that it was growing most rapidly. Camp, more than any one individual, created the American version of football that became the dominant college sport, and thus, in a way, shaped the course of all intercollegiate sport in America. The leader of American football played halfback in the first Harvard-Yale game played under rugby rules, and he stayed active in the game for the next half-century. He attended the 1877 football rules convention as a sophomore and continued for the next forty-eight years, dying of a heart attack while attending the 1925 NCAA meeting on rules.[1] Camp helped transform football from a relatively insignificant fall pastime in colleges to a gigantic commercial attraction which was the most visible sign of college life. To many, football was the primary college activity which stood for manliness and virility. Football appeared to contrast with the effete aspects of the institution which emphasized esoteric knowledge and the egghead.

Walter Camp came to represent the practical and the virile. Camp, born two years before the Civil War, lived close to Yale from an early age and attended a preparatory school adjacent to the Yale campus. It was natural for the seventeen-year-old son of a middle-class schoolmaster to attend Yale. As the country celebrated its centennial, Camp played as a freshman on Yale's championship team of the newly formed Intercollegiate Football Association. Camp soon became identified with America's dominating athletic college of the nineteenth century. Yale won at all its major sports, but football success was synonymous with Yale, as it won over 95 percent of its games in the years Camp was associated in some capacity, officially or unofficially, with the football team. Yale lost only fourteen games in the span of thirty-four years from 1876–1909, surely the greatest record in intercollegiate history.[2]

Camp and Yale athletics typified much of the new industrial society in the post-Civil War era. In 1882, a year after ending his six seasons of varsity football at Yale, Camp began a lifetime career at the New Haven Clock Company, one of Connecticut's largest industries. Camp, then, was part of the nineteenth-century laissez-faire capitalism which dominated the economic and political scene. Yale football and Walter Camp were much like the economic ideology of capitalistic America. Under that belief, the strong survived and prospered; the weak languished or perished. Camp, like his brother-in-law William Graham Sumner, the Social Darwinist, believed that the fittest survived.

Camp, according to most observers, was the principal reason for the unmatched success of Yale. One biographer has stated that Camp never coached a Yale football team,[3] but others claim he was the official coach from 1888–92 and the de facto coach before and after that time.[4] William H. Corbin, the captain of possibly the greatest all-time Yale team of 1888, which outscored its opponents 698 to nothing, had likely invited Camp to be his official coach in 1888. As captains controlled teams prior to the infusion of professional coaches by the twentieth century, Corbin probably asked Camp to be his unpaid head coach for the season. Corbin wrote sometime later that it had been his ambition since 1888 to place Camp "in the position of absolute authority as head coach."[5] At that time, 1902, Corbin hoped that Camp would "continue next year to act as head coach" while another man acted as field coach.[6]

The distinction between head coach, field coach, and captain does not appear as clear as that between coach and captain several generations later, but to understand Camp it must be clarified somewhat. Whether or not Camp was officially a head coach, it is clear that he was the individual who most Yale captains went to for coaching advice and direction for the team. Often the previous year's captain became the field coach, with Camp remaining the advisor of the field coach and the captain.[7] Camp was the continuity which tied Yale's remarkable teams together from year to year. W. W. "Pudge" Heffelfinger, probably the greatest tackle of the first half-century of American football, recalled to Camp that in the late 1880s and early 1890s the Yale football team was "closely tied together . . . with your advice and guidance."[8] In 1889, a Yale graduate wrote Camp saying that he hoped Camp would "be enabled to find time to coach" the team.[9]

It was natural for Yale boosters to want Camp's expertise, but numerous other colleges also sought his advice. One was Notre Dame instructor and new football coach James Kivlan, who in 1892 asked Camp to furnish him "with some points on the best way to develop a good football team."[10] Yale's dearest adversary, Harvard, also knew his importance. Harvard professor and dean LeBaron Briggs, associated with the college from the early 1870s, may have best summarized Camp's influence. "I knew him as a master of football," said Briggs, "whose advice—if the Yale captain would listen to it— meant inevitable defeat to the college I loved best."[11]

The advice of Camp came most often during coaching sessions at the Camp home during the evenings of the football season. Camp's wife, the former Alice Graham Sumner, would attend afternoon practice, taking notes on the proceedings of the team while Camp was in the office of the New Haven Clock Company. In the evening the team leaders would discuss the team's progress with the insightful Camp. This system is what Camp referred to in 1899 as the "Czar principle," whereby there was an "unnamed officer" with "one man directing and loyalty to him."[12] Camp was the Czar of Yale football.

Camp's control of football on the national scene was considerably different but no less important for the development of the game. He led the way in legislation which transformed English rugby to American football. Camp was Yale's representative to the Intercollegiate Football Association meeting in 1880, when he suggested probably the most radical rule change in rugby football in its history.

Camp convinced the student-led rules convention to allow a team in possession of the ball to retain it after a player was tackled and "down." In rugby, when a player was downed, the ball would be played in a "scrummage." Both sides gathered about the ball en masse and each attempted to kick the ball in the direction of the other's goal. There was much pushing, shoving, and hacking of the opponents shins in this endeavor. When the ball came out of the scrum, a player would then pick it up and run toward the opponent's goal. What was developing in American rugby was a kind of heeling, dragging, or snapping of the ball backwards out of the chaotic scrummage. As the players gave the ball a downward and backward movement with the foot, a teammate would pick up the ball and run with it.[13] A rule, however, was needed to differentiate clearly between the offense and defense.

To Camp and other collegians, the rugby scrummage was not logical or rational. To a future clock entrepreneur, what should be more important than to rationalize football? Like industrial mass production, football would be systematized as to who controlled the ball, giving it a greater semblance of order. Camp's new scrimmage rule read:

A scrimmage takes place when the holder of the ball . . . puts it down on the ground in front of him and puts it in play while on side . . . by snapping it back with his foot. The man who first receives it from the snap-back shall be called the quarter-back. . . .[14]

The innovation of Camp produced a new type of game with both a center (snapper-back) and a quarterback.

Camp's insightful use of the scrimmage led to the development of distinct strategy as found in the modern game, but it lacked one element. There was no provision for relinquishing the ball. A team could keep control of the ball, and it would do so even if a player were tackled behind the goal resulting in a safety, as there was no penalty in the scoring system. A team could retain the ball indefinitely if it did not kick or fumble the ball. When in the second half of the 1880 Thanksgiving Day championship game Princeton was pushed back toward its goal by Yale, the Princeton captain directed his players neither to kick nor to lateral the ball, thus preventing fumbles. Princeton maintained the ball, kept the game scoreless, and retained the championship it had won the previous year.

Following another year when the "block game" was used by both Yale and Princeton, resulting in another scoreless game, Camp suggested incorporating the notion of "downs," whereby a team was given three attempts to make five yards (or lose ten yards) or give up possession of the ball. The five-yard, three-down rule created the need for five-yard chalk lines on the field, creating the "gridiron" effect and thus a new name for the American football game.

The resulting gridiron game of downs and yards to be gained led inventive collegians to create efficient machine-like tactics and strategy. Much as Harvard dropout Frederick W. Taylor was doing for scientific management of the workplace at the Midvale Steel Company in Philadelphia, Camp was producing "work" efficiency on the "play" field at the same time.[15] Yale, under Walter Camp, had the smoothest running football machine, emphasizing team cooperation rather than individual effort. Signals for calling plays when a team had undisputed possession followed naturally. Camp first devised four plays which were called by nonsense sentences. When the sentence "Look out quick Deac" or any part of it was yelled, it meant that Henry Twombly would receive the ball from the quarterback and run through the line. "Play up sharp Charlie" was another signal for a different back to run. Simple were the signals, and soon Princeton used letters of the alphabet, while Harvard and Penn employed both sentences and letters.[16]

The evolution of signals was part of the development of strategic offensive plays aimed at the adversary. Even before the scrimmage line was created, the elementary forms of running interference for the ball carrier began. Under Rugby Union rules, no player could be in advance of the ball; thus no one could interfere with a player attempting to make a tackle. If a teammate of the ball carrier was ahead of the ball, he was "off-sides" and could not legally interfere. In England, there was an upper-class understanding in rugby, as in other sports, that the spirit of the rules was as important as the rules themselves. In America, the letter of the rules might be observed, but the spirit of the rules was much undervalued. As Camp remarked, "The Rugby code was all right for Englishmen who had been brought up upon traditions as old and as binding as the laws themselves," but Americans lacked those traditions.[17] Just as Americans "heeled" or "snapped" the ball out of the scrimmage in violation of the spirit of the rules, teammates began guarding the ball carrier by running alongside him and interfering with the tacklers. Yale, with Camp as captain in 1879, and Princeton evidently first used this strategy.[18] With the scrimmage and retention of the ball, this tactic became more valued. By 1882 and the yards and downs rule, officials were increasingly lax in the enforcement of the "off-side" rule.[19] Once accepted, Camp said, interference became the "keynote of the American game."[20]

As a result of the Americanization of rugby through the innovations of Camp and others, football soon emphasized mass formations with organized interference in an effort to make five yards in three attempts. Camp continued to be innovative, including his numerical system of scoring for touchdowns, extra points, field goals, and safeties in 1883, and the first all-American team, which he selected in 1889. His impact upon rule changes, which led to mass plays and accompanying loud cries of brutality, however, stands out in the development of college football.

The Development of Mass Plays and Cries of Brutality

What was occurring in the Americanization of rugby football in the 1880s was a more rational or businesslike approach to the sport. A more efficient system was being developed, so that the team which became the most professionally organized would profit the most in terms of victory. How the game was played from the standpoint of personal enjoyment or aesthetic sense was much less important than was the final result of the contest. If mass plays to produce five yards and an eventual touchdown or a field goal could be achieved, it was far more important to the collegians than if the experience of participation was enjoyable during the contest. Mass plays resulted because that was the strategy which served to produce winners.

Brutality intensified under the new Intercollegiate Football Association rules which Camp molded, but it was not a new phenomenon. Football, when frosh-soph class battles were in vogue, had its violent element. After Rutgers and Princeton inauguarated soccer football, one could hear the call: "Let us have no more wholesale maulings [of the] brutal foot-ball matches."[21] Following a fray with Yale, a distraught Rutgers student exaggerated:

> We fought from noon till nearly dark:
> Our dead and dying strewed the park.[22]

Yale, the constant winner, often became the point of barbed comments for ruffian behavior. The "Yale team have cultivated a habit of . . . mauling their antagonists with double fists," complained Tufts college.[23] Harvard charged Yale players with jumping on downed players with their knees while striking with closed fists as Yale "prepared to win . . . by means which gentlemen would never stoop to."[24]

In the early 1880s, charges of brutality increased as it appeared that brute force rather than agility and skill were coming to dominate the scrimmage game.[25] The newly formed faculty athletic committee at Harvard voted to ban football in 1883 because the rules allowed players to strike opponents three times with closed fists before being ejected.[26] Yet, five days later, Harvard was playing Yale at the Polo Grounds in New York City.[27] Meanwhile, at the University of Pennsylvania, the faculty, provost, and trustees were discussing whether or not to continue football under existing rules.[28]

Penn did not ban football for its brutality, but Harvard soon did. The three-member Harvard faculty athletic committee decided to attend four of the Intercollegiate Football Association league games the next fall. In each game, the trio saw "brutal fighting with fists" and a lack of gentlemanly behavior, "the spirit that scorns to take an unfair advantage of an opponent." The game, they reported to the Harvard College faculty, was "brutal, demoralizing to the players and to the spectators, and extremely dangerous."[29] Football was a disgrace to the university, and they wanted it banned for a year. The faculty concurred. The same Harvard athletic committee viewed other colleges playing football a year later and concluded that brutality had almost disappeared.[30]

After a year's absence, Harvard rejoined the Intercollegiate Football Association, but the question of football violence among the dominating colleges continued. Even a supporter of football complained in a popular journal of roughness, injuries, and brutality, while Harvard authorities continued their assault upon the game.[31] Dudley Sargent, a medical doctor, head of Harvard's physical education program and chairman of the athletic committee, wrote to the student president of the Intercollegiate Football Association asking that group to change its rules. Sargent wanted to prevent "brutalities which so nearly destroyed one of the best and most attractive of our out door sports."[32] The game remained essentially the same, however, when Harvard met and beat Princeton in the fall of 1887. A Princeton man recalled the encounter which forced him out of the game before it concluded "due to sheer weakness from loss of blood." The bleeding from breaking his nose early in the game, being kicked in the chest, and cut in the scalp and face, combined with a bruised shoulder and strained knee ligaments were the Princeton player's memories from his toughest playing day.[33] Harvard students had not learned the gentlemanly game hoped for by the faculty.

Following the season of 1887, the Intercollegiate Football Association passed a radical rule that nearly assured mass plays and increased charges of brutality. The Association, with Camp leading the way, ruled that tackling below the waist to the knees be allowed for the first time.[34] The low tackle did much to reduce the effectiveness of open field dodging which had been a feature of most games up to this time. The open style of play was dropped in favor of mass plays, when victory resulted from the closed formations. For the next six seasons, ingenious captains and coaches developed a series of close formation wedges to make the necessary five yards in three attempts and counter the more effective low tackle. Two innovative football coaches from the University of Chicago and the University of Minnesota, Amos Alonzo Stagg and Henry L. Williams, revealed the new strategy in their 1893 *Treatise on American Football.* Their book diagrammed the Princeton wedge, the Yale modification of the Princeton play, Harvard wedges, a split wedge, a feint wedge, and the famous flying wedge.[35]

No football play ever devised was more dangerous, or more ingenious, than Lorin F. Deland's flying wedge, first used by Harvard. The Boston businessman was neither a Harvard graduate nor a football player. He was, however, interested in adapting military strategy, especially Napoleon's first principal on the concentration of force, to football. Deland contacted Bernie Trafford, the Harvard captain, and the two discussed Deland's football strategy. Trafford called his men together for a summer practice to test the Deland football theories. The closed July practices were not entirely secret, for colleges then as now had their spying systems. Yale heard that Harvard was testing a new strategy, but it did not learn the details of the play that would startle the football world. An informant wrote Camp that summer: "'Now I fancy no complicated maneuvers can be made to work with certainty. . . . To work them at all would require a standard of team play which Harvard is not usually up to."[36]

The flying wedge was practiced in secret during the fall but never tried in a game until the Yale contest, concluding the season. Harvard, with a scoreless tie at the beginning of the second half, put the ball into play. The rules then allowed the team which was kicking off to either kick to the opponents or to merely touch the ball with the foot, pick it up, and pass it back to a teammate who could run with it. Deland ingeniously thought of using the latter method with one man over the ball and the other players divided into two groups well back and on each side of the ball. The five heaviest Harvard men were in one group, about 25 yards from the ball, while the four faster runners were in the other, possibly 20 yards from the ball. In the middle of the diagonally placed groups a single player acted as a decoy runner. Upon a signal, with the heavier men starting somewhat sooner and running at full speed, the other group angled to form an apex or "V" aimed at one of the Yale players. The ball was passed to one of the flying wedge as it rammed into the Yale forward wall. Legend has it that the play gained to the Yale 25-yard line before the flying wedge broke down, but the gain was only about 20 yards.[37] Nevertheless, the flying wedge was a sensation, probably the most feared play in football history.

Brutality and the Crisis of 1894

The dynamics of the flying wedge caught the imagination of football players and fans across America, leading to the appearance of greater violence. Nearly every team experimented with some form of the flying wedge, introducing aspects of mass momentum plays into their regular scrimmage attack. President Eliot of Harvard, the leading educator in America, condemned football with its increasing violence, saying:

> The game of foot-ball grows worse and worse as regards foul and violent play, and the number and gravity of injuries which the players suffer. It has become perfectly clear that the game as now played is unfit for college use.[38]

It was only natural that strong opposition would arise over a game that looked like mass mayhem and which had players such as Yale's Frederic Remington, who dipped his football jacket in a slaughterhouse pool of blood to make it look more businesslike.[39]

In 1893, after the first full year of the flying wedge, a Harvard graduate asked the Harvard Board of Overseers to investigate the merits and evils of football and to compile statistics regarding the game.[40] Robert Bacon of the Board of Overseers asked Yale's Walter Camp to chair a committee to determine the degree of brutality in football. A blue-ribbon committee of six was struck, consisting of two ministers, a judge, a life insurance executive, and Bacon and Camp. The committee was dominated by men from the Big Three, Harvard, Yale, and Princeton, but it was Camp who did most of the work. Over a thousand questionnaires were sent to coaches and former players, as well as high school and preparatory school administrators.[41]

In early 1894, Camp began collecting the data. Of the ex-players, Camp asked the questions: What were their football experiences; what injuries had they received; were the injuries permanent; and how might the game be improved? Camp compiled the data and concluded for the committee that Harvard, Yale, and Princeton players during the previous eighteen years had an "almost unanimous opinion" that football has been a "marked benefit" both physically and mentally.[42]

Camp, though, was selective in what he chose to be published in his book, *Football Facts and Figures*.[43] One of Yale's players, William Corbin, captain of the great 1888 team, replied that when he played, the use of interference had not come into general use. The game, he said, "was more open than at present, and the dangers [of] the present style of interference and 'mass plays' were absent."[44] His comments remained in the report, but a Harvard player's comments were deleted by Camp. The ex-player had said that the rules of the game needed to be amended to "keep it free from injuries to the players."[45] Camp also excised from the book the statement that 20 percent of the ex-football players reported some permanent injury.[46] Yet, the comments of Walter "Pudge" Heffelfinger, the ex-Yale great and probably the greatest player of the first half-century of football, were included. Heffelfinger replied, "During all the years I have played I have known no one personally who has been seriously injured."[47]

School headmasters and college faculty reported divergent opinions. While one man would say that football was "the grandest of all games and must be saved," another would state that radical changes in the rules were needed.[48] William T. Reid, a California prep school headmaster and father of a future Harvard star football player and coach, wanted football to be "modified or replaced by one less violent."[49] William Milligan Sloane, Princeton professor and the individual most responsible for sending an American team to the 1896 Olympics, was a supporter of all forms of sport. Sloane praised football, shortly before sailing to France for an 1894 meeting at the Sorbonne which brought about the re-establishment of the Olympic Games. Like the Olympics, Sloane believed that football contributed to manly health, and it had fewer injuries than "most other vigorous autumn and winter games."[50] The publication of the selected documents favorable to football in *Football Facts and Figures* did much to allay fears that football was ruinous to young men's health.

The publication of Camp's book was fortunate for football, for the game had suffered a crisis in leadership the same year. Several incidents added to the troubled times in intercollegiate football. President Grover Cleveland abolished the annual Army-Navy football game following an 1893 season report which found 24 Annapolis players admitted to the hospital, 82 sick days for the team, and an additional 60 excuses from drill for injuries.[51] At the same time that Harvard, Northwestern, and other colleges were considering abolishing football, others, such as Cornell, were limiting games to college grounds.[52] While these activities were taking place, the University of Pennsylvania and Wesleyan withdrew from the Intercollegiate Football Association during the football season because of new eligibility rules which they opposed. This left the Association with only two members, Yale and Princeton, as Harvard had withdrawn four years before.[53]

With the disintegration of the Intercollegiate Football Association, there was no acknowledged organization for the needed rule revisions. The University Athletic Club of New York City, sensing a void in leadership, requested that Harvard, Yale, Princeton, and Pennsylvania form a rules committee for governing football play. These four institutions agreed to send delegates. Yale's Walter Camp was chosen for the important position of secretary. The group quickly changed the football rules, abolishing mass momentum plays in which more than three men were moving forward before the ball was put in play.[54]

With the abolition of the flying wedge and some other types of mass momentum plays and the publication of the laudatory *Football Facts and Figures,* some of the football turmoil was quelled. However, the situation between Harvard and Yale deteriorated to new depths. The 1894 football game between the two rivals resulted in foul play and broken bones. Harvard players alone had a broken leg, collar bone, and nose, while several Yale players went to the hospital with head injuries.[55] Harvard's faculty voted to abolish intercollegiate football because of broken bones, broken rules, and broken promises, but the eventual decision was to break athletic relations with Yale in the major sports.[56] The split in athletic relations was reflected in the rules committee of 1895. Harvard and Penn separated from Yale and Princeton and joined Cornell to form their own rules-making body.

The chaos over contending rules found its way into the important universities in the Midwest. Amos Alonzo Stagg, athletic director of the University of Chicago, chastised the eastern colleges for not creating one set of rules. Stagg, the former Yale star, wrote Walter Camp warning him that if the older colleges would not act effectively, the western colleges "shall certainly get out a set ourselves."[57] The eastern powers, sensing the likelihood of another set of contending rules from the newly created "Big Ten" conference in early 1895, responded by joining together once again. To maintain their athletic power further, the eastern group asked all colleges to submit their suggestions for reform.[58] The committee which ruled football became, for the first time, alumni-controlled. Walter Camp was joined by alumni from the other colleges. The alumni rules committee, led by Walter Camp, never satisfactorily came to grips with the problem of excessive physical violence in football.

As the century came to a close, the question of football brutality was not settled, and it would not be for more than a decade. A larger question was why, if football had a significant violent element, would it not have been eliminated by college authorities who were recognized as being in a position to act? What was there in American society that gave sanction to a game which so many could call brutal?

Football and Manliness:
A Measure of the American College

The freedom of college men to form their own extracurriculum in the nineteenth century was not, of course, a freedom without restrictions. College faculties everywhere by the end of the century formed athletic committees in an attempt to prevent football and other sports from encroaching upon academic interests. Football as played in the 1890s, though, must have looked like an extension of freedom into anarchy to a number of professors and administrators. Even if college faculties and presidents had favored abolishing football, they probably could not have done it, as forces much larger than college officials were at work. American football, with its violent element, fit well into the American mentality which demanded manliness and the virile features of society. The perceived function of football as a facilitator of manly qualities was a potent force in making the sport a featured activity on most college campuses.

Theodore Roosevelt, before becoming President, was speaking for that part of America which was concerned with the possible loss of virility as the nation became urbanized and abandoned a tough, frontier mentality. Roosevelt and others feared a national decay. "If we lose the virile, manly qualities," he wrote the year before he led the Rough Riders in Cuba against the Spanish, America would "reach a condition worse than that of ancient civilizations in the years of decay."[59] He told youthful readers that "the love of athletic sports . . . has beyond all question had an excellent effect in increased manliness."[60] In the midst of the 1890s' football crisis emanating from charges of brutality, Roosevelt, a Harvard graduate, wrote Walter Camp that he was "utterly disgusted" with Harvard President Eliot and his faculty's call for a ban on football. Roughness, said Roosevelt, was an advantage of football. A man in the real world, he said, "can't be efficient unless he is manly." Reacting to the charge of violence, he told Camp that he "would a hundred fold rather keep the game as it is now, with the brutality, than give it up."[61]

Roosevelt, the symbol of the strenuous life, was a spokesman for manly virtues in college life and in national life, but he certainly was not alone. In a country which saw the decline of manly virtues at the end of the nineteenth century, there was a need for new concrete and symbolic forms of manhood.[62] This was especially true for the collegiate sons of both middle-class and more socially elite parents. Football, considered the most manly of college sports at the close of the nineteenth century, could provide the proof that colleges as institutions, as well as college men, were virile. Athletic prowess of a college football player was a marked contrast to the pale, dyspeptic scholar of an earlier time.

Football was new proof of an urban manhood in a country searching for its signs, as America increasingly entered the world's political stage. Senator Henry Cabot Lodge, spreading his imperialistic gospel of Anglo-Saxon superiority, celebrated his twenty-fifth class reunion by praising vigorous athletics, and told President Eliot so. "The time given to athletic contests and the injuries incurred on the playing field," he said to the Harvard class of 1896, "are part of the price which the English-speaking race has paid for being world-conquerors."[63] Charles F. Thwing, president of Western Reserve, agreed and praised football as "a game of hearts" in which pluck and enthusiasm characterized the Anglo-Saxon race.[64] Professor Bronson of Brown University echoed the same sentiments when he praised football and other sports as America entered the arena of world politics. "National robustness" through continued athletic exercise must be preserved, Bronson said, to offset the weakness produced by "city life and greater ease."[65] A medical doctor at the University of Pennsylvania, J. William White, was never more convinced of the value of football to the making of men than after an 1896 Thanksgiving Day football game played in vile weather. The game was fought out in a driving northwest rain and snow in a "quagmire of ice-cold mud . . . with pools of icy water on the surface." After a hard fought Penn victory, he praised the team. "Those eleven frozen, purple, shivering, chattering players" were to be honored, he said, "by every one who loves manliness and courage."[66]

Football was, then, more than just a rough college game. It was a symbol of college and national virility. As a medical doctor wrote Camp during Camp's investigation of the football question in 1894: "If our nation survives, the man of the future must be able to elbow his way among rough men in the foul air. . . ." Football, he said, "furnishes good ideals of courageous manhood."[67] This was important to the life of colleges which were often thought to be "effete and impractical."[68] Thus, when Theodore Roosevelt called upon his countrymen "not for a life of ease but for the life of strenuous endeavor," he could use the football metaphor: "Hit the line hard: don't foul and don't shirk, but hit the line hard."[69]

College presidents and some faculty could be persuaded of the need for the virile element and for the preservation of football. Even the leading college educator, Charles Eliot, reinforced the argument. For two decades beginning in the 1880s, Eliot, while voting on several occasions to ban football at Harvard, would write publicly that "effeminacy and luxury are even worse evils than brutality."[70] Other presidents agreed. Princeton's Francis Patton, who saw no reason for men to forfeit their manliness by being Christians, valued football. It was through football, Patton believed, that "some of the very best elements of manhood may emerge."[71] President William Rainey Harper of Chicago, who hired Amos Alonzo Stagg "to develop teams which we can send around the country and knock out all the colleges," did not think the game was brutal. He considered that masculine football was the "great American college game."[72] Notre Dame's president, John Cavanaugh, said in the early 1900s that he would rather see young men playing the dangerous game of football and receiving "a broken collar bone occasionally than to see them dedicated to croquet."[73] Historian Edwin Slosson, who was opposed to football, noted not only that colleges often showed a tendency toward femininity but that college presidents were nearly unanimously in favor of the game.[74]

Though college presidents often spoke out against the brutal nature of football, they generally praised it, as Slosson said, for fostering manly virtues. Presidents, hired and fired by boards of trustees, usually did not take stands in opposition to those who paid their salaries. As boards of trustees were supportive of intercollegiate athletics in the latter 1800s, it was natural for presidents not to create controversies by calling for drastic actions when football crises occurred. Those who did were sometimes called unmanly themselves, a term that presidents might fear. One reply to Camp's 1894 questionnaire made the point. Football, an ex-football player wrote, "can never suffer while patronized by the numbers and class of people, who almost entirely compose the audiences at today's great contests, unless it is *legislated against by Presidents* of Colleges, who I am sorry to say have *missed their gender.* . . ."[75] Some presidents may have "missed their gender" relative to manly sports, but not most.

More and more, presidents and their institutions reflected the dominant business ethic as colleges became universities and universities expanded into "Big Education," paralleling "Big Business."[76]

Governing boards in the late nineteenth century, like presidents, spoke for America when they endorsed football and other sports on the college campus. Boards more and more were drawn from the business elite to set policy in American colleges and universities. They began to set athletic policy as well.[77] Condoning the commercial and business aspects of athletics, governing boards increasingly agreed to the hiring of professional coaches and the erection of large stadiums which could seat far more than the number of students and staff. The brutal nature of mass plays in football probably mirrored the businessmen's world, as did the commercial aspect of football. An observer of the American scene tried to draw business and football into perspective. "The spirit of the American youth, as of the American man," the editor of *Nation* wrote in 1890, "is to win, to 'get there,' by fair means or foul; and lack of moral scruple which pervades the struggles of the business world meets with temptations equally irresistible in the miniature contests of the football field."[78] That, however, was part of manly American society as it moved toward the twentieth century. Football brutality and its appearance of manliness was one measure, and an important one, of late-nineteenth-century American higher education.

VIII

College Track: From the Paper Chase to Olympic Gold

FOOTBALL DOMINATED LATE-NINETEENTH-CENTURY intercollegiate sports, while crew and baseball were supreme before the rise of the gridiron game. Track and field became the fourth major college sport of the 1800s, and, like the other three, was imported from the British Isles. Track, of course, was much older than British history or even written history. One may recall that Odysseus won the foot race in Homer's *Iliad* when the goddess Athena made Aias slip in manure, causing the victim to spit out cow dung rather than receive the silver bowl which went to the winner. While the silver trophy remained symbolic of track success, track and field in America never attained the status of baseball, crew, or football, or of running in ancient Greece. Track's impact was nevertheless felt by the 1890s outside the college world. Track, along with crew, was important to the development of international intercollegiate athletics, and it was the performance of collegians on track teams which gave America dominance after the Modern Olympics were internationalized in 1896.

The British Background of Track and Field

American intercollegiate track and field, like crew, baseball, cricket, and football, received its impetus from athletic contests imported from Britain. Running activities, however, unlike cricket and crew, were not well organized at the English public schools or the two great universities in the first half of the nineteenth century. While Oxford and Cambridge competed in cricket and crew in the 1820s, there were no intercollegiate track contests until the 1860s. In Britain, there was a tendency for the elitist public schools to introduce organized sports before the universities adopted them. This was true of running events.

Possibly the earliest track meet at a public school was the hare and hounds run at Rugby, begun in the 1830s.[1] Thomas Hughes, two decades after he had participated in sports at Rugby, described the cross-country run in his *Tom Brown's Schooldays*. At the "Big Side" hare and hounds meet, two well-known Rugby runners were chosen to be the hares, each with two bags of torn-up newspapers as scent. The newspaper fragments were scattered over the nine-mile run by the hares who were given a few minutes' head start before the forty or so young Rugbyite hounds were released to follow the scent. Crossing fields, ditches, and streams, the boys attempted to catch the hares before they reached a local landmark where ale, bread, and cheese awaited those who completed the run. Young Tom Brown and his friend Harry East ran until their legs gave way and never finished the journey. Thomas Hughes described it:

> "Well," said Tom mopping away, and gulping down his disappointment, "it can't be helped. We did our best anyhow. Hadn't we better find this lane, and go down it, as young Brooke told us?"
> "I suppose so—nothing else for it," grunted East. . . .
> So they tried back slowly and sorrowfully, and found the lane, and went limping down it, plashing in the cold puddly ruts, and beginning to feel how the run had taken it out of them. The evening closed in fast, and clouded over dark cold, and dreary.[2]

Hughes's Rugby episode had a strong impact on the development of running in both England and America.

Eton, an even more elite English public school than Rugby, introduced another type of cross country run in 1845, a steeplechase. The race, about three miles long, included plowed fields, several jumps, and other challenges. It became an annual event and was soon joined by dashes, hurdle races, and other running events.[3]

At mid-century, track and field was awakened at Oxford and Cambridge. Exeter College at Oxford, which had a steeplechase, added a number of events, ranging from the 100-yard dash to the two-mile cross country contest with twenty-four jumps. Halifax Wyatt, who had suggested the college meet, won the cross country event, running in flannel pants through the muddy terrain.[4] Other colleges at Oxford soon followed Exeter's model, and inter-college contests began by the 1860s. Cambridge, too, followed the lead of Oxford, and by the close of the 1850s the Cambridge University Athletic Club put on its own track meet. The ten events of the 1859 meet included the quarter-mile (58 seconds), mile (5 minutes, 14 seconds), high jump (5'6"), fourteen-pound shot put (37'3"), and the cricket-ball throw (98 yards, 5").[5] The growth of track and field at England's two universities naturally led to a call for an Oxford-Cambridge meet.

Students of the two universities negotiated an eight-event meet at the Christ Church College cricket grounds on the Oxford University campus in March 1864. Each of the university's varsity teams won four events. Two representative performances were the mile run in four minutes, 56 seconds, and the quarter-mile in 56 seconds.[6] Even with the status of varsity competition, track and field never became as important as crew, cricket, or football in England or baseball, crew, or football in America. In England, according to an Oxford man, there was generally the need for "the encouragement of bribery" to get men to participate by offering valuable silver cups or trophies for winning performances.[7] A faculty member at Cambridge complained in 1873 that the track athlete, unlike the rower, looks to "the mustard-pot in the silversmith's window, which, now, alas! must be visible before an athlete will jump over a foot stool or run around a grassplot."[8] So while track grew in British universities, it was never as attractive, except for prizes, as were the team sports.

Tom Brown and the Paper Chase Arrive in America

American colleges followed where the British led. Within three years of the 1857 publication of *Tom Brown's Schooldays,* the Rugby novel had made an impact on running and other sports in America.[9] At Andover Theological Seminary in Massachusetts, the imported Rugby game of hare and hounds, or paper chasing, was the "rage" in 1860.[10] But at Andover and other institutions of higher learning, interest in paper chasing was periodic at best until organized track meets spread in the 1870s. Yale students tried the English game of hare and hounds in 1870, but it seems to have died almost as soon as it was introduced.[11]

Harvard experimented with the sport of hare and hounds in 1876, just one week before the inaugural Thanksgiving Day championship football game. Harvard hares were given a fifteen-minute start, trailing paper scent over a seven-mile course around Cambridge. Jumping fences, running through backyards, evading irritated property owners and their dogs, Harvard students completed their first paper chase.[12] Whether it was because of angered land owners or exhausted runners, there appeared to be no more chases for three years, until the Harvard Athletic Association sponsored another race. Harvard's popular football captain, Robert Bacon, may have given the sport a new boost when he participated in a ten-mile paper chase which included about forty hounds and two hares.[13]

At about this time other colleges were taking up the paper chase. New York City's Columbia University began hare and hound racing following the 1878 Thanksgiving Day race sponsored by the Westchester Hare and Hounds Club.[14] Princeton formed a Hare and Hounds Club in 1880 and held local runs. Princeton challenged Columbia to a twelve-mile run in the spring of 1881, but Columbia did not accept the invitation.[15] Nearly a decade passed before two colleges met in a paper chase. By then the name of the sport would be changed to cross country.

Cross country runs of collegians and athletic clubs were popular enough for the formation of the National Cross-Country Association in 1887.[16] The term "cross country" began to replace the paper chase and hare and hounds as the accepted name, and the need to scatter paper also began to fade. The runners, however, continued to be called "harriers," and the tradition has continued. Three years after the National Cross-Country Association held its first championship, the University of Pennsylvania beat Cornell in the first intercollegiate cross country race in 1890. Cornell continued to take an active part and suggested forming the Intercollegiate Cross Country Association of Amateur Athletics of America in 1899. The Association held its first championship in November, with Cornell winning the six-mile cross country race, followed by Penn, Columbia, and Princeton.[17] By the twentieth century, cross country, transformed from paper chasing, had arrived on American college campuses, though not in a dynamic way. Track and field was also progressing at the same time in a more forceful manner.

Track: A James Gordon Bennett Regatta Addendum

Track and field is not always separated in the public's mind from cross country running, but it was for the most part in the nineteenth century. Because the English kept the distinction, it was logical for Americans to do the same. It is not entirely clear when track contests arrived on college campuses. Footracing was known in colonial times. Ben Franklin's College of Philadelphia (University of Pennsylvania) had a footracing championship in 1770.[18] This, however, was probably an isolated incident. Not until the mid-nineteenth century did interest in track and field arise. This was evidently first seen at Princeton.

Princeton was a logical site for the development of college track because of its strong Scottish background. Scots had a long tradition of running and field events. The organized contests were known as Caledonian Games; Caledonia being the Roman name for Scotland from the days of antiquity. Scots coming to America naturally brought their games with them. Caledonian Games were first recorded in America in Boston in 1853. Scottish Princeton had a track and field meet as early as 1859, with a Scot, S. J. Humphries, winning a traditional Caledonian contest, the hop-step-jump, today called the triple jump, with a distance of over 40 feet.[19] Annual contests, though, did not appear until Scottish immigrant and Caledonian performer George Goldie was hired in 1869 by the new Princeton president and Presbyterian minister from Scotland, James McCosh. Goldie became director of Princeton's new gymnasium. Soon Princeton students were participating in track contests which they called Caledonian Games.[20]

Princeton was not the only college experiencing the growth of track around 1870. Nor were the Caledonian Games the sole model for the growth of track and field. At Columbia, George Rives, who had recently graduated, traveled to England to attend Cambridge University. He observed the Oxford-Cambridge track and field meet of 1868. The meet was only in its fifth year, but Rives was impressed and wrote home encouraging Columbia students to form an athletic association. The association held its first meet in 1869, basing it on a combination of running events found at the Oxford-Cambridge meet and field events patterned after the Caledonian Games, then popular in New York City.[21] Yale students were also able to participate in running in 1869, as a four-mile race was contested at icy Hamilton Park in January. The next year the Yale crew sponsored a three-mile run with substantial prizes of $15, $10, and $5 for the first three places. It probably was not surprising that conditioned crew members won the money, the winner covering the three miles in just short of 19 minutes.[22]

More important than the growth of track at any single campus was the stimulus given by a first generation Scottish-American and owner of the New York *Herald*, James Gordon Bennett, Jr. Bennett, whose father had gained great wealth after founding the *Herald*, was a nineteenth-century nouveau riche playboy and sport promoter. While his greatest love was yachting, his lifetime sporting interests included polo, tennis, pedestrianism (long-distance running-walking contests), horse racing, and later auto and airplane racing.[23]

Bennett, cognizant of the attention the elite intercollegiate regatta of 1873 was receiving, offered a prize trophy for a two-mile run at the Hampden Park track in Springfield, Massachusetts, during the regatta. The prize, valued at $500, according to one estimate, was offered less than two weeks before the scheduled event when Harvard's William Blaikie, representing Bennett, sent a letter to various colleges announcing it.[24]

The race gained a good deal of interest, partly because of the eligibility controversy of the first American intercollegiate track meet. Six men were entered in that race, though only three competed. The reluctance to contend for the lucrative prize stemmed in part from the fact that Duncan Bowie of McGill University in Montreal was entered. Bowie met Bennett's only requirement, by being a college student. Bowie, however, ran in Caledonian races in a number of American cities at which valuable prizes were offered and professional runners contested. He had won a considerable amount of money in 1872 at the sixteenth annual New York Caledonian Club celebration, where he won three races and the hop, step, and jump. His mile victory alone was worth $90, about one-third of a laborer's annual salary.[25] Cornell's Edward Phillips, especially, challenged Bowie's eligibility and received William Blaikie's support. Blaikie and Phillips were nevertheless overruled, and Bowie was allowed to compete. The Harvard and Dartmouth representatives withdrew, probably knowing that they were outmanned. leaving only Amherst's Otis Benton and Cornell's Phillips to do battle.[26]

At 11:00 a.m., while the Harvard-Brown freshman baseball game was in progress at Hampden Park, the three racers lined up for the start of the race. Hundreds left the ball game to go to the track grandstand, causing the game to be temporarily suspended. McGill's representative, Bowie, nearly six feet tall and weighing 147 pounds, wore running tights and a small straw hat. Amherst's Benton, like Bowie, was also trained in running and even had his trainer with him. The 5' 8½" athlete wore a Robinson Crusoe-like goat-hide outfit as he waited at the starting line of the circular half-mile track. Phillips of Cornell, a wiry 144 pounds on a nearly 5' 9" frame, wore shorts and a white Merino wool shirt. The two twenty-one-year-old Americans flanked the Canadian, one year their elder, as they awaited the start.[27]

"Go" barked the starter, and the runners were off before the shouts and cheers of the attending collegians. Phillips at first, then Bowie, and finally Benton took the lead. They remained close as they moved into the fourth and final lap. With a quarter-mile to go, the three runners were abreast, but Amherst's Benton was spent. With 200 yards to the finish, he fell to the grass infield, face down, completely exhausted. Phillips drove on, but it was Bowie who flashed his speed and showed his endurance as he pulled away and looked back before crossing the finish with a slight smile on his face. Bowie showed his Caledonian race experience, winning with energy to spare.[28]

While the winning time of 11 minutes, 18.5 seconds seemed far from the mark of under 10 minutes set in an Oxford-Cambridge meet, the excitement of the race did much to ensure a second and expanded meet the following year. Bennett again provided "massive silver prizes" for the contest at Saratoga, New York, the new site of the intercollegiate regatta. This time, five events were scheduled; 100-yard dash, one-mile, three-mile, 120-yard hurdles, and seven-mile walk. About thirty students from eight colleges participated in what Bennett's newspaper dubbed the New York Herald Olympic Games. The rules of the 1874 track meet restricted participation to students who were eligible to be on college crews.[29] A Cornell student ran the mile in less than five minutes, but that was still almost half a minute off the best pace recorded in the Oxford-Cambridge meets. A Wesleyan crew member won the three-mile race, indicating again that rowers were probably the best trained for endurance events. Yale sent two of its baseball stars, and they returned home with silver cups for winning the hurdles and 100-yard dash. Princeton also had a winner, as intercollegiate track expanded and more athletes contended for the costly prizes. The "decided incentive to athletic sports," as a Harvard student described the Bennett trophies, was a key to the increased participation. Lucrative pot-hunting was important to the development of "amateur" track and field in American colleges.[30]

The intercollegiate track meet at the annual intercollegiate regatta stimulated colleges to form track associations and to hold regular intramural meets on the individual campuses. Only Columbia, Yale, Princeton, and Cornell had track clubs before the 1873 event sponsored by Bennett.[31] Bennett's meet stimulated both Williams College and the University of Pennsylvania to organize and hold track meets in the fall of 1873. Following the 1874 meet, Amherst, Stevens, Rutgers, and Harvard began to sponsor field days for track athletes.[32] A Harvard man, proud that his college had joined others, wrote: "At last we have the various foot contests so well known in the British universities."[33]

Nearly all the newly formed college track clubs found it expedient to follow the lead of Bennett by offering expensive prizes for which the men would compete. Harvard purchased cups for prizes by charging an entrance fee of fifty cents, double the price of a ticket to most professional baseball games of the early 1870s.[34] Princeton's Caledonian Games of 1874 provided $15 gold medal first-place prizes and $10 gold medal second prizes for each of fifteen events. The outstanding athlete of the meet was given a $50 gold medal.[35] At Yale, money prizes were offered at its track meet. The three-mile walk and the three-mile run were awarded $25, enough to hire a private servant to tend a student's room at Yale for a year. Only $10 was presented to the 100-yard dash winner.[36] The *Spirit of the Times* chastised the action of paying for performances as a "mercenary undertow." As a result, Yale changed its offerings from cash to prizes worth a certain value, as Princeton and others were doing.[37] It was probably more hypocritical, but it met the standards of nineteenth-century upper-class amateurism. Dartmouth began its own track and field meet by offering silver cups and silverware as prizes for fifteen first- and second-place winners. The one-and-a-half-day event, made possible by a faculty-sanctioned vacation, even provided for a professional runner exhibition. Norton Taylor, a forty-six-year-old with the same resting pulse, ran 10 miles in less than an hour, a significant feat in the nineteenth century.[38]

With colleges showing interest in forming athletic associations to promote track, the regatta-sponsored track meet was bound to grow. Even southern colleges, notably Virginia and William and Mary, were invited, though they did not attend.[39] The 1875 regatta, the grandest of all nineteenth-century American college rowing festivals, doubled the number of track events as part of its addendum to the gala affair. Two of the events, a three-mile run and a seven-mile walking contest, were open only to university graduates. Prizes for the ten events were worth $2000 or more, including silver goblets or cups for the undergraduates and gold watches for the alumni.[40] The winners came from six of the ten competing colleges—Amherst, Cornell, Harvard, Union, Williams, and Yale. A feature of the meet was the performance of William Taylor of Harvard's crew, who, after rowing in the regatta the day before, won both the three-mile and seven-mile walks—events he was eligible for as a recent graduate.[41] Ironically, the intercollegiate track meet was growing at exactly the same time that the Intercollegiate Rowing Association was about to disintegrate. When Yale and Harvard could not win in the large crew meet, they decided to withdraw to compete only against each other. As the rowing association began to fall apart, the track athletes decided to form their own organization.

The IC4A Is Born

Wanting a greater identity and more freedom of action, the trackmen decided to take direct control of their annual meet, removing it from the hands of the regatta committee. Following an invitation from the presidents of the Harvard and Yale athletic associations, ten colleges met on December 4, 1875, to form a track and field association. The result of the Springfield, Massachusetts, meeting was the creation of the Intercollegiate Association of Amateur Athletes of America (IC4A), with Creighton Webb of Yale at the helm.[42] A constitution was quickly adopted in a harmonious meeting, giving track and field management to a committee of students directly involved in the sport. The three-member games committee had representatives from Harvard, Yale, and Wesleyan, indicating once again the central position of Harvard and Yale in the development of intercollegiate sports. As with earlier intercollegiate sport development in crew, baseball, football, and cricket, the athletes who were competing were the ones who wanted to be free to make the important decisions in their sport. In track and field, the process took three years to accomplish, as the first three annual meets had been the product of a newspaperman and sport promoter, James Gordon Bennett, Jr., and the prestigious and commercialized regatta.

The IC4A held a second meeting in early January in New York City to determine the site and set the schedule for the annual meet. The IC4A decided to continue meeting at Saratoga the day following the regatta. Saratoga was chosen because of the useful publicity associated with the regatta and the decision of the Saratoga Citizens Committee to build a 440-yard track only a short walk from the major hotels.[43] The convention also decided to increase the number of events. The fifteen events included six running races, from the 100-yard dash to the three-mile run, the one- and three-mile walks, high and long jumps, and the mile run and mile walk for graduates. The program was rounded out with the shot put, a baseball throw, and a 200-yard, three-legged race.[44]

One of the early decisions of the IC4A has remained for over a century. The group decided "not to invite the Englishmen or foreigners of any description to compete."[45] This may have been done to insure that no foreign athlete, such as McGill's Duncan Bowie in 1873, would invade the American scene. More likely, the non-foreigner clause was passed to acknowledge the decision of the Intercollegiate Rowing Association not to invite foreign universities to compete.[46] Competition between American collegians and English collegians would not occur in track for another two decades, and then it was outside of IC4A control.

A second decision of the IC4A of some social importance was to insure that all prizes were of equal worth.[47] Previously, one silver cup for winning the graduate three-mile walk might be worth double that of the student three-mile run. Earlier silverware prizes did not necessarily come from the same sponsor, and the values varied widely. As "pot-hunting" was important in track and field, the value of a prize could easily sway who and how many athletes would contend for a certain event.[48] With the 1876 decision, the 440-yard trophy would be equivalent to the high-jump or 120-yard-hurdle award—and a valued pursuit.

The first meet of the IC4A was held at the Glen Mitchell trotting park of Saratoga; because the promised track had never been constructed. The meet followed the regatta, which was won by Cornell for the second straight year and after which Harvard rowers withdrew to more successful competition with Yale only. The regatta over, seventy-one competitors contended for the silver trophies of track. On an "insufferably hot" day with a good attendance, H. W. Stevens of Williams won the 100-yard dash in a sluggish 11 seconds, while J. W. Pryor of Columbia won the high jump with a 5'4" mark, considerably short of the remarkable world's record of Oxford's Marshall Brooks of 6'2½" set in the Oxford-Cambridge meet of 1876. Princeton's J. M. Mann was a double winner as he threw the baseball over 386 feet and tossed the sixteen-pound shot almost 31 feet, helping Princeton to win the first IC4A title, with four individual champions.[49] The track and field side show to the regatta was, according to one source, gaining more interest than the centerring crew meet.[50] That was probably wishful thinking; few spectators showed up for the second day of track competition even though it was a beautiful day, with a cool Saratoga breeze.

With the death of the intercollegiate regatta at Saratoga, the IC4A looked for another site for its annual games. The IC4A had made a good connection in 1876 when it chose Daniel M. Stern as its meet referee. Stern was a member of the New York Athletic Club, the leader in American track and field. The NYAC facility at Mott Haven became the IC4A site for the next half a dozen years. Separated from rowing, the IC4A was able to develop in its own way, holding meets at three sites in New York City until the early 1900s.[51]

The IC4A continued to be the dominant track and field event in colleges until well into the twentieth century. Beginning in 1880, either Harvard or Yale won every IC4A meet for seventeen consecutive years. In the first three decades only six colleges, all present-day Ivy League institutions, were winners, including Columbia, Cornell, Pennsylvania, and Princeton.[52] For a short while, the IC4A embraced two non-track events with the 1880 introduction of a two-mile bicycle race and a tug-of-war contest. The tug-of-war lasted a dozen years, and the bicycle race continued after that. By 1894 and the first American collegiate competition in international track and field, American collegians had several world records, including Georgetown's Bernie Wefers 9.8' in the 100-yard dash and 22.6' in the 220-yard dash. A decade before America participated in the Modern Olympics in 1896, Charles Sherrill of Yale had introduced much of the world to the sprinter's crouch start, and Mike Murphy, his coach, was to become the dominant professional track coach in the world.[53]

International Track: The Yale-Harvard Connection

By the 1890s, Americans were as ready to challenge the world in track as they were to test their strength in military might. America had already become the most productive industrial power, had completed its continental manifest destiny, and had officially announced that the western frontier no longer existed. It was natural for the nation, as it was for individuals and institutions within it, to challenge others outside the continental limits. Americans, since the Revolutionary War, had measured themselves against the British model. Americans might have disliked the mother country, but the British culture served as a standard for America to judge itself.[54]

Americans tested their culture in sports with the British as they did in the arts, literature, or industrial production. In sports, though, it was easy to compare. Unlike the arts, the final result on the scoreboard was the measure. Americans had sent individuals or teams to challenge the English since the first decade of the nineteenth century, when heavyweight Tom Molyneux challenged and lost twice to the English champion, Tom Cribb. The first great victory over the British in sport occurred when John C. Stevens's *America* took a yachting victory in 1851 over fifteen English vessels and captured the "America's Cup." Yet, in that same decade, American writers still unfavorably compared Americans to the British. "Nobody supposes that native Americans," wrote a *New York Herald* writer, "can play cricket, or any other game requiring muscular force, agility and endurance" as do the British.[55] At the same time, a journalist for the popular weekly *Spirit of the Times* believed that Americans "shall have in the rising generation muscular development which may shame our British friends."[56]

Not until after the Civil War did any collegians attempt to challenge the British, and it ended in a defeat for the Harvard crew in the famed Oxford-Harvard meet. On the heels of Harvard's loss, the *Nation* called for an Anglo-Saxon Olympics every four years, bringing together athletes in rowing, yachting, cricket, baseball, and track and field.[57] While the Anglo-Saxon quadrennial did not materialize, American collegians increasingly faced the English in such sports as baseball, crew, football, and lacrosse in the 1870s and 1880s.[58]

Collegiate track and field competition with the British began a quarter-century after crew, but it occurred at an important time for the development of international sport. Only two years before the internationalization of the Olympic Games in 1896, Yale challenged Oxford to a track meet. Charles Sherrill, the Yale dash man of a few years before and at the time a lawyer, arranged the meeting.[59] The Yale-Oxford meet was stimulated by Yale's success at the IC4A competition which it won in both 1893 and 1894. Yale, the acknowledged athletic power among American colleges, was a logical institution to challenge Oxford, winner of its two previous contests with Cambridge. Though the meeting between Oxford and Yale was the first international contest at the collegiate level, it was not unexpected. The earlier rowing match between Harvard and Oxford had set a precedent, and an Oxford-Yale race would have taken place in 1891 if Yale had not lost to Harvard's crew.[60] Even in track, an American contingent from the Manhattan Athletic Club competed in the English championships in 1891, winning four events.[61] The collegians knew that American athletes were competitive with the best of both Oxford and Cambridge and that most of the world's track records were held either by English or American athletes.[62]

On July 16, 1894, the first collegiate international track and field meet took place at the Queen's Grounds at Kensington in London, England. On a wet and chilly day, there were nevertheless nearly 10,000 spectators. The contest for the best of nine events included five running events, high and long jump, hammer throw, and shot put. The traditional English three-mile run was dropped, benefiting Americans, who generally ran nothing longer than the mile. A match of styles was clearly seen in the 100-yard dash. The two Americans started in the newer crouch position, while the two Oxford men took the traditional leaning, upright stance. The old style won this time by about a yard in 10.4 seconds, as both Oxford men surpassed the best of Yale. The 120-yard hurdle race may have been the turning point of the match. The hurdles were run on grass, a British tradition. The American who was leading at the eighth flight fell, allowing the Oxford man to win in 16.6 seconds. The meet was not decided, however, until the last, highly contested event in which Oxford won the half-mile in a fraction over two minutes. The English elites had won five events to three, with the high jump being a tie. That event had more than unusual drama as Swanwick, the Oxford high jumper, attempting to break the tie at 5′ 8¾″, knocked out a front tooth when his knee hit it.[63]

The Americans naturally analyzed their loss. Some charged Yale with inadequate preparation. Not only had the Americans failed to have a trainer accompany them to England but once there they trained too little and too irregularly in an attempt to avoid staleness. In both the quarter- and half-mile races, the Yale men led, but were caught at the finish, while in the mile race, the lack of stamina was clearly shown throughout the race. The Americans also complained of the cold, rainy weather, the grass course for hurdles, and running around the track in a clockwise rather than the usual counter-clockwise direction.[64] Nationalistic Americans had taken Yale for their own, and they did not want to feel inferior to the best stock of the English.

To Yale and to America, the significance of an athletic victory the next year was apparent. For Yale, 1895 was important, for athletic relations had been broken with Harvard over a football game the previous fall, and athletic contests between the two institutions in all major sports were banned. Yale was obviously looking for other dual competition in track and field, which they had first begun with Harvard in 1891. On a more significant national level, it was important for America's most visible collegiate athletic institution, Yale, to defeat the British. By early 1895, America was deeply involved in a boundary dispute between Venezuela and the adjoining colony of British Guiana. The American charge that Britain had violated the Monroe Doctrine, then nearly three-quarters of a century old, was exacerbated by John Bull's occupation of a Nicaraguan port. America, wrote Secretary of State Richard Olney, "is practically sovereign on this continent." This belief was reinforced by President Cleveland, who took the position that Britain arbitrate its problems with Venezuela or face a military confrontation with the United States. President Cleveland addressed Congress later in the year, stating that it was "a grievous thing to contemplate the two great English-speaking peoples of the world as being otherwise than friendly competitors in the onward march of of civilization."[65] As the Harvard-Oxford crew race had been contested at the height of the Alabama claims resulting from the Civil War, the Yale-Cambridge track meet was contended in the midst of antagonistic British-American relations.

The relations between the two Anglo-Saxon nations seemed to be only slightly more trying than the negotiations needed to produce a track meet between representatives of England and America. That process showed the confused state of relations between the two elite English universities and the American colleges as well as the open conflict between Harvard and Yale in the mid-1890s. Originally the IC4A Executive Committee invited Oxford and Cambridge to select a representative team from the British universities for a meet in America consisting of first- and second-place winners of the 1895 IC4A championships. The IC4A Executive Committee, however, did not first get individual American colleges to agree to the proposition, and Yale, Princeton, and Columbia voted against the challenge, while Harvard abstained. Harvard and Yale's reluctance to be involved caused Oxford and Cambridge to decline the challenge. Oxford and Cambridge then challenged the two to a dual meet, probably not knowing that they had broken athletic relations.[66] Nevertheless, Harvard suggested to Yale that a three-way competition be held between a combined Harvard, Yale, and Penn team and a team from Oxford, Cambridge, and a third English college. Harvard's refusal to team up with Yale placed Yale in an uncomfortable position. Yale could agree to compete alone with the English, but Yale, an alumnus noted, "can hardly suggest that Penn should be joined after Oxford & Camb[ridge] have ignored her."[67] Harvard, in justifying its rejection of a joint Harvard-Yale team, noted that there was "no Oxford and Cambridge in America" and to accept participation with Yale would be to claim a pre-eminence which the American public does not acknowledge. "Yale," Harvard historian and athletic authority Albert B. Hart said, "is incontestably the most athletic institution in America, and it is entirely suitable that she should meet representative English athletes."[68]

Yale decided to go ahead without Harvard and agreed to meet Cambridge, the winner of the Oxford-Cambridge meet, in a fall contest. The meet was scheduled for New York City's Manhattan Field shortly after an extraordinary international track meet was held at the same site. Just two weeks before the collegiate contest, an "all-American" track team running under the colors of the New York Athletic Club faced an "all-English" team as representatives of the London Athletic Club. What was predicted to be a close match between the two countries ended with the annihilation of the English, eleven events to none. In doing so, the Americans set four world records: Charles Kilpatrick's half mile in 1 minute 53.4 seconds; Bernie Wefers' 100-yard dash in 9.8 seconds, and 220-yard dash in 21.6 seconds; and Michael Sweeney's remarkable 6′ 5⅝″ in the high jump.[69] The defeat could not have been more complete and was probably the most surprising and one-sided victory of

America over the British in any sport since the America's Cup triumph in 1851. The Americans must have truly enjoyed twisting the British lion's tail in athletics; only a few months later that satisfaction would return after America's diplomatic triumph in forcing Britain to back down on its demands over the Venezuela boundary dispute. According to one British writer, the London Athletic Club defeat at the hands of the NYAC "came as a crushing surprise to most Englishmen at that time."[70]

Yale also wanted to prove its and America's superiority on the track. With the involvement of a number of Yale and Cambridge athletes who had competed with the NYAC and the LAC, Yale won eight of eleven events.[71] The Cambridge men only won the quarter-mile, half-mile, and mile races. As Americans had made excuses the year before, the British were quick to point out that their runners were not used to the warm autumn weather in New York City, nor did the Cambridge men get the opportunity to test the Americans in any event longer than the mile.[72]

Within four years, Harvard and Yale combined to challenge Oxford and Cambridge, losing first in England and winning a return match in 1901.[73] Before those events took place, though, American collegians had a significant impact on the Modern Olympics when they were expanded in 1896 to include others, in addition to Greeks.[74]

Princeton, William Milligan Sloane, and the 1896 Olympics

The international version of Modern Olympics were the creation of French aristocrat Baron de Coubertin. Coubertin's fixation on an international athletic festival was based on what he erroneously believed was the amateurism of the ancient Greeks. To accomplish his goal of setting up quadrennial Olympic games, Coubertin looked for sport leadership first among the English and then among the Americans. He came in contact with a professor of history and political science at Princeton, William Milligan Sloane.[75] Sloane, whose specialty was French history, met in August 1893 with Coubertin and a cast principally of French gentlemen to discuss an eight-point amateur-Olympic proposal. Seven of the points dealt with questions of amateurism, and the eighth regarded the possibility of an Olympic revival.[76] Later that year Coubertin traveled extensively in America, visiting the Chicago World's Fair and at least nine universities, from Harvard to Stanford. He stayed with

Sloane at Princeton for three weeks. Shortly before Coubertin departed for France, Sloane arranged a meeting for him with sport figures from the eastern elites, Harvard, Yale, Princeton and Columbia, in an attempt to drum up support for his Olympic idea.[77] Coubertin appreciated that effort.

Sloane seemed to be the obvious choice of Coubertin to get America involved in the Olympics. When Coubertin organized the International Olympic Committee, Sloane became the American representative. Though he was no aristocrat, Sloane's urbanity allowed him to move in their circles. Reflecting those among whom the Olympic idea arose, Sloane believed that "the more the higher classes of different nations get to know one another the less likelihood is there of their fighting."[78] Nevertheless, even as the eastern elite colleges were increasingly becoming involved in international contests, there was little enthusiasm for participation in the Olympics. Only Sloane and Princeton showed any eagerness to be represented. At Yale, Walter Camp was asked to respond for the athletic program, but as one advisor to Camp said: "Do not put yourself to any inconvenience."[79] Harvard was only a little more responsive. When two Harvard students asked permission for leaves of absence to attend the games, Dean LeBaron Briggs allowed the honor student and senior Ellery Clark to leave, but refused permission to freshman Jim Connolly.[80] Connolly quit Harvard to attend the games. Though Harvard officials were not sympathetic toward undergraduates participating, two did so, and another four graduate students or alumni of Harvard also participated.[81] Most of them, however, ran under the sponsorship of the Boston Athletic Association.

At Princeton, Sloane was successful in promoting the trip to Athens. Sloane, a member of the athletic committee, arranged for four juniors to take six weeks off for the journey. The most important was Robert Garrett, whose widowed mother was a member of a wealthy Baltimore banking family who owned the Baltimore and Ohio Railroad. Garrett's mother financed not only Garrett but the other three.[82] Of the Princeton four, only Garrett was dominant, as he won both the shot put and the discus and came in second in the long jump and the high jump.[83]

Through the active participation of Sloane and Princeton's four athletes, and the involvement of six Harvard or ex-Harvard men, America was represented by collegians. Competing against the other twelve nations present, the American collegians won nine of the twelve track and field events and came in second in five more. Impressive as that might appear, the American Olympians would have lost all but the high jump if they had competed and accomplished the same times and distances in the Yale-Cambridge meet of 1896. For example, Thomas Burke of the Boston Athletic Association won the Olympic 100 meters in 12 seconds—the Yale winner in the Cambridge meet did an equivalent distance in less than 11 seconds. Robert Garrett won the Olympic shot put at 36′ 2″—the Yale winner did it in 42′ 2″. Only Olympian Ellery Clark would have succeeded in the Yale-Cambridge meet with his winning 5′ 11¼″ high jump.[84]

Despite the lack of representation of the best American track and field athletes, the Olympics showed an Anglo-Saxon superiority. The only non-Anglo-Saxon winner was Spiridon Loues, the Greek marathon winner who became the hero of the 1896 Athens games. The domination by American athletes gave them more than just pride in their country. It was one more symbol of the growing belief of Americans in their superiority. The American success was the harbinger of future Olympic triumphs and of flag-waving patriotism. In the words of Senator Henry Cabot Lodge only months after the Athens conquest, "It is the spirit of victory which subordinates the individual to the group, and which enables that group, whether it be a college or a nation, to achieve great results and attain high ideals." The great results were part of the "march of imperialism," according to Lodge.[85] In their own way, a small group of principally college track and field athletes contributed to the belief in Anglo-Saxon superiority and the quest for world domination for which Lodge and the imperialists stood.

The success of the American collegians in 1896 stimulated others besides William Milligan Sloane to become involved in future Olympics. Four years later the Athletic Association at the University of Pennsylvania voted to send a track team to the Paris Olympics. A group of thirteen, including some alumni from the University of Pennsylvania, garnered nine of the sixteen first-place medals taken by the Americans.[86] As was the case four years before, all track events were won by Anglo-Saxons, with the exception of the marathon. American college athletes were contributing heavily to that sense of superiority expressed in Englishman Rudyard Kipling's poem of a few years before, "The White Man's Burden":

Take up the White Man's burden—
    Send forth the best ye breed—
Go bind your sons to exile
        To serve your captives' need. . . .[87]

Collegiate participation in the Olympics not only reflected America's increasing involvement in track and field but symbolized a larger role of athletics in defining America's place in the international scene. It would continue to do so throughout the twentieth century.

In only a generation, track and field had expanded from local paper chases and as an auxiliary of the intercollegiate regattas of the 1870s to international collegiate and Olympic competition. The expansion had occurred primarily under student leadership and control, with some help from alumni and faculty, such as Princeton's William Sloane. The freedom of students to control much of their athletic destiny was a major feature of intercollegiate sport. Freedom, as will be seen, was never complete in track and field or any other sport. Varying outside forces came to exert pressure and jeopardize the control which students had commanded from the first. No group came to challenge student autonomy more than did college faculties.

IX

Student Control and Faculty Resistance

WALTER CAMP, ATHLETIC ADVISOR of Yale, said it best: "Neither the faculties nor other critics assisted in building the structure of college athletics." Camp wrote in 1885 that though the faculty placed some obstacles in the way, "it is a structure which students unaided have builded."[1] This was true at Yale, and it was true at most in stitutions of higher learning in America. Students had indeed been free to develop their extracurricular activities, with athletics being the dominant one by the latter quarter of the nineteenth century. That freedom, however, was jeopardized by several contending groups, faculties being the most vigorous.

The faculties of the individual colleges continually resisted the encroachment of student athletics upon the life of the institution. Faculty members were caught between their perceived notion that exercise was of value to students' health and their consternation that uncontrolled athletics led to educational abuses. Andrew Davis, a Harvard graduate, looked favorably upon intercollegiate athletics and indicated that college sport from the 1860s prospered "in proportion to the encouragement given by the faculties, but which thrives even where it is discouraged by official frowns."[2] An obvious tension existed between students' love of athletics and faculty's concern for educational integrity.

Student Associations Support Intercollegiate Teams

Students were almost the sole force in developing athletics within the larger college extracurriculum, including the first five intercollegiate sports. Crew, baseball, cricket, football, and track and field were all contested intercollegiately by the early 1870s. Later in the nineteenth century other intercollegiate sports would be developed under student leadership. These included the first intercollegiate contests in rifle (1877), lacrosse (1877), bicycling (1880), tennis (1883), polo (1884), cross country (1890), fencing (1894), ice hockey (1895), basketball (1895), golf (1896), trap shooting (1898), water polo (1899), swimming (1899), and gymnastics (1899). Teams were usually organized under an elected captain who was chosen for the next year at the conclusion of the season. The captain's responsibilities were not dissimilar to those of a latter-day professional coach. The captain set up training procedures, organized practice, chose the starting line-up, and made important decisions during contests. Much of the team's success was centered around his leadership qualities. The captains became the campus heroes. The muscular captains of the late nineteenth century, according to the president of Massachusetts Institute of Technology, Francis Walker, replaced the campus leaders of the mid-1800s who were noted for their "speech-making, debating, or fine writing."[3]

The captain and team were given substantial support through a student organization created on nearly every campus between the 1870s and 1900. The purpose of the student athletic association was to provide financial assistance to relieve athletes of the entire expense of their sports and to give moral support for college athletics. At first these groups were set up for individual teams, such as football or baseball, but soon they were combined to support all the teams which students desired to promote. Representative athletic associations were formed first in the east—Harvard (1874), Princeton (1876), Rutgers (1876)—but soon spread westward and southward—Michigan (1876), Missouri (1886), Duke (1887), Stanford (1891), and Oregon (1893).[4]

Athletic association support came originally from dues which might be fifty cents or one dollar a year. Later, fund-raising drives, such as concerts, musical shows, or other theatricals, were conducted by the associations to further the athletic fortunes of individual institutions. Early on, athletic associations were also in-

volved in obtaining subscriptions from a high percentage of the
student body to support teams. This was often accomplished under
severe social pressure, and might have been, in another form, pun-
ishable as extortion. Supporters of college athletics generally did
what needed to be done to provide for the favored teams.[5] Eventually the athletic association manpower necessary to coerce student subscriptions was used to collect gate receipts, the principal
method of financing college athletics before the turn of the century.

As important as the athletic association was to the success of
an institution's teams, it seldom had a powerful position in directing athletics. The power remained with individual teams, manifested principally by the all-powerful captain and the student manager of each team. The athletic manager was instituted to ease the
task of the captain by taking on many of the administrative tasks
such as corresponding with individuals, arranging for games, checking on athletic eligibility, and looking after team finances. The
team managers and team captains would therefore get much of the
credit for athletic success and bear the brunt of team failure. When
problems arose which reflected negatively upon the reputation of
the institution, the captain and manager received most of the criticism. It was, in fact, the problems which the captains and managers could not or would not control that led to faculty regulation
and control.

Faculty Weigh Student Freedom against Responsibility

The freedom which students had to construct intercollegiate athletics, without the necessary responsibility to academic and other
concerns, led directly to faculty actions. Intercollegiate athletics, the
dominant aspect of the extracurriculum, could operate in a laissez-
faire climate outside of faculty control only so long as it had little
deleterious effect upon academic interests and the good name of
the institution. When this occurred, and it emerged quickly, faculty
at most colleges responded by restricting student freedom or banning some actions. "The necessity of regulation," a Harvard athletic committee report noted, "implies the existence of abuse."[6]

If in the eyes of the faculty the students involved in athletics
misused their freedoms, faculty in the tradition of "in loco parentis" would attempt to curtail their activities. The paternalism in
American college faculties was breaking down slowly in the latter
half of the nineteenth century, but it was never far from the sur-

face. When faculty members believed that students were devoting too much time to athletics, were wasting money on their games, were winning or participating dishonorably, or were bringing professionalism into the extracurriculum through paid coaches or subsidized athletes, they were prone to curtail the actions.

In the early days of intercollegiate athletics, before faculty athletic committees, the entire college faculty would often sit in judgment regarding athletic and other problems. This was not unexpected, for post-Civil War faculties traditionally spent untold hours discussing such subjects as students being off-campus without permission; drinking or playing billiards; throwing snowballs on campus; making noise during study hours; missing required morning chapel; or printing indiscretions in the student newspaper. In fact the faculty at Princeton as late as 1882 resolved "that every professor should feel it to be his duty . . . to look after the morals and behavior of the students in the classroom, chapel, and elsewhere."[7] The expansion of the organized extracurriculum by the 1870s increased the paternalistic faculty's concerns, as not only intercollegiate athletics grew but other activities grew as well, such as bands and orchestras; glee, banjo, and dramatic clubs; and student publications.

Two institutions, Yale and Princeton, exemplify the attempt by faculties to deal with the extracurriculum and its most important component, athletics. They may be the two best examples of faculty involvement in institutions with major athletics, for they show some marked differences in the approach in the second half of the nineteenth century. Yale, by 1900, was always the institution used to illustrate the student control of athletics. Princeton, in contrast, was the first college known to have a faculty committee to regulate athletics and was constantly meddling in student athletics.

Shortly after the Civil War, the Yale faculty recognized the need to regulate intercollegiate athletics, even though in later years it would claim a hands-off policy. Yale action began when the faculty voted in 1868 to deny a petition by the Yale baseball team to play three away games. The next year the team petitioned again, and the faculty relented, allowing the request with the understanding that no Yale student spectators accompany the team.[8] Within three years the faculty restricted games to Wednesday and Saturday afternoons, a somewhat more lenient policy than that of the Harvard faculty, which the same year limited contests to Saturdays and other holidays.[9]

When football arrived on the Yale campus in the early 1870s, and the team was refused permission to leave campus to play games, the team used the precedent of the baseball team to petition the faculty. The faculty still refused, stating that the baseball team had "no standing permission to leave town to play games."[10] Soon, however, the faculty relented and football joined baseball in participating in away games. By 1878, the football team was given permission for the first time to miss class recitations for an out-of-town encounter.[11]

By the 1880s, Yale had established itself as the dominant athletic institution in America, and the faculty had committed itself to a hands-off policy. The faculty was primarily concerned that athletes attend class and keep up their scholarship. Of course the Yale faculty could and did hold the threat of prohibition. At one point in the 1880s, the Yale faculty posted a warning that athletic contests might be banned if students showed disorderly conduct.[12] Yet, a Princeton man was probably correct when he accepted as fact that "there is probably not another university in the land where students have more direct control of college athletics than Yale where athletics are less under Faculty rules and where there is less friction . . . between students and Faculty."[13]

The laissez-faire system at Yale appeared to the Yale faculty and president to work effectively. The success at Yale was clearly evident by the 1880s as it had won eight of ten baseball championships, five of six football championships, and seven of ten dual championships over Harvard in crew. When Walter Camp, Yale's athletic advisor, pointed out that twenty of twenty-six championsips came to Yale in the three major sports, he was crediting it to the Yale system of undergraduate control. "Managers and captains," he later said, "are absolute in their power, the rest of us bearing ourselves with proper modesty and decorum in offering here and there bits of advice."[14] Agreeing with Camp was Eugene Richards, a math professor and staunch supporter of Yale athletics as well as a believer in the hands-off policy. "Faculty control," he wrote, "should limit itself to the requirements of the college work, and hold each man liable for that."[15]

Not until the time just before the NCAA was being formed, in 1905, did Yale seriously consider greater faculty control. The situation arose only after a muckraking journalist and member of the first Yale football team, Clarence Deming, revealed an enormous athletic reserve fund of over $100,000 and an annual athletic income at Yale equal to one-eighth of the total gross income of the university.[16] Yale professor William Beebe raised the question of the need for a university athletic committee to investigate "the raising and spending of money for athletics."[17] Within a month, an investigating committee was probing abuses of athletic management. After a great deal of discussion and rancor during the fall and winter, and a tabled resolution which called for the elimination of football at Yale if gate receipts were collected, the Yale faculty agreed to leave the principal management of athletics in the hands of the undergraduates.[18] Students maintained control at Yale, but the same could not be said at most other colleges in America, certainly not Princeton.

The Princeton situation was quite different from that of Yale and more similar to that of other colleges. Princeton first played baseball against Rutgers a year after the conclusion of the Civil War, but there was much more excitement when Yale initiated a challenge to come to Princeton the next year to play a ball game and to stay over for Princeton's Class Day of 1867. Princeton's faculty and especially the president did not favor the visit, "fearing lest so large a crowd of strangers might produce a good deal of disturbance." The students, however, visited faculty members and convinced them to give their permission.[19] Permission to travel to away games was of greater concern to Princeton's faculty, as it was to most college authorities. The same year that the president of Cornell indicated that he would not allow a team of thirty college men to "agitate a bag of wind," with a football team from Michigan, seventeen footballers were given permission to take a night boat to New Haven for a contest. The Princeton team had first made arrangements with Yale and then asked permission. The Princeton faculty resolved not to grant future permission unless the teams applied before scheduling the contest.[20]

As intercollegiate contests expanded, students kept constant pressure on faculty for greater freedom to participate in out-of-town contests. At Princeton a major confrontation occurred between the faculty and the president over a proposed trip to New England. The baseball team desired to be absent from campus for five days at the end of the term, just before final examinations. The proposal to play Yale, Amherst, and Harvard was first turned down by the faculty when President James McCosh was in attendance. Three days, later, a team committee appeared before the faculty to plead its case. The faculty, this time without the president present, reversed itself from a 7–3 vote opposing to a 9–2 vote granting permission. President McCosh was furious. Not only did he note that the team would not return for the Sabbath, the faculty had overturned a decision which he had helped make. The faculty, burned by the fury of the Scottish Presbyterian president, gave an eleven-point justification for its action, including its belief that there was an understanding that because Harvard and Yale had played at Princeton, a return game was expected. In addition, Princeton lost both previous games and a "loss of honor" would result from a refusal to play the return games.[21] This incident, which is one of the longest entries in Princeton's Faculty Minutes, which date back to the 1700s, points out the seriousness with which faculty and presidents viewed their role in limiting student freedom to participate in intercollegiate athletics.

Athletics were not the only concern of the Princeton faculty. Students organized a Glee Club in 1874. By the early 1880s, the Glee Club and athletic teams were increasingly asking to miss more classes and, what was probably more important to the leaders of Presbyterian Princeton, to be absent from chapel. When the Glee Club traveled more than any of the athletic teams at Princeton, the faculty decided to take an action which evidently no other American college had as yet taken. It struck a committee to set common policy, especially as it related to away games and performances. On April 29, 1881, the Princeton faculty formed a Committee on Athletics and the Musical Clubs.[22]

The First Faculty Athletic Committee

Princeton's action in forming an athletic committee is recognition that intercollegiate athletics and other aspects of the extracurriculum were commanding more time of the faculty than they were willing to expend. Many faculty members would have been happy if intercollegiate athletics and the problems they created would have disappeared. After all, the faculty was in no position to manage athletics which students themselves had initiated. About all they could do was to attempt to check the excesses and veto those aspects they deemed harmful. Faculty could not spend significant amounts of time directing athletics, nor did most of them have the knowledge or interest to do so. The faculty could, however, appoint an athletic committee of those who had either some knowledge or some interest in athletics. That small group could then deal with details such as determining the number of away contests, setting the time of contests, establishing rules of eligibility, and resolving questions of professionalism.

The Princeton faculty appointed a three-member committee in 1881 which included William Milligan Sloane, who fifteen years later would be instrumental in sending an American contingent to the first modern Olympics. The committee's first action was to propose a list of regulations to the student-run athletic teams, emphasizing time and place of contests. Athletes could be absent from Princeton no more than eight days a term, and then only if they were members of either the football or baseball teams. Members of the cricket, lacrosse, rowing, or other athletic teams were not so privileged, as they could participate out-of-town only during vacations or on Saturday afternoons. In addition, all athletes would need parental permission to participate away from Princeton.[23]

The Princeton faculty, keeping rather close watch over its athletic committee, continued to add responsibilities to the committee's regulatory functions. The athletic committee began to fix dates for baseball and to approve of the baseball trainer or coach.[24] When the athletic committee decided to ban baseball contests with all professional clubs, however, the students reacted vigorously and with a degree of deviousness.

The question of collegians playing professional baseball teams was not unique to Princeton. A number of major eastern colleges had begun to play the pro teams. For instance, Harvard and Yale played more games against pro teams in the National Association of Professional Base Ball Players and the National League in the 1870s than they did against other colleges.[25] College faculties questioned this association, for they had a long tradition of attempting to inculcate morality into socially elite young men. They distrusted any association with professional baseball players, whom they deemed socially inferior, with lower standards of manners and morals.[26] President Charles W. Eliot of Harvard, a Boston Brahmin, and his faculty were imbued with this class bias. Eliot, in 1882, attempted to get other colleges collectively to ban competition with professionals, but his action failed.[27] The Princeton faculty, however, believed the position was a good one and prohibited baseball practice or competition with professionals.

The Princeton baseball captain for 1883, John Harlan, believed the faculty interference was ill-conceived and devised a plan to defeat the action. Not only did two members of the Board of Trustees write a letter to the faculty protesting the action but Captain Harlan duped the faculty into believing that games with professionals were less morally harmful than were games with some amateur teams. Harlan procured a game with an amateur team of workers from a New Jersey patent pill manufacturer. Just before the game, Harlan told the amateur team of the Princeton faculty action, indicating that the unruly demonstration of behavior of an amateur team might help to restore games with professionals. Harlan told his story:

> I had previously sent complimentary tickets to the faculty telling them that I had succeeded in getting a non-professional nine for a practice game. Many of the Faculty came. I presume they never saw such an exhibition of ruffianism as those good fellows gave us. The pitcher came out in a red undershirt, and with one shoe off; and the way they howled and quarrelled among themselves, and with the umpire, and with me, was astonishing. The result was so convincing that when I appeared at the next Faculty meeting, with a copy of the rules adopted by the professional league, parts of which [forbade] swearing, card playing, gambling, and boisterous conduct, etc., I carefully read, the Faculty unanimously rescinded the rule made a few weeks before.[28]

The faculty was fooled, but the athletic committee and entire faculty remained active in their attempt to control athletics. In 1884, the faculty passed a regulation that no professional athlete, oarsman, or baseball player could be employed to coach or to practice with the team. It was ironic to allow collegians to play against pros, but not to be coached by them.[29] But that was no more surprising than when the Princeton faculty, which required all contests to be played on the home grounds of the two teams, granted permission to play the annual Yale-Princeton football game in New York City.[30] Obviously, one of the problems that the Princeton faculty and athletic committee had was to keep some control over a growing student extracurriculum which threatened the life of the institution. As Princeton's Woodrow Wilson later said: "The side shows are so numerous, so diverting—so important if you will—that they have swallowed up the circus, and those who perform in the main tent must often whistle for their audiences."[31] The non-educational atmosphere existed elsewhere, and Harvard was no exception.

Harvard Develops the Athletic Committee Concept

The Harvard faculty found similar disquieting tendencies in inter-collegiate athletics and chose, like Princeton, to take action. At Harvard, too, baseball was the initial focus of faculty attention. Five years after Harvard students formed their first baseball club, the team concluded a forty-four game schedule, twenty-six of them during term time of the 1870 school year. The following year the Harvard faculty banned baseball on days other than Saturdays and holidays. Within two years the faculty eased the restriction somewhat, by allowing four games during weekdays.[32] By the early 1880s, the faculty was concerned with the number of away games, nineteen of a twenty-eight schedule. Faculty members were also disturbed with the type of teams being played and the atmosphere surrounding intercollegiate athletics. The result, like that at Princeton, was the formation of a faculty athletic committee.[33]

The Harvard athletic committee of three faculty members was poised for immediate action. Two of the members came from the college proper, Charles Eliot Norton, cousin of President Eliot and professor of fine arts, and John W. White, professor of Greek. The third member was a medical doctor and director of the Harvard gymnasium, Dudley A. Sargent. At their first meeting they adopted rules for Harvard athletics which included an injunction to stop all competition against professionals and to disallow the hiring of coaches without the consent of Sargent. These two class-biased decisions based upon elitist amateur concepts were accompanied by another which was intended to keep the "hoi polloi" away from intercollegiate contests: the decision to build a fence around the athletic field. The athletic committee justified the enclosure by indicating that it would "protect the grounds and exclude objectionable persons."[34]

The issue of enclosing a field would not likely cause students any concern, but actions in the area of professionalism would be disturbing. A faculty ban of games with professional baseball teams would hurt Harvard's preparation for important games, especially with Yale, which had no restrictions. Harvard's athletic committee contacted Yale and asked if it would also consider not playing against professionals. Even though Yale refused to act, the Harvard committee concluded unanimously: "We could not waver from our first step."[35] For the next several years, Harvard President Eliot and the athletic committee attempted, without success, to get other colleges to prohibit competition against professionals.

The faculty was also disturbed about the entrance of professional coaches in both baseball and crew. Harvard's paid baseball coach was fired by the athletic committee in 1882, irritating the students.[36] The committee was in favor of the upper-class British concept of amateurism and decided that Harvard would allow the employment of "a gentleman amateur to assist in the gymnasium and superintend games."[37] Harvard's athletic committee attempted to get other colleges to go along with its rule, but it was no more successful than with its desire to rid competition against professional teams.[38]

The Harvard athletic committee kept up the pressure to eliminate pro coaches. In 1884, William Bancroft, the successful paid crew coach, was dismissed by the committee, angering the students, who wanted an explanation. The committee replied: "To the Public we have given no reason, and have none to give."[39] It is no wonder that Harvard students continued to believe that their faculty operated with a "spirit of secrecy and exclusiveness."[40] The athletic committee took its authoritarian stand one step further when it restricted freedom of the press by pressuring the editorial staff of the *Harvard Crimson* into not publishing negative letters of former crew captains regarding the dismissal of Bancroft.[41]

The running feud between the Harvard crew and the athletic committee continued as students fought to regain autonomy over their program. The crew circumvented the athletic committee the next spring by privately asking a professional, George Faulkner, to aid them in their rowing. Only when Faulkner was taken to the annual Yale boat race, quartered with the crew, and seen coaching them on the river was the ruse discovered.[42] Harvard did win the race, which was far more important to the crew than whether it hired a pro coach. It is probably significant that in the next dozen years, after faculty athletic committee meddling, Harvard won only once against Yale, the institution which had a faculty hands-off policy.[43]

As thorny as the crew problem was, it was not as disruptive as the action of the Harvard athletic committee to abolish football. While the committee was wrestling with the professional coaching issue in crew, it was troubled by the lack of gentlemanly decorum on the football field. Following the 1883 game with Yale, the committee informed the football team that football as played under present rules was banned. The committee was most disturbed with the student-controlled Intercollegiate Football Association rule which disqualified a player for "striking with closed fist" only after the third incident in a game.[44] Only because the Harvard student representative pressed the Football Association to change its rule before the 1884 season was the Harvard team allowed to play. Still, the Harvard athletic committee kept a close watch over the game by attending a number of contests, watching specifically for objectionable play. The paternalistic faculty members reported at the conclusion of the season that football as then played was "brutal, demoralizing to players and spectators, and extremely dangerous." As the committee believed that football placed a premium on unfair, yet profitable play, it asked the Harvard faculty to prohibit the game.[45] The faculty concurred.

The meddlesome Harvard athletic committee was under attack by students principally, while alumni were also becoming more interested in the success of Harvard athletics. In the spring of 1885, the Harvard faculty determined that a new athletic committee should be created to reflect student and alumni interests. A five-member committee was formed with two undergraduate leaders in athletics and a graduate with athletic interests as representatives, along with director of the gymnasium, Sargent, and a medical doctor from the area.[46]

The new committee appointed by President Eliot looked closely at the intercollegiate football situation during the year of Harvard's abolishment and concluded that the objectionable features of the game had disappeared. The committee, in recommending a resumption of football, stated that no sport could take the place of football, that "roughness, unaccompanied by brutality and unfair play, often tends to develop courage, presence of mind, and a manly spirit."[47] If true, even the most antagonistic academic could hardly disagree with the development of manly character, a chief component of the justification of sport in the latter nineteenth century. With the committee's sanction, football continued once again at Harvard.

Many faculty, however, questioned the development of positive character attributes with regard to athletic participation. Faculty continued to complain of the number and intensity of athletic contests disturbing serious academic work, of ungentlemanly behavior, of injuries and brutality, of unhealthy moral influences of big city games, of financial inducements to attend college, and of waste and extravagance under student management.[48] There was so much faculty discontent at Harvard that following an investigation by a committee of the Harvard Overseers, the athletic committee of five was abolished, and a new nine-member committee was established.

As Harvard was the educational leader in America, the new 1888 athletic committee, formed of three students, three alumni, and three faculty, became the model for many institutions of higher learning. The new committee was no longer under faculty appointment or control, though the Harvard faculty was to continue to have a significant influence over athletics. Beginning in 1888, the athletic committee was to have "the entire supervision and control of all athletic sports" under the authority of the Harvard controlling body, the Corporation. The committee was at the same time "subject to the authority of the Faculty of the College."[49] The ambivalence over where power lay—faculty, governing boards, or athletic committee, but no longer chiefly the students—was a major question for colleges in the latter years of the nineteenth and throughout the twentieth-century.

The crisis over power erupted at Harvard in 1895, despite a statement by a Harvard faculty member two years earlier that "there is now no such thing as 'Faculty interference' with the management of athletic sports."[50] In that year, following an inordinately brutal football game between Harvard and Yale, the Harvard faculty voted by a 2 to 1 margin to abolish football. The athletic committee, however, voted unanimously to continue the game by reforming it.[51] The battle lines were drawn. The athletic committee correctly claimed that it alone had been charged by the Harvard Corporation to carry out the supervision of athletics. The committee asked the Corporation to clearly define its powers relative to the faculty of Harvard College. "Does the continuance or abolition of intercollegiate football," Chairman James Barr Ames queried the Corporation, "rest with the Committee or with the Faculty?" Ames, the Dean of the Law School and former Harvard baseball captain, wanted to know if his committee was to have "responsibilities without power."[52] The situation was resolved temporarily, though not entirely satisfactorily, when the Corporation sided with the committee, and the faculty rescinded its resolve to ban football.[53]

The power struggle certainly was not over at Harvard or at other colleges. Eight years later, the Harvard faculty asked the athletic committee to once again abolish football. Again the committee refused, indicating that "football is only one of many distractions in college life."[54] In another three years, in the midst of the 1905–6 national football crisis, both the faculty and the Board of Overseers asked the athletic committee to ban football. A whole series of student, alumni, and Corporation maneuvers, including the involvement of President Theodore Roosevelt and a radical reform of football rules, prevented the abolition of football at Harvard.[55] The Harvard situation had clearly shown the conflict between students and faculty, and indeed, between pro-athletic factions of the faculty and those who believed athletics were anathema to the intended purposes of institutions of higher learning.

A Crack in Faculty Control

By the turn of the century, boards of athletic control had been created by faculty at most institutions of higher learning in America. In many ways the athletic committees had become buffers between the students who wanted complete faculty hands-off and the faculty, many of whom wanted severe restrictions or abolishment of intercollegiate sports. The conflict over the power of faculty athletic committees led many colleges to add students and alumni to them. Students were needed for their technical knowledge and to somewhat pacify them through representation. Yet the committees had been created originally on the principle that students could not be trusted to manage their own sports effectively. The alumni were included because their influence over all aspects of higher education was growing in the latter decades of the nineteenth century. Furthermore, college alumni were an integral part of college athletics, involved in the financial stability and often the coaching of teams.

Students often resented the loss of freedom to run their own extracurricular programs. The president of Northwestern University reflected this feeling when he wrote in his annual report of 1896 that many of the students "seemed to think that the University was meddling with matters that did not properly come with its jurisdiction."[56] Students, nevertheless, recognized that they often had little choice but to accept faculty and athletic committee rulings. When, at Cornell, the faculty restrained itself on an athletic governance issue, students thanked the faculty for its "refusal to introduce . . . an element of paternalism into . . . athletic interests."[57] This was in response to Cornell professor Burt Wilder, who suggested that only one faculty rule was needed to control intercollegiate athletics, rather than eleven rules passed by the newly formed "Big 10" conference in the Midwest. "No student," he proposed, "shall have

leave of absence for the purpose of engaging in an athletic contest."
Wilder, giving no credence to the student's loss of freedom to pursue unhindered their extracurriculum, believed that Cornell should
be the first institution to issue a "declaration of independence [from]
the existing athletocracy."[58] Like a number of other faculty members, Wilder felt a loss of faculty power to control the educational
mission of higher education.

As alumni were increasingly added to athletic committees, faculty saw an even greater erosion of their power. Alumni support
of athletics, particularly financial, often meant alumni governance.
A case in point is Dartmouth in the 1890s and early 1900s. After a
series of poor athletic teams at Dartmouth, the alumni association
in 1892 asked the Board of Trustees to place athletics in the hands
of the association.[59] The trustees agreed by creating an alumni
athletic committee. With greater alumni control, Dartmouth's athletic fortunes began to rise. The alumni took over the operations of
the gymnasium from physical educators, and they built a new
athletic field. William Tucker, an original member of the Alumni
Committee on Athletics, soon became the Dartmouth president.
After a dozen years in office, Tucker could look with pride at
athletics and the general growth of Dartmouth. He attributed much
of the success to Dartmouth's alumni, with its "distinct and well
organized movement."[60] A year later, during the football crisis
following the 1905 season, a battle broke out between faculty and
alumni over athletic governance. The faculty petitioned the trustees
to restore to the faculty a wider control over athletic affairs. The
trustees quickly concluded that the Alumni Committee on Athletics
should continue to "determine the athletic policy of the College,"
and the case was closed.[61]

Not only had students seen a loss of freedom to control athletics
over the previous generation but faculties too had seen their powers
diminished. The Dartmouth case was to be repeated at many other
institutions by the early 1900s. As the twentieth century progressed,
students lost complete control over their games, and faculties were
generally impotent when important decisions were made.

In retrospect, it appears that by the early 1900s, athletic committees, no matter what their composition, could not solve independently major problems of athletics in higher education. At the same
time as the NCAA was being formed in 1905, philosopher and
dean of Brown College, Alexander Meiklejohn, stated that only
through cooperation and mutual understanding of the colleges

could athletic difficulties be resolved. He, like many others before him, indicated that students could "not be trusted to manage their own contests." Neither, he wrote, could athletic committees solve athletic problems because there was "no provision for intercollegiate cooperation in the management of athletics."[62] Until institutions relinquished some of their own independence to a larger body could a semblance of order be achieved in intercollegiate athletics. As students lost their freedom to manage athletic contests without interference from faculty and others, individual colleges increasingly lost control of athletics to outside forces. The movement toward inter-institutional control arose.

X

The Early Failure of Faculty Inter-Institutional Control

WHEN CHANCELLOR MACCRACKEN of New York University in 1905 called for an inner-institutional faculty conference to decide whether intercollegiate football should be banned or reformed, the resulting birth of the National Collegiate Athletic Association was not the first attempt to bring about faculty control of intercollegiate athletics. Neither was the creation of the Intercollegiate Conference of Faculty Representatives (Big Ten) in 1895. The movement toward inter-institutional faculty control of athletics began a generation before the NCAA, when faculties from Princeton and Harvard Universities independently formed faculty athletic committees. Concern about the inability or unwillingness of students to control their own athletic programs initiated these faculty responses. Within a few years a move by faculty to create inter-institutional control of student games was begun in eastern colleges. Though these faculty reforms were structurally unsuccessful, they were the harbingers of faculty-controlled athletic conferences and a national athletic body.

A theme of rugged individualism on the part of college students running their own extracurricula pervades the period before the NCAA was born. Like the industrialists who favored a laissez-faire policy in the late nineteenth century, students were reluctant to share with their academic superiors authority in athletics, a non-academic area. Similarly, there was strong resistance to giving up individual institutional autonomy over college sports in favor of greater control and the collective good. Nevertheless, as America advanced into the Progressive Period of the 1890s and 1900s with increasing social legislation, American college athletics progressed in a similar direction. By 1905 and the creation of the NCAA, it was apparent to a number of college faculties and administrations that a generation and more of principally hands-off attitudes toward student-controlled intercollegiate athletics had not been effective. By the early 1900s, there was a growing belief that unless some type of collective action above the level of student control were taken, intercollegiate athletics might not survive at some institutions. Only a crisis in football, the dominating college game from the 1890s on, brought to an end the lengthy period of rugged individualism in college athletics.

The First Attempts at Inter-Institutional Control

Almost from the beginning of intercollegiate sports, there was a concern for institutional control of athletics. President James Mc-Cosh in 1874 alerted his Princeton Board of Trustees to the problems of athletics. "It is a nice question," McCosh reported, "whether evils may not arise from sports in no way under control of the College authorities."[1] In due time, by the early 1880s, the Princeton faculty took action by forming the first college faculty athletic committee, in an attempt to settle athletic questions. In the remaining two decades of the nineteenth century, nearly all colleges formed autonomous athletic committees of faculty members when problems arose.

Despite attempts to do so, leading eastern colleges had not joined together in athletics to create inter-institutional policies by the early twentieth century. Each institution, to the contrary, would draw up its own athletic rules. Conflicts arose when the regulations of one college gave it an athletic advantage over another. Institutional athletic committees acting individually, without some form of inter-institutional control, led to almost constant arguments over eligibility rules and conditions of competition, such as the choice of officials or the use of professional coaches. As a result of inter-institutional athletic conflicts, calls for cooperative efforts to solve athletic problems were heard. Harvard and Princeton again led the way. Yale, the third member of the so-called Big Three, for two decades rejected efforts to form inter-institutional athletic rules.

Charles W. Eliot, Harvard's longtime president, pointed the way toward inter-institutional control in 1882 when he wrote a letter to other New England college presidents. "Our Faculty," Eliot's letter started, "wishes me to inquire if your Faculty would think it expedient first to prohibit your baseball nine from playing with professionals and secondly to limit the number of matches. . . ."[2] Eliot indicated that his faculty was ready to take action against professionals, but believed that common action would be more effective. The faculty of Harvard's chief rival, Yale, considered Eliot's proposal but took no action.[3] The Yale faculty inaction is the first of a generation-long series of hands-off actions by Yale faculty and administration with regard to inter-institutional control of athletics. This policy itself was largely due to Yale's unquestioned athletic supremacy during this period—the administration apparently felt there was little reason to tamper with success. The cooperative effort proposed by Eliot failed, and Harvard took action unilaterally to control professionalism.[4]

The next year, the Harvard athletic committee sent a letter to Yale requesting its faculty to call a conference of leading colleges to discuss common intercollegiate athletic problems. When the Yale faculty declined, the Harvard athletic committee went ahead and issued a call for a late December 1883 meeting. The issue of professionalism, especially of professional coaches, was the primary concern. Several weeks before the meeting, Dudley A. Sargent of Harvard's three-member athletic committee visited five other colleges to obtain a cross-section of opinions about the use of professional coaches in colleges. Sargent talked to, among others, Walter Camp of Yale, the athletic committee of Princeton, a professor at Columbia, the Amherst physical educator, Edward Hitchcock, and the president of Williams.[5] Sentiment, according to Sargent, was decidedly against professional coaching.

The issue of professionalism was on the minds of the faculty conferees when eight institutions met in New York City on December 28, 1883. This first gathering of faculty predated the Big Ten's first conference by eleven years, and was twenty-two years to the day before the original meeting of the NCAA.[6] Yale did attend the first meeting, along with Harvard, Princeton, and five lesser athletic institutions: Columbia, Penn, Trinity, Wesleyan, and Williams. By the time the conference had developed several resolutions, Yale had withdrawn. Among the eight resolutions passed by the conference were the following: (1) no professional athlete should be employed as a coach of any college team; (2) no college team should play against a non-college team (including professional teams), and games should be contested only on one of the college's home grounds; (3) athletes were to be limited to four years of athletic participation; and (4) each college should set up a faculty athletic committee to approve rules and regulations, and the colleges who accepted the resolutions would compete only against others who did the same.[7]

The resolutions were sent to twenty-one eastern institutions with the condition that when five colleges adopted them they would become binding. The Harvard faculty accepted them by a 25–5 vote, and the Princeton faculty and trustees adopted them unanimously. No other colleges voted to support the resolutions.[8] Thus the first attempt at inter-institutional control was unsuccessful. The defeat was to a great extent due to the lack of consensus by various college faculties on individual resolutions. For instance, the Harvard athletic committee debated whether colleges should be able to participate against amateur, but non-collegiate teams, and whether some athletic contests might be played on neutral grounds rather than on home fields. Dudley Sargent believed that any modification of the eight resolutions would weaken all of their work. "If the rules could not be accepted as they were," Sargent stressed, he "would vote to abandon joint action entirely and let each college fall back upon its own regulations."[9]

While the twenty-one college faculties debated the issue, students became aware of the resolutions and, in near unanimity, opposed them. The student-controlled Intercollegiate Association of Amateur Athletes of America (IC4A) meeting in late February 1884 was nearly unanimously opposed to the faculty resolutions. From a Lehigh University athlete who claimed that professional coaches were necessary, to Amherst students who favored only the four-year rule, to Columbia athletes who felt that it was none of the business of faculty how athletics were governed, students opposed the meddling of faculty.[10] A Harvard senior commented that the resolutions were "objectionable in themselves and objectionable on the grounds that we were not consulted, but mainly objectionable on the principle they violated, that of non-interference."[11] Princeton students passed a satirical circular protesting the athletic action of their faculty, while the Columbia students called for an intercollegiate student convention to oppose faculty interference.[12] At least one faculty member, Yale's E. L. Richards, agreed with the students.

He wrote to Princeton professor William Milligan Sloane, chairman of the faculty conference, that "the management of athletic sports might wisely be left to the students."[13]

The student-faculty conflict over the nature of intercollegiate contests was to continue for the next generation. Students saw athletics as their own creation and their responsibility, to conduct as they saw fit. Faculty generally reacted only to what they saw as the evils of college sports. The 1883–84 faculty conference represented this conflict clearly. The popular journal *Spirit of the Times* prophesied rather accurately during this first faculty conference attempt at inter-institutional control:

> Students and professors look at athletics from totally different standpoints, . . . [professors believing] that between them is a chasm which affords no tenable middle ground; that the students are unwisely stubborn in support of their own ideas; and that this obstinancy will, sooner or later, drive the strong army of authority to attain by harsh action, what might have been done by timely concession and compromise.[14]

With the failure of the members of the conference of 1883–84 to ratify the resolutions, individual colleges returned again to their own rules regarding eligibility, participation against professionals, and the hiring of professional coaches. Complaints continued among faculties. Following the football season of 1886, President McCosh of Princeton, concerned about the athletic excesses of the period, sent a circular to other eastern college presidents urging once again intercollegiate cooperation to eliminate athletic abuses. McCosh proposed that Harvard, as the oldest American college, should issue the call for another convention.[15] The Harvard faculty replied that Harvard would gladly be present at such a meeting provided that Yale would be represented. Yale, led by Walter Camp, had no such notion. The Yale position had not changed since 1884, when Camp wrote in support of student control, saying that "college athletic organizations if left to themselves would soon work out their own salvation."[16] Following Yale's refusal to be involved in the third attempt at inter-institutional faculty control, President McCosh's proposal died stillborn.[17]

The Brown Conference of 1898

More than a decade would pass, and the birth of the midwestern "Big Ten" Intercollegiate Conference of Faculty Representatives would occur, before another major effort to bring about eastern inter-institutional faculty control would surface. Individual colleges increasingly formed athletic committees, often composed of faculty, alumni, and undergraduates, as professionalism and questionable ethics made inroads into intercollegiate sports. But because each college tended to set its own standards, there were often acrimonious charges that one institution's rules gave it an advantage over another in the quest for victory. The idea of a permanent organization of colleges working cooperatively to achieve uniform rules was, of course, not new when it was suggested in the mid-1890s by the chairmen of athletic committees of several eastern colleges.[18]

Many problems had arisen since the previous 1886 attempt at mutual rules, primarily with football and baseball which loomed large on most eastern campuses in the 1890s. The question of eligibility in football caused particular problems, as "tramp athletes" transferred with impunity from one college to another primarily to participate in athletics. Fielding H. Yost, later a famous football coach at Michigan, was a good example. Competing as a hefty, six-foot-tall, 195-pound tackle for West Virginia University, Yost "transferred" to Lafayette College in Pennsylvania. Yost was ready to play in the most important football game in Lafayette's history when it contested the University of Pennsylvania. Penn had a thirty-six-game undefeated streak in 1896 when Yost made his appearance. In one of the great games of the nineteenth century, Lafayette upset Penn 6–4 with "freshman" Yost playing left tackle. He almost immediately transferred back to West Virginia University to complete work on a law degree, which he received half a year later.[19]

In addition to the tramp athlete question, athletes at many institutions could participate more than four years, and often played as students while attending professional schools such as law and medicine. Normal progress toward a degree often was not a condition of participation. Students were often paid in one form or another to play football and baseball. Payment of college baseball players to compete for summer resorts was commonplace, and there was no agreed-upon definition of an amateur athlete. Nor was the question of hiring professional coaches resolved. In addition, as football grew to be an ever-larger spectacle, the questions of pre-season and summer practices and commercialization through large gate receipts became prominent concerns. With all these issues, the overriding question of the place of athletics in American higher education was in need of resolution.

On February 18, 1898, four days after the sinking of the battle-ship *Maine* in Havana harbor, faculty, alumni, and undergraduate representatives from seven colleges met to do battle in their own way with the questions which for colleges were nearly as inflammatory as the question of possible war with Spain. All the colleges of the present-day Ivy League, with the conspicuous exception of Yale, met in Providence, Rhode Island, with Brown University as host. Each of the seven colleges—Brown, Columbia, Cornell, Dartmouth, Harvard, Penn, and Princeton—sent three representatives, faculty, alumni, and student, to meet in an attempt to find joint answers to vexing athletic questions of the previous decade or so.[20]

The original meeting of the Brown Conference of 1898, which was closed to outsiders and the press, began in the afternoon and continued past midnight.[21] All major issues were discussed, including eligibility of undergraduates and graduate students, athletic scholarships, summer baseball for pay, contests held on grounds other than those of the college, professional coaches, excessive gate receipts, and faculty control of athletics.[22] No decisions were made concerning the principal questions, but a special committee was created to conclude the work of the conference.

Wilfred Munro, the Brown University professor who chaired the meeting, was given the responsibility of heading a committee of the conference, composed of seven members, all of whom were faculty members. No students or alumni were represented. The committee of professors met several times during the spring of 1898. The first drafts of the committee report probably showed truer feelings of the faculty than did the published report. An early draft charged that many of the abuses which have existed in inter-university athletics were due to "athletics being vested solely in undergraduates," while "most of the quarrels are due primarily to the actions of graduates." The faculty, according to a pre-published outline, desired to "weed out" any "student who has entered the university for athletic purposes solely."[23] The inflammatory statements were either eliminated or toned down in the final draft. So too was the negative statement about "gladiatorial contests" which was changed to the somewhat more positive "public spectacles."[24] Even with editorial changes, which were probably made to create less anxiety or agitation among students and alumni, the 1898 Report on Intercollegiate Sports was a strongly worded document.

The Brown Conference Committee Report stands out as a potent call from faculty for cooperative action to cure the evils of intercollegiate sports. "We are not engaged," the final report asserted, "in making athletes."[25] What the committee wanted to do was to prevent college athletics "from interferring with the mental and moral training of the students."[26] The committee also knew what it did not want in college sports. It did not want college athletes to be tainted with professionalism and commercialism. The Report spoke out for the upper-class British sport model found at Oxford and Cambridge, where a gentlemanly game of enjoyable competition transcended "victory at all costs."

The attainment of excellence in athletics was not a high priority of the faculty-controlled Brown Conference Committee. "We should not seek perfection in our games, but, rather, good sport," the report read.[27] But seeking perfection, or at least excellence, was exactly what college athletes wanted to do in the 1890s. Because college students desired to beat other college teams, they had already developed an elaborate, rationalized system of rigid practice schedules and training systems, had hired coaches and recruited athletes, and had created methods of raising revenue. Historically, American college athletics had been commercialized from the first railroad-sponsored contest between Harvard and Yale in 1852.[28] Athletics had been professionalized by the next decade, when the first professional coach was hired by Yale in 1864 to enable the Yale crew to defeat Harvard for the first time.[29]

There is a touch of irony in the issue of excellence and winning, which students and alumni favored, and the Brown Conference Report's concern for gentlemanly participation advocated by faculty. Harvard's president Charles W. Eliot, the leading exponent of the British model of moderation in sports, had been one of the first college spokesmen for attaining pre-eminence in athletics at Harvard. Eliot had championed superiority in athletics as early as 1869. In his inaugural address upon assuming the Harvard presidency, Eliot said: "There is an aristocracy to which sons of Harvard have belonged, and, let us hope, will ever aspire to belong—the aristocracy which excels in manly sports. . . ."[30] Eliot's inaugural was a challenge to Harvard students to be the best not only in intellectual concerns but in athletics. The statement was not lost upon the ears of Yale faculty; lovers of Yale athletics quoted Eliot's own inaugural words for many years, saying that Eliot had "expressed a desire to win in athletics; that Harvard had set the pace for Yale and drawn them in to it."[31]

Harvard's premier philosopher, George Santayana, apparently

knew the spirit of America better in the 1890s than did the Brown Conference Committee when he, too, called for an athletic aristocracy similar to that of Eliot's a generation before. Santayana said that athletics at the highly competitive level were for the few who could excel, were played as a "dire struggle" in a situation analogous to war, and were valued by society because of the degree of perfection reached. Students who played the contests might never have thought about it, but they would likely have agreed with Santayana. For it was Santayana who said that in athletics, as in all performances,

> the value of talent, the beauty and dignity of positive achievements depend on the height reached, and not on the number that reach it. Only the supreme is interesting: the rest has value only as leading to it or reflecting it.[32]

Students would almost certainly have ridiculed an early Brown Conference Committee draft statement which claimed that "there is very little fun in watching a college team which has been so trained and perfected that it can win every game during the season."[33] And Santayana would probably have concurred with the students. Intercollegiate contests in America did not have the tradition of gentlemanly play for recreation and fun—they had been played for more than a generation emphasizing excellence and winning.[34] The Brown Conference Committee Report could not change the thrust of sport in American colleges, though it would attempt to do so.

Neither the Brown Conference philosophy nor its twenty proposed rules were accepted in American college athletics. Nor was its suggestion that a yearly conference be called to consider regulations and the proper development of athletics. Nevertheless, the athletic rules and the suggestion for annual meetings on athletics were not entirely forgotten.

The twenty rules suggested by a group of faculty from prestigious institutions gave colleges throughout the United States athletic guidelines as they worked toward faculty athletic control. To attempt to ensure order in institutional control with significant faculty direction, the Report stated that (1) each institution should form an athletic committee with faculty representation on it; (2) the athletic committee would approve all coaches, trainers, captains, and team managers; (3) no athletic competition would take place without athletic committee approval; (4) any student participation in more than one sport would require athletic committee approval; and

(5) the athletic committee would ensure that all athletes were bona fide members of the institution.

To ensure that college athletes would be bona fide students, the Brown Conference would require that (1) only students in good academic standing would be eligible to participate; (2) special or part-time students could not participate until they had attended college for one year; (3) students deficient in studies in one university department could not participate in athletics if they transferred to another department in the same university; and (4) no student admitted without passing the university entrance examination, or convincing governing authorities that he was capable of doing a full year's work, would be eligible for athletics.

The Brown Committee also prescribed the length of athletic eligibility. The Report recommended that (1) students be allowed no more than four years of eligibility; (2) students transferring from one institution to another could not participate in intercollegiate athletics for one year; (3) only freshmen would be allowed to participate on freshmen teams; and (4) no freshman could participate on both the freshmen and varsity teams.

The Brown Conference faculty group hoped to better control the nature of practices and contests. To this end they recommended that (1) teams were not to practice during college vacations, except ten days prior to the opening of the fall term (even then football was given some priority—principally to prevent injuries); (2) all contests were to be held on college grounds; and (3) students of the competing colleges were to be given preference in the allotment of seats to contests.

Finally, the Brown Conference Report placed a stamp of approval on what the faculty members believed would be an amateur code in the fight against encroaching professionalism in college athletics. The proposed amateur code stated that (1) no student could participate in athletics if he had previously played for money, such as a baseball player at a summer resort or an athlete who received financial support to participate on a college team; (2) no student could participate in athletics if he had ever taught sports for financial gain; and (3) no student would be eligible in athletics if he received board free at special dining facilities for athletes (training tables) or if he owed money for training table meals.[35]

In general, the Brown Conference Report of 1898 came out strongly in favor of faculty and athletic committee control of truly amateur contests, in which bona fide student athletes would participate without excessive commercialism. While the goals of the Report were exemplary for the upper-class ideals of nineteenth-century, British-like, amateur sport, the attempt to place those ideals into a fiercely competitive, win-oriented, and less class-restrictive American society was to prove unsuccessful. Some individual athletic committees did accept a number of the specific rules as their own, and in so doing moved colleges closer to uniform eligibility rules.[36] Yet colleges chose not to take collective action on the rule proposals. The Brown Conference suggestion for yearly conferences "to consider regulations and the proper development of the athletic sports" did not bear fruit at this time.[37] Colleges were still reluctant to commit the direction of athletic programs to an annual conference in which faculties would have a strong influence. They were likewise reluctant to have the extracurriculum taken away from student management. A dilemma in athletic governance resulted.

The Dilemma of Athletic Governance

The 1898 Brown Conference showed the difficulty of attempting to regulate intercollegiate athletics through non-student groups, such as faculty-initiated athletic committees or annual conferences, while at the same time allowing students at the individual compuses to manage the details of athletic practicing, arranging competition, hiring officials, and financing the teams. Yet this is evidently what many institutional leaders desired. A year before the Brown Conference, a committee of the Harvard Corporation dealing with sports recognized that "athletics were apart from the ordinary affairs of the college, and a matter which the Faculty could not well control." Nevertheless, this 1897 Corporation committee concluded that "the undergraduates, under careful general restriction, ought to be given so far as possible, a *free hand* in the management of their sports."[38] Harvard, the leader of faculty control of athletics since the 1880s, recognized the principle of student management of athletics while consistently violating this principle with athletic committee actions. Wrote Harvard athletic committee chairman Ira N. Hollis in 1900:

> It is at present the settled policy of the Athletic Committee to leave the management of sports and contests in the hands of students so far as it is compatible with good behavior and good scholarship.[39]

According to Hollis, "Contests should have their beginnings among the students, and should be controlled by the Committees."[40] With control in athletic committee hands and the management in student hands, a continuous tension and conflict inevitably followed at Harvard and elsewhere.

At Columbia, the chairman of the athletic committee, George Kirchwey, attempted to play the middle ground, as did Harvard's Hollis and many other institutional leaders. Kirchwey wrote in the early 1900s that "the failure of the system of unregulated student control does not necessarily involve the adoption of the alternative system of direct control by the university authorities."[41] A major problem of turn-of-the-century intercollegiate sport was that there were no clearly defined athletic policy makers, nor was it clearly established who would manage athletics.

Yale, among the leading eastern colleges, had a policy which apparently created the least amount of internal conflict, but was the most controversial externally. Yale favored student and alumni control and management of athletics. Yale had no athletic committee and saw no need for one. President Arthur T. Hadley continued the Yale policy of opposing faculty involvement in athletics, and this opposition at Yale for the last two decades of the nineteenth century kept the premier athletic college from participating actively in faculty- or college president-initiated conferences of the 1880s and 1890s. Hadley, referring to the Brown Conference, said:

> We believe that the responsibility for carrying out of the measures intended to promote honorable athletics must of necessity fall upon the shoulders of academic public sentiment, graduate and undergraduate, and that action of a faculty which is construed as assuming this responsibility tends to weaken its force in the places where it really belongs.[42]

Yale was, indeed, in the rear guard, as it supported student freedom and control of athletics. The travail which other colleges were experiencing in the governance of athletics, as evidenced by the Brown Conference and its predecessors, was not felt strongly at Yale until the twentieth century. Yale's established hands-off athletic policy remained even during the trauma that hit college sports in the early 1900s.

Seven years after the Brown Conference, a crisis of immense dimensions arose in intercollegiate football. In response to a profusion of questionable ethical acts, of brutality, and of fatal injuries, college authorities questioned whether football should be reformed or perhaps abolished. Chancellor MacCracken of New York University invited representatives of eastern colleges to meet and to resolve the issue in early December 1905. Out of this meeting came a call for a national conference of faculty representatives on December 28, 1905. It was from this meeting that the future National Collegiate Athletic Association was formed.[43] Over sixty colleges from across the nation met in an attempt to resolve the crisis in football. The officials at Brown University saw no need for another regional meeting.[44] The Brown Conference, which had failed in 1898 to solve major athletic problems, was not to be reconvened in 1906 as an eastern attempt to come to grips with vexing questions. The NCAA, though, would eventually address the issues on a national level.

From the 1880s, there had been a move away from student control of intercollegiate athletics toward increased faculty control, both at the local level and between colleges. The formation of faculty athletic committees at institutions was the first step. The inter-institutional athletic conferences of the 1880s and 1890s, though failures, increased the university faculty and administrative governance in the most visible extracurricular activity in colleges. The leading colleges of the east were experiencing great difficulty in breaking down the long tradition of hands-off policy and of student-run games. Not until after the 1905 crisis in football did colleges on a national level join together as they sought order in athletic affairs. Eventually the NCAA addressed the issue of inter-institutional governance of athletics, but the search for order continued to be an elusive goal throughout the twentieth century. That search for order was enhanced, yet in many ways complicated, by the rise of the professional coach.

Football was an important part of the extracurriculum which helped to free students from the classical curriculum in the early 1800s. Yale students with top hats are shown kicking a football in 1807. (*Library of Congress*)

Class battles, such as Winslow Homer's 1857 "Bloody Monday" football game at Harvard, were part of the initiation rites for freshmen at most colleges during the 1800s. (*Harper's Weekly* I (1857), 489.)

Rowing, the first intercollegiate sport, was also the first international college contest. Oxford's four beat Harvard's crew on the Thames River in London in 1869 before a crowd estimated at a million spectators. (*Harper's Weekly*, Sep. 4, 1869, p. 585.)

Victorious Cornell crewmen in 1875 are hoisted on the shoulders of fans at the glorious intercollegiate regatta at Saratoga, where 30,000 spectators gathered among the social elites. (*Frank Leslie's Illustrated*, July 31, 1875, p. 368.)

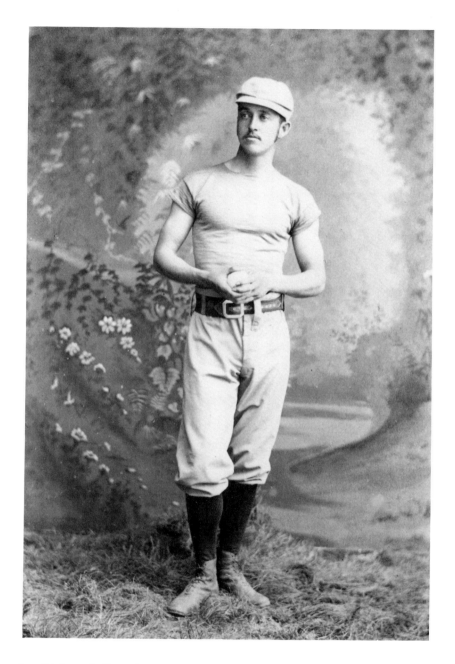

Lee Richmond, Brown's great pitcher, was the center of an amateur-professional controversy. A week before Richmond beat Yale for the college championship in 1879, he pitched a no-hitter against the Chicago White Stockings in his professional debut. (*Brown University Archives*)

Intercollegiate track and field began as an outgrowth of the annual college regatta in 1873. Participation was stimulated by offers of expensive silver trophies, with some participants known as "pot hunters." (*Harper's Weekly,* June 18, 1881, p. 401.)

Rutgers beat Princeton six goals to four in the first intercollegiate football game in 1869. The game was similar to soccer, which soon lost out to rugby football. (*Rutgers University Archives*)

THE HARVARD-McGILL FOOTBALL GAME.

Montreal, 1874.

Harvard brought rugby football to American colleges after it was introduced to the game by Montreal's McGill University in 1874. The next year Yale took up rugby, and it seldom lost for the next half-century. (*Harvard Graduate Magazine*, 1905, p. 423.)

Princeton and Yale were the football powers of the generation after the colleges Americanized rugby. The annual Princeton-Yale football game in New York was a prominent event of the elite social calendar by the 1880s. (*Harper's Weekly*, Dec. 7, 1889, p. 977.)

Running interference in front of the ball carrier was one major transformation of English rugby to American football. The play is depicted by artist Frederic Remington. (*Harper's Weekly*, Dec. 2, 1893, p. 1152.)

A FRIENDLY GAME OF FOOT BALL WITH YALE.

The *Harvard Lampoon* satirized Yale's aggressive play as "brutal" within several years of the beginning of intercollegiate contests. (*Harvard Lampoon*, Nov. 21, 1879, p. 88.)

With the development of roughness in football, players invented noseguards and earguards as the preliminaries to helmets, shown in an 1893 Frederic Remington drawing. (*Harper's Weekly*, Nov. 18, 1893, p. 1101.)

Mounting injuries and unethical play created investigations into the value of football. Injuries, though, often were considered part of the price of building manliness in the colleges. (*Harper's Weekly*, Aug. 31, 1891, p. 844.)

College faculties, such as that of Harvard, took action by banning football for brief periods of time. The Harvard faculty voted three times to ban football. (*Harvard Lampoon*, 1883.)

O. F. Schmidt

Some faculty members, including Professor Woodrow Wilson at Wesleyan College in the 1890s, helped coach football and other sports. (*St. Nicholas*, Nov. 1912, p. 19.)

Few college presidents spoke out against the excesses of intercollegiate athletics, though Harvard's Charles Eliot was an exception. He wanted football banned but could not gather enough support among the forces who controlled it. (*Harvard University Archives*)

Masses of spectators came to support college football. As depicted in this 1893 photograph, Princeton is about to unleash its version of the "flying wedge" upon Yale before 50,000 spectators at New York's Manhattan Field. (*Frank Leslie's Illustrated,* Dec. 7, 1893, p. 370.)

It took a key death in the critical year of 1905 to produce drastic rule changes, including the forward pass, and the creation of the NCAA to give a semblance of order to football. (*Literary Digest*, Dec. 4, 1909, p. 997.)

EDUCATION. IS THERE NO MIDDLE COURSE?

Well before the twentieth century, the "dumb" jock had been caricatured in contrast to the sickly looking "brain." Thomas Nast, the superb cartoonist, may have been first, in 1879, to do so. (*Harper's Weekly*, Aug. 30, 1879, p. 696.)

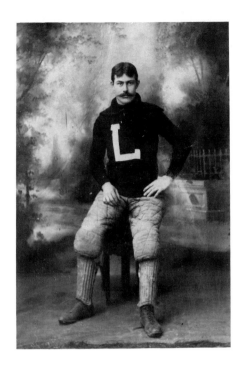

Athletes from an early time were often more concerned with participation in sports than in academics. Fielding H. Yost, the legendary coach, transferred from the West Virginia law school to Lafayette in order to play in a game against Pennsylvania in 1896. (*University of West Virginia Archives*)

Yale's football captain, James Hogan, was given a two-week vacation in Havana, Cuba, after the football season at the turn of the century. It was paid out of a "slush fund" controlled by Yale's athletic boss, Walter Camp. (*McClure's Magazine,* June 1905, p. 116.)

Harvard started the stadium-building mania of the twentieth century when it constructed the first steel-reinforced stadium in 1903. (*Harper's Weekly*, Dec. 9, 1905, p. 1783.)

XI

The Rise of the
Professional Coach

THE PROBLEM OF INTER-INSTITUTIONAL CONTROL was made even more
difficult and pressing by the rise of the professional coach. The premium placed upon winning by individual institutions was extremely
high prior to the advent of professional coaches, but it intensified
when an individual's coaching career was dependent principally
upon turning out winners. "Players like to win," argued a former
Yale all-American football player, Frank Butterworth, "but head
coaches and especially paid coaches, had to win."[1] Each coach
wanted to develop advantages which would give him and his team
the winning edge. Uniform rules determined by inter-institutional
action might take away the freedom of the pro coach to win using
whatever method he devised to accomplish his task.

The introduction of the professional coach into college sport did
as much as anything to accomplish the rationalization of intercollegiate athletics. The pro coach began with the Yale crew in 1864, and
by the early 1900s the coach's organization for victory was rather
highly developed. The pro coach so dominated the athletic program
among leading colleges that he was, at times, paid more than the
highest salaried professor, and he was becoming as visible as the
college president on the college campus. The saga of the professional coach does much to explode the myth that there was ever a
lengthy period when the amateur spirit pervaded college athletics.
Intercollegiate athletics, almost from the first, had the professional

spirit. This was exhibited in the drive for excellence, and the professional coach manifested this drive from an early period.

The Beginning of Professional Coaching: The Crew Situation

Four decades after the first American professional college coach was hired by the Yale crew, Caspar Whitney, America's foremost professional writer on amateur sports, believed that the professional coach was "the most serious menace of college sport today." Said Whitney, "Let those who value mere winning above all else have their professionals. . . ."[2] Winning, of course, was what most individuals involved in "amateur" college sport desired by the early 1900s. It was not easy to discern what was considered next in importance to victory.

The desire to win, and the freedom of students (and eventually alumni) to pursue that goal, brought about the rise of the professional coach. Those who idealized college athletics as amateur were destined to be disillusioned. An editor of the *Harvard Bulletin* dreamed along with Whitney: "Some day it may seem good policy to say that graduate coaching, even, shall be put away, and that the undergraduates alone shall be responsible for their crew, their nine, their eleven. If that time ever comes," he wrote hopefully, "college athletics will then be truly sports."[3] Nevertheless, one thing prompted the professional coach, and that was the desire to excel over others—to be victorious.

Yale, the eventual dominating athletic power of the era, initiated professional coaching in colleges the year Caspar Whitney was born. In 1864, a dozen years after the first Harvard-Yale boat race, the Yale crew hired a gymnasium instructor from New York City to produce a group of trained rowers and defeat Harvard for the first time in their dual championships. The clear victory in the three-mile race, by over 40 seconds, proved to Yale that the professional coaching of William Wood was far superior to student training by one of their own.[4] Yale kept hiring pro coaches into the 1870s. By that time other, smaller institutions, "freshwater colleges," began to compete in the Rowing Association which Harvard had created.

Massachusetts Agricultural College started the proliferation of professional rowing coaches who were hired seasonally through student initiative. When the Aggies completely surprised Harvard and Brown in winning the 1871 regatta with pro coach Josh Ward, it set other small colleges to thinking that they, too, might beat mighty Harvard. A Dartmouth crew was started, and a professional coach was hired after students, alumni, and friends subscribed a hefty $2,000 for the team. Massachusetts returned with Josh Ward, and Bowdoin entered with coach George Price. But that was not enough to win the next regatta, as Amherst, with pro coach John Biglin, garnered the victory. When the race was completed, even members of the Harvard crew, which had never had a pro coach, believed that they would have won with a professional trainer.[5] In the third year of the regatta, eight of the eleven crews were guided by professional coaches: the three Ward brothers, Josh, Ellis, and Hank guided Massachusetts, Amherst, and Columbia; Biglin took over Dartmouth, while Price remained at Bowdoin; Fred Sinzer led Wesleyan; John Blew headed Trinity; and Henry Coulter was at Cornell. Most, if not all, had rowed professionally. Only Harvard, Yale, and Williams remained out of the professional coaching ranks.[6] This time, even with the preponderance of pro coaches, the two best crews were Yale and Harvard, by far the two largest colleges among the group racing.

The third regatta was the last time the Association would allow pro coaches, for it voted in early 1873 to ban them following the race that summer.[7] No trainers or coaches were to be allowed unless they were undergraduates or graduates of the colleges represented. Thus, at an early period there was a distinction between alumni and non-alumni coaches. Even if an alumnus were paid, he was considered an amateur coach. This distinction remained until well into the twentieth century, when some "amateur" alumnus coaches working only during the season were receiving more money to coach than were full-time professors.

The action to ban pro coaches was never completely enforced. The next year the crew of Wesleyan used the same coach of the previous year, Fred Sinzer, to train for the Saratoga Regatta, and nearly beat Columbia for the championship.[8] A year later Dartmouth, which had finished sixth and fourth the two previous years, sent two of its crew to New York City to improve their stroke and hired George Englehardt to teach the entire crew the new method.[9] Dartmouth improved its time by 50 seconds over the three-mile course, but the crew ended up only fourth behind Cornell, Columbia, and Harvard. After 1876, both Harvard and Yale had withdrawn from the regatta, and they returned to their dual meets, leaving the regatta to die. A number of colleges dropped rowing as it was expensive, and they no longer had the chance to gain prestige and to advertise their institutions at the expense of Harvard and Yale.

The First Great American Pro Crew Coach: Charles Courtney

Of the few colleges that remained active in rowing, Cornell, Columbia, and Pennsylvania were the three most significant outside of Harvard and Yale. Cornell, though, produced the first great professional crew coach in American colleges. It was Cornell's Charles Courtney who said, "If you want to win you must first beat Columbia," and Cornell learned to do that on a regular basis.[10] Courtney coached Cornell crews from 1883–1916, a period of thirty-four years. His rowers won 98 meets, many of them regattas, and lost only 46 in that period. At the intercollegiate regatta begun at Poughkeepsie, New York, in 1895, Courtney's crews won 14 of 24 titles, never finishing below third. The record included seven sweeps in which Cornell's varsity eight, varsity four, and freshman eight all won in the same year. No other college had even one sweep during Courtney's years.[11] Prior to his hiring at Cornell, Courtney was first an amateur and then a professional rower. He was undefeated in 88 amateur races up to 1877. He received national acclaim for winning the amateur rowing championship contested at the Centennial Exposition in Philadelphia, the same year Cornell won its second consecutive rowing championship at Saratoga. The next year he turned professional to cash in on his fame, even though he had succeeded financially in amateur rowing.[12] A natural contest was one with the Canadian, Ned Hanlan, who had won the professional competition at the Philadelphia Centennial. In 1878, the first of three Courtney-Hanlan matches took place. Some 20,000 spectators watched the Canadian pro win a close five-mile race at Lachine, Quebec, and collect the enormous $10,000 prize. Although a charge against Courtney of throwing the match was made by the *New York Times,* the second match created a greater furor in professional rowing.[13]

The next year, the twenty-nine-year-old Courtney challenged the world's best single sculler, Hanlan, five years his younger. The two were scheduled for a race for a $6,000 prize on Lake Chautauqua in western New York. A large, temporary grandstand was erected; tickets for observing the race on steamboats were sold for $5.00; and a special rail line was built to carry spectators to the site. The contest, though, never took place. During the night before the contest, Courtney's boat was sawed in half, and he refused to row in any other. Courtney's supporters claimed Hanlan's men did it as Hanlan was drunk and would have lost the next day. Hanlan's people charged Courtney with destroying the boat to prevent an embarrassing loss. The mystery has never been solved, but because Courtney never beat Hanlan, a stigma hung over his head throughout his life as the loser who ruined his boat to prevent another loss.[14]

Courtney's position was complicated further the next year when a third encounter with Hanlan was arranged on the Potomac River in Washington, D.C. Both houses of Congress adjourned for the event, and President Rutherford B. Hayes was in attendance, along with an estimated 100,000 spectators. Hanlan was so superior, that before Courtney reached the turning post to return to the finish line where the race began, Courtney dropped out, turned around, and began his return to the finish. Unsuspecting spectators near the finish believed that Courtney was leading. Hanlan, sensing the worst, rowed with unrelenting effort and passed Courtney before they reached the finish line. Courtney's behavior, some believed, led to the downfall of professional sculling in America.[15]

No wonder, then, that at the announcement of the hiring of Charles Courtney by Cornell in 1884, there would be detractors. The *New York Times* asked what was the intention of the Cornell crew: "Do they intend to saw their boat, to drink poisoned tea, or to run foul of sunken wires in case they find themselves overmatched in the coming regatta?" The *Times* praised the Harvard faculty for forbidding the employment of professional coaches. "If college boys cannot learn to row without associating with persons like Courtney," the paper went on, "perhaps they would be quite as well off if they devoted a little more time to classics and mathematics and a little less to rowing."[16] Cornell students knew of Courtney's past when he was hired, but the year before, Courtney had helped the Cornell crew for ten days prior to the Lake George Regatta in which Cornell beat Penn, Princeton, and Bowdoin. They valued his rowing expertise above what some called questionable ethics.[17]

Cornell had picked a winning coach to continue its winning tradition. Cornell had won back-to-back intercollegiate regattas at Saratoga in 1875 and 1876. In 1881, its crew had traveled to the Henley Regatta in England in an unsuccessful effort to beat the English.[18] Courtney, however, improved upon the previous record. From the mid-1880s to the mid-1890s Cornell never lost a race, varsity or

freshman. Despite Cornell's excellence in the period, Coach Courtney could not convince either Harvard or Yale to compete in rowing. While Harvard rowed against Columbia, and Yale competed
against Penn, neither would row against Cornell. Why? According
to a Penn graduate from that time, it was because "Cornell was too
fast."[19] Neither Harvard nor Yale appreciated competing against the
"mechanics" from Cornell, and losing to them was unbearable. So
Courtney did what he could to show the world what his crews could
do. In 1893, the Cornell and Penn crews journeyed to Lake Min-
netonka near Minneapolis for a meet. Two years later he took his
crew to Henley for Cornell's second attempt to win a cup. But that
was a loss and a social disaster.

When Cornell was invited to Henley to row for the Grand Challenge Cup, Courtney was in the first year of a three-year contract
calling for $1,200 and reaching $1,500 the third year.[20] The well-
paid coach, secure in his job, sailed to England with his crew, but
was ill and missed the opening heat when Cornell contested the
Leander Boat Club of London. The Leanders were traditionally a
powerful crew composed of former Oxford and Cambridge rowers.
British society was in mass attendance in the small town of Henley,
west of London on the Thames River. The scene was charming and
peaceful, and the rich and well-born were everywhere along the
one-mile, 550-yard course, women wearing "gay dresses and the
men sport[ing] bright blazers." The river was "cram jam full of
craft of every description, punts, canoes and skiffs," noted a member of the Cornell crew.[21] Beneath the glitter was a mutual dislike
between the English and the Americans, often tempered by an
American admiration of British culture. The 1895 American involvement in the Britain-Venezuelan boundary dispute probably increased
nationalistic feelings on both sides of the Atlantic.

Any ill-will which existed between the two countries was raised
to a fever pitch at the start of the Cornell-Leander race. For Courtney, though in bed at the time, the memory of the incident remained
for a lifetime. As the two crews lined up for the starter's signal, the
wind was blowing full force in the face of the Leander crew, while
Cornell was sheltered by the boat house. "We had a great advantage," wrote a Cornell rower. "We were sure to win that heat and
Leander was scared. So scared," he said, "that they could not get a
good start. So they dropped out and gave us the heat."[22] The Leander
crew, though, said that the starter had begun the race before they
were ready. What was most disturbing to the British way of think-

ing was the American reaction when the Leander crew stopped. The American crew, according to the standards of the British, should have done the sporting thing and discontinued so that a restart could have been held, but the Americans "rowed over" for an easy victory. The incident confirmed in the English mind that Americans cared only about winning and would do most anything to accomplish victory. The sympathizer of the British amateur spirit, Caspar Whitney, would have agreed, for he had previously noted that "the ideal of the English Universities is gentlemanly sport, not victory."[23]

Courtney felt otherwise, and he was especially opposed to the treatment of his crew by the spectators and the British press. He said that if he had been in the launch at the start, he would have been willing to have his crew recalled, as Cornell "wanted to win on our merits, or not at all." He was not there, the crew did not restart, and the press and spectators vilified the American crew. "We were treated in the most brutal sort of manner," Courtney was quoted as saying.[24] A team member reported that "many a taunting remark was made to our fellows."[25] As one Englishman was heard to say after Cornell lost the next heat, satisfying English pride: "Serves you right for yesterday."[26] Courtney was so angered at the English that he vowed, "I would not go back to England for the whole island," and he never did.[27]

The 1895 Henley experience and later events showed clearly another side of Charles Courtney and professional coaching in America—that of the autocratic coach. When intercollegiate sport began, if anyone was in an authoritarian position it was the captain. In fact, it was often the captain who hired the coach in the early stages of professionalism of coaches. Once the pro coach was successful and was asked to continue, it placed him in a stronger position to dictate policy. Courtney, unlike most, if not all, other coaches in the 1890s, had a multi-year contract which began with his 1895 crew. He could move even closer to dictatorial powers, symbolic of the twentieth-century coach, while he jeopardized the freedom of students to control athletics as they desired. An example occurred at Henley while Cornell was practicing for the regatta. The crew elected one member to be captain, but Courtney objected to the choice. He demanded that Chick Freeborn be put in place of newly elected Captain Sharpe. According to one account, Courtney threatened his crew that if the change were not made, he would resign as coach. "If you know enough about rowing and have enough confidence in your own ability to get along without me," Courtney told the rowers, "well and good." He threatened his crew that unless they elected a captain of his choice "and do it at once, my responsibility as coach and trainer will cease." If the Cornell crew lost, Courtney wanted no one associated with Cornell "to say that I neglected to do my duty by the university, by the crew or by myself." He closed his speech with a statement any experienced coach might have said who was driven by a desire for excellence and winning: "I've got reputation to lose. You, gentlemen, have one to make."[28] The crew acquiesced; the elected captain, Sharpe, resigned, and Courtney's choice, Freeborn, replaced him.

Two other incidents give a glimpse of Courtney's domineering position following his many coaching successes. In 1897, he removed five members of the varsity crew for eating strawberry shortcake against his orders. His crew, composed mostly of second stringers, won the intercollegiate regatta at Poughkeepsie.[29] Courtney was not always so fortunate in deciding what course to take regarding obedience and the striving for victory. As part of his rational approach to winning, Courtney logged careful daily records each year. The 1904 season saw Cornell lose to Syracuse in the Poughkeepsie Regatta. Courtney blamed Captain Coffin for lacking discipline in training. Following a nine-second loss to what he called a "third class college crew," he wrote in his diary that "no crew ought to win that has trained as this year's Cornell Varsity has trained." Courtney, berating himself as well as his captain, wrote a record for future reference: "If I had done what I knew to be my duty I would have dropped him from the crew early in the season for I knew he was not training as he should. He was drunk," Courtney revealed, "the day of the freshman banquet and I knew it."[30] Courtney's judgment, or lack of judgment, and his power to act on it was just one aspect of the dominant position the pro coach had attained in the latter nineteenth and early twentieth century. Similar problems would be thrust upon the college coaches as they increasingly took power or had it handed over to them at the turn of the century.

The Rational Approach of Harvard Coach William Reid

If crew initiated professional coaching into college sport, it was football in which the pro coach came to dominate by the early years of the twentieth century. William Reid of Harvard is a good example of the very well-paid coach who took a highly rationalized approach to attempt to bring about a football winner. Reid further represents the transition between the graduate coach, one who participated in football and returned soon after graduation to coach for a short period, and the full-time coach who desired to make his living at coaching. Reid never became the latter, but he might have if his psychological and physical being had been more constituted to the rigors of professional coaching.

Bill Reid, Jr., came to Harvard from Belmont, California, where his father was a preparatory school headmaster. William Reid, Sr., ironically had opposed hiring individuals to coach amateur sports a decade before his son would become a highly paid coach at Harvard.[31] Bill, Jr., graduated from Harvard in 1901 after participating for four years on the baseball team and two years on the football squad. As a catcher he was baseball captain during both his junior and senior years. He is possibly the only Harvard catcher who played an entire season without an error, the year Harvard won eighteen and lost only two one-run games. In football Reid played on or coached the only two Harvard teams to beat Yale in the decade and a half following 1890. The Harvard baseball team won three of four series from Yale during Reid's four years there. Reid was, then, a winner as far as Harvard was concerned, and it was only natural to turn to him for coaching.

In the fall following his graduation, he was asked by the football captain to be the head coach. This was in the Harvard tradition of using young football alumni as graduate coaches. It was an honor to be chosen and to do what one could for the glory of the alma mater. The twenty-two-year-old Reid gained some acclaim when Harvard went undefeated and beat Yale 22–0, the worst defeat inflicted upon Yale by Harvard up to that time. The fact that Harvard had played an ineligible player, Oliver Cutts, who was later shown to be a professional, while Yale had been forced to drop an ineligible player, Edgar Glass, took some shine, but not much, off the rare Harvard victory over Yale.[32] Reid stuck around Harvard long enough to pick up a masters degree and coach the baseball team to a 21–3 record the following spring. He then married and returned to his father's California preparatory school as the assistant headmaster.[33]

Reid might have returned earlier to Harvard to again coach football had Harvard not been embroiled in the whole question of hiring professional coaches. Harvard certainly needed professional coaching if its losses to Yale by wide margins in 1902 and 1903 were any indication of the effectiveness of its alumni coaches. Shortly after the second straight shutout by Yale, former Harvard football players created the Harvard Graduate Football Association and offered to hire Bill Reid at $3,000 to coach football. The touchy question of a paid football coach, however, was tabled—killed—by the Harvard Athletic Committee.[34] There was a paradox, if not hypocrisy, in the athletic committee's refusal to pay a head coach, when the committee had sanctioned the $500 payment of an assistant coach for the past four years.[35]

Another year and another shutout loss to Yale later, the Harvard captain asked the athletic committee for permission to hire Bill Reid for the 1905 season. By this time the athletic committee was feeling the pressure to purchase the best alumni coach available. The twenty-six-year-old Californian was offered the high salary of $3,500 to coach the football team. There was probably only one other football coach paid more than that in the early 1900s. George Foster at Columbia was paid $5,000 after his team defeated Yale, Foster's alma mater.[36] But Reid would not come east for that salary, so the committee voted to allow the alumni to subscribe an additional $3,500 for "extraordinary expenses" to secure Reid. The extra money was subscribed almost at once.[37] With the $7,000 package, Reid would be paid nearly double the salary of the average professor at Harvard, 30 percent more than the highest paid professor, and nearly as much as Charles Eliot, Harvard's president since 1869.[38]

It is somewhat surprising that a young man who lost twenty pounds in his first coaching bout at Harvard four years before should want to return to the pressures of coaching. When contacted a year earlier about the possibility of coaching, Reid admitted, "I am of a very nervous temperament and very much addicted to worrying . . . and I don't know whether I could last a good stiff campaign or not." Yet, the offer to return to Harvard was, he said, "one of the most delightful things I have ever experienced."[39] And the money was also acceptable, as he had been making only $1,500 at the Belmont school.

Reid believed that to win, Harvard must have a thoroughly organized and systematized plan of attack—a rationalized approach. He looked at the previous shutout losses to Yale and the number of Harvard players who had become ineligible because of poor academic records. Reid concluded that though no one was particularly to blame, "it is rather the natural result of a failure to conduct our football on rational business principles."[40] What Reid wanted was a rational approach like that of Yale, which among other qualities had the organizational leadership of athletic advisor and coach of coaches Walter Camp, and a private academic tutoring system for athletes paid for out of gate receipts. As Camp said: "The organizer wins in athletics as he does in business."[41] Reid favored a systematized approach akin to the father of scientific management in industry, Frederick W. Taylor.

Reid set about to create such logical procedures, and he had much catching up to do. Two months prior to his hiring, he journeyed across the nation to check out the coaching situation at Harvard. While there, he called a meeting of thirty-five of the most promising football players. At the meeting he emphasized strongly the need for academic eligibility. Each man indicated to Reid that he would stop cutting classes, if he had been in the habit. Reid naturally knew a great deal about the Harvard faculty members and their attitudes toward students. He wrote that "most any professor will pass any man in the course who is regular in attendance[,] who gets in his reports . . . , and who shows anything like a decent interest in his work."[42] The second action Reid took with his future players was to indicate, from reports received from previous coaches, what each player's weaknesses were and what the individual should do before the next season to correct them.[43]

Reid arrived as the full-time football coach in March 1905, and he systematized his approach by beginning a diary of football commentary that eventually reached something short of 1000 typewritten pages of football notes, comments, and records. But that was only a small part of his plan for out-organizing and out-scoring Yale, the one true test of his rational program. In the half-year before the football season began, Reid organized winter gymnasium workouts using weights and wrestling, as well as holding spring and summer practice. Reid wanted, in effect, year-round physical activity, focused on football. He canvassed all 4,000 Harvard students, developing a card catalogue including weight and possible team position. Contacting former players and coaches, Reid obtained written documents on how to play every position on the team. He traveled a considerable distance to contact Lorin Deland, the former Harvard coach and inventor of the flying wedge a decade and a half before, to discuss signals and plays. The new coach met with the team physician, Dr. Nichols, for advice on proper diet and cleanliness. He began a search for a team trainer for better treatment of injuries and improved use of safety equipment. In search of the best equipment, Reid ventured to the Spalding manufacturing plant in New York and obtained a copy of the order placed by Yale. While in New Haven, scouting the Yale baseball team, he artfully obtained samples of all equipment being constructed for the Yale team, including shoes, head gear, shoulder, elbow, hip, and knee pads, and special harnesses for injuries. He had photos taken of punting for the coaches' biomechanical analysis and for showing players correct form. Reid's imaginative mind considered such things as building a new football shoe for punters and the use of ribbons of leather on the kicking shoe to give the ball a greater spiraling effect.[44]

To look for future football material he set up Harvard Clubs at several of the preparatory schools which fed athletes to the major eastern institutions. To this end, he invited the Andover baseball team to Harvard to see the Harvard-Princeton baseball game. Reid also gave the mandatory speeches before alumni clubs and the academies, and he wrote articles for newspapers and magazines. The new Harvard coach acted as if he were in the eye of a hurricane as he strove to make Harvard a winner.[45]

Three areas of Reid's effort, the scholarship of athletes, the recruiting of athletes who had dropped out of school, and the scheduling of games, give further proof of the impact that professional coaches had on intercollegiate athletics. Reid lamented his inability to motivate all of his potential squad to achieve academically. One, Preston Upham, was a 225-pound prospect who left campus for periods of three or four days, missed classes, gambled, entered street brawls, and seemed to Reid to have had "absolutely no filial or moral sense." Reid nevertheless went to see his parents and his classmates, talked to each of his professors (who complained that when Upham was in class he often slept), and planned with Upham a daily study schedule. Reid hired a private tutor just before spring examinations, but to no avail. Upham returned to night excursions in Boston, got into a row and knocked out three Boston policemen. Reid and others, however, through work with newspapermen, kept the incident out of the newspapers and Upham away from likely Harvard expulsion. All was to no avail, as he failed his examinations, was dismissed from Harvard, and ended up as a telephone linesman in Kansas City.[46] Upham was only one of forty men with whom he worked whose academics were weak. This was at a time that "no man of even ordinary ability," according to Reid, "can possibly fail to get through Harvard if he attends his lectures regularly and does a little work with some thinking."[47] Tracking his athletes academically was one of the most trying tasks which Reid felt he needed to do at Harvard.[48]

Keeping athletes eligible was one thing; bringing back athletes who had been dismissed or had quit Harvard was another. The most bizarre case was that of Harry LeMoyne, "one of the greatest natural athletes that Harvard has ever had."[49] He had left college because of academic problems as well as feeling remorse over the death of two students he roomed with during his freshman year. Reid was determined to get LeMoyne, who was working on a sheep ranch at Hagerman, Idaho, back into Harvard. He visited LeMoyne's parents a number of times to see if they would support him if he returned. Reid then talked to individuals at the Harvard Scientific School about LeMoyne's academic deficiencies and secured a tutor for him. This accomplished, Reid procured a room, rent-free, which LeMoyne might use. The coach then got an advertising agency to acquire a free railroad pass from Idaho, and he got several prospective jobs for LeMoyne to earn his board. Having done all this, Reid and others began to attempt to contact LeMoyne by letter and telegram. When this failed, Reid arranged with a storekeeper in Hagerman, Idaho, to have the messages delivered to LeMoyne by horseback. Hearing nothing, Reid got one of LeMoyne's friends to visit him. The hard-working coach never received a direct reply from LeMoyne. Reid recorded that after exhausting "every means in my power to bring him around" it had all been useless, "something of a wild goose chase."[50] Reflecting back upon the LeMoyne case as the season was about ready to start, Reid confessed that "the endeavor to get LeMoyne back here was not wholly legitimate."[51] And it wasn't.

The pressure that winning placed on Reid put him in a paradoxical position with regard to academic achievement and recruiting athletes. The same could be said about the scheduling of opponents. Should one schedule opponents of comparable competitive ability, or should a coach rig the schedule to produce the greatest number of victories? Reid, and the athletic leaders of major colleges at this time, had little difficulty reconciling this, as if it were not an ethical question. Reid and others before and after him chose victories. That is a principal reason Harvard from 1890 to 1910 competed against Princeton only twice, and then only the two years Harvard and Yale had broken relations. Besides not liking Princeton's "mucker" type of play, Reid revealed, even before he took the job, that "to play Princeton two weeks before Yale we'll wreck ourselves sure."[52] Thus, Reid spent a great deal of time working out a schedule that would bring victories while keying on "The Game" with Yale to close the season.

Reid's basic approach was to schedule so that Harvard could "lick our opponents in increasing strength as the season progressed and as our team developed."[53] This remembrance of Reid four decades after the fact was only inaccurate in details, for the final game was, without question, the focal point. Reid, in 1905, scheduled four easy games first (Williams, Bowdoin, Maine, and Bates) to try out his men. He then considered a stronger team, such as Amherst, to secure a "fighting spirit" in his team. Reid discussed with his advisors playing Columbia, Syracuse, Cornell, or Penn State in place of Amherst, but each was stronger than Harvard was willing to play. He finally dropped Amherst from consideration and settled on the Springfield YMCA Training School.[54] Wesleyan was considered for a mid-week game as an easy tune-up for a tough Army team to follow, but the idea was dropped because someone might have been injured. Reid wanted to meet the West Point team before Army would acquire any experience playing any of the other Big Four colleges (Penn, Princeton, and Yale) and while Harvard could take "advantage from whatever nervousness the Cadets may feel."[55] Following Army was a game with Brown. Reid had been assured by the Brown coach before finalizing the schedule that he "would not develop a team of such nature that it would reach a climax" at their game.[56] The Carlisle Indians of Pennsylvania would follow Brown. Even before Jim Thorpe came to the government Indian school, Reid was concerned that it was recruiting from other Indian schools.[57] After the Indians, the season was to conclude with Penn, Dartmouth, and Yale. The choice of Dartmouth between the Penn and Yale games was a difficult one for Reid to make. Though he wanted to give Dartmouth "a most unmerciful whaling," he was not sure that Harvard could do it. Yet, reasoned Reid, "if Dartmouth seems too strong we will have to cut her out entirely. . . . If we cannot feel absolutely sure of Dartmouth," he believed, "then I would rather let her go and play Holy Cross."[58] He was reassured, and after months of thinking and negotiations, Harvard came up with an eleven-game schedule, including nine home games in its new, nearly 40,000-seat stadium.

When the regular season began, the intensity which Reid gave to his job increased. The pressure to produce victories began to mount on Reid, and his constitution could not take it. By the time the first game was played, Reid had already lost six pounds from his slender 165-pound frame at the beginning of the fall season. He was repeating his experience of the 1901 season when, as a twenty-two-year-old coach, he admitted that he worried himself "into a state of practical uselessness."[59] Whether it was attempting to attain parental consent for an athlete to participate, choosing the best eleven players, deciding on the formations and plays, checking the mounting injuries and even diseases including gonorrhea, questioning the judgment of assistant coaches, disputing the eligibility of opposing players, objecting to the choice of officials, or, most important, having anxiety about the next game, Reid worked himself into a state of near-paralysis.[60] By the season's end, he was drinking and taking drugs for sleeping, which were slipped into his drinks by Herbert White, one of Reid's athletic advisers.[61]

Reid was torn by the anxiety of a stressful season which saw defeats by Penn and Yale and a tie by Dartmouth. Reid's 8–2–1 season was a bitter disappointment. He continued to coach the following year and ended with an 11–1 season. The one loss, however, was a shutout by Yale for the second consecutive year. He said that he "looked upon the two years as a failure," despite losing only three games.[62] A quarter-century later, though, he realized that he had laid the foundation, through his rational plans, for Harvard's later victories over football power Yale.

When Reid resigned at the close of the 1906 season, he wrote an article for the *Harvard Graduates' Magazine* intended to sway those who wanted Harvard to win into believing that a paid coach was necessary. At a time when Harvard policy makers and the athletic committee were fighting a last-ditch battle to preserve the amateur coaching ideal, Reid claimed that if Harvard returned again to "charity" coaching, the team would be "wiped off the field every time we compete." Reid saw the dichotomy of "a paid coach . . . and self-respect, or charity coaching and a loss of self-respect."[63]

When writing the article, Reid may have had in mind the man who would become head coach in 1908, Percy Haughton. Haughton had played with Reid at Harvard and had given Reid advice and assistance when he was coaching. Haughton continued the rational approach that Reid had brought to coaching at Harvard. According to a contemporary, Haughton used "intensive analysis, executive thoroughness, and commanding influence . . . and [a] rational and highly developed degree of team play."[64] Reid was happy when the mantle was passed; the leadership he had brought to Harvard was surpassed by the "peerless Haughton."[65] The successful, rational coach had arrived.

Harvard and the Great Debate over Professional Coaching

William Reid and Percy Haughton were in the middle of the professional coaching debate at Harvard, America's most important educational institution and last bastion of the so-called "amateur" system of coaching. Harvard had begun discussing the issue of professional coaching in the 1870s and 1880s, and a significant number of the leaders at Harvard were still attempting to preserve an amateur form in the first decade of the twentieth century. In 1882, Professor Charles Eliot Norton proposed allowing professional coaches so that Harvard might compete equally with other colleges. This feeling divided the athletic committee, for that body, led by Dudley Sargent, had opposed moving intercollegiate athletics away from the amateur sport ideal.[66] Norton was, in fact, in favor of the English system of amateur coaching, but he thought it was unfair that only Harvard would uphold the system, knowing that pros produced winners. The dilemma for Norton was made manifest when the attempts at faculty inter-institutional controls of the 1880s failed, and Harvard was left to fend for itself on the issue.[67]

For a generation Harvard waffled on the issue, first allowing and then opposing professional coaches in such sports as baseball, cricket, and crew. By the early 1900s the professional coaching issue was at a crisis stage at Harvard, as Yale won nearly all the time over its chief rival. The Harvard athletic committee, though wavering at times, clung to the concept of amateur coaching even as defeats, especially to Yale, mounted.

The professional coaching issue was central to the notion of what individuals believed sport was all about. Amateurism in sport was a nineteenth-century upper-class concept created by the English.[68] It was an elitist attitude contrived to keep the lower classes from mixing with their social superiors on the athletic field. It was an undemocratic, non-egalitarian concept designed to make amateurism appear to be superior to professionalism. It ran counter to the social and political forces of the nineteenth century, calling for freedom of opportunity regardless of class position. It was, therefore, a reactionary policy to preserve for the traditional power and social elite control over an important area of upper-class life—sporting activity.

In America, Harvard came closest to the English model of Oxford and Cambridge. Harvard's upper-class attitudes of the Boston Brahmins permeated the depths of the institution through its governing boards, president, faculty, and athletic committee. Nearly all the centers of power at Harvard attempted to channel students away from mass appeals toward elite attributes—the model being the Oxford-Cambridge one. Anthony Trollope saw this as early as the time of the American Civil War, saying that Harvard College "is to Massachusetts, and, I may almost say, is to all the northern States, what Cambridge and Oxford are to England."[69] In sport, of course, this meant the Oxbridge ideal of amateur sport and the rejection of the professional coach. No Harvard president would have done as ex-Yale man and president of the University of Chicago, William Rainey Harper, would do in 1891. Harper, who understood America but lacked elitist English ideals, hired a professional coach at Chicago, Amos Alonzo Stagg, another "Yalie." Paying Stagg a staggering salary for the time, $2,500, and giving him tenure as an associate professor, Harper told Stagg that he wanted him to develop teams which "we can send around the country and knock out all the colleges."[70] How different this was from the Harvard attitude which justified amateur coaching by looking socially upward and geographically eastward. "The fact that the English university oarsmen have scorned professional help," commented a Harvard publication, "is an argument which cannot be easily disposed of."[71] Ira N. Hollis, chairman of the Harvard athletic committee, had acquired the Harvard attitude in the early 1900s when he opposed professional coaching "simply as useful in producing teams for competitive purposes."[72]

Was competition to produce excellence and winning what really mattered? To Yale it obviously was. When Yale needed professional coaches, it hired them. With Walter Camp advising, professional coaching was not needed in football until Yale started losing to Harvard in the second decade of the twentieth century. In the Harvard-Yale rivalry in crew and football in the years before 1905, Harvard won only three crew matches in the previous twenty-one contests, the exact number of wins Harvard recorded in the preceding twenty-one football games. Harvard, generally without professional coaches and without the stability of a Walter Camp, seldom won its important games. A Harvard publication confessed that victories never compensate for the loss of gentlemanly sport. "It is not pleasant to be beaten by Yale year after year," the periodical stated. "All Harvard men want to win our full share of victories, but, after all, the ultimate end of athletics is not to defeat Yale. If it were, then the employment of a professional coach would be wise."[73] The amateur apologist, Caspar Whitney, pleaded for the Oxbridge of America to forsake turning to the professional coach. "You, Harvard, show the world that at least one American university recognizes sport for sport's sake, and even in defeat, cherishes it as such above sport for the mere sake of beating a rival."[74]

The pressure at Harvard, however, to consider that winning, and winning over Yale, mattered as it did in other American colleges was mounting. The rear-guard Harvard Board of Overseers voted in 1907 to recommend to the athletic committee that it do all that it could do to attain inter-institutional control to abolish professional coaching.[75] Half a year later, the athletic committee voted on a motion to ban unilaterally all paid coaching after the academic year 1909–10, but it lost. With the defeat, the committee went on record in favor of "abolishing paid coaches, *acting in conjunction with the University's important rivals,* after 1909–10."[76] Other institutions refused. Harvard by this time had already hired James Wray, who would lead Harvard to seven victories in the next eleven crew contests with Yale, and would soon hire Percy Haughton, who would lose only twice to Yale in the next nine years. Harvard had been pulled reluctantly to sanction the professional model which turned out winners in the spirit of the American competitive society. And the scoreboard stood: professional coach one, amateurism nothing.

XII

Amateur College Sport: An Untenable Concept in a Free and Open Society

THE RISE OF the professional coach was a major force in the early movement in American intercollegiate athletics to adopt a professional model. By the late nineteenth and early twentieth century, it was clear that the professional model produced victories. Only those with idealistic blinders on, such as *Outing* editor Caspar Whitney, believed that the amateur sport model would outlast a professional one in America. Only Whitney, or someone of his ilk, could claim in 1894 that professional sport was dead in America and that true amateurism had conquered all. Men's intercollegiate sport had accepted much of the spirit of professionalism as its own. Yet college athletics expressed an amateur ideal during this period, as it did nearly a century later. One might say that Americans for well over a century have tended to profess amateurism while they have exhibited the professional spirit in most areas of "amateur" sport. This was no more apparent than in intercollegiate athletics. Why have Americans accepted the professional model, and why have they felt the need to justify their actions in the name of amateur athletics?

The historic amateur-professional dilemma in college sport required, as all dilemmas do, a choice between equally undesirable alternatives. The collegiate dilemma might be stated as follows: if a college has truly amateur sport, it will lose prestige as it loses contests; if a college acknowledges outright professional sport, the college will lose respectability as a middle-class or upper-class institution. The unsatisfactory solution to the dilemma has been to claim amateurism to the world, while in fact accepting a professional mode of operation.

The term amateur has been a charged one. Historically, since the mid-nineteenth century, the word "amateur" as used in sport has stood for positive values in relation to "professional," which has had negative worth. Amateur has meant good and elevated; professional has meant bad and degraded. The exaltation of the amateur and the debasement of the professional, as has been noted, was a function of nineteenth-century British social class elitism.

Amateurism as Defined by the British

"Ancient amateurism is a myth," classicist David Young boldly stated in his perceptive *The Olympic Myth of Greek Amateur Athletics*.[1] The heart of amateurism, he has pointed out, is social elitism, born in Victorian England by the upper classes to exclude those of the working class.[2] Though the ancient Greeks had no concept of amateurism, the English social elite developed the myth and then passed their own amateur legislation as if they had past precedent to rely upon. In the 1870s, the elite British Amateur Rowing Association separated itself from plebeian types by passing an amateur law. In so doing it gave us one of the many negative definitions of amateurism which have plagued sport since then. The upper-class rowers ruled that no person is an amateur "who is or ever has been by trade or employment for wages a mechanic, artisan, or labourer or engaged in any menial duty."[3] Since then, nearly every definition of an amateur in sport has been a negative one. Thus, an amateur is a person who has:

- never competed in an open competition;
- never competed for public money;
- never competed for gate money;
- never competed with a professional; and
- never taught or pursued athletics as a means of livelihood.

Amateurism has almost always been defined in terms of what it is not, rather than what it is. There appears never to have been a successful, positive, workable definition of amateurism, even as amateurism has served principally the social and economic elite since the mid-1800s. The philosopher Paul Weiss was basically right when he stated:

> A rich man does not need to become a professional player. Since he has more leisure time than most, he also has more time to devote to sport. As a consequence, he may become an amateur athlete. . . . By and large the line between amateur and professional is mainly a line between the unpaid members of a privileged class and the paid members of an underprivileged class.[4]

Harold Harris, the late classical historian, echoed the same theme in his volume *Sport in Britain*. Harris believed that "the distinction between professional and amateur had been purely one of social class."[5] The British amateur attitude was carried to America, but because America lacked entrenched classes, at least to the degree that Britain had them, the amateur attitude would never flourish in practice as it did in the elite-led sports in Britain.

If amateurism has not been defined in negative terms (for example, an amateur is one who has never participated for remuneration), then it has generally been defined as a state of mind determined by the motives of the athlete. The athlete participates only for the love of the sport. Amateurism, to many, has been an attitude, not a state of being.[6] If amateurism is an attitude determined by the athlete, it leads to a perplexing problem—a dilemma of rather large dimensions. First, external judges can never prove the motives, the state of mind or attitude, of the amateur. Second, the historic claiming of positive virtues of the amateur relative to the professional is a false concept. There is simply no evidence that an amateur is more virtuous than a professional. In fact, the reverse may be true, for the amateur at the upper levels of competition often received financial advantage for participation in amateur sport—certainly a hypocritical stance. This has been the situation in collegiate sport since the 1880s, and a few cases before that.

The paradoxical or self-contradictory situation in intercollegiate athletics since the 1870s demands documentation, for there are those who believe that at one time American college athletics were purely amateur, a paragon of athletic amateur virtue. There are two problems with that belief. First, one must believe that amateur athletics equate with virtue, second, that they were once without a professional element. The first is debatable; the second is simply not true.

Professionalism in Nineteenth-Century College Athletics

Inroads of professionalism into college athletics prior to the twentieth century have been noted throughout this volume. Eight categories have been chosen which indicate the characteristics of professionalism which existed in nineteenth-century American college sports:

1. competition for valuable, non-cash prizes;
2. competition for money prizes;
3. competition against professionals;
4. charging money at the gate;
5. costs of a training table not borne by the athlete;
6. payment of athletic tutors by others than the athlete;
7. recruitment and payment of athletes; and
8. payment of a professional coach.

While a number of the categories may not appear to be truly in the professional realm to late twentieth-century observers, it is important to note that they were considered to be so by many people in the nineteenth century. Thus, it is logical to think of professionalism in nineteenth-century not twentieth-century terms.

Whether non-cash prizes should be considered part of the professional element is debatable. More than a century ago, as today, few questioned a non-cash prize if its value were small. Early on, though, collegians were receiving very valuable prizes for victories in crew, especially, and also in track and field. In the very first intercollegiate competition between Harvard and Yale at Lake Winnipesaukee, New Hampshire, in the summer of 1852, the prize for the winning Harvard crew was a pair of expensive black walnut oars.[7] College crews continued to row for costly prizes for the next generation, leading to the opulent 1870s when, at the fashionable intercollegiate regatta rowed on Lake Saratoga, silver goblets were offered, worth double what an average laborer might earn in a year.[8] It is probably not surprising that the first intercollegiate track contests, held in conjunction with the intercollegiate regatta, included valuable prize trophies. A Harvard student noted that it was worth several months of intense practice to win one of the track prizes at Saratoga.[9] Dartmouth College, which held its own track and field contests in the 1870s, offered such prizes as opera glasses, silver inkstands, silverware, and the works of Thomas

Macaulay, John Milton, and William Shakespeare.[10] There is no question that nineteenth-century college athletes were competing for expensive prizes, often at the expense of just a love of sport.

If competing for non-cash prizes was a somewhat questionable professional practice, it was less doubtful when monetary prizes were offered. Harvard probably started it all in the 1850s when its four-oared crew, including a graduate student and future Harvard president Charles Eliot, rowed in a meet which had a $100 first prize. That was more than enough to pay for their rowing shell.[11] By the next decade, Harvard was competing for purses as high as $500 in Boston regattas.[12] In track and field several colleges were offering gold medals for individual track events. Yale offered money prizes until the practice was questioned by a reputable sporting journal.[13]

Competition against professionals, like the competition for cash and non-cash prizes, was moving towards the professional model in intercollegiate sports. Again, Harvard's crew was involved, when its athletes competed against professional scullers in the 1850s. Harvard even once split the first prize with professionals after defeating their pro rivals.[14] More than crews, college baseball teams competed against professionals. Almost as soon as professional teams were formed, colleges picked them out for good competition. Yale played 60 percent of its games against professionals from 1868–74. Harvard, in 1870, won thirty-four games and lost only nine—eight being to professional teams.[15] Charles Eliot, who was president of Harvard by this time, eventually attempted to rid Harvard of the practice of playing professionals through inter-institutional controls. He failed. Students, who controlled college athletics, did not want to give up this aspect of the professional mode.

Charging money at the gate was also considered by some to be an agent of professionalization akin to competing against professionals. Harvard faculty believed that collecting money at its contests gave an "undesirable professional tone" to college athletics. The faculty felt so strongly about gate receipts that they banned them on the campus in the 1870s. Students were so determined to collect them that they left the campus to participate in baseball games in Boston so that they could collect money from spectators.[16] By the 1880s and 1890s, most colleges had accepted the idea of charging spectators. And, of course, Harvard eventually succumbed to the temptation. Harvard even built the first reinforced concrete stadium in America in 1903 and could then extract tribute from 40,000 spectators for its annual football game with Yale.

One might question whether these activities were really anti-amateur in the pure sense of playing the game for love of the sport. Similarly, one might question another characteristic of professionalism, the training table. Creating the training table, which began with crew in the 1860s, was intended to produce winning teams through better food. In the 1800s, it was generally thought that amateur athletes should pay for the general cost of board and that only the additional cost of training table extras should be borne by athletic funds. Yet it was increasingly common for the entire food costs to be picked up by athletic associations, giving the athlete a "free ride."[17]

Another way of paying athletes was to use athletic funds to provide them with tutors. To keep athletes eligible was a problem for Ivy League schools then as now. Yale, the "jock" school of America for the half-century following the 1870s, was also the richest school athletically. Until 1905, Yale was paying for athletic tutors out of a secret fund kept under Walter Camp's control.[18] Yale, though, was only one of a number of institutions which tried to keep its athletes academically eligible using professional means.

Yet, the tutoring of students was never the concern which recruiting of students to participate in athletics and the payment of athletes were. The recruiting of athletes, however, was predated by half a century by the recruiting of sub-freshmen for college literary societies. Literary and debating societies formed around the ferment of the American Revolution and were the first organized extracurricular activities. It was important to competing literary societies to recruit preparatory students to enhance their society in the eyes of the others.[19] Recruitment occurred early in athletics also. After the first intercollegiate baseball game in history between Williams and Amherst in 1859, Williams charged Amherst, the winner, with recruiting its pitcher from a blacksmith's shop.[20] Some years later, Hamilton College successfully advertised in the *New York Clipper* for a pitcher and catcher for its baseball team, to the dismay of Cornell, which had to play Hamilton.[21] By the end of the century, the William and Mary baseball team was petitioning its faculty with the following strange request: "We wish to request that, if we should secure a 'pitcher' and would provide for his support at the college hotel, you would allow him to matriculate free of charge."[22] The faculty opposed the action because they considered it "professionalism." Recruitment for the major sports of rowing, baseball, football, and track and field were common by the twentieth century. A number of the athletes were being paid to participate. At Columbia, in 1899, five men of the football team had their tuition, board, and room paid for through illegal actions of the student manager of the team. Other colleges were taking similar actions as college sport was moving toward the professional model.[23] Pennsylvania State College was one of the first to legalize the recruitment and payment of athletes when in 1900 the Board of Trustees sanctioned athletic scholarships to include room, board, and tuition.[24]

While recruiting and paying athletes extended the amateur model to the extreme, it was no greater challenge than the change from amateur to professional coaches. The professional coach may have been the single most important element in intercollegiate professionalism. In the opinion of many advocates of amateurism in college sport, the pro coach was anathema. It began in crew at Yale during the Civil War, and within a generation there were professional coaches in the major sports of rowing, baseball, football, and track and field, as well as a number of minor sports.[25]

By the early twentieth century, there was probably no college in America which was able to preserve amateurism in men's sport, as competition for money and non-money prizes, contests against professionals, collection of gate receipts, support for training tables, provision for athletic tutors, recruitment and payment of athletes, and the hiring of professional coaches pervaded the intercollegiate athletic scene. Professionalism had invaded college sports and had defeated amateurism as it was understood in the nineteenth century.

To conduct athletics in a professional mode while calling them amateur was both a self-contradiction and an hypocrisy; a pretense at virtuous character without possessing virtue. To call collegiate sport amateur was in fact playacting, the ancient Greek definition of the term hypocrisy. Intercollegiate athletics, which had many virtues according to numerous individuals, was acting the part of amateur sport while playing like professional athletics. Thus, the amateur-professional athletic dilemma developed. If a college had truly amateur sport, it would lose contests and thus prestige. If a college acknowledged outright professional sport, the college would lose respectability as a middle-class or higher class institution. Be amateur and lose athletically to those who were less amateur; be outright professional and lose social esteem.

The solution to the dilemma, then, was to claim amateurism to the world while in fact accepting professionalism. The solution worked amazingly well, but it was not honest intellectually, thus the dilemma. Why did this occur? Why was there a need for colleges to espouse amateurism while practicing professionalism? Could amateurism ever have worked in American colleges as it did at Oxford and Cambridge? If not, what in American society precluded amateurism in intercollegiate athletics?

A Professional Model and an Ideology of Freedom and Equality

A dominating nineteenth-century American ideology, based upon freedom and equality, would not allow the British upper-class concept of amateur sport to permeate American college sport. The United States may have begun with ideas of political freedom and equality of rights, but the liberal ideology was transformed in the nineteenth century to a freedom, or equality, of opportunity.[26] As the English historian J. R. Pole has so aptly stated, "Equality of opportunity was the chief meaning that Americans could now hope to extract from a tradition which had been handed down to them as equality of rights."[27] Americans had rejected the British concept of a fixed status system based upon birth, wealth, and education, and it had telling implications for "amateur" intercollegiate sport.

The amateur concept involved a system of privilege and subservience that would not and could not hold up in American society. Americans repudiated an antiquated system that did not meet the criterion of freedom of opportunity to achieve excellence in college sport. To achieve excellence, the professional model proved to be far superior to the amateur model. As Americans opposed the aristocratic social system of England with its monarchy, House of Lords, landed nobility, courtiers, privileges, sinecures, and pensions that characterized the English state and church, and Oxford and Cambridge, Americans did not accept the tenets of amateurism.

It might be argued that the pervasive ideological belief of freedom of opportunity led to a breakdown of amateurism and to a logical accent on professionalism in college sport. With a greater freedom of opportunity in America, it is likely that the American college developed differently from the system of higher education in England. One of the major differences was that until the nineteenth century, Oxford and Cambridge had a monopoly of higher education in England. Those two universities dominated the entire period of the development of intercollegiate sport. In America no two institutions, such as Harvard and Yale, could control higher education even though they might have chosen to do so. In America, there was greater freedom and opportunity to found colleges and to develop them to the extent that private, state, or local monies were available. Thus, in America great private institutions such as Harvard, Stanford, and Yale evolved as well as outstanding state-supported institutions such as California, Michigan, and Wisconsin. There was no upper-class control of higher education and no upper-class control of athletics, with its elitist concept of amateurism, as occurred at Oxford and Cambridge.

Even if America's most elite institutions had wanted to develop amateur sport based on the Oxbridge model, they could not have succeeded. There simply was no easy way to control sport in a select group of colleges, because there was no way to control the quality or quantity of institutions of higher education. Any individual, group, or level of government could found a college, and any college which wanted to raise intercollegiate athletics to a level of excellence was free to do so with a commitment of time, effort, and financial backing. Freedom of opportunity was a pervasive element in the development of the American college and its athletics. Oxford and Cambridge, for instance, had no equivalent to the American intercollegiate experience in crew in the 1870s. In America, small colleges had the freedom to develop crews as Yale and Harvard had done before them. Thus, the farmers from Massachusetts Agricultural College, or the mechanics from outback Cornell, or the Methodists from Wesleyan could produce crews and challenge the established colleges from the colonial era and garner victories at the intercollegiate regatta. The egalitarian principles were more dominant than any elitist desires that might have existed at Harvard or Yale, the closest equivalent to Oxford and Cambridge which America had to offer. Separate, dual competition between Harvard and Yale, in an attempt to keep themselves socially and athletically above the fray as Oxford and Cambridge did for generations, meant that both Harvard and Yale would eventually lose athletic esteem and prestige. Harvard and Yale could not long remain athletically superior to, and separate from, the newer and less prestigious institutions in America.

In a similar way, the upper-class amateur ideal of participating for the enjoyment of the contest and for no other motive, including financial considerations, could not easily exist in a society whose freedom of opportunity ideology allowed all to seek excellence through ability and hard work. Intercollegiate athletics fit well into that ideological model, and a meritocracy based upon effort and talent resulted in college athletics from an early time. Achieved status in colleges and in athletics became the American way, rather than the ascribed status as seen in England's elitist universities and their athletics.[28]

The English amateur system, based upon participation by the social and economic elite and rejection of those beneath them from participating, would never gain a foothold in American college athletics. There was too much competition, too strong a belief in merit over heredity, too abundant an ideology of freedom of opportunity for the amateur ideal to succeed.[29] It may be that amateurism can never succeed in a society which has egalitarian beliefs. It may be that amateur athletics at a high level of expertise can only exist in a society dominated by upper-class elitists.

This historic amateur-professional dilemma, which existed almost from the beginning of intercollegiate athletics in American colleges, remained into the early years of the twentieth century and well beyond. American colleges practiced a type of professionalism, and yet they claimed amateurism. The dilemma resulted from the need to protect college sport from outside criticism by using acceptable amateur language while at the same time desiring the prestige and status which came from a highly professionalized model that produced excellence and winning.

XIII

Eligibility Rules in a Laissez-Faire Collegiate Scene

THE DEVELOPMENT OF the professional model and its emphasis upon excellence and winning had a dramatic impact upon the recruitment of athletes and the need for eligibility rules. From an early period in American intercollegiate athletic history, there was pressure to bring in athletes with little regard for academic considerations. This, like nearly all other aspects of intercollegiate sport, began under student control. Recruiting expanded under the professional coach, and as the twentieth century progressed, recruiting and keeping athletes scholastically eligible for athletic competition became a full-time job.

Conflicting eligibility rules probably led to more problems between colleges than any other concern in the late 1800s and early 1900s. They were also a principal reason why colleges were forced to consider inter-institutional controls following a period of laissez-faire mentality in which each college determined for itself what eligibility rules it would use. Thus in the generation before the NCAA was formed, attempts to solve a myriad of eligibility disputes tested the patience of students, coaches, alumni, faculty, and college administrators. Included among the concerns were the participation of graduate students and alumni; the recruitment and eligibility of freshmen; the question of bona fide students; the status of non-degree, "special" students; and the residency of transfer students and athletic "ringers." Attempts at solving the eligibility problems would bring about significant changes in the governance of intercollegiate sport and would have an impact on the role of the NCAA. The laissez-faire mentality of individual institutions would only gradually fade away.

An Early Eligibility Question—Graduate Participation

When Harvard and Yale started intercollegiate athletics in an 1852 crew meet, there were no eligibility rules and no eligibility problems. Most rowers of the Yale and Harvard crews were members of the junior classes. However, one member of that Harvard crew, Joseph Brown, the captain and coxswain, was later involved in the first eligibility controversy. Brown had been out of school two years when the two institutions met again in 1855, but there he was barking out orders as coxswain of the Harvard boat.[1] Yale had a legitimate complaint, but it allowed Brown to compete, though he was not a Harvard student. If the same thing had occurred half a century later, Yale would have cried foul. Yale then would have demanded an affidavit from Harvard indicating that he was eligible, and if he were not, would have protested vigorously to the Harvard captain and the athletic committee to withdraw him. This time, though, with no rules, Yale preferred to make an agreement with Harvard to disallow alumni to participate in the future.

This first intercollegiate eligibility rule remained until 1869 when Harvard crossed the waters to challenge Oxford. The Harvard captain asked Yale to suspend the rule for that year so that a Harvard law student, Joseph Fay, could compete against Yale at the same time that most of its first crew was in London. Yale agreed, but regretted it when Harvard won its fourth straight contest over Yale.[2]

For two colleges to agree on eligibility rules was difficult, as winning was what mattered; but it was clearly a thornier issue when multiple institutions were involved. The graduate question arose at the intercollegiate regatta in 1873, when twelve colleges heatedly debated the point. The association of rowing colleges agreed in an 8–4 vote to prohibit any person from rowing for one college who had graduated at another.[3] This was probably most detrimental to Harvard, which had sizable professional schools in medicine, divinity, and especially law, from which athletes were often chosen. Harvard argued that "the equality between colleges can only be established by allowing each to enjoy its fullest resources." To allow Yale to select athletes from its large scientific school as well as the traditional "academic" college at Yale was unfair, Harvard reasoned, if it debarred to Harvard such groups as law students.[4]

The whole notion of graduate student participation in the 1870s and 1880s was confused, as graduate education was in its infancy in America. To be studying law or medicine was not necessarily to be in graduate school at that time, for they were generally considered professional schools. A person who was a college graduate might attend a professional school, but it was not necessary. For instance, Harvard did not restrict its law school to college graduates until 1893, a first in America.[5] For institutions with professional schools, it was possible to attract athletes who had played four years, and then get another two or three years of eligibility from an experienced athlete. A record may have been approached by Carl Johanson, an eight-year football veteran at Williams, Harvard, and Cornell. At Cornell he attended law school for three years, though football may have been his major interest. In 1892, he not only played but also coached the team, one which included "Pop" Warner, the legendary twentieth-century coach.[6] President William Howard Taft recalled that during his days at Yale in the late 1870s, a man could "grow old in college athletics."[7] Two-thirds of an 1880s Harvard baseball team were members of Harvard professional schools, four in law school and two in medical school.[8] This fact came to the notice of President Eliot, and charges of a type of professionalism were brought against Harvard athletics. One Harvard graduate opposed "calling back a bearded host of graduates" to play sports.[9] The Harvard Athletic Committee felt the same way and passed a motion in 1890 to allow athletic participation only to degree candidates or special students in Harvard College or the Scientific School.[10]

Harvard was not alone in its concern over graduate and professional school participation in athletics. The Harvard athletic committee action was almost surely triggered by the 1889 Intercollegiate Football Association eligibility controversy. "Certain questions of amateur standing" caused Yale and Wesleyan to call for a special convention of the five-member league's Graduate Advisory Committee. The football season was well under way at the time of the meeting, and it was only weeks before the important league match-ups. Earlier that fall two veteran Princeton players returned for post-graduate study, while two other stars entered Princeton as special students. Charges of professionalism and questionable eligibility brought Walter Camp to propose a nearly five-hundred-word eligibility resolution. It called for bona fide students who attended school for the entire year and a certain number of recitations each week, and who had never received any financial considerations for athletic participation. Princeton's representative, Duncan Edwards, felt that the resolution was aimed principally at Princeton's undefeated team, which threatened Yale's unbeaten streak of four years. Edwards rose to amend the motion by prohibiting participation of all students in professional departments and all post-graduates. This would have eliminated four players each at Harvard, Penn, and Yale. Edwards's amendment was defeated by those schools affected plus Wesleyan, and the Camp motion passed.[11]

Harvard, which was scheduled to play Princeton next, immediately challenged fifteen Princeton players under the new rule, practically the entire squad. Edwards retaliated by protesting against four Harvard men.[12] A second meeting was necessitated to rule on the protests. Trying to save face for the Intercollegiate Football Association for passing ex post facto legislation, Wesleyan moved to table, and effectively kill, the Harvard protest of Princeton players. In a 3–2 vote, with Harvard and Yale in the minority, the motion was tabled. Immediately, Edwards withdrew his protest against the Harvard players.[13] The season continued two days later with the Harvard-Princeton game. No players were eliminated, but the Association was on its way to destruction over eligibility concerns, as Harvard withdrew in less than a week.

The participation of graduates was only part of the controversy, but it was a significant concern. It was especially odious to some if the player attended professional or graduate school "for the foot-ball season only."[14] When Harvard broke relations with Princeton and withdrew from the football league, it began a major effort to form a dual league with its chief rival Yale. In those negotiations, which went on for about a decade, the notion to ban graduate participation was a point at issue.[15]

The graduate question was kept alive within the now four-member Intercollegiate Football Association and elsewhere. In 1893, with growing charges of professionalism in college football, Yale proposed what became known as the "undergraduate rule." Only Penn, which was building a football powerhouse using graduate students and special, non-degree students, was opposed to the new proposal.[16] When it passed, the issue was not settled. The same Yale resolution was introduced a few weeks later at the intercollegiate track league (IC4A) meeting. This time it was defeated, with Penn leading the attack. To further confuse the issue, Harvard and Yale agreed to not apply the undergraduate rule for their annual football game, leaving each college to judge for itself what eligibility rules to enact.[17] The Harvard-Yale action moved eligibility legislation back a generation and solved none of the problems created under student-managed athletics.

The return to individual college eligibility policies was set off when Yale undergraduates, in a mass meeting, voted 502 to 440 to oppose an inter-institutional agreement to ban graduate student athletic participation made by their athletic leaders at the football meeting.[18] Law students had originally organized the meeting, for they believed that their athletic rights at Yale had been abridged. Other students protested the Yale decision to apply the football ruling unilaterally, to all its major sports. Walter Camp saw clearly the negative effect Yale's unitary action would have on the success of Yale athletics. Speaking about the possibility of Yale losing games, Camp said: "If we allow a question which is one of internal policy to militate against Yale's outside interests in regard to other colleges we shall only be doing ourselves an injustice."[19] Camp believed strongly that Yale, which traditionally had the strongest aversion to inter-institutional controls, should not hurt itself through solitary restrictive legislation. Yale, true to its history, refused to send a delegate to a meeting in 1893 called by Brown University during the crisis to discuss eligibility rules. The meeting, on shaky grounds when it began, collapsed when Columbia, Dartmouth, Penn, and Princeton withdrew from negotiations.[20]

Penn, a principal beneficiary of professional school and graduate participation, reopened the possibility of rescinding the ban on graduate participation during the fall of 1893. When the football association refused to budge on the matter, the Penn captain was furious. "If that's a fair sample of the spirit of American independence that exists in our colleges," captain H. A. Mackie declared, "then I never want to win a game of football." Penn tendered its resignation, and Wesleyan followed suit.[21] Princeton and Yale were the sole remaining members of the once-powerful Intercollegiate Football Association, which set the national standards for football. The crisis of eligibility was not solved satisfactorily, but a number of schools either banned graduate student participation or required one-half or one year of residency before competition.[22]

The concern over graduate participation was not addressed effectively on a national level until after the football crisis of 1905. At that time not only was there a focus on the brutality of football but the ethics of recruitment and eligibility were much discussed. With the leadership of Harvard, the Big Three of college sports finally agreed to ban graduate students in all four major sports.[23]

The elite schools of the east could lead in eligibility matters for only a limited time, with their reluctance to take collective action. The "Big Ten" conference in the Midwest was already showing signs of leadership that it would eventually wrest from the eastern schools. In 1895, the presidents of seven Midwest universities organized the "Big Ten" in order to bring about more athletic order and ethical standards. Eight of the twelve presidential rules dealt with eligibility. The conference decided that graduate students could participate for the minimum number of years required to obtain a graduate degree, which was shortly changed to a limit of two years.[24] Following the 1905 football crisis, the "Big Ten" decided that graduate students were no longer welcome on the athletic field. The "Big Ten" acting collectively, in contrast to eastern hesitancy at inter-institutional controls, also took a giant step in eligibility legislation. At the same time that it banned graduates, it prohibited freshman eligibility.[25]

Freshman Eligibility: More Athletic than Educational Concern

Eventually inter-institutional action eliminated athletes at both ends of the student spectrum. If the graduate prohibition eliminated the perpetual athlete, the freshman rule was intended primarily to curb recruiting practices, with some minor concern that the scholarship of freshmen might be improved if they did not attend college solely to play athletics.

Freshman eligibility seemed to be of no concern in the early years of intercollegiate competition. Most athletes played on freshman teams and saw little varsity action. Freshman team intercollegiate competitions became significant events in the 1870s. For a freshman team to beat an arch rival in baseball or to win the freshman race at the intercollegiate regatta was of some importance. Some colleges began to stack the freshman team with upperclassmen and graduate students to turn out winners. Harvard, which may have had tougher standards than a number of other institutions in the 1880s, had a senior pitch for its freshman team against Yale. When football became important in the 1880s, the freshman football team often appeared to be a varsity team because of the number of non-freshmen participating. The 1888 Harvard freshman football team, for example, included a majority of starters who were not freshmen; the captain was enrolled in the law school until the day after the Yale game. Having accomplished what he had gone to Harvard for, he left the campus.[26] Harvard and Yale were unsuccessful in negotiating agreeable freshman eligibility rules, so the Harvard athletic committee drew up its own rules intended to restrict its freshman team to freshmen.[27]

At that time, President Eliot suggested that one way to curb athletic excesses would be to prohibit all freshman intercollegiate participation.[28] He had some support from other athletic leaders, such as Walter Camp, but student opinion was generally favorable toward freshman being eligible for varsity competition. Yet a group of faculty representatives from eastern colleges meeting at Brown University in 1898 did not oppose freshman varsity eligibility.[29] Eliot's argument was that freshman participation during the fall football season caused "interference with their studies at the worst possible time." His statistics at Harvard showed that the number of failing grades of freshman footballers in 1898 surpassed the combined total of "A's" and "B's."[30] With this and other evidence, the Harvard athletic committee voted to prohibit freshmen from participation on varsity teams until one year of residency. This was contingent, however, on its principal opponents, Yale, Princeton, Pennsylvania, and Cornell, passing similar legislation.[31] Again, the lack of a successfully negotiated inter-institutional agreement blocked the action of Harvard. Yale was the primary stumbling block. Replying to a Princeton athletic committee inquiry about freshman eligibility, Walter Camp replied that Yale "could not, no matter how much you may think it wise, take the power from the hands of our undergraduate managers."[32]

That was basically true until 1906, when the football crisis of the previous fall was being resolved. The main argument for the ban on freshman varsity participation, according to an experienced Yale athletic negotiator, Samuel Elder, was "to diminish the proselyting by some colleges from the preparatory schools."[33] Elder believed that in a crisis where ethical considerations of eligibility were highly visible, if his college did not unite with Harvard and other colleges to ban freshman eligibility, "Yale will get a savage black eye in the papers and from the public."[34] Because of public sentiment and not because of any academic considerations, Yale felt forced to accept the wishes of Harvard, and also of Princeton, to limit eligibility to three years, as the triad had also banned graduate eligibility.[35] At almost the same time, faculty from the midwestern "Big Ten" schools passed legislation to prohibit both freshman and graduate eligibility.[36] A "hands-off" policy was no longer tenable. Yet many schools, especially smaller ones, continued to use whomever was available, including some who were not bona fide students.

Bona Fides: Specials, Transfers, and Tramps

Graduate students, freshmen students, and non-students—all were eventually banned from men's varsity intercollegiate athletics. The issue of bona fide students was a kind of catch-all phrase that faculties enjoyed using. Faculty members, more than any others, desired to maintain scholastic standards and not to bring individuals into college solely for athletic purposes. When faculty athletic committees were first organized in the 1880s and 1890s, they were often content to define eligibility in terms of amateurism and bona fide students. The problem with those two concepts was in trying to define them. Everyone knew what a bona fide student was until a special case came up. Was a student bona fide as soon as he enrolled? Did the student need to attend for a period of time to show that he was serious about school, not only about athletics? Was a star athlete who suddenly "transferred" schools a bona fide student or only a bona fide athlete? Was a "special" student, one who was admitted in a non-degree program, a bona fide student? Was a part-time student really bona fide?

Being a bona fide student had one thing in common with being an amateur athlete; they both required intent on the part of the individual. Being an amateur demanded that an individual participate for the enjoyment of the sport and not for financial reward. Being a bona fide student assumed that the athlete was attending college for an education and would not withdraw after a season or after eligibility expired. American society generally demanded written rules, outlining specific and tangible regulations, but placed little faith in the spirit of the rules, an aristocratic notion. To write an eligibility rule based upon intent and unprovable motives was not wise. As one could not prove whether an individual plays "sport for sport's sake" as an amateur, neither could one certify that one desires to be a full-time, bona fide student. Americans, it has often been pointed out by elite British sportsmen, were restricted only by the letter of the rules, not the spirit of the rules.[37] It stood to reason, then, that lacking a gentlemanly spirit of fair play, colleges would pass restrictive eligibility legislation as they would increasingly add umpires and referees in most of their college sports to control the lack of gentlemanly behavior.

The 1889 crisis in the Intercollegiate Football Association, more than any other single event, produced agitation over bona fide students. Walter Camp defined a bona fide student-athlete for the association as one who matriculated for the entire school year, and pursued a regular course which required at least five lectures or recitations each week. If challenged, the player had to furnish to an advisory committee a certificate signed by three faculty members stating that the student was upholding the rule, as well as produce a "personal affidavit duly verified under oath" to the same.[38] When the Football Association passed the Camp motion but refused to apply it ex post facto to Princeton's newly acquired but former star players for that season, Harvard withdrew from the league.[39]

The rule sponsored by Camp, however, said nothing about the "special" student who attended college in a non-degree program. Most colleges had a number of "special" students, probably as one means of increasing revenue without lowering enrollment or graduation standards. Student athletic leaders soon saw the possibilities of using the "special" category to harbor athletes, just as universities learned nearly a century later to use federal subsidies to stockpile students who were economically deprived but athletically gifted. Importing athletes under the name of "special students" was a sham, according to a Harvard man in 1890.[40] Wesleyan College threatened to break athletic relations with Trinity College if it did not pass a rule to prevent special students from competing.[41] A Columbia special student in 1898 signed up for ten hours of certain courses where no attendance was taken, merely to be eligible to play football. The faculty was forced to redesign its rules for athletic eligibility to require special student attendance at fifteen hours of courses, evidence of passage of exams, and one year of residency.[42] The one year or half-year residency rule was becoming more common in the 1890s, as institutions attempted to prevent athletic misuse of college enrollment policies.

Perversion of enrollment strategies was no more clearly evident than that found in the transfer of students for athletic purposes. The idea of restricting the right of an individual to transfer from one college to another and be able to participate in all collegiate activities seems unfair when seen from the point of view of an individual in a free society. But from an 1896 University of Pennsylvania view-point, it would have been just and honorable to have ruled as illegal Fielding H. Yost's famous "transfer" from West Virginia University to help Lafayette College break Penn's string of thirty-six football victories.[43] Not that Penn was itself opposed to obtaining transfer students who were proficient in athletics. One notable example among many at Penn was Andrew Smith. First attending Penn State College in 1901, Smith starred in a game against the University of Pennsylvania in October 1902. Two days later he was working out with the University of Pennsylvania team, but continued to play three more games for Penn State before transferring to Penn. He competed for Penn through 1904, earning all-American honors, after which he dropped out of school.[44]

Transfer students such as Andy Smith were so common by the early years of the twentieth century that they achieved the infamous title of tramp athletes. They were, though, not new on the intercol-legiate scene. As early as 1873 Syracuse hired some tough Irish men to row for its crew after allowing them to take an analytical drafting course.[45] Shortly thereafter three Princeton football players matricu-lated at Columbia and immediately helped Columbia defeat Yale in a football game.[46] By the 1890s the practice was becoming common in midwestern colleges. At Michigan, the athletic program went one step farther by requiring neither transfer nor enrollment. Seven mem-bers of the Michigan football team had no connection at all with the institution.[47] These activities occurred nationally and prompted the need for stricter eligibility rules, including a transfer rule. By the early 1900s, a number of institutions across the nation required a period of residence, usually a year or half a year, before these stu-dents could participate athletically.[48]

Recruiting and Granting Athletic Scholarships

Whether athletes were brought in as transfers, freshmen, or gradu-ate students, there was the tendency to make the matriculation more secure with financial inducements. At the December 1905 meeting which set in motion the formation of the NCAA, the chancellor of Allegheny College in Pennsylvania, W. H. Andrews, indicated that for colleges in his area there were no eligibility rules and that re-cruitment and financial offers to athletes were rampant. "We go out after men for the sake of baseball and football, offering all sorts of inducements," Andrews lamented. "It isn't a thing unknown among us for a man to go from the football team of one college to the football team of another in mid-season. Scholarships are offered to promising players. Professionalism is winked at."[49] That was not a new revelation, for some colleges had been offering financial advantages to athletes as early as the 1870s and began passing rules to attempt to end the practices by the early 1880s.

Financial considerations for participation were first evident in baseball, though they may have occurred earlier in crew. For instance, John Ostrom, the captain of the Cornell crew, had a $30-a-month college job as janitor. Another oarsman saw the janitorial position as an athletic sinecure. He wrote president Andrew White that he could "serve the university as an oarsman as well as a janitor if I can get the position." If he obtained the position, he said that he would show his appreciation at the Saratoga Regatta at the end of the year.[50] Yet the problem of athletic financial inducements appeared greater in baseball. The College Baseball Association, comprised of six eastern colleges, took the first concerted action to end the practice of offering financial inducements to promising players. In 1881, it passed a rule that no player was eligible whose college expenses were paid by baseball interests.[51] The other two major sports, crew and football, were also involved. According to one college professor in the early 1880s who undoubtedly exaggerated, the major college baseball, boating, and football teams were composed of "about two or three dozen young men in each college, whose expenses are paid by their fellows."[52] James McCosh, the Presbyterian minister from Scotland who was president of Princeton, need not have been so shocked when he discovered in 1883 that one young man had entered Princeton to play football, not study.[53] At Harvard, the young historian Albert B. Hart was not as naive, recognizing that by the 1880s some young men "became regular members of the college in order to develop and exhibit their skill as athletes."[54]

The 1889 Intercollegiate Football Conference controversy brought out for public scrutiny the practice of recruiting and subsidizing athletes, which had been going on for some time. The dirty athletic laundry of Princeton and Harvard was hung out by the press. When Harvard challenged the eligibility of fifteen Princeton footballers, it was in part a response to the recruitment of four experienced athletes who came back to Princeton for the 1889 season. It might have been five except that the first-year law student, Highland Stickney, ended up at Harvard rather than Princeton. Stickney revealed two letters from Princeton's star halfback, Knowlton "Snake" Ames, who had tried to procure Stickney's services for the season. Ames, who himself played baseball for pay, wrote Stickney that he could get him a "scholarship" which included free "board, tuition, etc." The athletic men at Princeton, Ames said, "get by all odds the best treatment in any of the colleges."[55] True possibly, but Stickney ended up at Harvard. Stickney was working the system for all that it was worth. He had previously written Bill "Pa" Corbin, the previous football captain at Yale, asking what Yale could do for him. Corbin telegraphed Walter Camp: "Stickney wrote. Have received good offers from Harvard and Princeton to play football. What will you give[?]"[56] Princeton's captain, Edgar Allan Poe, was convinced that Stickney and two other Harvard men had received financial inducement to play football at Harvard.[57] At the same time, an athlete at the University of Pennsylvania indicated that a Harvard man had offered him a scholarship, pecuniary compensation, and a railroad ticket if he would leave the Penn law school and enter Harvard's law school so that he could play baseball.[58] And these were only some of the accusations being made among the athletic powers.

Other eastern colleges of lesser athletic renown increasingly emphasized recruiting and tendering of athletic scholarships. Columbia, which had languished in all major sports except crew, pushed for athletic recognition in football in the late 1890s, hiring a former Yale player as coach and paying a majority of its starting team through free tuition, board, and lodging.[59] The Methodists at Wesleyan raised money to enable a baseball player to return to college and uphold the athletic prestige of his alma mater.[60] Farther north, Dartmouth alumni organized a committee to raise money so that traveling expenses of preparatory students being recruited for athletics could be defrayed.[61] Pennsylvania State College was possibly the first college to sanction athletic scholarships when in 1900 the Board of Trustees offered scholarships to talented Penn State athletes who had been at the institution for at least one year.[62]

Payments to attend college intensified nationally as the practice spread from the eastern schools elsewhere. In the 1890s, abuses were found in the south. For example, the William and Mary baseball team attempted to get the college to allow a pitcher to receive a tuition waiver while the team would pick up expenses at a local hotel.[63] Not far away, Randolph-Macon College students were recruiting townies and semi-pro athletes to fill out its baseball team, until the faculty banned the practice.[64] Farther south, the University of Georgia learned the law-school trick early when it enrolled an inferior student academically, but superior athletically, in the law school, which had no admission requirement.[65] Actually the situation was no better at many other southern colleges which were only beginning to take up athletics following the leadership of the east.

Athletic recruitment practices in the West also reflected the eastern models. Apparently, the freedom to compete for victories and the prestige gained from them brought with it the freedom of procuring athletes, often without regard to academic standards. College histories reveal hundreds of cases of the recruitment and payment of students as well as the hiring of non-students to fill out athletic teams. Students at the University of Kansas recruited a farm boy for their football team in 1895, obtained financing from Lawrence citizens, and paid the young man's parents to release him. Townspeople also hired a footballer, entered him as a law student, and saw him disappear from school at the season's end.[66] One should not get the idea that only the larger colleges and universities were actively recruiting and paying their athletes. Nearby in Kansas, Fairmont College and Friends University severed relations over two such athletes.[67] Nor should one believe that only students sanctioned shady recruiting practices. At the University of Nebraska, a young man arrived in Lincoln in March 1903 intending to enroll and play baseball. When the registrar refused admittance, the university chancellor enrolled him two weeks later in the law school. It was likely that the baseball team profited while the law school did not.[68]

A decade before, Walter Camp had warned colleges about the kind of professionalism which he saw in burgeoning recruitment and offers of athletic scholarships. He predicted a situation which did occur half a century later. Foretelling the point-shaving and throwing of college basketball games in the 1940s and early 1950s, he wrote: "A man who begins by selling his skill to a college may someday find himself selling an individual act in a particular contest—selling races, selling games."[69] Historically, however, this kind of scandal in college athletics has not been common, although it has existed.

The Eligibility Situation by the Time of the NCAA

What was much more common than Camp's concern was the intensity of recruitment, bringing athletes onto campuses which claimed to be educational institutions, not athletic clubs. The year the NCAA was initiated, 1905, showed clearly some of the major eligibility concerns. James Hogan, captain of the Yale football team, graduated that year, ending a four-year career. The mature Hogan was two years older than the Yale head coach in 1904. He had lived in a suite in Vanderbilt Hall, the most luxurious of Yale's dormitories, and ate free meals at the University Club. His tuition was paid, and he received a scholarship of $100 per year. In addition, Hogan and two others had the privilege of receiving the entire profits of selling score cards at the popular baseball games. To earn some additional money, Hogan became an agent for the American Tobacco Company, for which he earned a commission on each cigarette pack sold in New Haven. When his last Yale game was concluded, the twenty-nine-year-old, three-time all-American and honor student was given a two-week vacation in Cuba with all expenses paid by the Yale Athletic Association. The association categorized the payments as "miscellaneous expenses."[70] If Hogan had not been bought by Yale to participate in athletics, it appeared to some that he had been.

Yale's chief rival, Harvard, sent no one on a Caribbean junket, but during the years that Hogan was making a financial success of his college football career, Harvard had several interesting eligibility questions arise in baseball including that of Orville "Home Run" Frantz. An imposing batter, Frantz was probably the outstanding college first baseman of his time. Frantz was also holder of a prestigious George Emerson Lowell scholarship. One of the two Lowell scholarships was usually awarded "to a deserving student who has shown excellence in athletics." Yet Frantz was only a "C" student. When a New York newspaper charged Harvard with procuring trained athletes, athletic committee chairman Ira Hollis raised the question of the scholarship held by Frantz. "To outsiders," Hollis told President Eliot, "it might seem that the University is insincere. . . ." Eliot gave a scribbled reply: "Corporation have accepted the trust and propose to execute it."[71] Frantz kept his scholarship, but the athletic committee declared him ineligible for a different reason. Eight years before, Frantz, had received $36 plus expenses for playing baseball in Wellington, Kansas.[72] Stripped of his eligibility, Frantz was made head baseball coach the following year.

Incidents similar to those of Harvard and Yale were repeated at other institutions across the country. A Yale graduate coaching at the University of Chicago, Amos Alonzo Stagg, was excoriated by one writer in 1905 for purchasing his athletes. Like John D. Rockefeller, who granted some of his millions to build the University of Chicago and allowed it to acquire professors by paying them more than most college presidents, Stagg was allowed to use a large Rockefeller trust fund to secure needy athletes. Wrote an early twentieth-century writer: "Chicago University is bartering her gold-fed academic prestige for a muscular leg, and using funds endowed for needy students to offset the bids of rivals of equal culpability."[73] But Stagg was only "keeping up with the Joneses," the chief one for him being the University of Michigan.

Chicago's rival, Michigan, had its own recruiting successes. When Fielding H. Yost took over as coach of Michigan in 1901, he brought a player, Willie Heston, from Stanford University where he had previously coached. Heston was an experienced football player, having earlier graduated from a teacher training institution. At Michigan he scored over a hundred touchdowns in four years, making him famous enough to sell his own Willie Heston Cigars. Also arriving from Palo Alto was the failed scholar but fine athlete George "Dad" Gregory. Yost also had the help of the Michigan admissions office, which allowed an outstanding high school athlete to enroll without first completing his high school degree. By 1905, Yost's point-a-minute teams were undefeated in 55 consecutive games. Michigan finally lost to Stagg's Chicago Maroons, 2–0, in a game before 25,000 fans, the largest crowd in midwestern collegiate history. The "Big Ten" conference followed the 1905 season with the passage of restrictive eligibility regulations, retroactively applying them to active players. Michigan rejected the decision and withdrew from the conference.[74] With Michigan out of the conference, Stagg's team had the opportunity to win even more regularly, while continuing its own recruiting ploy using Rockefeller money.

In the west and in the east, recruitment and subsidization of athletes was a common concern. By the time of the 1905 football crisis and the organization of the first successful national inter-institutional athletic body, a university dean could say that "there is not an eastern college in which the 'professional' rule has not been broken again and again in recent years."[75] More and more were there reports of sub-freshmen athletes who would write colleges requesting, for instance, "all expenses during the year—board, room, tuition, books, etc.—and one hundred dollars besides."[76] Bill Reid, the Harvard football coach in 1905 and 1906, reported on West Coast recruiting problems after returning to California. He specifically condemned St. Mary's College and Santa Clara College in California. Using another Catholic school analogy, Reid charged that they "have been fully as bad as Georgetown used to be."[77]

The need for uniform eligibility rules had arrived by 1905. Eligibility rules, whether passed by individual colleges or as inter-institutional legislation, tended to diminish student freedom to participate. Graduates, freshmen, transfers, specials, and even earnest students with marginal grades lost their freedom to participate in one of the institution's extracurricular activities. Institutions were unable to eliminate individual wrongdoers and tried to solve the problem by eliminating groups of students, some of whom were innocent victims of the system. Individual freedom was lost in the process, just as student freedom had been forfeited when the professional coach came into existence. The inter-institutional NCAA would eventually further restrict student freedom to participate and, by the latter half of the twentieth century, restrict the freedom of individual institutions to control their own academic and athletic affairs. That process on a national level only began in the crisis year of 1905.

XIV

Brutality, Ethics, and the Creation of the NCAA

IN AMERICAN INTERCOLLEGIATE HISTORY, no year has been as momentous as that beginning in mid-1905. It was a watershed year, as important to the direction that college athletics would take as the contemporary publication of Upton Sinclair's *The Jungle* was to creating legislation in the meat packing industry. In both cases the time was ripe to change laissez-faire policy by establishing national guidelines over brutal and unethical practices. One dealt with animals and the other with athletes, and some saw similarities between the two, particularly with regard to football. Not surprisingly, President Theodore Roosevelt was intimately involved in the reform of both meat packing and intercollegiate athletics.

Football disputes were the stimulus to the whole reform movement and the creation of the National Collegiate Athletic Association that year. Football completely dominated all other college sports combined. The dean of Brown University, Alexander Meiklejohn, pointed out the ambivalent nature of football on the college campus. On the one hand he believed that football was the most important social force for good in colleges. On the other hand, he saw that "its influence for evil is becoming so apparent in the forms of unfairness, untruthfulness, and brutality as to threaten the most vital interest of the college training."[1]

The corrupting side of athletics, especially football, gained most of the attention in the 1905–6 school year. Frederick Jackson Turner, the historian, spoke for that element in early 1906. Football, Turner said, had become a commercialized and professionalized business. In his censure of early twentieth-century football, the originator of the frontier theory of American history condemned coaches and student managers who scoured the country for athletic material. He also knew from experience that faculties were kept busy "playing a game of hide and seek with the man who sells his athletic skill for personal gain." To Turner, it was an "absurd idea" that football was "the test of the excellence of a university and the proper means of advertising it."[2] Turner's sentiments had been expressed in one way or another in speeches, newspapers, and popular magazines, and they reached a crescendo following the 1905 football season. Reform or even abolishment of football was almost assured.

The Muckrakers and Theodore Roosevelt

The crisis in football and of all college sport occurred in the midst of progressive reform, as President Theodore Roosevelt began his second term in office. The new journalistic muckrakers previously had exposed corporate corruption, political graft, labor racketeering, and adulterated foods. They rather suddenly directed some of their rapier-like pens at college athletics. Nationally circulated, middle- and upper-middle-class magazines took up the cudgel and hammered away at college sport throughout the 1905 year. *McClure's Magazine*, the leader of them all, started off with an exposé of professionalism in college sport, tearing into eastern institutions such as Columbia, Penn, Princeton, and Yale. *Outlook* called the disease in colleges "bacillus athletics," which fed on commercialism. *Collier's* told of the purchasing of football victories in "Big Ten" institutions. *Nation* clamored for the abolition or radical reform of football. Even the usually dignified *Harvard Graduates' Magazine* contributed to the raking of muck as its anonymously authored article, following the 1905 football loss to Yale, led all periodicals in a scathing attack upon what it called Yale's premier but unprincipled athletic program.[3]

Possibly the most important article was that in *McClure's Magazine*. Henry Beech Needham was one of the leading muckrakers, although not as well known as Lincoln Steffens, Ida Tarbell, Ray Stannard Baker, or Finley Peter Dunne.[4] His two-part series in the spring and summer of 1905 ran concurrently with Tarbell's character study of John D. Rockefeller and Steffens's piece on tarnished politics in Ohio in the same magazine. It was significant because it attacked the most prestigious eastern institutions for prostituting college athletics. The article featured the gamut of winning-at-all-cost behavior: illegal inducement to athletes, hiring tramp athletes, payment of high salaries for summer baseball, faculty collusion with athletes, cheating in the classroom, squandering of athletic monies, diabolical practices of professional coaches, seeking lucrative gate receipts and building costly stadiums, and continuing brutality in football.[5]

Needham's condemnation of athletics at college preparatory schools, especially Andover and Exeter, undoubtedly caught the notice of the schoolmasters. Only two years before, a group of seventy headmasters asked the Intercollegiate Football Rules Committee to modify the rules to eliminate the dangerous mass plays of football.[6] Endicott Peabody, founder and headmaster of the Groton Preparatory School, was disturbed to the point that he requested President Roosevelt to invite the "Big Three" colleges to an early fall White House meeting.[7]

Even before this, Teddy Roosevelt was clearly aware of the athletic situation and was ready to enter the battle for reform. Roosevelt was a master at political timing who, as historian Robert Wiebe has shown, could turn other's "contributions into dramatic personal victories."[8] Shortly after the publication of Needham's first article, Roosevelt presented an address at Harvard University and spoke of the matter of intercollegiate sport. "Brutality in playing a game," Roosevelt intoned, "should awaken the heartiest and most plainly shown contempt for the player guilty of it; especially if this brutality is coupled with a low cunning."[9] Shortly thereafter, he met with Needham while vacationing at Oyster Bay on Long Island. As Roosevelt often did, he exchanged ideas with muckrakers, using ideas which they generated for his own purposes.[10]

Action soon followed Roosevelt's words. Endicott Peabody's letter to Roosevelt pointed out that athletic dishonesty was ruining intercollegiate sports. Peabody believed that if Roosevelt used his office to hold a meeting of the Harvard, Yale, and Princeton coaches, he could "persuade them to undertake to teach men to play football honestly."[11] The idea was, of course, that the eminent position of the "Big Three" would allow reform to filter down to the lesser institutions. Roosevelt agreed to his friend's idea and to the trickle-down theory of athletic reform.

Roosevelt invited two representatives each from Harvard, Yale.

and Princeton to meet with him and the new Secretary of State Elihu Root. An early October luncheon was set for the White House. Harvard was represented by coach Bill Reid and team physician Dr. Edward Nichols. Yale sent Walter Camp and head coach John Owsley. Princeton was led by head coach Arthur Hildebrand and Professor John B. Fine from the athletic committee. At the meeting the President discussed football in general and noted incidents of unfair play of each of the three colleges. He told them that he wanted to see if the spirit of fair play could be improved. After the representatives had discussed the situation, Roosevelt asked the three older men, none of whom were the head coaches, to draw up some kind of agreement for clean and ethical football. As the train carrying the six headed north from Washington, D.C., a message intended for the nation was constructed.[12]

The train-ride memorandum was telegraphed to Roosevelt and almost immediately released by Walter Camp to an interested public. The nation's athletic leaders, as recognized by Roosevelt, stated:

> At a meeting with the President of the United States, it was agreed that we consider an honorable obligation exists to carry out in *letter* and in *spirit* the rules of the game of football, relating to roughness, holding and foul play, and the active coaches of our universities being present with us, pledge themselves to so regard it and to do their utmost to carry out that obligation.[13]

While there were expectations that the moral suasion of the President and the three elite institutions would reach the entire collegiate scene, the nature of football was such that questionable practices and serious injuries would continue. In the American game of football, as in other sports, the desired result of the contest—victory—dominated the concern for playing the game. It was most difficult for the three signatories to carry out the spirit of the rules when the football players, according to a Harvard athlete, had been taught for years the "tricks of the trade" in deceiving the officials.[14] If the three leading football powers could not have confidence in each other, it was not likely that a national call for upholding the spirit of the rules would be successful. Roosevelt, if not intercollegiate athletics, would come out ahead for borrowing from the muckrakers and appearing to be a leader who was cleaning up one more area of corruption in American society. The hoped-for results, however, never emerged.

Harvard's Threat, Reid's Ruse, and More Brutality

Less than a month after the White House meeting, members of the Harvard governing boards, spurred on by Harvard President Eliot, were considering abolishing football. News of this secret discussion soon reached coach Bill Reid and his football advisors, who feared the worse for their game. They quickly met and decided that the best plan to avert a ban of football at Harvard was to release a letter condemning football as then played. According to Reid, the group secured a copy of President Eliot's recent criticisms of the game "and embodied all of his suggestions in the letter, with a manner of expression as close to his own as we dared use."[15] The clever ruse was not revealed for two decades. The letter, signed by Reid, was more effective than any muckraker's article, because the called-for reform came from an active participant. The content of the letter, though a ploy, is revealing. Reid addressed his stratagem to the Harvard Graduates' Athletic Association, a group which he felt would be helpful in saving football at Harvard. He wrote:

> After several years of experience with Intercollegiate football, after careful consideration of criticisms which have been made of the fine game, and after the many honest but fruitless efforts to change it so that these criticisms could be avoided, I have become convinced that the game as it is played to-day has fundamental faults which cannot be removed by any mere technical revision of the rules.
>
> Although I am willing to admit that the necessary roughness of the game may be objectionable to some people, that appears to me to be much less serious than the fact that there is a distinct advantage to be gained from brutality and the evasion of the rules—offenses which, in many instances, the officials cannot detect because they are committed when the players and the ball also are hidden from the eyes of the umpire. For these reasons I have come to believe that the game ought to be radically changed.
>
> I therefore respectfully request your Association, which represents the Alumni of the University, immediately to appoint a Committee whose duty it shall be to make a careful investigation of the subject, and to report such thorough-going alterations in the game as will remove the unfair advantage now obtained from violations of the rules, will put a higher premium on skill, make mere weight and strength of less value, and will produce a more scientific and interesting sport.[16]

Not only had the Harvard football authorities bested the Harvard ruling bodies by strongly calling for reform before the policy makers voted officially to ban the game, they also beat Walter Camp and Yale to the reform punch. Reid confirmed this when he confided in his diary: "By getting this letter printed now . . . Harvard will be in the front seat of the band wagon and some of Yale's fire will be stolen."[17]

As events would show, it was important for Harvard football leaders to appear to be in the forefront of reform. The letter had been released only three days before the important Penn football game. At Franklin Field in Philadelphia, Penn had watered the field the night prior to the game as it had done in 1900 and 1901. Penn came onto the field with new, long cleats to enable the team to maneuver on the muddy field, while the Harvard team attempted to use their regular cleats. Falling and fumbling, Harvard lost 12–6 in a game lacking civility and sportsmanship. While the field-soaking incident led Harvard to break relations with Penn for nearly two decades, a slugging disqualification brought more attention.[18]

This act of brutality caught the attention of President Roosevelt. With the score tied at six, Bartol Parker, the Harvard center, slugged his Penn counterpart in the face and was disqualified. Roosevelt, only a month after the "Big Three" White House conference, called Coach Reid to Washington, D.C., again and asked for an accounting of the incident, the first major violation of the agreement. Reid explained the situation to the President following a dinner at which the German ambassador was present. Parker, Reid said, had been hit in the groin several times by the Penn center. Parker told the umpire, but no action was taken. When the Penn player repeated the action, Parker socked him and the official threw him out. "Mr. President," Reid asked Roosevelt, "what would you have done under similar circumstances?" The President looked at Reid, spoke vehemently through his teeth as he often did, and replied, "It wouldn't be good policy for me to state," agreeing that the Harvard player had some justification for his actions. The incident was closed as far as Roosevelt was concerned, and Reid returned to Cambridge.[19]

Two weeks later another act of aggression occurred in Harvard's stadium, jammed with 43,000 spectators. This time Yale was the accused, and the incident set a chain reaction in motion. Late in the first half of a scoreless tie, Harvard's nearly two-hundred-pound Francis Burr awaited a Yale punt, signaling a fair catch. Two Yale players approached him, one hitting him low and the other high.

James Quill, leaping high in a position parallel to the ground, struck Burr squarely in the face. With blood spurting from Burr's broken nose, the fans began a storm of hisses. Major Henry L. Higginson, an influential Harvard man who fifteen years before had presented his alma mater with thirty-one acres for an athletic field, told Coach Reid to take his team off the field.[20] Reid, however, refused the order. Harvard fans, as well as those who opposed both football and brutality, would not let the incident go away.[21] Nor would Theodore Roosevelt.

Roosevelt, whose favored Harvard team had now been shut out by Yale four straight years, called Reid to the White House once again. Roosevelt was particularly upset about the umpire, Paul Dashiell, a faculty member at the Annapolis Naval Academy and a member of the Football Rules Committee. While Dashiell was probably the best-known official in America, he had refused to penalize Quill for slugging or unnecessary roughness. At the time Dashiell was up for appointment as professor of chemistry at the Naval Academy, an appointment Roosevelt controlled. The promotion was, according to Reid, "the ambition of his life." Reid had told Dashiell after the game that he would never again officiate a Harvard game. In addition, Reid was asked by Roosevelt to give his opinion of Dashiell.[22] Roosevelt's reaction to Reid's explanation was that he didn't "know whether that kind of a man was fit to teach the boys at Annapolis."[23] The President in the meantime asked Dashiell to explain his actions.

Dashiell was worried about the damage the Harvard-Yale game had done to football, and he undoubtedly realized the potential harm his involvement had on his own career. The $100 he received for officiating the game, equivalent to well over $1000 eight decades later, was small relative to that which Roosevelt could do to him as commander in chief of the armed forces. "I am deeply sorry, Sir," Dashiell wrote to the President, "from every personal feeling, that the matter should have been brought to you in so unfavorable a light. . . . I regret the injury that it has done the game, now in so critical a condition. . . ."[24] Dashiell was never officially exonerated for his officiating, indeed he never again officiated a Harvard-Yale game. He did, however, remain on the rules committee, and Roosevelt, after a six-month delay, made Dashiell's Naval Academy appointment.[25]

Dashiell's officiating controversy in the Quill-Burr brutality affair was generally kept private, yet it was one of the incidents in a public storm whipped up by a Harvard graduate over its relations with Yale in athletics. An unnamed individual close to the Harvard scene wrote an article for the *Harvard Graduates' Magazine* which was published only days after the Quill incident. The anonymous author out-muckraked the muckrakers. He condemned Yale authorities, including President Arthur Hadley, for having cringed before the athletocracy led by dictator Walter Camp. He inferred that the athletic leadership of Yale and its win-at-all-cost athletic policies caused the public to believe that college athletics "are like gin-stunted jockeys to the crowd at a horse-race, or like the gladiators butchered to make a Roman holiday." Yale, he said, "persistently opposed every attempt to curb, or regulate, or purify athletics." The frontal attack against Yale was augmented with a back-handed compliment with much truth in it, that Yale should be given "full credit for organizing and maintaining the most remarkable athletic system ever seen in an American or an English university."[26]

Yale men were naturally furious about the article and that the *Harvard Graduates' Magazine* would even consider publishing it. To Camp, the magazine "violated the very commonest decencies of journalism."[27] James T. Curtis, secretary of the Spalding sporting goods company and a Yale man, was boiling mad when he aimed his invective at the "Mugwamp cranks" at Harvard.[28] Lewis S. Welch, the editor of the *Yale Alumni Weekly*, concluded that the article, published by a party to the insult, was an "anonymous libel" written by an individual who should have been excluded from Harvard for being "mentally and morally weak."[29] It is ironic that only a couple of weeks before, Harvard's President Eliot had been asked by the Yale president to present the inaugural lecture, a gift from a Harvard alumnus to Yale for the bettering of relations between the two institutions.[30]

The MacCracken Conference: Abolition or Reform

The elite confrontation, fought between the two most important collegiate institutions, who unfortunately lacked upper-class gentlemanly manners, was reflective of the entire intercollegiate athletic scene. The same day of the Quill-Burr debacle, Harold Moore, a halfback of Union College, died of a cerebral hemorrhage in a pile-up during a game with New York University. The death triggered an instant reaction from the chancellor of New York University, Henry MacCracken. He immediately telegraphed President

Eliot asking if he would call a conference to either reform or ban football.[31] Eliot, however, declined to become involved because he believed that college presidents "certainly cannot reform football, and I doubt if by themselves they can abolish it."[32] Eliot remained rational, while others, such as the New York University chancellor, worked on emotional energy. Eliot did not want an immediate meeting of college presidents and told MacCracken that there should be a cooling-down period. "Deaths and injuries," Eliot telegraphed a reply to MacCracken, "are not the strongest argument against football. That cheating and brutality are profitable is the main evil."[33] Reform, though, often is accomplished from an emotional, not rational approach to pressing problems.

MacCracken, turned down by Eliot, took action himself. He sent invitations for a conference on football to nineteen institutions which New York University had played against for the past two decades. In his letter calling for an early December conference, he first asked: "Ought the present game of football be abolished?" If not, he wanted some agreement for a thorough reform. If the institutions voted to abolish football, he wanted to get a feeling as to what game or games might replace football. He also believed that this preliminary conference should lead to a second conference, one of a national nature to be held after Christmas.[34]

Two-thirds of the institutions invited sent delegates, about half of whom were college presidents. Though they lacked the prestige that a Harvard or Yale would have lent to the group, the MacCracken conference nevertheless attacked with vigor the issue at hand. Thirteen colleges sent faculty or administrators to the Murray Hill Hotel in New York City on December 8, 1905. One college, Columbia, had just banned the game, and others were considering similar action.

Columbia came to the meeting presenting a closed agenda of President Nicholas Murray Butler. He wanted to ban football nationally and reform all college athletics. By ending football, Butler believed it would be the "first step in a general overhauling of the whole athletic situation in American colleges."[35] Butler's Columbia had gone through half a dozen years of athletic turmoil. The chairman of the athletic committee and dean of the law school, George Kirchwey, at one point threw up his hands over the football situation, claiming that the entire athletic system rested on a false basis and its evils were incurable.[36] During the 1905 football season, a mini-riot occurred at a Columbia-Wesleyan game. Players, fans, and Columbia coach Dick Morley rushed onto the field after a Wesleyan player "gathered up his legs" and crashed into the back of an already downed Columbia runner. Newspapers reported that Morley struck the Wesleyan player who had injured the Columbia man, and order was restored only after police rushed onto the field.[37]

At season's end Columbia acted quickly and strategically, announcing the banning of football at Columbia while students were home on a Thanksgiving break.[38] Columbia President Butler had earlier contacted Harvard's Eliot to see if Eliot would back a new, national football rules-making body to replace what a Columbia trustee termed was the "self-perpetuating, non-representative, pigheaded" old rules committee headed by Walter Camp.[39] Eliot refused to be involved with any rules committee in which Camp might be involved. Yale, Eliot said, would surely appoint Camp to any new committee. Camp, Eliot believed, was "directly responsible for the degradation and ruin of the game." The trouble with Camp, Eliot told his peer at Columbia, was that he was "deficient in moral sensibility—a trouble not likely to be cured at his age."[40] With no help coming from Harvard, Columbia went its own way, unilaterally banning the game with hopes of influencing others. The first chance was at MacCracken's meeting in New York City.

A resolution that "the present game of football as played under existing rules be abolished" was promoted by Columbia and presented to the thirteen institutions. Columbia, New York University, and Union College (whose player died) were joined by Rochester and Stevens Institute to ban football. Had two other colleges joined the abolitionists, this small, but significant group of college authorities would have united with Columbia in its move to eradicate football as then played. Reform, however, not abolition, was favored by a majority of the colleges represented, led by West Point and Wesleyan.[41]

To accomplish the reform, the convention set up a special committee to consider rule changes to end dangerous, brutal, and mass plays. The convention also decided that a more representative, national group should join it in an annual meeting to discuss mutual problems. The thirteen colleges decided that individuals chosen to be representatives at the national meeting should not be involved in the professional aspect of athletics. That is, they decided to eliminate anyone who had ever received compensation from athletics including players, coaches, umpires, referees, directors, or committeemen, with the exception of college faculty members.[42]

For the next three weeks following the MacCracken conference, there was a wild power scramble among a number of institutions as the conservative old football rules committee and the new national group of reformers were about to meet. There was a natural tendency for the old rules committee to want to remain in power and to dictate the rules of play to all the colleges. After all, it was essentially this group which took rugby football as its game and transformed it in the previous generation into the most favored college sport, American football. The members of the football rules committee knew well that they represented the elites, Harvard, Yale, and Princeton, and a couple of tokens.

The upstart reformers knew that the time was ripe for change. MacCracken charged the Football Rules Committee as being the rule of the few elite, an oligarchy, comparable to the Russian grand dukes. "Over there," the N.Y.U. Chancellor's analogy went, "it is the Russian people against the Russian grand dukes. Here it is the football people against the football grand dukes . . . , a committee of misrules. . . ."[43] MacCracken's opinion was supported east and west by many others, including presidents from Columbia and California. Nicholas Murray Butler of Columbia called the rules committee "self-perpetuating, irresponsible, impervious to public opinion and culpable in refusing to heed the increasingly dangerous character of the game."[44] President Benjamin Ide Wheeler of the University of California condemned Camp's self-appointed committee which had "promised reforms, but have done nothing. . . . We will revise the rules ourselves, and the changes will be radical."[45]

Harvard, not Columbia or California, was the crucial figure in the power equation. Harvard was the unquestioned educational leader, and its president, Charles Eliot, was by far the most noted educator in America. The most visible Harvard graduate, Theodore Roosevelt, was President of the United States, and he was intricately involved in the reform process.[46] Eliot wanted the game abolished and told Roosevelt so. Roosevelt thought that Harvard would be "doing the baby act" if it took the foolish course President Eliot advised.[47] Roosevelt determined that he would do what he could to help reform the game, saving it from possible abolition.

If Roosevelt was distressed by Eliot and by the old rules committee headed by Camp, he felt comfortable with the membership of the Harvard Graduates' Athletic Association special committee. It was set up to formulate a new set of Harvard-sanctioned football rules in early December 1905, at the same time the MacCracken conference was being held. Bill Reid chaired the seven-member

committee, while LeBaron Briggs, dean of Harvard College, served
as an established voice of the university. Roosevelt probably knew
each of the members personally. There were five former or current
Harvard coaches, a team physician, and Briggs, all of whom favored
football.[48] While the Harvard committee spent about a month determining the rules by which it would continue to play, Camp's old
rules committee determined it would continue to control the game.

Camp's committee also met in early December but made little
progress, and Camp called a meeting for December 15. It was delayed by both Harvard's Reid and Paul Dashiell, the Harvard-Yale
official and member of the old rule-making body. Reid's delaying
action was designed to allow time for the Harvard graduate committee to develop rules which Reid could take to Camp's committee.[49] The Harvard Athletic Committee further pressured Reid not
to meet with Camp's group until it could give instructions to Reid.
It was finally decided to meet on December 29, though the Harvard
Athletic Committee would not authorize Reid to vote on any question without first referring back to the Harvard athletic officials.[50]
"We are in a great muddle here," Reid informed Camp, and he felt
he and Harvard "must proceed with extreme care."[51]

The NCAA Begins with a Compromise

While Reid was delaying the old rules committee, MacCracken's
invitation to national colleges to meet on December 28 was gathering its own momentum. The MacCracken group of sixty-eight institutions met in New York City the day before Camp's committee was
scheduled to convene in Philadelphia. There was a noticeable lack
of representation by the larger universities such as Harvard, Yale,
Princeton, and Chicago, all of whom had members on the old Football Rules Committee. The reform group, nevertheless, met at the
Murray Hill Hotel and formed a permanent organization, eventually
named the National Collegiate Athletic Association, with Palmer
Pierce of West Point as president. The NCAA then began a lengthy
and emotional debate over the future of football and decided to form
its own rules committee of seven. It instructed its committee to meet
with the old committee the next day. The object was an amalgamation or merger of the two groups, if possible. If the Camp committee
refused, the reform group would form its own rules.[52]

The new rules committee of the NCAA, headed by Henry Williams, a physician and the coach of Minnesota, met the old group

more than halfway as they traveled to Philadelphia for a meeting. In an informal session the two groups discussed joining together. The Camp committee deliberated for some time, hesitated about the idea of an amalgamated committee, and decided that each committee member should first confer with his own institution. They would then meet again and either accept or reject the proposal.[53]

In the fortnight which followed, the Harvard alumni committee produced a score of ethical rules and technical rules in an attempt to eliminate brutality and open up the game from the preponderance of mass plays at the line of scrimmage. Reid at the same time was required by the athletic authorities to obtain acceptance of the rules by the amalgamated group or Harvard would bar the game.[54] The Harvard rule changes called for more officials and increased penalties for unfair or brutal play. To open up the game, the Harvard group suggested increasing the distance to be gained from 5 yards to 10 yards in three attempts, creating a neutral zone between the two opposing teams at the line of scrimmage, and introducing the forward pass.[55]

Bill Reid, with rules in hand, had instructions from Harvard to withdraw from the old rules committee and support the reform group as he journeyed on January 12 to the Hotel Netherland in New York City. He knew that Harvard would not be standing alone, because Theodore Roosevelt had told Paul Dashiell of the Naval Academy to support the merger.[56] Reid had first warned Camp that the merger was a necessity. "If by having a meeting we can settle the question of amalgamation," he telegraphed Camp two days before the meeting, "I should advise having one, if not, it hardly seems worthwhile." He also told Camp that he would withdraw from the old committee, hoping that other members would do the same in forming a merger.[57]

On the day of the meeting, the two groups met independently. Reid joined the old group at first, and, as he had indicated to Camp, soon left the Camp committee to join the reform group. Four hours of discussion and exchanges of notes then took place. The old committee proposed that its officers become the new officers of the merged rule group. The reformers rejected the idea. The reform committee withdrew its proposition for a reduced, five-member committee on rules. The two parties finally agreed that the full group of fourteen would form the amalgamated committee and that the old committee would provide the chairman, while the new committee would supply the secretary. Cornell's L. M. Dennis was chosen as chairman while James Babbitt of Haverford was selected for the key position of secretary. Babbitt immediately resigned in favor of Bill Reid, in a Machiavellian political move.[58] Harvard had outmaneuvered Yale and Walter Camp, thus removing Camp from the dominant position he had held for decades and placing a Harvard man, to the embarrassment and anger of Yale. When Reid began using his position as rules secretary to Yale's disadvantage, Yale President Hadley confided to Camp that Reid was "not playing fair [and] ought to be a lesson to us for the future."[59]

The newly merged committee of fourteen then set out to reform the rules by eliminating brutal conduct and bringing about a more open game. Reid, with his handful of demands from Harvard, figured out a way to make it appear that the proposed rule changes came from a number of colleges. He had earlier told the old rules committee that if the Harvard rules were not accepted, "there will be no football at Harvard; and if Harvard throws out the game, many other colleges will follow Harvard's lead, and an important blow will be dealt the game."[60] He asked that each committee member take several of the Harvard rules and champion them as his own.[61] The desire of Reid to push through the Harvard recommendations was hastened by the Harvard Overseers' action two days prior to the New York City meeting. The Overseers, who recommended Harvard policy, voted that there should be no further intercollegiate football at Harvard until they had a report on the acceptance of the Harvard proposals by the national rules committee.[62] That Reid was successful probably shows that the need to appease Harvard and keep football alive was far more persuasive than was the twenty-six-year-old coach.

During the next four months, eight meetings, partially subsidized by Albert Spalding's sporting goods company, were held to hammer out the rules. Attendance of the large committee in New York City was exceedingly good, except for Amos Alonzo Stagg of Chicago, Dr. Henry Williams of Minnesota, and James Lees of Nebraska. For instance, both the Texas and Oberlin representatives made all eight meetings.[63] All was not harmonious. Camp had been warned by an ex-Yale man who was an athletic leader at Penn that Harvard and Reid were "making a big Bluff" on the rules. The Penn athletic trainer, Michael Murphy, believed that "Harvard would not play any more football under Camp's Rules" because they were sick of being beaten by Yale.[64] Yet Yale was in no position to stonewall major rule reform, as Camp would have liked. Camp favored only one major change, which was the extension of the yardage needed to be gained in three downs from 5 to 10 yards. He was fearful that some of the proposed changes were "so radical that they would practically make a new game."[65] At the time, however, an internal investigation of Yale athletic excesses was being carried out by the Yale faculty. The revelation that Yale athletics had a huge $100,000 secret fund which was used to tutor athletes, give expensive gifts to athletes, purchase entertainment for coaches, and pay for trips to the Caribbean had been made by one of the muckrakers. The exposé by a former Yale athlete, Clarence Deming, had tarnished the Yale image, and it was in no position to appear in any way to be against reform.[66]

Yale was reluctant to hinder reform, and Harvard wanted to continue even after the Harvard Faculty of Arts and Sciences voted in February to prohibit football for 1906.[67] Camp, unwilling to do anything which might mar the game he so remarkably developed, and Reid, intent on saving the game for Harvard, came into conflict. Camp was willing only to push for the 10-yard rule. Others, including Reid, wanted to weaken the defense and strengthen the offense with innovations such as the forward pass. In the end, the major rule changes to prevent brutal play included prohibiting runners from hurdling the line, creating a ball-length neutral zone between the two teams, requiring six men on the offensive line of scrimmage to prevent massing behind the line, preventing tackling below the knees, and increasing the number of officials to four while adding larger penalties for violations. To open up play, the 10-yard rule in three downs and the forward pass were added.[68]

The forward pass was the most innovative of all the new legislation. When, against the wishes of Camp, it was introduced, there were questions of who could catch the ball, where it could be thrown from, where it could be caught, and what would be the result if the ball was not caught or touched? The final decision after much discussion was that one forward pass could be made from behind the line of scrimmage if it was thrown at least five yards to either side of the center to an end or a back. One strong limitation to forward passing was the rule that if the ball was not touched by a player on either side, the ball went to the opponent at the spot where the ball was thrown.[69] Later rules would make less severe penalties for the forward pass, but the committee wanted to be cautious at first. As one would guess, the forward pass was used very sparingly at first. There is some question as to what team first used the forward pass. Some believe that St. Louis University's Brad Robinson threw a pass to Jack Schneider in a September 1906 game against Carroll College. Still others credit Wesleyan College's quarterback, Samuel F. B. Morse, Jr., who completed a 20-yard pass to Irvin Van Tassel, a halfback, in October 1906. Yet, there was one made much earlier than this as two Kansas colleges experimented with the forward pass in a game held on Christmas Day, 1905. Fairmont College's Bill Davis threw a pass to Art Solter against Washburn College.[70] Whoever gets credit, the forward pass eventually created the modern exciting game, especially after 1912 when penalties were removed for incomplete passes.

The forward pass and other legislation intended to eliminate mass plays and unethical physical contact helped convince a majority of Harvard's Corporation and Overseers that the new game should be given at least one more year to prove that it was worthy of college men. The May 1906 votes of the Harvard policy makers were 15–9 to sanction football by the Corporation and 17–6 by the Overseers.[71] President Eliot, who voted no, remained unconvinced. "It is childish," Eliot said, "to suppose that the athletic authorities which have permitted football to become a brutal, cheating, demoralizing game can be trusted to reform it."[72] Eliot had failed to convince his own trustees to ban the game, something that a small group of colleges accomplished, including Columbia, New York University, Union, Northwestern, California, and Stanford.

The NCAA: A Ruling Body Lacking Power and Prestige

Harvard remained in football but, along with Yale, Princeton, and a number of other influential colleges, did not immediately join the NCAA. While the NCAA would eventually become extremely powerful, similar to a monopolistic cartel,[73] it began as a small group of colleges lacking unity or real power to legislate intercollegiate reform.

The weakness stemmed from two basic causes. First, the prestigious colleges did not readily desire to see another group usurp power which they traditionally held. In other words, the Big Three which dominated football were reluctant to have the NCAA create its own football rules committee and eliminate the power which the dominating colleges had wielded for a generation and more. Of the institutions which had membership on the old football rules committee, only Pennsylvania joined the NCAA that first year. This left

Harvard, Yale, Princeton, Cornell, the Naval Academy, and Chicago out of the new organization. Columbia, Brown, and every member of the "Big Ten," except Minnesota, refused to join. Not one West Coast college enrolled in the NCAA, though because they lacked national prestige, it was not as important to the stature of the NCAA.[74] The NCAA, nevertheless, would have been delighted even to have a Stanford or California join. NCAA leadership under Captain Palmer Pierce of West Point attempted to remedy the prestige factor by making overtures to the traditional football powers to join the organization. It was plain to see that if a Harvard, Yale, or Chicago had joined, other colleges likely would have done so.

The second weakness of the NCAA came from the laissez-faire mentality of individual institutions. Individual autonomy did not disappear when the NCAA created the first national inter-institutional collegiate organization. The leader of the Amateur Athletic Union, James E. Sullivan, criticized the independence of colleges, claiming that their athletics lacked organization and had a "go it alone" attitude.[75] Even with criticism such as Sullivan's, the NCAA nevertheless was created on the principle of individual autonomy, and it was written into the NCAA constitution and by-laws. The object of the NCAA, according to its constitution, was to regulate and supervise college athletics nationally, yet the by-laws would contain no national eligibility rules. As mandatory eligibility rules were "judged impracticable," by Palmer Pierce and the NCAA, they were left to each institution to enact and enforce.[76] Englishman James Bryce made an observation the same year the NCAA was created. Americans, he said, were the most individualistic of all people, and "they are not the people among whom the art of combination has reached its peak."[77] He was right. Home rule dominated the NCAA for the first half-century of its existence. The individual colleges agreed collectively to act individually.

Moral force, not political force, was the keystone of NCAA power in the early years. Yet its lack of numbers at the first annual meeting in December 1906 even made moral suasion difficult. Only 39 institutions had joined the NCAA, and only 28 sent delegates, far short of the 68 colleges represented one year before. Three years later, only three of the seven original Football Rules Committee institutions had joined the NCAA—Pennsylvania, Chicago, and Harvard— but two-thirds of the "Big Ten" schools had joined. Membership had grown to 67 by then.[78] With Harvard, Brown, and Columbia in the east and a number of the large state universities becoming members, the NCAA was on much firmer ground than it was three years before.

The importance of the founding of the NCAA was that it gave a national focus to the numerous problems facing intercollegiate athletics. It was not able to solve the problems, except for producing uniform playing rules for various sports, but it was a vehicle for discussing them. It also produced guidelines for institutions who wanted to bring greater order to this important part of college life. If an institution wanted to achieve faculty control of athletics, it had the voice of the NCAA behind that choice. If a college wanted to limit recruiting and the granting of athletic scholarships, the NCAA guidelines could be used. If a single school or league wanted to eliminate professional athletes or those who played summer baseball for pay, the NCAA studies and recommendations would be helpful. The freedom of an individual institution to carry out its own athletic program was not jeopardized by belonging to the NCAA—at least not at first. The early years of the NCAA were, then, a time when a slow process took place, moving from the individualism of institutions to collective control for the good of intercollegiate athletics. Athletic evolution, not unlike human evolution, is a long and uneven process.

XV

The Swarthmore Case:
An Addendum on Freedom

A LIBERAL ARTS COLLEGE located outside of Philadelphia at Swarthmore was small, peace-loving, and Quaker. The time was 1907. The Swarthmore incident came about during the turmoil surrounding football ethics and brutality. While Swarthmore was not one of the athletic powers of the east, it was represented at the original MacCracken meeting to "ban or reform" football late in 1905, and had voted with the 8–5 majority to reform rather than abolish the game. It sent a delegate to the original meeting of the NCAA that same December, and it was a charter member of the NCAA. Unlike Columbia and Union colleges in the east, Swarthmore continued to play football under the reformed rules.

Anna T. Jeanes decided she might accomplish at Swarthmore that which Harvard President Charles Eliot could not—ban football. Jeanes, a millionaire heiress in her mid-eighties and without relatives, wrote Swarthmore, among other charitable organizations, into her will. She bequeathed large sums of land or money for a women's hospital, Quaker homes and infirmaries for the aged, and schools for blacks. Swarthmore College, according to her will, was to inherit her coal lands and mineral rights, worth what was believed to be between one and three million dollars. It was contingent upon whether or not Swarthmore "shall discontinue and abandon all participation in Intercollegiate athletics, sports, and games."[1]

When Jeanes died in 1907, Swarthmore had a momentous question to solve. Should it accept a conditional gift of a million or more to drop athletics, forever restricting the freedom of college authorities to act while giving them much greater financial independence? Or should it reject the largest endowment ever offered Swarthmore? President Joseph Swain, perplexed, wrote to twenty-five college presidents asking for their advice. There was a range of responses. Minnesota's Northrop advised: "Money talks, as it always does, and I for my part would accept it." Benjamin Ide Wheeler of California emphatically stated that he "should not for a moment think of accepting as a bribe or a price, nor any other sum." Dartmouth's President Tucker replied that "Educational Freedom is a much greater endowment than money; don't accept it."[2]

With over forty pages of testimony to draw upon, President Swain formed his own conclusions to present to the Swarthmore governing board. Using William Penn's "holy experiment" as an example of the ideals of civil and religious liberty of the colonial period, Swain argued for Swarthmore's historic position of freedom of action. "Freedom," the president maintained, "is above the price of endowments."[3] Just as a college should not accept money to approve or disapprove the teaching of evolution, socialism, or human slavery, it should not accept money to either abolish or continue forever intercollegiate athletics. The issue of freedom was too important for that. Swarthmore athletics were preserved, not because they were intrinsically good but because to abolish them forever for a price would have made a mockery of institutional freedom.

In the half-century from the time of the first intercollegiate contest to the development of the NCAA, the question of the freedom to pursue athletics had been an important one. Even before the advent of intercollegiate contests, the issue of freedom to participate in sport had been fought between students, who looked at the extra-curriculum as their own domain, and faculty, who saw the entire collegiate experience as under their control. The faculty, at that time with their attitude of "in loco parentis," often viewed sport from a patriarchal-authoritarian position. By the early twentieth century, students had to a great extent lost control of athletics as the institutions began to exert dominance. A Yale faculty investigation into athletics in 1906 resulted in the faculty voting to "accept the wisdom of leaving the main management of athletic matters in the hands of undergraduates. . . ."[4] This, however, was not in concert with the direction which intercollegiate sport was taking in America. Actions of faculties and presidents, mandates of boards of trustees, and decisions of professional coaches and graduate managers of athletics eroded student freedom to control their own games.

The decision of Swarthmore College to reject a potentially enormous endowment and to not abolish intercollegiate sports, and the unilateral action of Columbia University's faculty and president to ban football two years earlier, showed the extent that students no longer controlled their own sports. After all, neither institution asked students whether they wanted to continue athletics as a part of the extracurriculum. Student freedom to participate in athletics under their own terms continued to deteriorate in the twentieth century. This, of course, was not totally different from the loss to administrative control of other extracurricular activities such as music, drama, or journalism. The difference was that intercollegiate athletics seldom became part of the curriculum; unlike glee clubs or acting societies, it was not considered "academic"—probably a throwback to medieval mind-body dualism. Student losses included the traditional custom of choosing their own coaches. Some also lost the opportunity to participate if they fell into certain categories. Graduate students could not participate at all. Freshmen and transfer students were forbidden the opportunity to participate immediately upon matriculation, as new eligibility rules came to dominate. By the 1920s, student athletes were not free to quit college to participate in professional football because of the collusion of the colleges and the professional league.[5]

Students sometimes voluntarily gave up power that had been theirs from the beginning. At other times the power was taken by competing groups such as faculties or trustees. Students gave up their freedom to coaches or alumni in order to turn out winning teams or for financial security. Once students gave up control for the sake of victory, it was difficult to reverse this decision. The benefits gained when athletic authority left students' hands and entered others' was plain—greater stability and continuity from year to year and success in winning for those programs with the most able leadership. But the losses were also real. Assimilation of athletics into the administrative echelon of the institution left students with fewer rights, less freedom, and a lack of control over their own athletic lives.

Swarthmore, unintentionally, was making a statement about student control of athletics when it made a decision to favor institutional freedom over financial security. Students, Swarthmore leaders were saying, did not have control; the institution did. No one had asked the students if they wanted intercollegiate athletics. The extracurriculum had seemingly begun as the expression of student freedom in three major areas—intellectual, social, and physical, as shown by the examples of literary clubs, fraternities, and sports. The students were free until the institution decided that they would not be. Institutional leaders throughout America in the twentieth century had to determine for each college how much authority the college would exert over student games.

College athletics, because of the overwhelming interest taken in them, have tended to the extremes—anarchy or license on the one hand and authority or totalitarianism on the other. Student control tended toward the former, institutional control tended toward the latter. Student-controlled intercollegiate athletics had been lost primarily because students lacked the responsibility to run them without conflicting with academic values. In addition, while students wished to remain free to control their own sports, they wanted to be helped financially by alumni and professionally by coaches and trainers. Student freedom gradually lost out to the power of authority. By the early twentieth century, students had lost the freedom of the extracurriculum to the faculty; they had lost the freedom to run individual sports to the coaches and trainers; and they had lost the financial independence of intercollegiate athletics to the alumni and the college authorities.

From the first Harvard-Yale crew meet in 1852 to the initial meeting of colleges to form the NCAA in 1905, intercollegiate athletics had shown a transformation from a free competitive activity of students to a less free but more institutionally controlled activity. Stability and authority had been substituted for student freedom out of institutional necessity. Colleges would continue to contend with major questions, including the most important question—should colleges continue to allow highly competitive athletics to exist in institutions of higher learning? Joseph Swain's Swarthmore College had made a dramatic statement that it could not be bought off to prohibit intercollegiate sports. Freedom, a key concern in the history of college athletics, was a major part of the important decision. In athletics, as in the political life of a nation, an age-old question continued in need of an answer: Is it easier to restrain freedom from becoming license and anarchy or to prevent power from expanding into authority and total control?

EPILOGUE

A Twentieth-Century Meaning of American College Athletics

THERE IS A TENDENCY to define history as the story of change over time. In large part this is true of the developing period of intercollegiate athletics in America. Change has been stressed. For example, college sport developed from rather unorganized activities to more organized class battles, and from the initial, almost spontaneous, intercollegiate contests to highly rationalized athletics. There was change from student-directed athletics to institutional control; from the student captain to the professional coach. Rules of eligibility moved from a laissez-faire approach to a more highly regulated state. Change appeared to rule nineteenth-century sport.

As important as change is to our historical understanding of college sport, continuity is a significant factor. Continuity in men's intercollegiate athletics from the latter years of the nineteenth century through the twentieth century is in many ways more important than is the change. The athletic programs of the late twentieth century are patterned after those developed in the previous century. The commercialized, professionalized, and rationalized college athletics of the twentieth century were not accidents. The major colleges that have followed this model had good teachers. The role model for big-time athletics were the two most elite colleges in nineteenth-century America—Harvard and Yale. One should not be misled by the Ivy League emphasis on academics rather than athletics. Both the perceived evils and benefits of intercollegiate athletics began in eastern institutions led by the elites of the present Ivy League. The rest of American colleges have symbolically, if not actually, cloned Harvard and Yale and continued the tradition.

From an early time, those involved in higher education and college athletics placed winning and prestige well above whatever might have been in second place in creating commercialized, professionalized, and rationalized intercollegiate athletics. At Harvard and at Yale, students, alumni, presidents, governing boards, and even faculties created, or allowed the creation of, big-time athletics, which produced victories and presumably improved the public status of the two leading colleges. Financial favors to sub-freshmen recruits; intensive training before, during, and after the season; lack of or violations of eligibility rules; questionable ethics; payment of professional coaches well beyond faculty salaries; bowing to alumni athletic interests; and construction of stadiums for the public were all part of the Harvard and Yale athletic programs in the late nineteenth and early twentieth century, before the National Collegiate Athletic Association was born.

By 1906, the year the NCAA was officially formed, Frederick Jackson Turner, the historian, censored intercollegiate athletics when he spoke to his own University of Wisconsin alumni gathering. Football, Turner said, "has become a business, carried on too often by professionals, supported by levies on the public, bringing in vast gate receipts, demoralizing student ethics, and confusing the ideals of sport, manliness, and decency."[1] It could have been said at most any other time during the twentieth century by a critic of intercollegiate athletics.

From the muckraking journalists' writings during the crisis year of 1905 to the Carnegie Report on *American College Athletics* in 1929 to the American Council on Education's reform efforts in 1952 to the creation of the Presidents' Commission of the NCAA in 1984, big-time intercollegiate athletics have come under intense criticism. Much of the criticism has been aimed at those who controlled athletics. Yet, it has never been clear who has controlled athletics in individual colleges. If it was confused in the nineteenth century, it has remained so during the twentieth century. Surely by the early 1900s, it was evident that students had lost most of the control at the leading institutions. Who had control was far less well defined.

Faculties, which took the initiative to form athletic committees to set athletic standards in the generation following the early 1880s, garnered some of the control. The faculty athletic committees might dictate certain policies, such as the number of games to be played or whether a medical exam was required for participation. Nevertheless, when important questions arose, the tendency was for that decision to be made elsewhere. For example, when an 1880s Princeton football team wanted to play Yale in New York City, the Princeton trustees overruled the faculty ban to allow it to occur.[2] At the University of Michigan two decades later, the faculty-dominated Board of Control chose to abide by "Big Ten" rules but was overruled by the Michigan trustees. The trustees reconstituted the committee to better insure a withdrawal from the conference.[3] These were not isolated cases.

Governing boards increasingly came to exert control over athletics. This was probably natural, for, after all, boards did set institutional policy, and athletics were a significant factor in the publicity a college received. The changing composition of boards in the latter nineteenth century probably influenced their determination to become involved in athletic matters. Beginning after the Civil War, alumni were first elected to governing boards. By 1900, elected alumni made up one-third of the Yale and Cornell boards. Although it was one of the fears at that time that "alumni could see things only from the undergraduate's point of view," it is for just this reason that board members wished to have a say on decisions involving the most visible part of college, intercollegiate athletics.[4] Yet, early in the century, governing boards were only beginning their eventual dominant role in college sport. By the latter years of the twentieth century, a former college president of a big-time athletic institution could state that "governing boards are largely responsible for the debacle of corruption in Division I intercollegiate athletics."[5] Similarly, the president of the Carnegie Foundation for the Advancement of Teaching believed that governing boards were critical for solving problems in intercollegiate athletics, but he realized that "some trustees would rather see a Heisman Trophy than a Nobel Prize on campus."[6]

University presidents, not governing boards, have usually been singled out for having the opportunity to reform athletics. They also have been criticized for seldom doing so. Presidents, who throughout the nineteenth century had a great deal of power in controlling the destinies of higher education, rarely took initiatives in reforming intercollegiate athletics. One individual remarked in 1905 that President Eliot of Harvard was alone in attempting to rid college athletics of abuses. He said that for the previous twenty years Eliot "protested without the seconding voice of any other college president."[7] That was only a slight exaggeration.

Individually, university presidents have never been able to control intercollegiate athletics. There are at least two reasons for this. First, presidents head individual institutions, and control of intercollegiate athletics necessitates inter-institutional agreements. Full athletic cooperation among the institutions, which are constantly competing for resources and enrollment for their own survival, growth, and prestige, has not succeeded. That, however, may be more of an institutional problem than a purely presidential problem.

University presidents have a greater problem inherent to the control of intercollegiate athletics. The president is caught between demands of the faculty on the one hand and the demands of the governing board on the other. The two groups have often differed on the value of athletics. Presidents are hired and fired by boards, and it has been a rare president who has taken a stance on athletics which differs from the board. Presidents, however, have often opposed the faculty on athletic issues. The boards generally have been far more interested in financial concerns and the institutional image than they have have been about learning and academic considerations. As educational historian Lawrence Veysey has noted, college administrators were by the 1890s already more dedicated to the public image than to an academic philosophy.[8] Henry S. Pritchett, the early 1900s president of the Carnegie Foundation for the Advancement of Teaching, noted the ineffectiveness of presidents, especially those who stood for sound educational goals. Some of the presidents with solid educational policy, Pritchett said, were dismissed because of "the popular cry for greater numbers or winning athletic teams."[9] Almost eight decades later, the president of Alabama, Joab Thomas, made a similar comment. When Thomas hired a coach with a losing record to head the traditional football power, Thomas admitted, "There are a large number of people who think that if Bill Curry doesn't do very well that my days are very limited."[10] If the past is prologue, American institutions of higher learning can expect little reform to be initiated by college presidents.

The clarity of control over intercollegiate athletics, then, is at best murky and has been for the entire twentieth century. Students have lost it. Faculties, who early had a strong influence, often were superceded in their desires to protect the academic integrity of higher education. University presidents, who logically would have a major influence on all aspects of college life, have generally chosen to distance themselves from most aspects of athletics, with the exception of those athletic activities associated with attracting prestige to the institution. It is likely that presidents have felt their jobs threatened if they chose to diminish the non-educational aspects of big-time athletics. Alumni have often become involved after one of two events happened—athletic indebtedness or a losing season. Alumni pressure brought about the creation of the athletic director, originally called the graduate treasurer. Eventually, alumni came to dominate completely a number of athletic departments, controlling the finances and hiring and firing the coaches. Alumni also came to influence the governing boards through financial endowment and election to the boards. Probably the two most influential groups in athletics as the twentieth century progressed were alumni and governing boards.[11] This is ironic because neither alumni nor boards have been represented in the major inter-institutional organization of big-time athletics, the NCAA.

The powers behind big-time athletics, alumni and boards, do not legislate for the control of college sports. Neither group sends representatives to the NCAA. The NCAA is a combination of colleges with faculty representation. The faculty representatives, however, generally are not chosen by the faculty. Rather, they are presidentially appointed. If historian Veysey is correct, one can expect faculty representatives to be more concerned with the public image-building of athletics than with academic considerations. One would then expect that NCAA policy would reflect institutional promotion over educational goals. Thus, the commercialization and professionalization of intercollegiate athletics would likely take precedent over concerns for educating individual athletes.

From the standpoint of the promotional versus the educational aspect of college sport, little has changed from the pattern created by Harvard, Yale, and other eastern colleges in the nineteenth century. Coaches, though, have become increasingly important, and athletic directors have given greater stability to the commercial and professional efforts to create rationalized approaches to college sports. Students, who lost control from an early time, have seen their role diminished as they have seen their freedoms curtailed. As the twentieth century has progressed, student athletes can no longer transfer freely from one college to another and participate in extracurricular activities as other students are free to do. They are no longer free to sign professional athletic contracts, though other students are free to become professionals. Students are even forced to submit "voluntarily" to the constitutionally questionable practice of drug testing, when no other students are required to do so. The commercialization, professionalization, and rationalization of college athletics has had its costs, while it has produced an excellence in performance unknown to the rest of the world.

Twentieth-century big-time athletics became a ritual for nearly all major universities, symbolizing in physical form the intense competition for prestige existing among the various institutions. Winning athletic teams were the most visible signs of the contests for prestige taking place in all areas of university life. Nearly all universities stood for increasing undergraduate enrollment, attracting academically superior graduate students, obtaining prestigious, or "star" professors, maximizing faculty publications, accumulating university gifts and endowments, and increasing private and public research dollars. Prestige came from beautifying the campus, building a chapel, erecting a student union, and enlarging the library holdings—no less than constructing a permanent stadium or indoor playing arena. That Harvard had by the early twentieth century led the nation with forty endowed professorships was no less important, only less well known, than that it had built the first concrete stadium in America. At Yale, the establishment in 1890 of the Yale Alumni Fund drive and its national leadership in alumni giving added to its prestige, just as having Walter Camp lead Yale in athletics enhanced Yale's visibility.[12] With the success of Harvard and Yale as competitors in higher education and in athletics, it was not surprising that the twentieth century saw a ritualized cloning of Harvard and Yale.

APPENDIX

Firsts in American Men's Intercollegiate Sports (1852–1905)

Sport	Date	Competitors	Winner	Score
Crew	3 Aug. 1852	Harvard-Yale (2 miles)	Harvard	By 4 lengths
Baseball	1 July 1859	Amherst-Williams	Amherst	73–32
Cricket	7 May 1864	Haverford-Penn	Haverford	89–60
Football (Soccer-like)	6 Nov. 1869	Rutgers-Princeton	Rutgers	6–4
Football (Rugby—U.S.-Canada)	15 May 1874	Harvard-McGill	Tie	0–0
Football (Rugby—U.S. only)	4 June 1875	Tufts-Harvard	Tufts	1–0
Track and Field	20 July 1873	Amherst-Cornell-McGill (2-mile run)	McGill's Duncan Bowie	11 min. 18:5 sec.
Rifle	17 May 1877	Harvard-Yale	Harvard	By 20 points
Lacrosse	22 Nov. 1877	NYU-Manhattan	NYU	2–0
Bicycle	29 May 1880	Yale-Columbia (Part of IC4A track meet) (2-mile race)	Yale's W. P. Wurtz	7 min. 57 sec. by 20 yards
Tennis	7–8 June 1883	Amherst, Brown, Harvard, Trinity, Yale	Harvard's J. S. Clark (singles) J. S. Clark and P. E. Presbrey (doubles)	

Firsts in American Men's Intercollegiate Sports
(1852–1905) (*Cont.*)

Sport	Date	Competitors	Winner	Score
Polo	27 Nov. 1884	Penn-Wesleyan	Penn	16–10
Cross country	1890	Cornell-Penn	Penn	
Fencing	5 May 1894	Harvard-Columbia	Harvard	5–4
Ice hockey	Feb. 1895	Brown-Harvard	Brown	4–2
Basketball	9 Feb. 1895	Minnesota State School of Agriculture-Hamline	Minnesota State School of Agriculture	9–3
Golf	7 Nov. 1896	Yale-Columbia (6-man teams)	Yale	By 35 holes
Trap shooting	7 May 1898	Columbia, Cornell, Harvard, Penn, Princeton, and Yale		
Water polo	7 March 1899	Penn-Columbia	Penn	2–0
Swimming	8 March 1899	Penn, Columbia, and Yale (4-man, 200-yard relay)	Penn	2 min. 23 sec.
Gymnastics	24 March 1899	Amherst, Brown, Columbia, Cornell, Harvard, Haverford, Lafayette, Lehigh, NYU, Penn, Princeton, Rutgers, Swarthmore, Trinity, Union, Union Theological Seminary, Virginia, Wesleyan, and Yale	Yale (team) Yale's R. G. Clapp (individual)	
Wrestling	5 April 1905	Columbia, Penn, Princeton, Yale	Yale	
Soccer	2 Dec. 1905	Columbia-Cornell	Tie	2–2

NOTES

Preface

1. Lord Chesterfield, letter to Philip Stanhope, 22 Feb. 1748, in Earl of Chesterfield, *Letters to His Son* (London: J. Dodsley, 1775), Vol. I, p. 321.

Chapter I.   The English Background of Early American College Sport

1. James M. Whiton, "The First Harvard-Yale Regatta (1852)," *Outlook* LXVIII (June 1901), 286. Whiton's doctoral dissertation at Yale, "Ars Longa, Brevis Vita," was completed in 1861. During his life he was Rector of Hopkins Grammar School, New Haven, Principal of Williston Seminary, Easthampton, and Pastor of Congregational churches in Lynn, Massachusetts, Newark, New Jersey, and New York City.

2. Ibid., 287; and Charles F. Livermore, "The First Harvard-Yale Boat Race," *Harvard Graduates' Magazine* II (Dec. 1893), 226.

3. Whiton, "The First Harvard-Yale Regatta," 286.

4. "Cambridge University Swimming Club Account, 1882–1895," Add. 8088, Cambridge Univ. Library Mss.

5. Ibid.

6. Percy Manning, "Sports and Pastimes Pursued in Oxford and Neighborhood Down to About 1850," Vol. II, p. 373, Ms. Top. Oxon. d. 202, Oxford Univ. Library.

7. Ibid., Vol. III, p. 1.

8. Ibid., 166.

9. Ibid., 167.

10. "Memoranda Cantabrigiensia," *The Sporting Magazine* XXII, n.s. (May 1828), 30.

11. "Some Farther (sic) Passages in the Life of an Oxford Scholar . . . ," *The Sporting Magazine* XX, n.s. (June 1827), 74.

12. "Certain Passages in the Life of an Oxford Scholar," *The Sporting Magazine* XX, n.s. (June 1827), 74.

13. Joseph Strutt, *The Sports and Pastimes of the People of England* (London: Methuen, 1903 (originally 1801)), 101–2.

14. F. S. Ashley-Cooper, *Eton v. Harrow at the Wicket* (London: St. James', 1922), 17, 23.

15. Stephen Green, *Cricketing Bygones* (Bucks, England: Shire Publications, 1982), 4.

16. H. A. Harris, *Sport in Britain: Its Origins and Development* (London: Stanley Paul, 1975), 49, and Geoffrey Bolton, *History of the Oxford University Cricket Club* (Oxford: Holywell, 1962), 6.

17. Manning, "Sports and Pastimes," Vol. I, p. 151.

18. G. C. Drinkwater and T. R. B. Sanders (eds.), *The University Boat Race: 1829–1929* (London: Cassell and Co., 1929), 8.

19. Broadside about crew eights meeting at Iffley, near Oxford, on the Thames, 26 May 1818, in Manning, "Sports and Pastimes," Vol. I, p. 152.

20. *The Sporting Magazine* XXII, n.s. (Aug. 1828), 321–22; and "Oxford University Boat Club Miscellaneous Papers," G. A. Oxon, C257, Oxford Univ. Library.

21. Charles Wordsworth, "A Chapter of Autobiography," *Fortnightly Review* XL, n.s. (1 July 1883), 68. For a general account of rowing at Oxford and Cambridge, see Christopher Dodd, *The Oxford and Cambridge Boat Race* (London: Stanley Paul, 1983).

22. *The Sporting Magazine* XXIV, n.s. (June 1829), 125.

23. Ibid., July 1829, p. 250.

24. "Oxford University Boat Club Miscellaneous Papers."

25. Drinkwater and Sanders, *The University Boat Race*, 12.

26. "College Customs Anno 1734/5," *Publications of the Colonial Society of Massachusetts Collections: Harvard College Records* (Boston: Published by the Society, 1935), Vol. XXXI, pp. 383–84.

27. Courtland Canby, "A Note on the Influence of Oxford University upon William and Mary College in the Eighteenth Century," *William and Mary Quarterly* XXI (July 1941), 242.

28. "The Genesis of Foxhunting in Virginia," *Virginia Magazine of History and Biography* XXXVII (April 1929), 155–57; "The Equine F F Vs," *Virginia Magazine of History and Biography* XXXV (Oct. 1927), 329–70; *Virginia Magazine of History and Biography* VII (Oct. 1899), 173–74; and John Clayton, "Chesterfield County, Virginia, Letter to Samuel Durrent, Kent, England, 21 March 1739," in *Virginia Magazine of History and Biography* VII (Oct. 1899), 174.

29. "Journal of the Meetings of the Presidents and Masters of William

and Mary College, September 14, 1752," *William and Mary Quarterly* II (July 1893), 55.

30. "The First Description of Harvard [1642]," *Harvard Graduates' Magazine* XII (Dec. 1903), 206.

31. Douglas Sloan, *The Great Awakening and American Education* (New York: Teachers College Press, 1973), 19.

32. "Laws of Harvard College, May 4, 1655," *Harvard College Records*, Vol. XXXI, p. 330.

33. Harvard Corporation Records, Vol. I, 28 April 1712, p. 79, Harvard Univ. Archives.

34. *Harvard College Records*, Vol. XXXI, p. 154.

35. *The Laws of Yale-College* (New Haven, CT: T. & S. Green, 1774), 11.

36. Leon B. Richardson, *History of Dartmouth College* (Hanover, NH: Dartmouth College Publications, 1932), Vol. I, pp. 106–7.

37. University of Pennsylvania Board of Trustees Minutes, 10 March 1761, Univ. of Pennsylvania Archives.

38. Princeton Faculty Minutes, 26 Nov. 1787, Princeton Univ. Archives.

39. *The Black Book, or Book of Misdemeanors in King's College, New-York, 1771–1775* (New York: Columbia Univ. Press, 1931), 4.

40. See Frederick Rudolph, "The Collegiate Way," in his *The American College and University* (New York: Vintage Books, 1962), 86–109. For character building being the central focus of college life well into the nineteenth century see also Lawrence R. Veysey, *The Emergence of the American University* (Chicago: Univ. of Chicago Press, 1965), 28–29, 186–91, 238–40; Paul H. Mattingly, *The Classless Profession* (New York: New York Univ. Press, 1975), 44, 65–69; and Roger L. Geiger, *To Advance Knowledge: The Growth of American Research Universities, 1900–1940* (New York: Oxford Univ. Press, 1986), 3.

Chapter II. Sport, the Extracurriculum, and the Idea of Freedom

1. John H. Bartlett and John P. Gifford, *Dartmouth Athletics* (Concord, NH: Republican Press Association, 1893), 7.

2. Dartmouth Faculty Records, 6 Oct. 1835, Dartmouth College Archives.

3. Joseph F. Kett, *Rites and Passages* (New York: Basic Books, 1977), 51, and Oscar Handlin and Mary F. Handlin, *The American College and American Culture* (New York: McGraw-Hill, 1970), 11.

4. Thomas Jefferson did stimulate reform in 1779 at William and Mary

by creating an elective system, over one century before it was common in other colleges. See E. G. Swen, *Kentuckians at William and Mary before 1861* (n.p.: privately printed, 1948), 18. James McLachlan argues in "The American College in the Nineteenth Century: Toward a Reappraisal," *Teachers College Record* LXXX (Dec. 1978), 287–306, that college students generally looked favorably upon their curriculum and that the curriculum did change significantly. The jury is out on both statements.

5. See for instance "Early Laws of the College, 1783," in Walter C. Bronson, *History of Brown University, 1764–1914* (Providence, RI: Brown Univ., 1914), 508–19.

6. See Frederick Rudolph, *The American College and University* (New York: Vintage Books, 1962), 97–99, and Lowell H. Harrison, "Rowdies, Riots, and Rebellions," *American History Illustrated* VII (June 1972), 18–29.

7. These occurrences are documented in a number of college faculty minutes from colonial times well into the nineteenth century. For a useful summary of student rebellions, see: John S. Brubacher and Willis Rudy, *Higher Education in Transition* (New York: Harper & Row, 1968), 51–57.

8. Steven J. Novak, *The Rights of Youth: American Colleges and American Students, 1798–1815* (Cambridge, MA: Harvard Univ. Press, 1977), 11.

9. Ibid., 105.

10. George R. Cutting, *Student Life at Amherst* (Amherst, MA: Hatch & Williams, 1871), 91. A college professor at William and Mary felt the same frustration as students. In 1852, Silas Totten wrote of the "unsufferably dull" life with the "same duties, the same lectures, and the same studies . . . , another monotonous year." Quoted in Anne W. Chapman, "The College of William and Mary, 1849–1854," M.A. thesis, College of William and Mary, 1978, pp. 127–29.

11. G. S. Hall, "Student Customs," *American Antiquarian Society Proceedings* XIV (Oct. 1900), 101.

12. Thomas S. Harding, *College Literary Societies* (New York: Pageant Press, 1971), 341, 355, 370, and 481.

13. Rita S. Saslaw, "Student Societies in Nineteeenth Century Ohio: Misconceptions and Realities," *Ohio History* LXXXVIII (Spring 1979), 198–210, argues that literary societies were conservative organizations controlled by faculties to further classical studies. If it were true in Ohio, which is questionable, it was not true in many other colleges in the nation.

14. Princeton Faculty Minutes, 12 April 1825, Princeton Univ. Archives.

15. Dartmouth Faculty Records, 9 April 1829, Dartmouth College Archives.

16. Henry D. Seldon, *Student Life and Customs* (New York: D. Appleton, 1901), 133.

17. Thomas Jefferson's liberal action in establishing the elective system in 1779 was accompanied with the freedom to choose any number of credits and courses that William and Mary students desired. See Swen, *Kentuckians at William and Mary*, 18.

18. Handlin and Handlin, *American College and American Culture*, 40.

19. For greater discussion see Sheldon, *Student Life and Customs*, 148–64.

20. Jurgen Herbst, "The American Revolution and the American University," *Perspectives in American History* X (1976), 281, and Handlin and Handlin, *American College and American Culture*, 5.

21. *Seventh Census of the United States: 1850* (Washington, D.C.: Robert Armstrong Public Printer, 1853), lxi, and "From a Graduate's Window," *Harvard Graduates' Magazine* XIV (Dec. 1905), 220.

22. "College Customs Anno 1734/5," *Publications of the Colonial Society of Massachusetts Collections: Harvard College Records* (Boston: published by the Society, 1935), 383–84; "Early Laws of the College, 1783," in Bronson, *The History of Brown University*, 508–19; and *The Laws of Yale-College* (New Haven, CT: T. & S. Green, 1795), 11.

23. *A Collection of College Words and Customs* (Cambridge, MA: J. Bartlett, 1851), 150–61, and Sheldon, *Student Life and Customs,* pp. 98–102.

24. "Hamilton College," *University Quarterly* IV (Oct. 1861), 303.

25. John White in 1850 recalled his experiences. See John L. Sibley's Private Journal, Vol. I, 19 July 1850, p. 246, Harvard Univ. Archives. See also *A Collection of College Words and Customs*, 314, and Jennie Holliman, *American Sports, 1785–1835* (Durham, NC: Seaman Press, 1931), 150.

26. Sheldon, *Student Life and Customs*, 103–5, and Walter L. Munro, *The Old Back Campus at Brown* (Providence: Haley & Sykes, 1929), 34.

27. Dartmouth Faculty Records, 7 Sep. 1877; *Princetonian,* 22 Sep. 1876, p. 8; Princeton Faculty Minutes, 19 Sep. 1876, p. 522; and Malcolm Townsend, "A Cane Rush," in Norman W. Bingham (ed.), *The Book of Athletics and Out-of-Door Sports* (Boston: Lothrop, 1895), 225–37.

28. George H. Tripp, *Student-Life at Harvard* (Boston: Lockwood, Brooks & Co., 1876), 51.

29. *A Collection of College Words and Customs*, 96.

30. Ibid., 135.

31. John L. Sibley's Private Journal, Vol. I, 27 Aug. 1846, p. 74.

32. "A Sophomore in 1845," *Harvard Graduates' Magazine* IX (Dec. 1900), 205.

33. *A Collection of College Words and Customs*, 96.

34. Francis O. French, "Sophomore at Harvard," in *Exeter and Harvard Eighty Years Ago* (Chester, NH: privately printed, 1932), 71.

35. Ibid.

36. Richard M. Hurd, *A History of Yale Athletics: 1840–1888* (New Haven, CT: privately printed, 1888), 53.

37. Charles H. Haswell, *Reminiscences of an Octogenarian, 1816–1860* (New York: Harper, 1896), 81; Frank Presbrey, *Athletics at Princeton: A History* (New York: Frank Presbrey, 1901), 20; "Reminiscences of James C. Seagrave, Class of 1845," 4, Brown Univ. Archives; Carl F. Price, *Wesleyan's First Century* (Middletown, CT: Wesleyan Univ. 1932), 258; Henry B. Twombly, *Personal Reminiscences of a Yale Football Player of the Early 'Eighties* (n.p.: privately printed, n.d.), 7; Hurd, *A History of Yale Athletics*, 53; and Horace Coon, *Columbia* (New York: E. P. Dutton, 1947), 293.

38. Leon B. Richardson, *History of Dartmouth College* (Hanover, NH: Dartmouth College Publications, 1932), I, p. 106, and II, p. 493.

39. "A New Class Rush," *New York Daily Tribune*, 15 Oct. 1905, Sec. II, p. 3; 15 March 1905, Sec. V, p. 1; and 1 Oct. 1905, Sec. II, p. 3; H. A. Bellows, "Student Life," *Harvard Graduates' Magazine* XIV (Dec. 1905), 296; George P. Baker, "The Opening of the Year," *Harvard Graduates' Magazine* XIII (Dec. 1904), 255; Price, *Wesleyan's First Century*, 160; *Columbia Spectator*, 6 Oct. 1905, p. 1; and Thomas Dunn, "Class Scraps Begat Bruises and Arnica," *The Penn Stater* LX (May 1973), 8–11.

40. Nora C. Chaffin, *Trinity College, 1839–1892: The Beginnings of Duke University* (Durham, NC: Duke Univ. Press, 1950), 208.

41. Richardson, *Dartmouth*, II, p. 493.

42. A number of historians have emphasized the influence of political and historical ideological values of freedom and equality in America. Among them are Gordon S. Wood, *The Creation of the American Republic 1776–1787* (Chapel Hill: Univ. of North Carolina Press, 1969), 43, 562; Roger Burlingame, *The American Conscience* (New York: Alfred A. Knopf, 1960), 403; Rush Welter, *The Mind in America* (New York: Columbia Univ. Press, 1975), 83–84; David M. Potter, *Freedom and Its Limitations in American Life* (Stanford: Stanford Univ. Press, 1976), 46; and Raymond Aron, "On the Proper Use of Ideologies," in Joseph Ben-David and Terry N. Clark, *Culture and Its Creators* (Chicago: Univ. of Chicago Press, 1977), 6. Even Daniel L. Boorstin, who believed that Americans were not interested in ideologies and have rejected them, stated that "remarkable continuity" has existed in American life resulting from beliefs in equality and liberty. See his *America and the Image of Europe* (New York: Meridan Books, 1960), 52, 60–61.

43. Novak, *The Rights of Youth*, 12.

44. Ibid., 57.

45. Ibid., 76.

46. Ibid., 48.

47. Ibid., 53.

48. Leverett W. Spring, *A History of Williams College* (Boston: Houghton Mifflin, 1917), 61; "Letters from William and Mary College [ca. 1800]," *Virginia Magazine of History and Biography* XXIX (April 1921), 173; "Letters from William and Mary, 1795–1799," *Virginia Magazine of History and Biography* XXX (July 1922), 225; and Novak, *The Rights of Youth*, 129.

49. Novak, *The Rights of Youth*, 105.

50. James Axtell, *The School upon a Hill* (New Haven: Yale Univ. Press, 1974), 242.

Chapter III.   The First Intercollegiate Sport: Crew and the Commercial Spirit

1. Richard M. Hurd, *A History of Yale Athletics: 1840–1888* (New Haven, CT: privately printed, 1888), 5.

2. Robert F. Herrick, *Red Top: Reminiscences of Harvard Rowing* (Cambridge, MA: Harvard Univ. Press, 1948), 9.

3. John DeGrange, "100 Years of Yale-Harvard Rowing," 1, Harvard Univ. Archives.

4. Jennie Holliman, *American Sports, 1785–1835* (Durham, NC: Seeman Press, 1931), 156.

5. Melvin L. Adelman, *A Sporting Time: New York City and the Rise of Modern Athletics, 1820–1870* (Urbana: Univ. of Illinois Press, 1986), 189–93, and Samuel Crowther and Arthur Ruhl, *Rowing and Track Athletics* (New York: Macmillan, 1905), 3–13.

6. Adelman, *A Sporting Time*, 192.

7. *Spirit of the Times*, 13 Aug. 1859, p. 317; and DeGrange, "100 Years of Yale-Harvard Rowing," 1.

8. Guy M. Lewis, "America's First Intercollegiate Sport: The Regattas from 1852 to 1875," *Research Quarterly* XXXVIII (Dec. 1967), 639.

9. James Whiton, "The First Harvard-Yale Regatta (1852)," *Outlook* LXVIII (June 1901), 289.

10. *New York Herald*, 10 Aug. 1852, p. 2.

11. Whiton, "The First Harvard-Yale Regatta," 289.

12. Ibid., 287; and Herrick, *Red Top*, 78.

13. *New York Herald*, 10 Aug. 1852, p. 2.

14. Charles F. Livermore, "The First Harvard-Yale Boat Race," *Harvard Graduates' Magazine* II (Dec. 1893), 226.

15. *New York Herald*, 10 Aug. 1852, p. 2; *Boston Daily Evening Tran-*

script, 5 Aug. 1852, p. 1; Whiton, "The First Harvard-Yale Regatta," 287; and *A History of American College Regattas* (Boston: Wilson, 1875), 9.

16. *Boston Daily Evening Transcript,* 4 Aug. 1852, p. 2.

17. *New York Herald,* 10 Aug. 1852, p. 2.

18. Walter C. Bronson, *History of Brown University, 1864–1914* (Providence, RI: Brown Univ., 1914), 246; and "The History of Boating at Brown," *The* [Brown] *Brunonian,* Jan. 1870, p. 103.

19. George W. Orton, *A History of Athletics at Pennsylvania* (Philadelphia: Athletic Association, Univ. of Pennsylvania, 1896), 63.

20. *New York Herald,* 27 July 1859, p. 1.

21. John H. Bartlett and John P. Gifford, *Dartmouth Athletics* (Concord, NH: Republican Press Association, 1893), 5–6; "Dartmouth College," *University Quarterly* 1 (April 1860), 367; *New York Clipper,* 6 Aug. 1859, p. 24; and Robert F. Kelley, *American Rowing* (New York: G. P. Putnam's Sons, 1932), 75.

22. *A History of Columbia University, 1754–1904* (New York: Columbia Univ. Press, 1904), 172–73; and "Columbia College," *University Quarterly* III (April 1861), 394.

23. *Wesleyan Argus,* 28 June 1871, p. 282; and "Wesleyan University," *University Quarterly* II (Oct. 1860), 391.

24. F. O. French, "Sophomore at Harvard," *Exeter and Harvard Eighty Years Ago* (Chester, NH: privately printed, 1932), 90; and *New York Herald,* 27 July 1859, p. 1.

25. *New York Herald,* 24 July 1859, p. 3.

26. Ibid.

27. *New York Herald,* 27 July 1859, p. 1.

28. F. O. French, letter to his father, 17 May 1857, in French, *Exeter and Harvard,* 140.

29. Herrick, *Red Top,* 80–81.

30. James D'Wolf Lovett, *Old Boston Days and the Games They Played* (Boston: Little, Brown, 1908), 62–63, 213–14; and Alexander Agassiz, "Rowing Fifty Years Ago," *Harvard Graduates' Magazine* XV (March 1907), 457–58.

31. *New York Clipper,* 24 July 1858, 107.

32. Hurd, *A History of Yale Athletics,* 8.

33. *New York Herald,* 27 July 1859, 1; and *New York Clipper,* 6 Aug. 1859, p. 4.

34. Lewis, "Regattas from 1852–1875," 640.

35. *A History of American College Regattas,* 13.

36. As quoted in Lyman Bagg, *Four Years at Yale* (New York: Henry Holt, 1871), 371–73.

37. *New York Clipper,* 6 Aug. 1859, p. 124.

38. Ibid., 4 Aug. 1860, 123.

39. Ibid., 5 Aug. 1865, 130; Bagg, *Four Years at Yale,* 376; "Yale Col-

lege," *University Quarterly* II (Oct. 1860), 398; "The College Regatta," *Yale Literary Magazine* XXX (Oct. 1864), 11; and "College Beginning," *The American College* I (Oct. 1909), 36. The Harvard faculty formed a Committee on Boating and Regattas in the later summer of 1860, but decided that "no immediate action respecting boating was expedient." Nevertheless, less than two years later, the faculty prohibited Harvard from rowing Yale either during the term or in vacation. Again in 1864, the faculty considered prohibiting intercollegiate athletic contests but this time decided against such action. See Harvard Faculty Minutes, 10 and 24 Sep. 1860, 2 June 1862, and 9 and 16 May 1864, Harvard Univ. Archives.

40. *Spirit of the Times*, 6 Aug. 1859, p. 308.

41. Tracy Mehr believed that there was a period of relative purity in the first generation of student controlled college athletics when they were "relatively free from commercialism" and were used "as a means rather than an end." The present work shows that he was wrong on both counts before the first decade of intercollegiate athletics ended. See his "A Moment of Relative Purity in College Sport, 1850–1880," in Wayne M. Ladd and Angela Lumpkin (eds.), *Sport in American Education: History & Perspectives* (Washington, D.C.: American Alliance for Health, Physical Education, Recreation and Dance, 1979), 64–70.

42. Bagg, *Four Years at Yale*, 343; and Hurd, *A History of Yale Athletics*, 10.

43. "Yale College," *University Quarterly* III (April 1861), 444, and I (April 1860), 406; and *Harper's Weekly* IX (19 Aug. 1865), 517.

44. Yale University Faculty Minutes, 12 April 1864 and 8 June 1864, Yale Univ. Archives.

45. R. M. Hurd, "The Yale Stroke," *Outing* XV (Dec. 1889), 230–31; and *New York Clipper*, 6 Aug. 1864, 130.

46. *New York Times*, 30 July 1864, p. 3.

47. Hurd, "The Yale Stroke," 230.

48. Henry James, *Charles W. Eliot, President of Harvard University, 1869–1909* (London: Constable, 1930), Vol. I, p. 81.

49. *New York Clipper*, 4 Aug. 1860, p. 123; Edward F. Blake, "Shall I Join a College Boat Club?" *University Quarterly* I (July 1860), 105–6; William Blaikie, "Ten Years among Rowing Men," *Harper's Monthly* XLVII (Aug. 1873), 408; Clarence Deming, "College Boating in the Sixties," *Outing* XLIV (June 1904), 416; and Hurd, *A History of Yale Athletics*, 8.

50. *New York Clipper*, 5 Aug. 1865, p. 130.

51. Blaikie, "Ten Years among Rowing Men," 408.

52. *New York Clipper*, 1 Aug. 1868, p. 130; *A History of American College Regattas*, 24; and Bagg, *Four Years at Yale*, 382.

53. Yale Univ. Faculty Minutes, 19 Sep. 1866 and 13 Nov. 1867, Yale Univ. Archives.

54. *New York Clipper*, 27 July 1867, p. 127, and 1 Aug. 1868, 130; and Bagg, *Four Years at Yale*, 386.

55. "100 Years of Harvard-Yale Rowing," 3; and *A History of American College Regattas*, 27.

56. *A History of American College Regattas*, 34.

Chapter IV.   Crew: Internationalism, Expansion, and the Yale-Harvard Pullout

1. "Speech on the Johnson-Clarendon Treaty, in Executive Session of the Senate, April 13, 1869," in *Charles Sumner: His Complete Works* (Boston: Lee and Shepard, 1900), Vol. XVII, pp. 53, 90.

2. *The Congressional Globe*, 19 April 1869, p. 729.

3. Adrian Cook, *The Alabama Claims* (Ithaca, NY: Cornell Univ. Press, 1975), 75–102; Edward L. Pierce, *Memoirs and Letters of Charles Sumner* (London: Sampson Low, Marston, 1893), 385–87; and Thomas W. Bolch, *The Alabama Arbitration* (Philadelphia: Allen, Lane & Scott, 1900), 128.

4. *Harper's Weekly* XIII (29 May 1869), 338, and 24 July 1869, p. 466.

5. A. G. Sedwick, "The Harvard and Oxford Boat Race," *Nation* VIII (June 1869), 432.

6. William Blaikie, "The International Rowing-Match, 1869," *Harper's Monthly* XL (Dec. 1870), 50; and "Boat Racing," *Gentleman's Magazine* II (Jan. 1869), 174–75.

7. Blaikie, "The International Rowing-Match," 50.

8. Ibid., 55–56.

9. Ibid., 54–57.

10. *The Manchester Guardian*, 25 Aug. 1869, p. 945.

11. Blaikie, "The International Rowing-Match," 63, 67; and *New York Clipper*, 4 Sep. 1869, p. 170.

12. "The International Boat Race," *Frank Leslie's Illustrated* XXIX (11 Sep. 1869), 409; and Blaikie, "The International Rowing-Match," 60.

13. "The Boat-Races," *Nation* IX (2 Sep. 1869), 187–89.

14. Blaikie, "The International Rowing-Match," 65–66.

15. Joseph J. Mathews, "The First Harvard-Oxford Boat Race," *New England Quarterly* XXXIII (March 1960), 74–82.

16. *London Times*, 25 Aug. 1869, p. 10, and 27 Aug. 1869, p. 3.

17. John Blanchard (ed.), *The H Book of Harvard Athletics* (Cambridge, MA: Harvard Varsity Club, 1923), 50.

18. *New York Clipper,* 30 July 1870, p. 130; and Lyman Bagg, *Four Years at Yale* (New York: Henry Holt, 1871), 389–99.

19. G. H. Gould, President, and Robert Grant, Secretary of the Harvard University Boat Club, letter to I. H. Ford, President of the Yale University Boat Club, 17 May 1871, as quoted in Blanchard, *The H Book,* 56.

20. *New York Clipper,* 22 July 1871, p. 125, and 29 July 1871, p. 130.

21. "First Regatta of the National College Rowing Association at Ingleside, Near Springfield, Mass., July 21, 1871," 27-page pamphlet published by the Massachusetts Agricultural College, 1872 (Brown Univ. Archives), 12, 13, 17–18.

22. *New York Tribune,* 25 July 1871, as quoted in Douglas K. Fidler, "The First Big Upset: American Culture and the Regatta of 1871," *New England Quarterly* L (March 1977), 78.

23. *New York Clipper,* 3 August 1872, p. 140.

24. Ibid., 26 July 1873, p. 133; and J. R. W. Hitchcock, "The Harvard-Yale Races," *Outing* VI (July 1885), 401.

25. *New York Clipper,* 26 July 1873, p. 133; *Harvard Advocate,* 26 Sep. 1873, pp. 4–5; *Western Sporting Gazette,* 26 July 1873, p. 118; Richard M. Hurd, *A History of Yale Athletics: 1840–1888* (New Haven, CT: privately printed, 1888), 17–18; and Blanchard, *The H Book,* 58–62.

26. *The Cornell Era,* 16 Jan. 1874, p. 115, and 23 Jan. 1874, p. 126; and *Harvard Advocate,* 23 Jan. 1874, p. 129.

27. Frank Presbrey and James Moffatt, *Athletics at Princeton* (New York: Frank Presbrey, 1901), 507.

28. Cornell University Board of Trustees Proceedings, 28 July 1876, p. 138, Cornell Univ. Archives.

29. *The Cornell Era,* 27 Feb. 1874, p. 161.

30. Statement of referee William Wood, as quoted in *Harvard Advocate,* 1 Oct. 1874, pp. 5–6.

31. *Harvard Magenta,* 2 Oct. 1874, p. 6, and 3 Oct. 1874, p. 7; and Hurd, *A History of Yale Athletics,* 20.

32. *New York World,* 19 July 1874, pp. 1, 4–5.

33. *New York Daily Tribune,* 22 July 1874, p. 8.

34. *Harvard Advocate,* 15 Jan. 1875, p. 121; Presbrey, *Athletics at Princeton,* 507–10; and "The Intercollegiate Boat-Race," *Harper's Weekly* XIX (24 July 1875), 598. Providing buoys was a complicated maneuver. In an attempt to prevent future collisions such as that of Harvard and Yale in 1874, first Saratoga Lake was surveyed in the winter of 1875. Stone anchors were sunk every eighth of a mile, 100 feet apart. At the top of each anchor, a wire was attached to float just below the water level. Flags, representing the colors of the colleges were then attached. Thus, a three mile long, 100 foot wide lane was provided each crew. See Waterman T. Hewett, *Cornell University* (New York: University Publication Society, 1905), Vol. III, p. 161.

35. *Cornell Daily Sun,* 26 June 1897, p. 2; Hewett, *Cornell University,* Vol. III, p. 151; and *Western Sporting Gazette,* 12 July 1873, p. 87.

36. John N. Ostrom, letter to Andrew W. White, 17 Nov. 1875, in Andrew D. White Papers, Cornell Univ. Archives; and Hewett, *Cornell University,* Vol. III, p. 152.

37. B. W. Dwight, "Intercollegiate Regattas, Hurdle-Races and Prize Contests," *New Englander* XXV (April 1876), 256.

38. "Diaries," Vol. XIV, 14 July 1875, Andrew D. White Papers, Cornell Univ. Archives.

39. Dwight, "Intercollegiate Regattas," 255; and Hewett, *Cornell University,* Vol. III, p. 167.

40. *Harvard Crimson,* 30 Sep. 1875, p. 2; and Executive Committee of Harvard University Boat Club and Committee of Graduates, letter to W. F. Weld, 20 Dec. 1875, in *Harvard Advocate,* 10 Jan. 1876, p. 89.

41. Newspaper clipping, ca. July 1875, in "Boating Notes of John E. Eustes," 10, Wesleyan Univ. Archives.

42. Lewis S. Welch and Walter Camp, *Yale: Her Campus, Class-Rooms, and Athletics* (Boston: L. C. Page, 1899), 468.

43. *Yale Record,* Vol. IV, No. 13, undated, ca. Fall 1875, p. 15. A Cornell man noted: "In justice, the principal officers of the Association should have been conferred upon those two colleges, but owing to their arrogance, many smaller colleges were alienated, and these offices for the last two years were given to other colleges. This has stung them to the quick—they must lead or they will not remain." *The Cornell Review* III (Jan. 1876), 177.

44. *Harvard Advocate,* 1 Oct. 1875, p. 2.

45. *Spirit of the Times,* 22 July 1876, p. 641.

46. *Harvard Advocate,* 1 Oct. 1875, p. 2.

47. Harvard graduate, class of 1873, Letter to the Editor, *Harvard Advocate,* 22 Oct. 1875, p. 31.

48. G. H. Lohmes, "Athletics at Cornell," *Outing* XV (March 1890), 456.

49. *Harvard Advocate,* 21 Jan. 1876, p. 100.

50. Herbert T. Steward, *The Records of the Henley Regatta, 1839–1902* (London: Grant Richards, 1903), 225–26; and R. D. Burnell, *Henley Regatta: A History* (London: Oxford Univ. Press, 1957), 102.

51. See Albert B. Hart, "Harvard's Athletic Policy," *Harvard Gradutes' Magazine* IV (Dec. 1895), 209–14. When Cornell challenged Yale to a meet in 1889, George Adee, a Yale graduate, wrote Walter Camp, Yale's athletic advisor, 16 Dec. 1889, opposing the move. "Yale intends now and in the future to row races with Harvard University only. . . . This is Cornell's entering wedge and it seems to me that no time should be lost in presenting a steel surface to it." Camp Papers, Box 1, Folder 3, Yale Univ. Archives.

52. *New York Journal*, 24 June 1897, quoted in *The Cornell Era*, 2 Oct. 1897, p. 20.

53. Newspaper Clipping, ca. 26 June 1897, Crew Scrapbook, Clippings and Pictures, 1896–98, 40/1/10/6, Cornell Univ. Archives.

54. Ibid.; and *New York Herald*, 26 June 1897, p. 3.

55. *New York Sun*, 26 June 1897, p. 2.

56. Thomas C. Mendenhall, *A Short History of American Rowing* (Boston: Charles River Books, 1980), 26.

57. Hart, "Harvard's Athletic Policy," 212.

Chapter V.   The Rise of College Baseball

1. Jacques Barzun, *God's Country and Mine* (New York: Vintage Books, 1954), 151.

2. Samuel L. Clemens, *Mark Twain's Speeches* (New York: Harper & Brothers, 1923), 145.

3. "College Beginnings," *The American College* I (Oct. 1909), 36; and Harold Seymour, *Baseball: The Early Years* (New York: Oxford Univ. Press, 1960), 164.

4. David Q. Voigt, *American Baseball: From Gentleman's Sport to the Commissioner System* (Univ. Park: Pennsylvania State Univ. Press, 1983), 8–9.

5. "Lawrence Base Ball Club: 1858 Constitution," HUD 3514.1500, Harvard Univ. Archives; and *Harvard Graduates' Magazine* XXV (March 1917), 346–50.

6. Frank Presbrey and James Moffatt, *Athletics at Princeton* (New York: Frank Presbrey, 1901), 20, 67.

7. Andrew M. Modelski, *Railroad Maps of North America: The First Hundred Years* (Washington, D.C.: Library of Congress, 1984), 43, 56, 75.

8. "College Beginnings," *The American College* I (Dec. 1909), 221; and *New York Clipper*, 9 July 1859, p. 95, and 13 Aug. 1859, p. 132. Amherst students were familiar with both the Massachusetts and the New York rules in 1859. See George R. Cutting, *Student Life at Amherst* (Amherst, MA: Hatch & Williams, 1871), 112.

9. "College Beginnings," *The American College* I (Dec. 1909), 222–24.

10. *Franklin and Hampshire Gazette*, 1 July 1859, as quoted in ibid.,

11. College Beginnings," *The American College* I (Dec. 1909), 222–24.

12. John Bascom, "Athletics," *Williams Alumni Review* II (Oct. 1910), 13, and "John Bascom," *Dictionary of American Biography* (New York: Charles Scribner, 1929), Vol. I, p. 32.

13. Cutting, *Student Life at Amherst*, 113, 117. The day before the baseball game, the two colleges competed in an intercollegiate chess

match, Amherst winning. The chess champions were greeted with a similar reception by Amherst students when they arrived at Amherst.

14. *University Quarterly* II (Oct. 1860), 341, 371; II (July 1860), 164, 197; III (April 1861), 426; Marilyn Tobias, *Old Dartmouth on Trial* (New York: New York Univ. Press, 1982), 75; W. D. Sanborn, "Base Ball," in F. O. Vaille and H. A. Clark, *The Harvard Book* (Cambridge, MA: Bigelow, 1875), Vol. II, 269; and Presbrey, *Athletics at Princeton,* 67.

15. Voigt, *American Baseball,* Vol. I, 11.

16. Sanborn, "Base Ball," 271.

17. *The Princeton Lit.* as quoted by Presbrey, *Athletics at Princeton,* 75.

18. Edgar S. Kiracofe, "Athletics and Physical Education in the Colleges of Virginia," Ph.D. dissertation, Univ. of Virginia, 1932, 12; and E. Merton Coulter, *College Life in the Old South* (Athens: Univ. of Georgia Press, 1928), 268.

19. *Grant County* [Wisconsin] *Witness,* 4 Oct. 1866, p. 3; and Harold C. Evans, "Baseball in Kansas, 1867–1940," *Kansas Historical Quarterly* IX (May 1940), 176.

20. See Robert P. Brown et al., *Memories of Brown* (Providence, RI: Brown Alumni Magazine Co., 1909), 248.

21. Sanborn, "Base Ball," 274–80.

22. John A. Blanchard (ed.), *The H Book of Harvard Athletics, 1852–1922* (Cambridge, MA: Harvard Varsity Club, 1923), 297.

23. Ibid., 167–70, 297.

24. Ibid., 172–82; and Sanborn, "Base Ball," 302–19.

25. *New York Clipper,* 30 July 1870, p. 123.

26. Blanchard, *The H Book,* 178.

27. Sanborn, "Base Ball," 340.

28. Harvard Faculty Minutes, 22 May 1871 and 21 April 1873; and John W. White et al., "Athletic Report," 12 June 1888, HUD 8388.3B, Harvard Univ. Archives.

29. Yale Univ. Faculty Minutes, 8 Feb. 1871, 17 May 1871, 29 May 1872, and passim., Yale Univ. Archives; Princeton Faculty Minutes, 23 May 1872, and 1 June 1877, Princeton Univ. Archives; Dartmouth Faculty Records, 27 May 1872, 25 Sep. 1878, 28 Oct. 1878, 3 March 1879, and 29 April 1879, Dartmouth College Archives; and Rutgers Faculty Minutes, 28 May 1875, Rutgers Univ. Archives.

30. Blanchard, *The H Book,* 298; *Harvard Advocate,* 30 April 1875, p. 74; and *Yale Record,* 16 Sep. 1874, p. 21.

31. As quoted in Presbrey, *Athletics at Princeton,* 119.

32. *Harvard Advocate,* 23 May 1879, p. 89.

33. J. Lee Richmond, "Beating Harvard and Yale in Seventy-Nine," in

Robert P. Brown et al., (eds.), *Memories of Brown* (Providence, RI: Brown Alumni Magazine Co., 1909), 365.

34. F. C. Bancroft, telegrams to J. Lee Richmond, 27 May 1879, 28 May 1879, and 31 May 1879, "John Lee Richmond Files," Brown Univ. Archives; *Worcester Daily Spy*, 3 June 1879, p. 4; and David S. Neft et al., *The Sports Encyclopedia: Baseball* (New York: Grosset & Dunlap, 1974), 12.

35. *Harvard Advocate*, 6 June 1879, p. 97.

36. *Harvard Advocate*, 12 Dec. 1879, p. 79; and *Worcester Daily Spy*, 8 Dec. 1879, p. 4.

37. *Harvard Advocate*, 27 Feb. 1880, p. 1, and 12 March 1880, 27; and *New York Times*, 7 March 1880, p. 1.

38. *Worcester Daily Spy*, 29 June 1880, p. 4.

39. John H. Bartlett and John P. Gifford, *Dartmouth Athletics* (Concord, NH: Republican Press Association, 1893), 22.

40. Ibid., 28; Presbrey, *Athletics at Princeton*, 167; and Henry Chadwick, "Baseball in the Colleges," *Outing* XII (Aug. 1888), 407–10.

41. Harvard Athletic Committee Minutes, 28 Nov. 1889, Harvard Univ. Archives.

42. Notorized Document, Camp Papers, Box 2, Folder 46, and Box 20 Folder 564, Yale Univ. Archives.

43. *Boston Post*, 20 Dec. 1889, clipping in "1889 Football Controversy," HUD 10889.2, Harvard Univ. Archives.

44. Walter Camp, "The Two Problems of Amateur Athletics," *Outing* XIX (Dec. 1891), 199.

45. Orton, *Athletics at Pennsylvania*, 150.

46. Newspaper clipping, 19 Jan. 1898, Brown Univ. College Scrapbooks, 1897–1904, Brown Univ. Archives.

47. "Brown Conference Report on Intercollegiate Sports," HUD 8398.75, Harvard Univ. Archives.

48. Walter Camp's "Memorandum of Conversation on Day of Harvard-Penn Football Game, 1901," and T. S. Woolsey, letter to Walter Camp, 23 Dec. 1901, Camp Papers, Box 22, "Cutts Folder"; and H. W. Raymond, Yale Class of 1869, letter to Walter Camp, 12 June 1901, Camp Papers, Box 20, Folder 569, Yale Univ. Archives.

49. Philip R. Allen, East Walpole, MA, letters to Walter Camp, 30 April 1903, 14 May 1903, and 21 May 1903, Camp Papers, Box 1, Folder 17, Yale Univ. Archives.

50. The Yankees were then called the New York Highlanders.

51. H. S. White, Chairman of the Harvard Athletic Committee, letter to Dr. Nichols, members of the Athletic Committee and baseball coaching advisor, 11 June 1904, attached to the Harvard Athletic Committee Minutes, 13 June 1904, Harvard Univ. Archives.

52. Harvard Athletic Committee Minutes, 13 June 1904, Harvard Univ. Archives.

53. *Boston Post,* 25 Nov. 1889, in "1889 Football Controversy," HUD 10889.2, Harvard Univ. Archives.

54. Camp, "Two Problems of Amateur Athletics," 199.

55. *New York Daily Tribune,* 22 June 1908, p. 1.

Chapter VI.   From the Burial of Football to the Acceptance of Rugby

1. Thomas Wentworth Higginson, "The Gymnasium, and Gymnastics in Harvard College," in F. O. Vaille and H. A. Clark, *The Harvard Book* (Cambridge, MA: Welch, Bigelow, 1875), Vol. II, p. 187.

2. *John L. Sibley's Private Journal,* Vol. I, 3 Sep. 1855, p. 366, Harvard Univ. Archives.

3. A Sophomore and a Freshman, The Bawl of the Battle," (1853), Yed 5/F7/853b Folio, Yale Univ. Archives.

4. "Harvard University," *University Quarterly* II (Oct. 1860), 357. For two years, the *Harvard Magazine,* representing the reform element of Harvard students, campaigned to eliminate Bloody Monday as being "unfair, brutal, drunken" and "cowardly." As quoted in John A. Blanchard (ed.), *The H Book of Harvard Athletics* (Cambridge, MA: Harvard Varsity Club, 1923), 326. The term "Bloody Monday" probably began after 1860, when students still continued to have an annual fight or rush at Harvard, and it existed until 1917 and the entry of the U.S. into World War I. See Blanchard, 350.

5. *Sibley's Private Journal,* Vol. I, 3 Sep. 1860, pp. 536–40, and *New York Clipper,* 4 Sep. 1860, p. 172. Mock burials were not uncommon in colleges. The most common was probably the annual burial of Euclid's geometry. This ceremony at Yale included driving a red-hot poker through the volume, placing it in a bier, proceeding with drums, flutes, and fifes, and either burying the hated text or placing it on a funeral pyre. See *A Collection of College Words and Customs* (Cambridge, MA: J. Bartlett, 1851), 27, and Yale Faculty Minutes, 29 Nov. 1848, 31 Oct. 1849, and 20 Nov. 1849, Yale Univ. Archives.

6. "History, Army-Navy Football," R.G.–Superintendent, S.G.–Athlethics, Box No. 1, Folder No. 1, U.S. Naval Academy Archives.

7. *University Quarterly* III (Jan. 1861), 176.

8. Ibid., 216–17.

9. *Rutgers Targum,* Jan. 1869, p. 8.

10. Rutgers Faculty Minutes, 22 Feb. 1870 and 21 May 1872, Rutgers Univ. Archives; and *Rutgers Targum,* Dec. 1869, pp. 3–4, Dec. 1870, p. 1, May 1871, p. 7, Oct. 1871, p. 2, and Nov. 1871, p. 2.

11. Parke H. Davis, *Football the American Intercollegiate Game* (New York: Charles Scribner's Sons, 1911), 43.

12. B. W. Crowninshield, "Boating," in F. O. Vaille and H. A. Clark, (eds.), *The Harvard Book* (Cambridge, MA: Welch, Bigelow, 1875), Vol. II, p. 253. While Harvard eventually chose crimson and earlier magenta, Rutgers thought scarlet or cherry would be similar yet different from Harvard colors. See *Rutgers Targum*, May 1869, p. 5. A Princeton student suggested the color orange after studying William of Orange, Prince of Nassau in 1866. Princeton's faculty gave permission to its students to wear orange-colored ribbons in 1868. See Frank Presbrey and James Moffatt, *Athletics at Princeton* (New York: Frank Presbrey, 1901), 25, and Princeton Faculty Minutes, 12 Oct. 1868, Princeton Univ. Archives. Much earlier, Oxford had chosen Oxford blue in 1829 while Cambridge used Eton's blue color as its own in 1836. See *British Sports and Sportsmen: Athletic Sports, Tennis, Rackets, and Other Ball Games* (London: Sports and Sportsmen, 1931), 28.

13. *Rutgers Targum*, Nov. 1869, p. 5.

14. Larry Pitt, *Football at Rutgers: A History, 1869–1969* (New Brunswick, NJ: Rutgers Univ., 1972), 12.

15. *Rutgers Targum*, Nov. 1869, p. 5.

16. As quoted from the *New Brunswick Fredonian*, 8 Nov. 1869, in the *Milwaukee Journal*, 30 Nov. 1918, p. 10.

17. See Edward Hitchcock's average measurements for Amherst students from 1861–81 in Edward Hartwell, "Physical Training in American Colleges," *U.S. Bureau of Education, Circulars of Information, 1885–1886* (Washington, D.C.: U.S. G.P.O., 1886), 560.

18. *Rutgers Targum*, Nov. 1869, p. 5.

19. For a more complete account of the game see Davis, *Football*, 44–50, and Pitt, *Football at Rutgers*, 3–23.

20. Rutgers Faculty Minutes, 5 Nov. 1869, Rutgers Univ. Archives.

21. Ibid., 12 Nov. 1869.

22. Ibid., 21 Dec. 1869.

23. Davis, *Football*, 50.

24. Pitt, *Football at Rutgers*, 24–25, and Davis, *Football* 50. A. M. Weyand, *Football, Its History and Development* (New York: D. Appleton, 1926), 2, suggest that the two faculties banned the contest. This may be so, but the lengthy minutes of the Rutgers and Princeton faculties show no evidence of any discussion of football in that period.

25. Thomas J. Wertenbaker, *Princeton: 1746–1896* (Princeton, NJ: Princeton Univ. Press, 1946), 326.

26. *Rutgers Targum*, Nov. 1869, p. 5.

27. Richard P. McCormick, *Rutgers: A Bicentennial History* (New Brunswick, NJ: Rutgers Univ. Press, 1966), 13.

28. *Rutgers Targum*, Nov. 1870, p. 7.

29. Pitt, *Football at Rutgers*, 25, and *Rutgers Targum*, November 1870, p. 8.

30. Horace M. Lippincott, "Early Football," *General Magazine and Historical Chronicle* XXXIX (1937), 150, and Davis, *Football*, 51.

31. Parke H. Davis, "The Beginning of Football at Harvard," *Harvard Alumni Bulletin* XVIII (15 Dec. 1915), 216.

32. Davis, *Football*, 54. Most histories state that Schaff attended Rugby School in England, but this is apparently not true. See Albert B. Crawford (ed.), *Football Y Men, 1872–1919* (New Haven, CT: Yale Univ. Press, 1962), 28, and Richard P. Borkowski, "The Life and Contributions of Walter Camp to American Football," Ed.D. dissertation, Temple Univ., 1979, p. 19.

33. Blanchard, *The H Book*, 348.

34. Ibid.

35. See Davis, *Football*, 51–56, for the written Princeton and Yale rules and a discussion of rule differences. The codified Harvard rules can be found in Blanchard, *The H Book*, 609.

36. Cornell Faculty Minutes, 24 Oct. 1873, Cornell Univ. Archives, and *Cornell Review* I (Dec. 1873), 201.

37. Howard W. Peckham, *The Making of the University of Michigan, 1817–1967* (Ann Arbor: Univ. of Michigan Press, 1967), 77; Kent Sagendorph, *Michigan, The Story of the University* (New York: E. P. Dutton, 1948), 150, and *The Cornell Era*, 31 Oct. 1873, p. 60.

38. *Yale Record*, 15 Oct. 1873, p. 69. The letter is printed in full in the *Rutgers Targum*, Oct. 1873, p. 5. See also Richard M. Hurd, *A History of Yale Athletics, 1840–1888* (New Haven, CT: privately printed, 1888), 57, and Davis, *Football*, 59–61.

39. *Harvard Advocate*, 17 Oct. 1873, p. 41, and 31 Oct. 1873, p. 53; and Davis, "The Beginning of Football at Harvard," 219.

40. *Harvard Advocate*, 3 April 1874, p. 58.

41. *Yale Record*, 27 May 1874, p. 419.

42. *Harvard Advocate*, 15 May 1874, p. 103.

43. Blanchard, *The H Book*, 360–63. A pre-game photo is found on p. 315.

44. *Harvard Advocate*, 29 May 1874, p. 113.

45. Blanchard, *The H Book*, 359–64.

46. *Harvard Advocate*, 30 Oct. 1874, pp. 35–36. and *Harvard Magenta*, 20 Nov. 1874, pp, 53–54.

47. *Harvard Advocate*, 14 May 1875, p. 80.

48. Ibid. Davis, *Football*, 67–68, is incorrect stating that the first rugby uniforms were worn by Princeton and Pennsylvania at Germantown on 11 Nov. 1876.

49. as quoted in the *Harvard Advocate*, 5 Nov. 1875, p. 53.

50. Presbrey, *Athletics at Princeton*, 278.

51. As quoted in Davis, *Football*, 66.

52. Jotham Potter and W. Earle Dodge, Princeton Football Association, letter to the Football Associations of Harvard, Yale, and Columbia, 7 Nov. 1876, in Davis, *Football*, 67.

53. *Yale Record*, 10 Dec. 1873, p. 168, and 17 Dec. 1873, p. 184.

54. Davis, *Football*, 69–70.

55. Original Constitution of the Intercollegiate Football Association, Walter Camp Papers, Box 1, Folder 23, Yale Univ. Archives.

56. *New York Herald*, 25 Nov. 1887, p. 6.

57. Davis, *Football*, 361–62.

58. Ibid., 361–74.

59. *New York Herald*, 28 Nov. 1879, p. 9.

60. Ibid., 25 Nov. 1881, p. 9. The first head gear may have been worn by a Naval Academy player in the 1893 Army-Navy game. An Annapolis women fashioned a moleskin head gear for Cadet J. M. Reeves. See "History of Army-Navy Football," R.G.-Superintendent, S.G.-Athletics, Box No. 1, Folder No. 1, U.S. Naval Academy Archives.

61. Ibid., 26 Nov. 1881, p. 9. See also Presbrey, *Athletics at Princeton*, 304–5; and Hurd, *A History of Yale Athletics, 1840–1888*, pp. 63–64.

62. Davis, *Football*, 80.

63. *New York Herald*, 22 Nov. 1885, p. 7.

64. Ibid., 25 Nov. 1887, p. 6. For a fine account of the 1893 event, see Richard Harding Davis, "The Thanksgiving-Day Game," *Harper's Weekly* XXXVII (9 Dec. 1893), 1170–71.

65. Ibid.

66. *The Cornell Review* III (Jan. 1876), 177.

67. *New York Herald*, 25 Nov. 1892, p. 3.

68. Thorstein Veblen, *The Theory of the Leisure Class* (New York: Modern Library, 1934, originally 1899), passim.

69. *New York Herald*, 30 Nov. 1893, p. 6.

70. Ibid., 28 Nov. 1890, p. 4, and Jonas Viles, *The University of Missouri* (Columbia: Univ. of Missouri Press, 1939), 242.

71. Ethelbert D. Warfield, "Are Foot-Ball Games Educative or Brutalizing?" *Forum* XX (Jan. 1894), 653.

72. Robert W. Emmons, "Needed Football Reforms," *Harvard Graduates' Magazine* III (March 1885), 319.

73. Amos Alonzo Stagg and Wesley W. Stout, *Touchdown!* (New York: Longmans, Green, 1927), 190, 204. Stagg's Springfield YMCA Training School football team played in the first indoor game in 1891 at the Madison Square Garden against a pick-up team which included a number of Yale players. Ibid., 136.

74. *Chicago Tribune*, 29 Nov. 1895, p. 13. A Stanford man, writing about the Stanford-California Thanksgiving Day game of 1894, said that "nobody eats a Thanksgiving dinner anymore. . . . Thanksgiving has lost

every vestige of its original character so far as this community goes." W. R. Dudley, letter to Prof. Burt Wilder, Cornell University, 20 Feb. 1895, Burt G. Wilder Papers, 14/25/95, Box 1, Cornell Univ. Archives.

75. The "Big 10" banned Thanksgiving Day games after the 1905 season as part of a larger reform movement. See Stagg, *Touchdown!*, 255.

Chapter VII.   The Americanization of Rugby Football: Mass Plays, Brutality, and Masculinity

1. Hartford Powell, Jr., *Walter Camp* (Boston: Little, Brown, 1926), 21. For an interesting account of Camp's contributions, see John S. Martin, "Walter Camp and His Gridiron Game," *American Heritage* XII (Oct. 1961), 50–55, 77–81.

2. Powell, *Walter Camp*, 128. Powell notes that Camp resigned from all official connection with Yale athletics in 1910. Others say it was 1914. Yet, in 1916, he was asked to help coach Yale's football team which for the first time was beginning to lose to Harvard and its great coach Percy Houghton. See George T. Adee, New York broker, letter to Walter Camp, 7 Feb. 1916, Box 1, Folder 10, Camp Papers, Yale Univ. Archives (hereafter noted as YUA).

3. Robert O. Anthony, "Biography," in his *Guide to the Walter Camp Papers* (New Haven, CT: Yale Univ. Archives, 1982), 4.

4. L. H. Baker, *Football: Facts and Figures* (New York: Farrar & Rinehart, 1945), 272. Thomas G. Bergin, *The Game: The Harvard-Yale Football Rivalry, 1875–1983* (New Haven, CT: Yale Univ. Press, 1984), 39, notes the dates as 1889–92. Richard P. Borkowski, "The Life and Contributions of Walter Camp to American Football," Ed.D. dissertation, Temple Univ., 1979, pp. 81–82, shows in arbitrary graph form the years in which Camp coached extensively at practices, had limited attendance at practice but coached as an advisor, or had no connection with the team. He states that Camp had no connection only in the years, 1895–96, 1898, 1906, 1911–15, and 1920–24.

5. William H. Corbin, letter to Walter Camp, 24 Nov. 1902, Box 7, Folder 204, Camp Papers, YUA.

6. Ibid.

7. Powell, *Camp*, 88.

8. W. W. Heffelfinger, Minneapolis, letter to Walter Camp, 30 Nov. 1912, Box 13, Folder 348, Camp Papers, YUA.

9. George A. Adee, New York City, letter to Camp, 7 Nov. 1889, Box 1, Folder 3, Camp Papers, YUA.

10. As quoted in Powell, *Camp*, 89. See also "Dean Briggs Goes to Radcliffe," *The Harvard Bulletin* V (17 June 1903), 1.

11. James H. Kivlan, letter to Walter Camp, 20 Sep. 1892, Camp Papers, Box 19, Folder 512, YUA.

12. Lewis B. Welch and Walter Camp, *YALE: Her Campus, Classrooms, and Athletics* (Boston: L. C. Page, 1899), 454, 457, and Anthony, *Guide to the Walter Camp Papers*, 4.

13. Walter C. Camp, *Walter Camp's Book of Foot-Ball* (New York: Century, 1910), 32.

14. Convention of 12 Oct. 1880, as quoted in Davis, *Football*, 468.

15. Frank B. Copley, *Frederick W. Taylor, Father of Scientific Management* (New York: Harper and Brothers, 1923), Vol. I, pp. 116, 223–36. David Riesman and Reuel Denney, "Football in America: A Study in Cultural Diffusion," *American Quarterly* III (1951), 309–25, argue that American football fit well into American industrial society with its recurrent stopping of action, division of labor between backfield and line, and precise synchronization of men.

16. Camp, *Walter Camp's Book*, 69–71, and Davis, *Football*, 81.

17. Walter Camp, "Football in 1893," *Harper's Weekly* XXXVIII (2 Feb. 1894), 118.

18. Davis, *Football*, 73.

19. Ibid., 84.

20. Camp, *Walter Camp's Book*, 130.

21. *Rutgers Targum*, April 1871, p. 3.

22. Ibid., Nov. 1873, p. 1.

23. *Harvard Advocate*, 16 Nov. 1877, p. 58.

24. Ibid., 14 Nov. 1879, p. 56, and *Spirit of the Times*, 15 Nov. 1879, p. 365.

25. *University Magazine*, 20 Oct. 1882, as quoted in George W. Orton, *A History of Athletics at Pennsylvania* (Philadelphia: privately printed, ca. 1896), 107.

26. Harvard Athletic Committee Minutes, 22 Nov. 1883, HUA, and A Yale Player, "The Development of Football," *Outing* XV (Nov. 1889), 14.

27. Richard M. Hurd, *A History of Yale Athletics: 1840–1880* (New Haven, CT: privately printed, 1888), 66.

28. Univ. of Pennsylvania Board of Trustees Minutes, 3 Dec. 1883, 2 Dec. 1884, and 3 Nov. 1885, Univ. of Pennsylvania Archives.

29. Harvard Athletic Committee Minutes, 25 Nov. 1884, HUA. A dramatic newspaper account of the brutal Princeton-Yale Thanksgiving Day game of 1884 can be found in Frank Presbrey and James Moffatt, *Athletics at Princeton* (New York: Frank Presbrey, 1901), 317.

30. Harvard Athletic Committee Minutes, 4 Jan. 1886, HUA.

31. Alexander Johnson, "The American Game of Football," *Century Magazine* XXXIV (May 1887), 894.

32. Dudley A. Sargent, letter to Mr. Savage, ca. April 1887, in the Harvard Athletic Committee Minutes, 26 April 1887, HUA.

33. Luther E. Price, Princeton graduate of 1888, letter to Walter Camp, 2 March 1894, Camp Papers, Box 20, Folder 563, YUA.

34. Davis, *Football*, 476.

35. Baker, *Football: Facts and Figures*, 563. The famous Princeton Wedge was created in 1884. The players formed a stationary "V" or wedge with a runner inside the "V." It, like the flying wedge, was used only on a kick-off or after a fair catch, but it lacked the momentum of the flying wedge. See Presbrey, *Athletics at Princeton*, 314.

36. Theodore S. Woolsey, York Harbor, ME, letter to Walter Camp, 17 July [1892], Camp Papers, Theodore S. Woolsey Folder, YUA.

37. *New York Herald*, 20 Nov. 1892, p. 15, and *Boston Herald*, 20 Nov. 1892, clipping in Harvard Intercollegiate Sport Scraps, Begun 1892, HUD 8392.2F, HUA.

38. *Report of the President of Harvard College, 1893–1894*, p. 16, HUA.

39. Richard Harding Davis, "A Day with the Yale Team," *Harper's Weekly*, XXXVII (18 Nov. 1893), 1110. Remington was later the famous illustrator, painter, and sculptor of the American West.

40. Harvard Record of Overseers, 29 Nov. 1893, HUA.

41. Anthony, *Guide to the Walter Camp Papers*, 5–6, 18. The committee included Rev. Joseph Twichell (Yale Corporation), Rev. Endicott Peabody (Groton School), James W. Alexander (Equitable Life), Hon. Henry E. Howland, (New York City), and Bacon and Camp. Dr. Pepper of the University of Pennsylvania declined.

42. Manuscript form of conclusions, Brutality Committee Report of 1894, Camp Papers, Microfilm Reel 27, p. 1, YUA, and Walter C. Camp, Compiler, *Football Facts and Figures* (New York: Harper and Brothers, 1894), 233.

43. Compare Camp, *Football Facts and Figures* with letters in the Camp collection.

44. William H. Corbin, Headmaster of Pingry School, Elizabeth, NJ, letter to Walter Camp, 2 Feb. 1894, Camp Papers, Box 7, Folder 204, YUA, and Camp, *Football Facts and Figures*, 148.

45. Frederick L. Eldridge, New York City and Harvard Class of 1882, letter to Walter Camp, 26 March 1894, Camp Papers, Box 10, Folder 266, YUA. See Camp, *Football Facts and Figures*, 184–86.

46. Manuscript form, Brutality Committee Report of 1894, Camp Papers, Microfilm Reel 29, p. 2, YUA.

47. Walter Heffelfinger, letter to Walter Camp, 5 March 1894, Camp Papers, Box 13, Folder 348, YUA, and Camp, *Football Facts and Figures*, 209–10.

48. John S. White, Headmaster, Berkeley School, New York City, letter to Walter Camp, 13 March 1894, Camp Papers (uncatalogued in 1982), YUA, and William E. Peck, headmaster, St. Mark's School, Southborough, MA, letter to Walter Camp, 9 March 1894, Camp Papers, Box 20, Folder 541, YUA, and Camp, *Football Facts and Figures*, 76, 98.

49. William T. Reid, headmaster, Belmont School, California, letter to Walter Camp, 28 March 1894, Camp Papers, Box 20, Folder 572, YUA. Reid's letter was completely left out by Camp in the published report.

50. William M. Sloane, letter to Walter Camp, 12 May 1894, Camp Papers, Box 22, Folder 633, YUA, and Camp, *Football Facts and Figures*, 119.

51. "Sanitary Report of Naval Academy, January 1894," as found in "History, Army-Navy Football," RG—Superintendent, SG—Athletics, Box 1, U.S. Naval Academy Archives. The Army-Navy game was resumed in 1899.

52. Henry W. Rogers, President of Northwestern, letter to Charles W. Eliot, 5 Dec. 1894, Eliot Papers, Box 135, Folder 1048, HUA; Harvard Record of Overseers, 6 Dec. 1893, 20 June 1894, and 10 Jan. 1895, HUA; and Davis, *Football*, 99. The 1894 Harvard team had eight major injuries out of its first 11 players during the season, including a broken leg, a broken collar bone, a dislocated elbow, a wrenched neck, an injured jaw, and two ankle injuries. See "Athletics," *Harvard Graduates' Magazine* III (Dec. 1894), 249–53.

53. Davis, *Football*, 95.

54. Ibid., 98–99, 486–87. Paul J. Dashiell, a prominent football official teaching at the Naval Academy, was invited to sit on the committee.

55. Albert B. Hart, "Harvard's Athletic Policy," *Harvard Graduates' Magazine* IV (Dec. 1895), 209–14; Bergin, *The Game*, 57–58; and Blanchard, *The H Book*, pp. 403–4.

56. M. H. Morgan, Acting Secretary of the Harvard Faculty, letter to the Athletic Committee, 20 Feb. 1895, and 20 March 1895, in Harvard Athletic Committee Minutes, HUA. Earlier, the Harvard Board of Overseers had voted to discontinue football at Harvard. See Records of Overseers, 10 Jan. 1895, HUA. The Harvard Athletic Committee challenged the faculty's action. See James B. Ames, Chairman of Athletic Committee, letter to the Faculty of Arts and Sciences, 25 Feb. 1895, Harvard Athletic Committee Minutes, 25 Feb. 1895, HUA.

57. Amos Alonzo Stagg, letter to Walter Camp, 11 Jan. 1896, Camp Papers, Box 23, Folder 651, YUA.

58. The "Big Ten" was organized on 11 Jan. 1895 as the Western Intercollegiate Conference of Faculty Representatives. They called immediately for football rule reform to minimize injury. See Carl D. Voltmer, *A Brief History of the Intercollegiate Conference of Faculty Representa-*

tives with Special Consideration of Athletic Problems (Menasha, WI: George Banta, 1935), 5–8, and Howard Roberts, *The Big Nine* (New York: G. P. Putnam's Sons, 1948), 14–16. See also Davis, *Football*, 101.

59. Theodore Roosevelt, "The Law of Civilization and Decay," *American Ideals* (New York: G. P. Putnam's Sons, 1897), 371. For a study of manliness in the progressive era, see Gerald F. Roberts, "The Strenuous Life, the Cult of Manliness in the Era of Theodore Roosevelt," Ph.D. dissertation, Michigan State Univ., 1970.

60. Theodore Roosevelt, "The American Boy," *The Strenuous Life: Essays and Addresses* (New York: Century Co., 1902), 155–56.

61. Theodore Roosevelt, Civil Rights Commission, Washington, D.C., letter to Walter Camp, 11 March 1895, Camp Papers, Box 22, "1895–1906" Folder, YUA. See also his "Values of an Athletic Training," *Harper's Weekly* XXXVII (23 Dec. 1893), 1236, for need of virile activities.

62. See Peter N. Stearns, *Be a Man! Males in Modern Society* (New York: Holmes & Meier, 1979), 96–112. Stearns notes that the loss of individuality both in the workplace and of ownership of producing property, the rise of feminism, and the decline of patriarchal authority in the home—all signs of the validity of manhood—were instrumental in the attempt by men to define themselves in other ways including participation in the male domain of sports. Concern for effeminacy resulting from increased wealth in industrial America was voiced as early as 1819 by John Adams in a letter to Thomas Jefferson. See Daniel T. Rodgers, *The Work Ethic in Industrial America* (Chicago: Univ. of Chicago Press, 1978), 102.

63. "Senator Lodge's Speech," *Harvard Graduates' Magazine* V (Sep. 1896), 67.

64. Charles F. Thwing, "Foot-ball: A Game of Hearts," *Independent* X (3 Nov. 1898), 1260–61.

65. "Newspaper Clipping," 18 Nov. 1898, Bound Univ. College Scrapbook, 1897–1904, Brown Univ. Archives.

66. Speech by White, as quoted in Agnes Repplier, *J. William White, M.D.* (Boston: Houghton-Mifflin, 1919), 78–79.

67. John E. Richards, M.D., letter to Walter Camp, ca. early 1894, Camp Papers, Reel 28, p. 14, YUA.

68. John A. Garraty, *The New Commonwealth, 1877–1890* (New York: Harper & Row, 1968), 26; Lawrence R. Veysey, *The Emergence of the Modern University* (Chicago: Univ. of Chicago Press, 1965), 278; and Frederick Rudolph, *The American College and University* (New York: Vintage Books, 1962), 317. At the same time colleges were thought to lack virility, the rise of women teachers in the schools was raising major questions about the teaching of boys by women. Among those concerned were two leaders of progressive education around 1900 who believed that the schooling of boys by women might devirilize the male segment

of society. See Charles De Garmo (annotations), in John Frederich Herbart, *Outlines of Educational Doctrine* (New York: Macmillan, 1901), 188–89, and G. Stanley Hall, "Student Customs," *American Antiquarian Society Proceedings,* New Series, XIV (1900–1901), 91–92.

69. Roosevelt, *The Strenuous Life,* 20, 164.

70. *Report of the President of Harvard College, 1887–1888,* p. 10; *1892–1893,* pp. 14–15; *1901–1902,* p. 4; *1904–1905,* p. 46, HUA. Yale professor E. L. Richards, believed that with sports as vigorous as football, "We shall see the death of that effeminacy which is so rapidly undermining the American nation." See his "Intercollegiate Football," *New Englander* XLV (Dec. 1886), 1050.

71. As quoted in Guy M. Lewis, "The American Intercollegiate Football Spectacle, 1869–1917," Ph.D. dissertation, Univ. of Maryland, 1964, p. 84. For manliness also see Francis L. Patton, *Religion in College* (Princeton, NJ: Princeton Press, 1889), 6.

72. "Newspaper Clipping, 1896," Camp Papers, Box 22, "1896–1905" Folder, YUA, and Richard J. Storr, *Harper's University: The Beginnings* (Chicago: Univ. of Chicago Press, 1966), 179.

73. As quoted in Casper Whitney (ed.), "Is Football Worthwhile?" *Collier's* XLV (18 Dec. 1909), 25.

74. Edwin E. Slosson, *Great American Universities* (New York: Macmillan, 1910), 309, 503–5. For other presidents and college officials on the value of football and manliness, see: Calvin M. Woodward (compiler), *Opinions of Educators of the Value and Total Influences of Inter-Collegiate and Inter-Scholastic American Football as Played in 1903–1909* (n.p.: privately printed, 1910); Charles F. Thwing, "Football: Is the Game Worth Saving," *Independent* LIV (15 May 1902), 1167–74; and James B. Angell, "Are Foot-Ball Games Educative or Brutalizing," *Forum* XVI (Jan. 1894), 647–54. For a detailed account of athletics and virility in a group of midwest teacher preparatory institutions see: Ronald A. Smith, "From Normal School to State University: A History of the Wisconsin State University Conference," Ph.D. dissertation, Univ. of Wisconsin, Madison, 1969), 100–110.

75. Frank R. Peters, Butte, Montana, letter to Walter Camp, 29 March 1894, Camp Papers, Box 20, Folder 545, YUA. Emphasis added.

76. Possibly the most outspoken opponent of the business control of universities was Thorstein Veblen who wrote his treatise, *The Higher Learning in America* (New York: Viking, 1935 (1918)), in the first decade of the twentieth century. See particularly pp. 63–64, 81, 84.

77. For example, the Cornell trustees in 1890 passed a resolution supporting Cornell athletics for contributing to "the rapid, vigorous and healthy growth of Cornell University." They noted that athletics have "forcibly illustrated the beneficial influence of wisely directed athletic sports in the advantageous development of educational organization."

Cornell University Board of Trustees Proceedings, 22 Oct. 1890, Cornell Univ. Archives.

78. "The Future of Football," *Nation* LI (20 Nov. 1890), 395.

Chapter VIII.   College Track: From the Paper Chase to Olympic Gold

1. Shearman Montague, *Athletics and Football* (London: Longmans, Green, 1894), 47, and Samuel Crowther and Arthur Ruhl, *Rowing and Athletics* (New York: Macmillan, 1905), 347.

2. Thomas Hughes, *Tom Brown's Schooldays* (New York: E. M. Lupton, undated (1857)), 115.

3. "Eton Athletics," *Fifty Years of Sport: Eton, Harrow, and Winchester* (London, Walter Southwood, 1922), 97–99.

4. Percy Manning, "Sports and Pastimes in Oxford and Neighborhood Down to about 1850," Vol. II, p. 226, Ms. Top. Oxon. d. 202, Oxford Univ. Library, and Shearman, *Athletics and Football*, 41–43. For information on paper chasing at Oxford in the 1870s, see "Oxford University Hare and Hounds Club," GA Oxon b. 174, Oxford University Library. At one time there were 132 members of the Oxford Club running at least once each week.

5. W. Beach Thomas, *Athletics* (London: Ward, Lock, 1901), 99. Other events were the 100 yard (not recorded), half mile (2:24), long jump (19'6"), 250 yard hurdles—12 flights (36 seconds), and a sack race.

6. A. C. M. Croome (ed), *Fifty Years of Sport: Oxford and Cambridge* (London: Walter Southwood, 1913), Vol. I, p. 5.

7. Thomas, *Athletics*, 20, and Shearman, *Athletics and Football*, 49.

8. Rev. Henry A. Morgan, Fellow of Jesus College, Cambridge, letter to John E. Morgan, Feb. 1873, in John E. Morgan, *University Oars* (London: Macmillan, 1873), 338–41.

9. See "Amherst College" *University Quarterly* II (July 1860), 148; John Sweet, "A Plea for Amusements and Physical Culture," *The Bookseller* I (Sep.–Nov. 1860), 132; and Guy Lewis, "The Beginning of Organized Collegiate Sport," *American Quarterly* XXII (Summer 1970), 226. William Blaikie, an athlete and Harvard graduate of 1866, believed that the influence on American college sport by Thomas Hughes and *Tom Brown's Schooldays*, was "greater, perhaps, than that of any other Englishman." See William Blaikie, "American Bodies," *Harper's Weekly* XXVII (Dec. 1883), 770.

10. "Andover Theological Seminary," *University Quarterly* II (Oct. 1860), 334.

11. Lyman Bagg, *Four Years at Yale* (New York: Henry Holt, 1871), 534.

12. *Harvard Advocate,* 24 Nov. 1876, p. 56.

13. Ibid., 12 Dec. 1879, p. 83, and *New York Times,* 14 Dec. 1879, p. 7. See *Harvard Advocate,* 16 Jan. 1880, p. 107, for Harvard's rules for hare and hounds racing, and *Spirit of the Times,* 22 Nov. 1879, p. 384 for general rules of hare and hounds racing. It is possible that Teddy Roosevelt took part in 1879 for he was a friend of Bacon and in his senior year. Later Bacon became Roosevelt's presidential secretary in the early 1900s. See also David McCullough, *Mornings on Horseback* (New York: Simon and Schuster, 1981), 204.

14. *The* [Brown University] *Brunonian,* 14 Dec. 1878, p. 60; *Spirit of the Times,* 20 March 1880, p. 153; and E. H. Baynes, "The History of Cross Country Running in America," *Outing* XXIII (March 1893), 485.

15. Frank Presbrey and James Moffatt, *Athletics at Princeton* (New York: Frank Presbrey, 1901), 575.

16. Crowther and Ruhl, *Rowing and Track Athletics,* 348, and John A. Krout, *Annals of American Sport* (New Haven, CT: Yale Univ. Press, 1929), 189.

17. Crowther and Ruhl, *Rowing and Track Athletics,* 351, and Jack A. Weiershauser, "The History and Development of Track and Field Athletics in the United States," M.A. thesis, Stanford Univ., 1941, p. 14.

18. Horace M. Lippincott, *Early Philadelphia* (Philadelphia: J. B. Lippincott, 1917), 156.

19. Presbrey, *Athletics at Princeton,* 22.

20. Gerald Redmond, *The Caledonian Games in Nineteenth Century America* (Rutherford, NJ: Fairleigh Dickinson Univ. Press, 1971), 53–57.

21. Fred E. Leonard and George B. Affleck, *A Guide to the History of Physical Education* (Philadelphia: Lea & Febiger, 1947), 282; Redmond, *The Caledonian Games,* 52–55 and 76–77; Robert Korsgaard, "A History of the Amateur Athletic Union of the United States," D.Ed. dissertation, Teachers College, Columbia Univ., 1952, pp. 32–33, and Melvin L. Adelman, *A Sporting Time: New York City and the Rise of Modern Athletics, 1820–1870* (Urbana: Univ. of Illinois Press, 1986), 218. The formation of the New York Athletic Club in 1866 and the holding of its first meet against the New York Caledonians in 1868 was a strong influence in promoting track and field and possibly influenced Yale students to organize track.

22. Bagg, *Four Years at Yale,* 532–33.

23. John A. Lucas and Ronald A. Smith, *Saga of American Sport* (Philadelphia: Lea & Febiger, 1978), 162–67.

24. *Western Sporting Gazette,* 17 July 1873, p. 91. Caspar Whitney also noted the $500 cup in his *A Sporting Pilgrimage* (New York: Harper & Brothers, 1895), 231.

25. Redmond, *The Caledonian Games,* 81–82.

26. *The Cornell Era,* 12 Sep. 1873, p. 2, and 31 Oct. 1873, p. 59.

27. *Western Sporting Gazette*, 26 July 1873, p. 122, and "The Challenge Cup," *New York Herald*, 18 July 1873, p. 6, in "Records of '73 Boat Club," Wesleyan Univ. Archives.

28. "The College Regatta," *New York Tribune*, 18 July 1873, pp. 1, 5, in "Records of '73 Boat Club," Wesleyan Univ. Archives, and *Western Sporting Gazette*, 26 July 1873, p. 122.

29. *New York Herald*, 21 July 1874, p. 3.

30. *Harvard Advocate*, 1 Oct. 1874, p. 11; *Yale Record*, 12 Sep. 1874, p. 3; and Walter Camp, "Track-Athletics," *Century Magazine* LVIII (June 1910), 271.

31. Lewis, "The Beginning of Organized College Sport," 228, notes that only Columbia and Yale had track associations, but Cornell formed one in the spring of 1873 and Princeton held its Caledonian Games the same spring. See G. H. Lohmes, "Athletics at Cornell," *Outing* XV (March 1890), p. 458, and Presbrey, *Athletics at Princeton*, 404.

32. George W. Orton, *A History of Athletics at Pennsylvania, 1873–1896* (Philadelphia: privately printed, ca. 1896), 17; Redmond, *The Caledonian Games*, 83–85; *Rutgers Targum*, Oct. 1874, p. 5; *Harvard Advocate*, 19 Feb. 1875, p. 4; and J. Mott Hallowell, "American College Athletics: Harvard University," *Outing* XIII (Dec. 1888), 234–35.

33. As quoted in Crowther and Ruhl, *Rowing and Track Athletics*, 269.

34. Hollowell, "American College Athletics," 234.

35. Presbrey, *Athletics at Princeton*, 404.

36. See David F. Allmendinger, *Paupers and Scholars* (New York: St. Martin's Press, 1975), 88, for figures on room servant costs at Yale.

37. *Spirit of the Times*, 5 Dec. 1874, p. 403, and 12 Dec. 1874, p. 434.

38. *The Dartmouth*, 23 Sep. 1875, p. 43, 30 Sep. 1875, p. 57, and 19 Oct. 1876, p. 76, and Dartmouth Faculty Records, 18 Sep. 1876, 14 May 1877, 24 Sep. 1877, and 27 April 1878, Dartmouth College Archives. The day and a half athletic vacation became a tradition at Dartmouth. Amherst College also found Taylor running for money shortly after the Dartmouth incident. See *The Dartmouth*, 9 Nov. 1876, p. 118.

39. *New York Times*, 9 July 1875, p. 1.

40. *Harvard Advocate*, 1 Oct. 1875, p. 5.

41. John A. Blanchard (ed.), *The H Book of Harvard Athletics, 1852–1922* (Cambridge, MA: Harvard Varsity Club, 1923), 464.

42. The IC4A claims that it was founded in 1876, but it is clear that it met first in 1875 at the Springfield Massasoit House. See for instance, *New York Clipper*, 11 Dec. 1975, p. 91; *New York Tribune*, 6 Dec. 1875, p. 1; *New York Times*, 5 Dec. 1875, p. 6; *The [Wesleyan] College Argus*, 18 Dec. 1875, p. 71; and newspaper clipping, ca. 1876, in "Charles W. Wason Crew Scrapbook, 1876," 40/1/199, Cornell Univ. Archives. The 10 colleges included Amherst, Columbia, Cornell, Harvard, Princeton, Trinity, Union, Wesleyan, Williams, and Yale.

43. *New York Clipper,* 15 Jan. 1876, p. 331.

44. *Harvard Advocate,* 10 Jan. 1876, p. 93; *The Dartmouth,* 13 Jan. 1876, p. 281; and the *New York Times,* 17 July 1876, p. 1.

45. *Harvard Advocate,* 10 Jan. 1876, p. 93.

46. *The Dartmouth,* 13 Jan. 1876, p. 281.

47. *New York Clipper,* 15 Jan. 1876, p. 331, and *New York Times,* 6 Jan. 1876, p. 5. It may be significant that Amherst, one of the more egalitarian colleges in the nineteenth century, favored equal prizes. The motion for equal value prizes was introduced by Amherst's G. W. Cloak.

48. *Harvard Advocate,* 9 June 1876, p. 99.

49. *New York Clipper,* 29 July 1876, p. 138; *Spirit of the Times,* 29 July 1876, p. 657; and "The Intercollegiate Games," *Outing* XXVII (Nov. 1895), 159.

50. *The Dartmouth,* 14 Sep. 1876, p. 15.

51. The IC4A history is chronicled by John A. Lucas, "The IC4A Championships—A 100 Year History," IC4A Centennial Track Meet Official Program, 1976, pp. 7–9, 46–49. See also the *IC4A Record Book, 1876–1976* (Centerville, MA: privately printed, 1976), 87.

52. *IC4A Record Book, 1876–1976,* p. 85. Not until 1921 did a non-Ivy League college win a championship, when the University of California did so.

53. Sherrill, beginning in 1887, was a four-time IC4A champion in the 100 and three times in the 220. Some claim that he invented the crouch start, but others believe it was Yale's coach, Mike Murphy, who introduced it to him. Still others believe that Bobby McDonald, an Australian, got the idea from watching kangaroos start. See Ellery H. Clark, *Track Athletics up to Date* (New York: Duffield, 1931), 40–43; Michael C. Murphy, *Athletic Training* (New York: Charles Scribner's Sons, 1918), 32–33; and John Corbin "Starting and Starters," *Outing* XXII (May 1893), 154. Murphy's Yale and Pennsylvania teams won 15 IC4A championships in 21 years that he coached beginning in 1887. See Edward R. Bushnell, preface to Murphy, *Athletic Training,* x.

54. Reginald Horsman, *Race and Manifest Destiny* (Cambridge, MA: Harvard Univ. Press, 1981), 81; Robert H. Wiebe, *The Search for Order* (New York: Hill and Wang, 1967), 257; Dixon Wecter, *Saga of American Society* (New York: C. Scribner's Sons, 1937), 159–60, 388; John Dizikes, *Sportsmen and Gamesmen* (Boston: Houghton Mifflin, 1981), 214; and Francis Trollope, *Domestic Manners of the Americans* (New York: Vintage, 1949, originally 1832), 157. President Theodore Roosevelt wrote to Finley Peter Dunne in 1904 that an American Anglophobiac becomes "a hanger-on around any titled Englishman or Englishwoman of what he deems good social position whose acquaintance he can manage to scrape." See Elting E. Morison (ed.), *The Letters of Theodore Roosevelt* (Cambridge, MA: Harvard Univ. Press, 1951), Vol. IV, p. 1042.

55. *New York Herald,* 27 July 1859, p. 4.

56. *Spirit of the Times,* 6 Aug. 1869, p. 308.

57. "The Boat-Race," *Nation* IX (2 Sep. 1869), 188.

58. Collegians from Harvard, Princeton, Yale, and New York University contributed to an American lacrosse team in 1884 which defeated British teams in 8 of 9 games with one tie. Cambridge University was beaten 6–0. See Presbrey, *Athletics at Princeton,* p. 537, and Ross Mackenzie, "Lacrosse," *Outing* XXI (Oct. 1892), 79. Similarly athletes from Harvard, Yale, Princeton, and Dartmouth journeyed to England in 1889 for a series of baseball games. See Guy M. Hays, "Glorified Rounders: American Baseball in Britain, 1874–1914," M.S. thesis, University of Maryland, 1985, pp. 47–48.

59. Croome, *Fifty Years of Sport,* I, p. 74.

60. Lewis S. Welch and Walter Camp, *Yale* (Boston: L. C. Page, 1899), 484.

61. "International Track and Field Contests of 1895," *Outing* XXVI (Sep. 1895), 454.

62. Caspar Whitney, "Development of Athletics in the United States," *Fortnightly Review* LIV (Sep. 1893), 423; Croome, *Fifty Years of Sport,* I, p. 44; and John A. Blanchard (ed.), *The H Book of Harvard Athletics, 1852–1922* (Cambridge, MA: Harvard Varsity Club, 1923), 426.

63. Croome, *Fifty Years of Sport,* I, pp. 74–75; "Oxford vs. Yale," *Outing* XXIV (Aug. 1894), 137; "The Oxford-Yale Athletic Meeting," *Outing* XXIV (Aug. 1894), 115–17; and W. H. Greenfell, "Oxford v. Yale," *Fortnightly Review* LXII (Sep. 1894), 379.

64. W. B. Curtis, "Editorial Comments," *Outing* XXIV (Sep. 1894), 143–45.

65. Julius W. Pratt, *A History of United States Foreign Policy* (Englewood Cliffs, NJ: Prentice-Hall, 1955), 350.

66. "International Track and Field Contest of 1895," 460.

67. Attorney Samuel J. Elder, Boston, letter to Walter Camp, 8 June 1895, Walter Camp Papers, Box 10, Folder 264, YUA.

68. Albert B. Hart, "Harvard's Athletic Policy," *Harvard Graduates' Magazine* IV (Dec. 1895), 212.

69. John A. Lucas, "The First Great International Track Meet," *Sports Illustrated* XXXVIII (16 April 1973), pp. E8–E12.

70. W. Beach Thomas, *Athletics* (London: Ward, Lock, 1901), 262.

71. *The Sport Chronicle Annual–1896,* pp. 86–88, L416.d.84.18, Cambridge Univ. Library. The University of Pennsylvania cricket team won America's first college international competition in cricket, beating a combined team from Oxford and Cambridge by 101 runs three weeks before the track meet. See T. C. Turner, "Cricket," *Outing* XXVII (Oct. 1985), 12–14.

72. Croome, *Fifty Years of Sport,* I, p. 75.

73. Crowther and Ruhl, *Rowing and Track Athletics*, 410–13, and Thomas R. Fisher, 2nd, "With the Harvard-Yale Team in England," *The College Athlete* III (Oct. 1899), 163–70.

74. David C. Young, in "The Origins of the Modern Olympics: A New Version," *International Journal of the History of Sport* IV (Dec. 1987), 271–300, has shown clearly that the Modern Olympics began in Greece, not in 1896, but in 1859 when, through the idea of Panagiotis Soutsos and money of Evangelis Zappas, the Olympic Games were held at the Plateia Loudovikov in Athens.

75. Sloane was author of such volumes as *The Life of Napoleon*, *The French War and the Revolution*, and *The French Revolution and Religious Reform*.

76. John A. Lucas, *The Modern Olympic Games* (New York: A. S. Barnes, 1980), 32–33.

77. Ibid., 33–34; John J. MacAloon, *This Great Symbol: Pierre de Coubertin and the Origins of the Modern Olympic Games* (Chicago: Univ. of Chicago Press, 1981), 165–66; and Richard D. Mandell, *The First Modern Olympics* (Berkeley: Univ. of California Press, 1976), 83–84.

78. *New York Times*, 22 March 1896, p. 12.

79. George A. Adee, New York City, letter to Walter Camp, 23 May 1894, Camp Papers, Box 1, Folder 7, YUA.

80. Lucas, *Modern Olympic Games*, 43, and Mandell, *First Modern Olympics*, 116.

81. The others associated with Harvard were Arthur Blake, Thomas Burke, Thomas Curtis, and William Hoyt. Burke, a world class athlete, won the 100- and 400-meter races; Curtis captured the 120-meter hurdles; and Hoyt took the pole vault.

82. Frederic T. Fox, "Our First Olympians," *Princeton Alumni Weekly* (2 June 1964), 10, and Presbrey, *Athletics at Princeton*, 461. Sloane apparently decided that Princeton should represent the U.S. after the New York Athletic Club chose not to participate in the Olympics. Sloane did not know until mid-March 1896 that the Boston Athletic Association would also send athletes to the Games. See newspaper clippings, Francis Lane Scrapbook, Princeton Univ. Archives.

83. The other three Princeton men were Francis Lane, Herbert Jameson, and Albert Taylor. Jameson was second in the 400 run, and Taylor was second in the pole vault. Lane would likely have done better but seasickness during the journey left him weak for the entire period of the Games.

84. Compare *The Sporting Chronicle Annual–1896*, pp. 87–88, with D. G. A. Lowe and A. E. Porritt, *Athletics* (London: Longmans, Green, 1929), 331–34.

85. Henry C. Lodge, "Senator Lodge's Speech," *Harvard Graduates' Magazine* V (Sep. 1896), 67.

86. Edward R. Bushnell, *History of Athletics at the University of Pennsylvania.* (Philadelphia: Athletic Association of the Univ. of Pennsylvania, 1909), Vol. II, p. 100. Bushnell, who was a member of the team, claimed that Americans would have won additional events, but the French Committee scheduled important events for Sunday after assuring the Pennsylvanians that there would be no Sabbath competition.

87. Rudyard Kipling, "The White Man's Burden," *The Writings in Prose and Verse of Rudyard Kipling* (New York: Charles Scribner's Sons, 1903), 78.

Chapter IX.   Student Control and Faculty Resistance

1. Walter Camp, "College Athletics," *New Englander* XLIV (Jan. 1885), 139.

2. Andrew M. F. Davis, "College Athletics," *Atlantic Monthly* LI (1885), 676.

3. Francis A. Walker, "College Athletics," *Harvard Graduates' Magazine* II (Sep. 1895), 3.

4. John W. White, W. S. Chaplin, and A. B. Hart, "Athletic Report," 12 June 1888, p. 9, HUD 8388.3B, Harvard Univ. Archives (hereafter noted as HUA); *Princetonian*, 14 June 1876, p. 11; Richard P. McCormick, *Rutgers: A Bicentennial History* (New Brunswick, NJ: Rutgers Univ. Press, 1966), 105; Kent Sagendorph, *Michigan, The Story of a University* (New York: E. P. Dutton, 1948), 150; Jonas Viles, *The University of Missouri* (Columbia: Univ. of Missouri Press, 1939), 214; Nora C. Chaflin, *Trinity College, 1839–1892: The Beginnings of Duke University* (Durham, NC: Duke Univ. Press, 1950), 447; Orrin L. Elliott, *Stanford University; The First Twenty Five Years* (Stanford, CA: Stanford Univ. Press, 1937), 219; and Henry D. Sheldon, *History of the University of Oregon* (Portland, OR: Benforts & Mort, 1940), 122.

5. See, for example, Frank Presbrey and James Moffatt, *Athletics at Princeton* (New York: Frank Presbrey, 1901), 67, 117; E. L. Richards, "College Athletics," *Popular Science Monthly* XXIV (March 1884), 597; "Overseer Athletic Abuses Committee Report," ca. April 1888, HUD 8388.5, HUA, p. 1; and White, "Athletic Report," 27.

6. White, "Athletic Report," 16.

7. Princeton Faculty Minutes, 15 May 1882, Princeton Univ. Archives (hereafter noted as PUA).

8. Yale Faculty Minutes, 25 March 1868 and 2 June 1869, Yale Univ. Archives (hereafter noted as YUA).

9. Ibid., 10 May 1871, and Harvard Faculty Minutes, 22 May 1871, HUA.

10. Yale Faculty Minutes, 21 Oct. 1874, 6 Oct. 1875, and 27 Oct. 1875, YUA.

11. Ibid., 25 Oct. 1876; and Richard M. Hurd, *A History of Yale Athletics: 1840–1888* (New Haven, CT: privately printed, 1888), 60.

12. Yale Faculty Minutes, 19 May 1887, YUA.

13. Presbrey, *Athletics at Princeton*, 56.

14. Walter Camp, "Yale Athletics, A Review of Its History," *Illustrated American* (19 April 1890), 207; and Walter Camp, letter to H. B. Fine, Princeton, 17 Oct. 1901, Walter Camp Papers, Box 8, Folder 278, YUA. See Parke H. Davis, "Princeton Athletic Records, 1860–1910," bound manuscript, Princeton Univ. Archives, for Yale records in baseball and football leagues.

15. Eugene L. Richards, "Intercollegiate Athletics and Faculty Control," *Outing* XXVI (July 1895), 328.

16. Clarence Deming, "Money Power in College Athletics," *Outlook* LXXX (July 1905), 569–72.

17. William Beebe, letter to Walter Camp, 27 Sep. 1905, Walter Camp Papers, Box 3, Folder 69, YUA.

18. Yale Faculty Minutes, 13 Jan. 1906, 20 Jan. 1906, 20 Feb. 1906, and 31 May 1906, YUA. The Yale decision confirmed what the secretary of Yale College suggested shortly after the controversy began. Secretary Anson Stokes replied to Camp: "The system which leaves things mostly in students' hands with a general oversight by you [Camp] seems to me to be the best." See Anson Phelps Stokes, letter to Walter Camp, 12 Oct. 1905, Camp Papers, Box 29, Folder 827, YUA.

19. Presbrey, *Athletics at Princeton*, 80.

20. Princeton Faculty Minutes, 13 Nov. 1873, PUA.

21. Ibid., 1 June 1877, 4 June 1877, 11 June 1877, and 15 June 1877, PUA.

22. Ibid., 29 April 1881.

23. Ibid., 2 June 1882 and 13 Oct. 1882.

24. Ibid., 7 April 1883 and 9 April 1883.

25. John A. Blanchard (ed.), *The H Book of Harvard Athletics, 1852–1922* (Cambridge, MA: Harvard Varsity Club, 1923), 298; *Harvard Advocate*, 30 April 1875, p. 74; and *Yale Record*, 16 Sep. 1874, p. 21.

26. David Q. Voigt, *American Baseball: From Gentleman's Sport to the Commissioner System* (University Park, PA: Pennsylvania State Univ. Press, 1983), 80–84; Harold Seymour, *Baseball: The Early Years* (New York: Oxford Univ. Press, 1960), 51–55; and Steven A. Riess, *Touching Base: Professional Baseball and American Culture in the Progressive Era* (Westport, CT: Greenwood Press, 1980), 155.

27. Princeton Faculty Minutes, 18 Sep. 1882, PUA.

28. As quoted in Presbrey, *Athletics at Princeton,* 141, and Princeton Faculty Minutes, 4 May 1883, PUA.

29. Princeton Faculty Minutes, 13 Feb. 1884 and 17 Oct. 1884, PUA.

30. Ibid., 13 Feb. 1884, and Presbrey, *Athletics at Princeton,* 319–21, 336.

31. Woodrow Wilson, "What Is a College For?" *Scribner's Monthly* XLVI (Nov. 1909), 576. Wilson had been on the Princeton athletic committee in the 1890s.

32. Harvard Faculty Minutes, 27 May 1871 and 21 April 1873, HUA.

33. John W. White, "The Constitution, Authority, and Policy of the Committee on the Regulation of Athletic Sports," *Harvard Graduates' Magazine* I (Jan. 1893), 209, and Dudley A. Sargent, "History of the Administration of Intercollegiate Athletics in the United States," *American Physical Education Review* XV (1910), 252.

34. Harvard Athletic Committee Minutes, 15 June 1882, HUA.

35. Ibid., 17 Oct. 1882.

36. Ibid., 27 Sep. 1882.

37. Ibid., 5 Oct. 1882.

38. In December 1883, Dudley Sargent visited five colleges and eleven individuals to find out their opinion of professional coaches. Most professors at Amherst, Columbia, Princeton, Williams, and Yale opposed pro coaches. Harvard Athletic Committee Minutes, 10 Dec. 1883.

39. J. W. White, W. E. Byerly, and D. A. Sargent, Athletic Committee, letter to Mr. Storrow, crew captain, 19 Dec. 1894, in ibid., 19 Dec. 1894. See also 30 Oct., 13, 20 Nov., 4, 16, 18 Dec. 1884, HUA.

40. *Harvard Crimson,* 23 Feb. 1884, p. 20.

41. Harvard Athletic Committee Minutes, 10 Jan. 1885 and 8 Oct. 1885, HUA.

42. Ibid., 8 Oct. 1885 and 21 May 1886; and Charles W. Eliot, letter to D. A. Sargent, 19 May 1886, in ibid., 19 May 1886.

43. Harvard had won 18 of 25 previous crew contests with Yale.

44. Harvard Athletic Committee Minutes, 22 Nov. 1883 and 12 March 1884, HUA.

45. Ibid., 25 Nov. 1884.

46. Ibid., 8 Oct. 1885.

47. Ibid., 4 Jan. 1886.

48. See, for example, ibid., 21 Dec. 1886; A. B. Hart, "Report of the Secretary and the Work of the Previous Committee," in ibid., 27 Nov. 1888; and "Overseer Athletic Abuses Committee Report," 109, ca. April 1888, HUD 8388.5, HUA.

49. "Report of the Overseers, Presidents and Fellows," 15 Oct. 1888, Series II, U.A. II, 10.7.2, HUA.

50. White, "The Constitution, Authority, and Policy of the Committee on the Regulation of Athletic Sports," 217.

51. M. H. Morgan, secretary of the Harvard faculty, letter to the Athletic Committee, 20 Feb. 1895, and James Barr Ames, Athletic Committee Chairman, letter to the Faculty of Arts and Sciences, 25 Feb. 1895, Charles Eliot Papers, Box 100, Folder 4, HUA.

52. James Barr Ames, letter to President and Fellows, 25 March 1895, and Ames, letter to Martin Brimmer, Chairman of the Corporation, 25 March 1895, ibid., Box 264, Jan.–Mar. 1895 Folder, HUA.

53. "Report to the Overseers, Presidents and Fellows," 25 March 1895, Series II, U.A. II, 10.7.2, HUA., and Charles W. Eliot, *Report of the President of Harvard College, 1894–1895*, pp. 13–14, HUA.

54. Harvard Athletic Committee Minutes, 16 Feb., 9 March, 5 June, and 16 Nov. 1903, HUA.

55. R. B. Merriman, "Football Reform," *Harvard Graduates' Magazine* XIV (March 1906), 426–27. See also, Ronald A. Smith, "Harvard and Columbia and a Reconsideration of the Football Crisis of 1905–06," *Journal of Sport History* VIII (Winter 1981), 5–19.

56. *Northwestern University President's Annual Report, 1895–96* (Evanston, IL: Northwestern Univ. 1896), 24.

57. William F. Atkinson and 648 students, letter to the President and Faculty, ca. June 1895, Cornell Univ. Faculty Minutes, 14 June 1895, Cornell Univ. Archives.

58. Burt G. Wilder, letter to the Faculty, 1 Feb. 1895, Burt G. Wilder Papers, Box 1, 14/26/95, Cornell Univ. Archives.

59. Dartmouth College Records of the Trustees, Feb. 1892, Dartmouth College Archives.

60. Ibid., 30 Sep. 1905.

61. "Memorandum," ca. spring 1906, President Tucker Papers, #1, "Athletics, A-H," Dartmouth College Archives, and Dartmouth College Records of the Trustees, 25 June 1906. At Harvard in 1907, a committee report indicated that the Athletic Committee of three members each of students, alumni, and faculty did not "represent the Faculty point of view sufficiently, and that athletics are too strongly represented." Students at the same time felt that they were too little represented. "Report of the Joint Committee on the Regulation of Athletic Sports," *Harvard Graduates' Magazine* XV (June 1907), 644–45.

62. Alexander Meiklejohn, "The Evils of College Athletics," *Harper's Weekly* XLIX (2 Dec. 1905), 1752.

Chapter X.   The Early Failure of Faculty Inter-Institutional Control

1. Princeton Trustees Minutes, 22 June 1874, Princeton Univ. Archives (hereafter called PUA).

2. C. W. Eliot, letter to other college presidents, 11 Sep. 1882, as quoted in Luther W. Warren, "The Charles W. Eliot Centennial," *Journal of Physical Education* V (March 1934), 24; Dartmouth Faculty Records, 18 Sep. 1882, Dartmouth College Archives; and Yale Univ. Faculty Minutes, 4 Oct. 1882, Yale Univ. Archives (hereafter called YUA). The concern over professionalism had evidently followed Harvard's hiring of a professional baseball coach in 1881 and the participation against professional teams and thus contact with what were considered the lower-class elements of major league teams. The Harvard Athletic Committee forbade coach Robinson's employment following the 1882 season. See Harvard Athletic Committee Minutes, 17 June 1882 and 27 Sep. 1882, Harvard Univ. Archives (hereafter called HUA).

3. Yale Univ. Faculty Minutes, 11 Oct. 1882, YUA.

4. Harvard Athletic Committee Minutes, 4, 14, 17 Oct. 1882, HUA.

5. Ibid., 10 Dec. 1882.

6. John W. White, W. S. Chaplin, and A. B. Hart, "Athletic Report," 12 June 1888, HUD 8388.3B, HUA, and Dudley A. Sargent, "History of the Administration of Intercollegiate Athletics in the United States," *American Physical Education Review* XV (1910), 252–53.

7. White et al., ibid; *Harvard Crimson,* 14 Feb. 1884, p. 1; 22 Feb. 1884, p. 1; and 23 Feb. 1884, p. 1.

8. White et al., ibid., 14.

9. Harvard Athletic Committee Minutes, 7 March 1884, HUA.

10. *Harvard Crimson,* 26 Feb. 1884, p. 1.

11. Ibid., 22 Feb. 1884, p. 1.

12. Ibid., 6 March 1884, p. 1, and 12 March 1884, p. 1.

13. E. L. Richards, letter to W. M. Sloane, 18 Feb. 1884, as quoted in the *Harvard Crimson,* 21 Feb. 1884, p. 1.

14. As quoted in the *Harvard Crimson,* 24 Jan. 1884, p. 1.

15. *The* [Brown College] *Brunonian,* 18 Dec. 1886, p. 114, 125, and Bruce Leslie, "The Response of Four Colleges to the Rise of Intercollegiate Athletics," *Journal of Sport History* III (Winter 1976), 216.

16. Walter Camp, letter to the *New York Times,* as quoted in the *Harvard Crimson,* 1 March 1884, p. 2.

17. A. B. Hart reviewed the history of inter-institutional attempts to control athletics in the Harvard Athletic Committee Minutes, 27 Nov. 1888, HUA.

18. Newspaper clipping, 17 Feb. 1898, Brown Univ. College Scrapbook, 1897–1904, Brown Univ. Archives (hereafter called BUA).

19. John R. Behee, *Fielding Yost's Legacy* (Ann Arbor, MI: privately printed, 1971), 19–23, and Parke H. Davis, *Football: The American Intercollegiate Game* (New York: Charles Scribner's Sons, 1911), 451–53. Davis was the coach at Lafayette at the time. He was a Princeton graduate as was "Doggie" Trenchard, the West Virginia football coach.

20. Brown Univ. Faculty Minutes, 8 Feb. 1898, BUA.

21. *Brown Daily Herald*, 18 Feb. 1898, p. 1. Cornell sent no student representative. Professor Wilfred H. Munro, Brown, was elected chairman, with Harvard alumnus F. W. Moore chosen as secretary.

22. Ibid., 19 Feb. 1898, p. 1, and newspaper clipping, 19 Feb. 1898, Brown Univ. College Scrapbook, 1897–1904, BUA.

23. "Conference on Intercollegiate Athletics, 1898," early draft, BUA.

24. Ibid. Compare the early draft to the published document.

25. Wilfred H. Munro (Brown Univ.), Benjamin I. Wheeler (Univ. of California representing Cornell Univ.), James F. Kemp (Columbia Univ.), Louis M. Dennis (Cornell Univ.), Ira N. Hollis (Harvard Univ.), George S. Patterson (Univ. of Pennsylvania), and Henry B. Fine (Princeton Univ.), "Report on Intercollegiate Sports," ca. April 1898, p. 5, BUA.

26. Ibid.

27. Ibid., 9.

28. John A. Lucas and Ronald A. Smith, *Saga of American Sport* (Philadelphia: Lea & Febiger, 1978), 197–99.

29. Guy M. Lewis, "America's First Intercollegiate Sport: Regattas from 1852–1875," *Research Quarterly* XXXVIII (Dec. 1967), 642.

30. Charles W. Eliot, "Inaugural Address," 19 Oct. 1869, p. 22, HUA.

31. Quoting Yale Professor Thatcher, Harvard Athletic Committee Minutes, 10 Dec. 1883, HUA.

32. George Santayana, "Philosophy on the Bleachers," *Harvard Monthly* XVIII (July 1894), 181–90.

33. "Conference on Intercollegiate Athletics, 1898," early draft, BUA.

34. See Ronald A. Smith, "Winning and a Theory of Competitive Athletics," in William J. Morgan (ed.), *Sport and the Humanities: A Collection of Original Essays* (Knoxville: Bureau of Education Research, Univ. of Tennessee, 1980), 44–50.

35. "Report on Intercollegiate Sports," ca. April 1898, pp. 10–14, BUA.

36. See James F. Kemp, "History of Faculty Control at Columbia," *Columbia University Quarterly* IV (Dec. 1901), 39–40; C. W. Eliot, "President Eliot's Report," *Harvard Graduates' Magazine* IX (March 1901), 452; and Francis A. March, Jr., *Athletics at Lafayette College* (Easton, PA: Lafayette College, 1923) 152.

37. "Report on Intercollegiate Sports," ca. April 1898, p. 10, BUA.

38. Augustus Hemenway, Robert Bacon, and Theodore Roosevelt (Committee on Physical Training, Athletic Sports, and Sanitary Condition of Buildings), "Important Suggestions in Athletics," *Harvard Graduates' Magazine* VI (Dec. 1897), 195–96. Emphasis added.

39. Ira N. Hollis, letter to Charles W. Eliot, 19 Nov. 1900, Eliot Papers, Box 110, Folder 143, "Hollis," HUA.

40. Ibid.

41. George W. Kirchwey, letter to President Nicholas Murray Butler, Columbia, 14 July 1902, "Athletics" Folder, Columbia Univ. Central Files.

42. As quoted in Caspar Whitney, "The Guiding Hand of Faculty in College Sports," *Outing* XL (July 1902), 497.

43. See Guy Lewis, "Theodore Roosevelt's Role in the 1905 Football Controversy," *Research Quarterly* XL (Dec. 1969), 717–24, and Ronald A. Smith, "Harvard and Columbia and a Reconsideration of the 1905–06 Football Crisis," *Journal of Sport History* VIII (Winter 1981), 5–19.

44. As quoted in the Harvard Athletic Committee Minutes, 10 Jan. 1906, HUA.

Chapter XI.   The Rise of the Professional Coach

1. Frank S. Butterworth, "Honesty in Football," *Outing* XLV (Nov. 1904), 141.

2. Caspar Whitney, "The Sportsman's View-Point," *Outing* XLII (Aug. 1903), 630.

3. Article clipping, *Harvard Bulletin*, 1 July 1903, p. 4, in Charles W. Eliot Papers, Folder 144, Box 110, Harvard Univ. Archives (hereafter noted as HUA).

4. *New York Clipper*, 6 Aug. 1864, p. 130, and John DeGrange, "100 Years of Yale-Harvard Rowing," HUD 8952.66, HUA.

5. Leon B. Richardson, *History of Dartmouth College* (Hanover, NH: Dartmouth College Publications, 1932), Vol. II, p. 563, and *New York Clipper*, 3 Aug. 1872, p. 140.

6. *New York Clipper*, 26 July 1873, p. 133.

7. *Yale Record*, 16 April 1873, p. 249.

8. Harry C. Heermans, 1874 crew member, letter to the editor, 12 Sep. 1938, in "Collection of Recollections," Wesleyan Univ. Archives.

9. John H. Bartlett and John P. Gifford, *Dartmouth Athletics* (Concord, NH: Republican Press Association, 1893), 179.

10. Horace Coon, *Columbia* (New York: E. P. Dutton, 1947), 305.

11. Charles Van Patten Young, *Courtney and Cornell Rowing* (Ithaca, NY: Cornell Publications, 1923), 101, and Thomas C. Mendenhall, A

Short History of American Rowing (Boston: Charles River Books, ca. 1980), 20. Mendenhall claims that Courtney's crews won 101 meets and lost 46.

12. In 1873, two bettors split their earnings with Courtney after a Courtney win, making the amateur rower $450 richer. See Waterman T. Hewett, *Cornell University* (New York: Univ. Publishing Society, 1905), Vol. III, pp. 218–19.

13. Frank Cosentino, "Ned Hanlan—Canada's Premier Oarsman: A Case Study in 19th Century Professionalism," *Canadian Journal of History of Sport and Physical Education* V (Dec. 1974), 9–10.

14. Ibid., 11–12, and Young, *Courtney and Cornell Rowing*, 25–26.

15. Cosentino, "Ned Hanlan," 12–13, and Mendenhall, *History of American Rowing*, 14.

16. *New York Times*, 15 April 1884, p. 4 and *The Cornell Era*, 18 April 1884, p. 249.

17. *The Cornell Era*, 18 April 1884, p. 249.

18. The Henley competition was tainted with the charge that Captain Shinkel, because of a wager, lost one of the races by pretending to faint while Cornell was leading. He supposedly committed a similar act in a Vienna, Austria, race later that summer. See *The Cornell Review*, (Oct. 1881), 32–33, 37, and Samuel Crowther and Arthur Ruhl, *Rowing and Track Athletics* (New York: Macmillan, 1905), 76–77.

19. Crowther and Ruhl, *Rowing and Track Athletics*, 107.

20. Athletic Association contract signed on 11 Oct. 1895, Charles Courtney Papers, Box 1, 40/1/142, Cornell Univ. Archives (hereafter cited as CUA).

21. Wilton Bentley, Henley, letter to Ruth, 7 July 1895, Will Bentley Crew Letters," 40/1/m.228, CUA.

22. Ibid.

23. "The Oxford-Yale Athletic Meeting," *Outing* XXIV (Aug. 1894), 115.

24. *Mail and Express* newspaper clipping, July 1895, in "Crew Clippings, 1895–1898," 40/1/m.229, CUA.

25. Wilton Bentley, letter to Ruth, 8 July 1895, "Will Bentley Crew Letters," 40/1/m.228, CUA.

26. *New York Times*, 11 July 1895, p. 1.

27. *Mail and Express* newspaper clipping, July 1895, in "Crew Clippings, 1895–1898," 40/1/m.229, CUA.

28. Ibid., 13 July 1895.

29. Morris Bishop, *A History of Cornell* (Ithaca, NY: Cornell Univ. Press, 1962), 346.

30. Charles Courtney, "1904 Record of Training for Season," Charles Courtney Papers, Box 1, 40/1/142, CUA. The statement by Courtney's biographer, C. P. V. Young, that "Courtney always had absolute control

over his men, even over their habits and manner of life" was only figuratively true. His authoritarianism, however, was apparent. See Young, *Courtney and Cornell Rowing*, 90. Muckraker Henry B. Needham wrote that "Courtney is not only a dictator, he is the proprietor of the Cornell crews. See his, "The College Athlete," *McClure's Magazine* XXV (June 1905), 272.

31. William T. Reid, Belmont School headmaster, letter to Walter Camp, 18 March 1894, Camp Papers, Box 20, Folder 572, "William Reid," Yale Univ. Archives (hereafter cited as YUA).

32. The Cutts-Glass case is noted in Ira N. Hollis, Chairman Harvard Athletic Committee, 10 page letter to Charles W. Eliot, 23 Jan. 1902, Eliot Papers, Box 110, Folder 143 "Hollis," HUA; President Arthur T. Hadley, Yale, ten letters to Charles W. Eliot, 30 Nov. 1901–27 Jan. 1902, Eliot Papers, Box 117, Folder 260; and Hubert M. Sedgwick, "The New Yale-Harvard Athletic Agreement," *Frank Leslie's Weekly* XCII (6 Feb. 1902), 143.

33. "Harvard College, Class of 1901, 2nd Report," 88, and "4th Report," 346, H.U.A., and John A. Blanchard (ed.), *The H Book of Harvard Athletics, 1852–1922* (Cambridge, MA: Harvard Varsity Club, 1923), 305, 314.

34. Harvard Athletic Committee Minutes, 6 Jan. 1904 and 2 and 17 Feb. 1904, HUA.

35. Ibid., 10 Jan. 1901, 7 May 1902, and 21 Dec. 1903. William H. Lewis was the assistant coach. Lewis is probably the first black coach in intercollegiate history. He had played at Harvard in 1892 and 1893 after graduating from Amherst.

36. Henry B. Needham, "The College Athlete," *McClure's Magazine* XXV (June 1905), 118.

37. Harvard Athletic Committee Minutes, 14 Dec. 1904 and 17 Feb. 1905; Archibald C. Coolidge, "Professional Coaches," *Harvard Graduates' Magazine* XIV (March 1906), 394; and R. B. Merriman, "Proceedings of the Athletic Committee," *Harvard Graduates' Magazine* XIII (June 1905), 630–31.

38. For salaries see "Appeal for the Teachers' Endowment," *Harvard Graduates' Magazine* XIII (June 1905), 762.

39. Bill Reid, Belmont, CA, letter to W. Cameron Forbes, Boston, 2 Jan. 1904, Wm. T. Reid Papers, "1904 Folder," HUD 8010, HUA.

40. William T. Reid, "The Football Situation," *Harvard Graduates' Magazine* XIII (June 1905), 602.

41. Walter Camp, "Athletic Notes," in Camp Papers, Box 65, Folder 1, YUA, as quoted in Alan Sack, "The Commercialization and Rationalization of Intercollegiate Football: A Comparative Analysis of the Development of Football at Yale and Harvard in the Latter Nineteenth Century," Ph.D. dissertation, Pennsylvania State Univ., 1974, p. 54.

42. W. T. Reid, Jr., "1905 Football Diary," Vol. I, 3, HUD 10905.76, HUA. The 441-page diary is part of the rational approach Reid took to his Harvard coaching experience.

43. Ibid.

44. Ibid., passim.

45. Ibid.

46. Ibid., 17–20.

47. Ibid., 20.

48. Ibid., 15.

49. Ibid., 9.

50. Ibid., 9, 13–15.

51. Ibid., 98.

52. Bill Reid, Belmont, CA, letter to W. Cameron Forbes, 2 Jan. 1904, W. T. Reid, Jr. Papers, "1904 Folder," HUD 8010, HUA.

53. Handwritten ms., ca. late 1940s, p. 23, in Wm. T. Reid Correspondence, HUD 8010, HUA.

54. Reid Diary, 13.

55. Ibid., 7.

56. Ibid., 351.

57. Ibid., 81–82.

58. Ibid., 8.

59. Ibid., 228.

60. Ibid., passim.

61. Ibid., 400.

62. "Harvard College, Class of 1901, 25th Anniversary Report, 1926," p. 501, HUA.

63. William T. Reid, Jr., "Football and Coaching," *Harvard Graduates' Magazine* XV (March 1907), 400.

64. James L. Knox, "The Transition Period From 1891 to the World War," in Blanchard, *Harvard H Book*, 422.

65. "Harvard College, Class of 1901, 25th Anniversary Report, 1926," p. 502, HUA.

66. Harvard Athletic Committee Minutes, 27 Sep. 1882, HUA.

67. Ibid., 21 Jan. 1884.

68. David C. Young, *The Olympic Myth of Greek Amateur Athletics* (Chicago: Ares, 1985), 15–27. See Chapter XII for an interpretation of the concept of amateurism in American colleges.

69. Anthony Trollope, *North America* (New York: Alfred A. Knopf, 1951 (originally 1862), 242.

70. As quoted in Richard J. Storr, *Harper's University: The Beginnings* (Chicago: Univ. of Chicago Press, 1966), 179.

71. "Professional Coaching," *Harvard Graduates' Magazine* XII (Sep. 1903), 34.

72. Ira N. Hollis, letter to Charles W. Eliot, 19 Nov. 1900, Charles W. Eliot Papers, Box 110, Folder 143, "Hollis," HUA.

73. "Professional Coaching," 32.

74. Caspar Whitney, "The Sportsman's View-Point," *Outing* XLII (Aug. 1903), 630.

75. Record of the Overseers of Harvard College, 13 March 1907, HUA.

76. Harvard Athletic Committee Minutes, 21 Oct. 1907, HUA. Emphasis added.

Chapter XII.   Amateur College Sport: An Untenable Concept in a Free and Open Society

1. David C. Young, *The Olympic Myth of Greek Amateur Athletics* (Chicago: Ares, 1985), 7.

2. Ibid., 15–27.

3. Herbert T. Steward, *The Records of the Henley Regatta, 1839–1902* (London: Grant Richards, 1903), 229, 300. The statement "engaged in menial duty" was added in the 1880s. See also Harold Harris, *Sport in Britain* (London: Stanley Paul, 1975), 86.

4. Paul Weiss, *Sport: A Philosophic Inquiry* (Carbondale, IL: Southern Illinois Univ. Press, 1969), 192.

5. Harris, *Sport in Britain,* 140.

6. Weiss, *Sport: A Philosophic Inquiry,* 210.

7. James Whiton, "The First Harvard-Yale Regatta (1852)," *Outlook* LXVIII (June 1901), 286–89.

8. *New York Clipper,* 22 July 1871, p. 125.

9. *Harvard Advocate,* 9 June 1876, p. 99.

10. Ibid., 19 Oct. 1877, p. 34.

11. Alexander Agassiz, "Rowing Fifty Years Ago," *Harvard Graduates' Magazine* XV (March 1907), 458, and Charles W. Eliot, "In Praise of Rowing," *Harvard Graduates' Magazine* XV (March 1907), 532.

12. B. W. Crowninshield, "Boating," in F. O. Vaille and H. A. Clark *The Harvard Book* (Cambridge, MA: Welch, Bigelow, 1875), Vol. II, p. 263.

13. *Spirit of the Times,* 5 Dec. 1874, p. 403.

14. Agassiz, "Rowing Fifty Years Ago," 458.

15. *Yale Record,* 16 Sep. 1874, p. 21, and John A. Blanchard (ed.), *The H Book of Harvard Athletics, 1852–1922* (Cambridge, MA: Harvard Varsity Club, 1923), 182.

16. *Harvard Advocate,* 31 Oct. 1879, p. 38.

17. Brown Univ. Athletic Council Minutes, 10 Oct. 1899 and 29 March 1900, Brown Univ. Archives.

18. *New York Post,* 18 Jan. 1906, in the Columbia Univ. Football Scrapbook, Columbia Univ. Archives.

19. George R. Cutting, *Student Life at Amherst* (Amherst, MA: Hatch and Williams, 1871), 19–20, and Henry D. Sheldon, *Student Life and Customs* (New York: D. Appleton, 1901), 125–33.

20. "College Beginnings," *The American College* I (Dec. 1909), 221–24. The charge was false, for pitcher Henry D. Hyde was a full-time student in 1859, graduated in 1861, and became a prominent lawyer in Boston.

21. *The Cornell Era,* 23 May 1884, p. 302.

22. College of William and Mary Faculty Minutes, 24 Feb. 1898, College of William and Mary Archives.

23. "Report to the Advisory Committee of the Columbia University Athletic Association," ca. spring 1900, in "Athletics," Columbia Univ. Central Files.

24. Pennsylvania State Univ. Board of Trustees Executive Board Minutes, 31 July 1900, Penn State Room, Univ. Archives.

25. See Chapter XI for a lengthy discussion of professional coaching development.

26. See Chapter II for a discussion of the ideology of freedom and equality. See also Robert E. Lane, *Political Ideology: Why the American Common Man Believes What He Does* (New York: Free Press, 1962), 17; Carl N. Degler, "Egalitarianism," *Encyclopedia of American Political History* (New York: Charles Scribner's Sons, 1984), Vol. II, pp. 481–88; E. Digby Baltzell, *The Protestant Establishment: Aristocracy and Caste in America* (New York: Random House, 1964), 7; Rush Welter, *The Mind of America, 1820–1860* (New York: Columbia Univ. Press, 1975), 118; and Rowland Berthoff, "Peasants and Artisans, Puritans and Republicans: Personal Liberty and Communal Equality in American History," *Journal of American History* LXIX (Dec. 1982), 588. Berthoff argues that equality of opportunity is an euphemism for unbounded personal liberty which has often dominated over communal equality and the general welfare in America .

27. J. R. Pole, *The Pursuit of Equality in American History* (Berkeley: Univ. of California Press, 1978), 129.

28. For a worthy discussion of amateurism and the heredity-ascribed versus talent-achieved status, see Barrington Moore, Jr., *Social Origins of Dictatorship and Democracy* (Boston: Beacon Press, 1966), 484–91. For a discussion of the infusion of professionalism in American culture and higher education, see Burton J. Bledstein, *The Culture of Professionalism* (New York: W. W. Norton, 1976), passim. For a strong argument that athletics naturally tend toward professionalism when excellence is desired, see James W. Keating, "The Heart of the Problem of Amateur Athletics," *Journal of General Education* XVI (Jan. 1965), 261–72, espe-

cially p. 265. For an example of English upper-class arrogance favoring amateur sport over professional sport, see that of an Oxford don, N. L. Jackson, "Professionalism and Sport," *Fortnightly Review* LXVII (Jan. 1906), 156–61. For an integrative attempt to show the transformation of the traditional British aristocratic sportsman's attitude in America to a popular gamesmanship in which social class is important, see John Dizikes, *Sportsmen and Gamesmen* (Boston: Houghton Mifflin, 1981), passim. Unfortunately Dizikes did not mention college sports, nor did he consider amateurism, a central consideration of the elitist sportsman.

29. Daniel L. Boorstin, in *America and the Image of Europe* (New York: Meridian Books, 1960), 58, makes the point that in America a college student was "required to show what he could do in order to acquire a status, but in England a student at Oxford or Cambridge was offered a position of status by being a student."

Chapter XIII.   Eligibility Rules in a Laissez-Faire Collegiate Scene

1. Guy M. Lewis, "America's First Intercollegiate Sport: The Regattas from 1852–1875," *Research Quarterly* XXXVIII (Dec. 1967), 640.

2. Walter Camp, "Call for a High Standard in College Athletics," *Harper's Weekly* XLIV (8 Jan. 1898), 46.

3. *Yale Record,* 16 April 1873, p. 249, and *Harvard Magenta,* 4 April 1873, p. 69.

4. *Harvard Advocates,* 11 Dec. 1874, p. 89.

5. Samuel Eliot Morison, *Three Centuries of Harvard, 1636–1936* (Cambridge, MA: Harvard Univ. Press, 1936), 338.

6. *Seattle Daily Times,* 24 Oct. 1931, newspaper clipping, 31/5/1495, Cornell Univ. Archives.

7. "Taft Condemns Commercialization and Proselyting College Athletics," *New York Times,* 29 Dec. 1915, p. 8.

8. John A. Blanchard (ed.), *The H Book of Harvard Athletics, 1852–1922* (Cambridge, MA: Harvard Varsity Club, 1923), 267.

9. William R. Bigelow, "Harvard's Better Self," *New England Magazine* (Dec. 1890), clipping in Charles W. Eliot Papers, Box 239, "Publicity" Folder, Harvard Univ. Archives (hereafter noted as HUA), and "Report of the President of Harvard College, 1888–1889," p. 12, HUA.

10. Harvard Athletic Committee Minutes, 14 Jan. 1890, HUA.

11. Parke H. Davis, *Football: The American Intercollegiate Game* (New York: Charles Scribner's Sons, 1911), 87–88, 478–80.

12. Ibid., 89–90.

13. Ibid., 90, 480.

14. Newspaper clipping, 30 Nov. 1889, in "1889 Football Controversy," HUD 10889.2, HUA.

15. See Harvard Athletic Committee Minutes, 1 March 1890, HUA, and James B. Ames, member of Harvard-Yale Conference Committee, letter to Walter Camp, Yale representative, 2 March 1890, Walter Camp Papers, Box 2, Folder 46, Yale Univ. Archives (hereafter noted as YUA).

16. Davis, *Football*, 95, 483.

17. Ibid., 95, 484.

18. *New York Times*, 2 Feb. 1893, p. 3.

19. Ibid.

20. Henry B. Needham, "The College Athlete," *McClure's Magazine* XXV (June 1905), 115–16.

21. *New York Times*, 28 Oct. 1893, p. 2, and Davis, *Football*, 95, 484–85.

22. "Report of the President of Harvard College, 1894–1895," HUA, and Brown Athletic Committee Minutes, 9 Dec. 1893 and 20 Jan. 1894, Brown Univ. Archives. Walter Camp indicated that Amherst, Cornell, NYU, Princeton, Swarthmore, Wesleyan, Williams, and Yale rejected graduate participation while Brown, Columbia, Fordham, Georgetown, Penn, Rutgers, Stevens, Trinity, and Union would allow graduates to play. See Camp, "College Athletic Outlook," *Harper's Weekly* XXXVII (1 April 1893), 315.

23. Harvard Athletic Committee Minutes, 31 Jan. 1906, 14 Feb. 1906, and 24 June 1906, HUA, and Yale Athletic Committee Minutes, 5 Feb. 1906, Walter Camp Papers, Box 49, 1906 Folder, YUA. Yale had to form an athletic committee, taking power from students, to meet and negotiate the rules with Harvard and Princeton. President Arthur Hadley of Yale pressed for this, fearing that Yale would lose status without an agreement. Hadley told Camp: "We certainly ought not allow Harvard and Princeton to go ahead without us." Hadley, letter to Camp, 26 Jan. 1906, Camp Papers, Box 49, 1906 Folder, YUA.

24. *Boston Daily Herald*, 19 Jan. 1895, p. 1; Herbert Barton, "The College Conference of the Middle West," *Educational Review* XXVII (Jan. 1904), 45–49; Carl D. Voltmer, *A Brief History of the Intercollegiate Conference of Faculty Representatives with Special Consideration of Athletic Problems* (Menasha, WI: George Banta, 1935), 6–8; Kenneth L. Wilson and Jerry Brondfield, *The Big Ten* (Englewood Cliffs, NJ: Prentice-Hall, 1967), 52; and Howard Roberts, *The Big Nine* (New York: G. P. Putnam's Sons, 1948), 14–17.

25. *New York Post*, 22 Jan. 1906, p. 1; *Chicago Record-Herald*, 21 Jan. 1906, Part II, p. 1; and Wilson, *The Big Ten*, 74.

26. "Report of the President of Harvard College, 1888–1889," p. 226, HUA, and John W. White, "The Constitution, Authority, and Policies of

the Committee on the Regulation of Athletic Sports," *Harvard Graduates' Magazine* I (Jan. 1893), 226.

27. John W. White, Athletic Committee, "Annual Report, 1889–1890," to Charles W. Eliot, ca. March 1891, Box 262, Jan.–May 1891 Folder, UAI.5.150, HUA.

28. "Report of the President of Harvard College, 1888–1889," pp. 13–14, HUA.

29. "Brown Conference Report on Intercollegiate Sports," HUD 8398.75, HUA.

30. "Report of the President of Harvard College, 1897–1898," pp. 16–17, HUA.

31. Harvard Athletic Committee Minutes, 20 Feb. 1899, HUA.

32. Walter Camp, letter to H. B. Fine, Princeton Athletic Committee, 16 Oct. 1901, Camp Papers, Box 8, Folder 278, YUA.

33. Samuel J. Elder, Boston, letter to Walter Camp, 13 Jan. 1906, Camp Papers, Box 10, Folder 165, YUA.

34. Elder to Camp, 17 Jan. 1906, ibid., YUA.

35. H. A. Bellow, "New Eligibility Rules," *Harvard Graduates' Magazine* XIV (June 1906), 694, and "Tentative Eligibility Rules," ca. Feb. 1906, Camp Papers, Box 8, Folder 278, YUA.

36. Wilson, *The Big Ten*, 74.

37. It has often been commented upon that while upper-class English observed both the letter and the spirit of the rules, Americans were prone to search for openings within the rules to gain an advantage: gamesmanship not sportsmanship. See as examples, "American Croquet," *Nation* III (9 Aug. 1866), 115; G. Stanley Hall, "Student Customs," American Antiquarian Society *Proceedings* XIV (Oct. 1900), 118; John Corbin, "English and American University Athletics," *Outing* XXXIX (Oct. 1901), 32–33; Henry D. Sheldon, *Student Life and Customs* (New York: D. Appleton, 1901), 53; William H. P. Faunce, "Character in Athletics," National Education Association *Proceedings* XLIII (1904), 564; T. Cook, "Some Tendencies in Modern Sport," *Quarterly Review* CXCIX (Jan. 1904), 132, 142; Needham, "The College Athlete," 272–73; Caspar Whitney, "Who Is Responsible for the Commercialism of College Sports?" *Outing* XLVI (July 1905), 486; Ralph D. Paine, "The Spirit of School and College Sport: English and American Football," *Century*, n.s., LXXI (Nov. 1905), 112–16; Hilda W. Smith and Helen Kirk Welch, *Constance M. K. Applebee and the Story of Hockey* (n.p.: privately published, 1975), 43; Endicott Peabody, "The Ideals of Sport in England and America," *American Physical Education Review* XIX (1914), 277–83; Amos Alonzo Stagg and Wesley W. Stout, *Touchdown!* (New York: Longmans, Green, 1927), 57–58; "A French View of American Sport," *Living Age* CCCXXXIX (Feb. 1931), 655; and "Big League Baseball," *Fortune* XVI (Aug. 1937), 37.

38. Davis, *Football*, 478.

39. White, "The Constitution, Authority, and Policy," 229.

40. Bigelow, "Harvard's Better Self," n.p. In the 1960s and 1970s, a federal program provided economic opportunity grants. It sometimes became a vehicle for supporting athletes from economically deprived families.

41. Frank W. Nicolson, Wesleyan faculty, letter to S. V. Coffin, Middleton, 10 Jan. 1905, Athletic, Misc. File, Wesleyan Univ. Archives.

42. James F. Kemp, "History of Faculty Regulation of Athletics at Columbia," *Columbia University Quarterly* IV (March 1902), 170–71.

43. John R. Behee, *Fielding Yost's Legacy* (Ann Arbor, MI: privately printed, 1971), 22, and Francis A. March, Jr., *Athletics at Lafayette College* (Eaton, PA: Lafayette College, 1923), 91.

44. "Statement of the Faculty Committee on Athletics at Pennsylvania State College Regarding A. L. Smith," 12 Nov. 1904, Camp Papers, Box 45, Folder 543, YUA; Transcript from December 1904, *Penn State Collegian*, Camp Papers, Box 45, Folder 204, YUA; Edward R. Bushnell, *History of Athletics at the University of Pennsylvania* (Philadelphia: Athletic Association of the Univ. of Pennsylvania, 1909), Vol. II, p. 24; and Needham, "The College Athlete," 126–27.

45. William F. Galpin, *Syracuse University* (Syracuse, NY: Syracuse Univ. Press, 1952), Vol. I, p. 152.

46. Horace M. Lippincott, "Early Football," *General Magazine and Historical Chronicle* XXXVIII (1936), 31.

47. Voltmer, *A Brief History*, 4.

48. For eligibility rules for some southern colleges, see Edgar S. Kiracofe, "Athletics and Physical Education in Colleges in Virginia," Ph.D. dissertation, Univ. of Virginia, 1932, pp. 55–60.

49. *New York Times*, 30 Dec. 1905, clipping in the Columbia Univ. Football Scrapbook, Columbia Univ. Archives.

50. James D. Jarvis, Cauasotata, letter to President White, 16 Oct. 1875, Andrew D. White Papers, Film #17215, Cornell Univ. Archives.

51. Frank Presbrey and James Moffatt, *Athletics at Princeton* (New York: Frank Presbrey, 1901), 135.

52. "Teaching in American Colleges," *Nation* XXXV (30 Nov. 1882), 458.

53. Thomas J. Wertenbaker, *Princeton 1746–1896* (Princeton, NJ: Princeton Univ. Press, 1946), 329.

54. A. B. Hart, "The Status of Athletics in American Colleges," *Atlantic Monthly* LXVI (July 1890), 67. The *Harvard Advocate*, 17 Dec. 1880, p. 77, noted that "Some students come to college for the avowed purpose of engaging in athletic contests . . . and do not hesitate to say so openly."

55. *Boston Post,* 20 Dec. 1889, clipping in "1889 Football Controversy," HUD 10889.2, HUA.

56. William H. "Pa" Corbin, Fishkill Landings, NY, telegram to Walter Camp, 4 Nov. 1889, Camp Papers, Box 7, Folder 204, YUA.

57. Edgar A. Poe, letter to Walter Camp, 9 Nov. 1889, Camp Papers, Box 20, Folder 553, YUA.

58. *New York Sun,* 27 Nov. 1889, as quoted in the *Harvard Crimson,* 11 Dec. 1889, in "1889 Football Controversy," HUD 10889.2, HUA.

59. G. R. Neidlinger, Columbia player, letter to William P. Mitchell, Columbia Football Manager, 22 March 1900, and "Report to the Advisory Committee of the Columbia University Athletic Association," ca. Spring 1900, in Athletics Folder, Columbia Univ. Central Files.

60. Wesleyan Univ. Faculty Minutes, 26 March 1901, Wesleyan Univ. Archives.

61. "Men of Dartmouth," circular, ca. 1900, in President Tucker Papers, #1, "Athletics, A-H," Dartmouth College Archives.

62. Pennsylvania State Univ. Board of Trustees Executive Committee Minutes, 31 July 1900, Penn State Room, Univ. Archives.

63. College of William and Mary Faculty Minutes, 24 Feb. 1898, William and Mary College Archives.

64. James E. Scanlon, *Randolph Macon College* (Charlottesville: Univ. Press of Virginia, 1983), 162.

65. Thomas G. Dyer, *The University of Georgia* (Athens: Univ. of Georgia Press, 1985), 165.

66. Clifford S. Griffin, *The University of Kansas: A History* (Lawrence: Univ. Press of Kansas, 1974), 650–51.

67. John Rydjord, *A History of Fairmont College* (Lawrence: Regent Press of Kansas, 1977), 165.

68. Robert N. Manley, *Centennial History of the University of Nebraska* (Lincoln: Univ. of Nebraska Press, 1969), Vol. I, p. 299.

69. Walter Camp, "Undergraduate Limitation in College Sports," *Harper's Weekly* XXXVII (11 Feb. 1893), 143.

70. Needham, "The College Athlete," 124; Albert B. Crawford (ed.), *Football Y Men 1872–1919* (New Haven, CT: Yale Univ. 1962), 83; and *New York Post,* 18 Jan. 1906, clipping in the Columbia Univ. Football Scrapbook, Columbia Univ. Archives.

71. Ira N. Hollis, letter to Charles W. Eliot, 16 Jan. 1903, Eliot Papers, Box 110, Folder 243, "Hollis Letters," HUA.

72. Harvard Athletic Committee Minutes, 15 Jan. 1903, HUA.

73. Edward S. Jordan, "Buying Football Victories," *Collier's* XXXVI (11 Nov. 1905), 19.

74. Kent Sagendorph, *Michigan: The Story of the University* (New York: E. P. Dutton, 1948), 31; Behee, *Fielding Yost's Legacy,* 48, 62–72; and Wilson, *The Big Ten,* 62–63.

75. Alexander Meiklejohn, "The Evils of College Athletics," *Harper's Weekly* XLIX (2 Dec. 1905), 1751.

76. William H. P. Faunce, "Character in Athletics," National Education Association *Proceedings* XLIII (1904), 558.

77. William T. Reid, Jr., letter to Walter Camp, 16 April 1908, Camp Papers, Box 20, Folder 573 "William Reid," YUA.

Chapter XIV.   Brutality, Ethics, and the Creation of the NCAA

1. Alexander Meiklejohn, "The Evils of College Athletics," *Harper's Weekly* XLIX (2 Dec. 1905), 1751.

2. Frederick J. Turner, "Speech at Alumni Banquet, 31 January 1906," Turner Papers, Box 2, "Athletics," Wis/Mss/AL, State Historical Society of Wisconsin Archives.

3. See Henry B. Needham, "The College Athlete," *McClure's Magazine* XXV (June, July 1905), 115–28, 260–73; Clarence Deming, "Money Power in College Athletics," *Outlook* LXXX (July 1905), 569–72; Edward S. Jordan, "Buying Football Victories," *Collier's* XXVI (11 Nov. 1905), 19–20, 23, (18 Nov. 1905), 22–23, (25 Nov. 1905), 21–22, 24, (2 Dec. 1905), 19–20, 23, and (9 Dec. 1905), 19–20; and "From a Graduate's Window," *Harvard Graduates' Magazine* XIV (Dec. 1905), 216–23.

4. Louis Filler, *The Muckrakers* (University Park, PA: Pennsylvania State Univ. Press, 1976), 80–89, 216; J. C. Furnas, *The Americans: A Social History of the United States* (New York: G. P. Putnam's Sons, 1969), 868–71; and Herbert Shapiro (ed.), *The Muckrakers and American Society* (Boston: D. C. Heath, 1968), 21–23.

5. Needham, "The College Athlete," 115–28, 260–73. See Ida M. Tarbell, "John D. Rockefeller, A Character Study," *McClure's Magazine* XXV (July 1905), 226–49, and Joseph Lincoln Steffens, "Ohio: A Tale of Two Cities," ibid., 293–311.

6. "A Football Petition," newspaper clipping, 6 Nov. 1903 and 6 Feb. 1903, in Charles W. Eliot Papers, Box 110, Folder 144, "Athletics," Harvard Univ. Archives (hereafter noted as HUA).

7. Theodore Roosevelt, letter to Walter Camp, 24 Nov. 1905, in Elting E. Morison (ed.), *The Letters of Theodore Roosevelt* (Cambridge, MA: Harvard Univ. Press, 1952), Vol. V, p. 94, and Endicott Peabody, letter to Theodore Roosevelt, 21 Sep. 1905, Theodore Roosevelt Collection, Letters Received, Vol. 97, Library of Congress, in Guy M. Lewis, "The American Intercollegiate Football Spectacle, 1869–1917," Ph.D. dissertation, Univ. of Maryland, 1964, pp. 223–24.

8. Robert W. Wiebe, *The Search for Order: 1877–1920* (New York: Hill & Wang, 1967), 192.

9. Theodore Roosevelt, "The Functions of a Great University," Address at Harvard Univ. 28 June 1905, *The Works of Theodore Roosevelt* (New York: Charles Scribner's Sons, 1926), Vol. XVI, pp. 324–25.

10. See Theodore Roosevelt, letter to Henry Beech Needham, 19 July 1905, in Morison, *Letters of Theodore Roosevelt*, Vol. IV, p. 1378. Roosevelt also corresponded with such muckrakers as Lincoln Steffens, Roy Stannard Baker, Upton Sinclair, Frank Norris, and Finley Peter Dunne.

11. Endicott Peabody, letter to Theodore Roosevelt, 16 Sep. 1905, as quoted in Lewis, "The American Intercollegiate Football Spectacle," 223.

12. W. T. Reid, Jr., "1905 Football Diary," 273–74, HUD 10905.76, HUA.

13. *New York Herald*, 12 Oct. 1905, p. 1. Emphasis added.

14. Quoting Karl F. Brill, newspaper clipping, fall 1905, HUD 10905, HUA.

15. *Boston Herald*, 17 Oct. 1926, Sec. E, p. 7.

16. W. T. Reid, Jr., letter to John D. Merrill, Secretary of the Harvard Graduates' Athletic Association, 8 Nov. 1905, in the *Harvard Graduates' Magazine* XIII (Dec. 1905), 300. To compare Reid's letter to Eliot's opinions, see C. W. Eliot, "The Evils of Football," *Harvard Graduates' Magazine* XIII (March 1905), 383–87. See also *Harvard Crimson*, 9 Nov. 1905, p. 1, noting Eliot's criticisms and Reid's letter.

17. Reid, "Diary," 371.

18. Ibid., 384–85, and H. E. von Kersburg, Harvard football player, 1905, letter to Bill Reid, 17 July 1948, William T. Reid Correspondence, HUD 8010, HUA.

19. "Handwritten ms," Reid Correspondence, ibid., 19–20.

20. Reid, "Diary," 436–37.

21. See, for example, Richard Henry Dana, letter to Charles W. Eliot, 18 Dec. 1905, Charles W. Eliot Papers, Box 209, "Dana," HUA, who suggested a football investigation such as the insurance investigation of 1905.

22. "Handwritten ms., 13–14, Reid Correspondence, HUD 8010, HUA.

23. Handwritten ms. of William T. Reid, to H. E. von Kersburg, ca. Aug. 1948, p. 18, in Reid Papers, "Correspondence" Folder, HUD 8010, HUA. The quote was crossed out and replaced by "I'll have to give this matter further thought" so that "no offense could possibly be taken."

24. Paul J. Dashiell, Naval Academy, letter to Theodore Roosevelt, 7 Dec. 1905, in Charles W. Eliot Papers, Box 244, "Theodore Roosevelt" Folder, HUA.

25. Reid, "Handwritten ms," 13–14, Reid Correspondence, HUD 8010, HUA.

26. "From a Graduate's Window," *Harvard Graduates' Magazine* XIV (Dec. 1905), 216–23.

27. Walter Camp, letter to W. W. Skiddy, Stamford, CT, 8 Dec. 1905,

Camp Papers, Box 13, Folder 348, Yale Univ. Archives (hereafter noted as YUA).

28. J. W. Curtis, letter to Walter Camp, 1 Dec. 1905, Camp Papers, Box 48, 1904–5 Folder, YUA.

29. Lewis S. Welch, letter to President Arthur T. Hadley, 4 Dec. 1905, in George B. Adams Collection, Box 7, Folder 35, YUA.

30. Arthur T. Hadley, letter to Charles W. Eliot, 9 May 1905, Eliot Papers, Box 216, "Hadley" File, HUA. Eliot was asked to be the first lecturer on 13 Nov. 1905, to which he later agreed.

31. Henry M. MacCracken, telegram to Charles W. Eliot, 25 Nov. 1905, Eliot Papers, Box 227, "MacCracken" Folder, HUA.

32. Eliot, telegram to MacCracken, 26 Nov. 1905, as quoted in *New York Daily Tribune,* 29 Nov. 1905, p. 2.

33. *New York Daily Tribune,* 29 Nov. 1905, p. 2.

34. Ibid.

35. Butler, letter to Francis S. Bangs, Chairman of the Columbia Committee on Athletics, 12 Dec. 1905, Francis S. Bangs Papers, 1905–10 Folder, Columbia Univ. Central Files.

36. Kirchwey, letter to Nicholas M. Butler, 14 July 1902, Athletics Folder, Columbia Univ. Central Files.

37. *Columbia Spectator,* 9 Oct. 1905, p. 1; *New York Daily Tribune,* 8 Oct. 1905, p. 9 and 10 Oct. 1905, p. 4; *New York Herald,* 8 Oct. 1905, Sec. I, p. 1; and *New York Sun,* 8 Oct. 1905, Columbia Univ. Football Scrapbook, Columbiana Collection, Columbia Univ.

38. *Columbia Spectator,* 29 Nov. 1905, p. 1, and *New York Daily Tribune,* 29 Nov. 1905, p. 1. For a more complete account of the Columbia banning, see Ronald A. Smith, "Harvard and Columbia and a Reconsideration of the 1905–06 Football Crisis," *Journal of Sport History* VIII (Winter 1981), 5–19.

39. Francis S. Bangs, letter to Nicholas Murray Butler, 28 Oct. 1905, Bangs Papers, 1905–10, Folder, Columbia Univ. Central Files.

40. Nicholas Murray Butler, letter to Francis S. Bangs, 30 Oct. 1905, ibid.

41. *Columbia Spectator,* 11 Dec. 1905, p. 1. Voting for reform were Fordham, Haverford, Lafayette, Rutgers, Swarthmore, Syracuse, Wesleyan, and West Point. Guy Lewis was not correct in "Theodore Roosevelt's Role in the 1905 Football Controversy," *Research Quarterly* XL (Dec. 1969), 721, when he stated that "there was no opposition to the proposals that the group endorse football and initiate a reform movement" at the MacCracken meeting.

42. *Columbia Spectator,* 11 Dec. 1905, p. 4.

43. *New York Daily Tribune,* 21 Dec. 1905, p. 10.

44. *New York Evening Mail,* 4 Dec. 1905, in Columbia Univ. Football Scrapbook, Columbiana Collection, Columbia Univ.

45. *New York Daily Tribune,* 25 Nov. 1905, p. 1.

46. For instance, Theodore Roosevelt wrote H. S. White, Chairman of the Harvard Athletic Committee, suggesting that White should see Reid and discuss Reid's White House discussions. See H. S. White, letter to W. T. Reid, 14 Dec. 1905, Reid Papers, 1905 Folder, HUD 8010, HUA. Eliot and other Harvard officials were distressed at the injury situation after team physician, Dr. Nichols, published "The Physical Aspect of American Football" in the January issue of the *Boston Medical and Surgical Journal.* It showed that 175 days were lost from classes by the Harvard football team and 1,057 days of incapacitation due to injuries. See *Harvard Crimson,* 5 Jan. 1906, pp. 1, 3, 5.

47. Theodore Roosevelt, letter to Edward Deshon Brandegee, 7 March 1906, in Morison, *Letters of Theodore Roosevelt,* Vol. V, p. 172; Eliot, letter to Roosevelt, 12 Dec. 1905, in Henry James, *Charles William Eliot* (Boston: Houghton-Mifflin, 1930), Vol. II, pp. 156–57; and Roosevelt, letter to Eliot, 21 Dec. 1905, Eliot Papers, Box 244, Theodore Roosevelt Folder, HUA.

48. The other five members were Dr. E. Nichols, '86; Robert Wrenn, '91; William H. Lewis, '95; W. Cameron Forbes, '95; and Lorin F. Deland, inventor of the Flying Wedge. Briggs was in the class of '75; Reid in the class of '01.

49. H. S. White, Chairman, Harvard Athletic Committee, letter to W. T. Reid, 14 Dec. 1905, Reid Correspondence, 1905 Folder, HUD 8010, HUA; Walter Camp, letter to William T. Reid, Jr., 15 Dec. 1905, Camp Papers, Box 20, Folder 572, Wm. Reid Folder, YUA; Prof. J. B. Fine, Princeton, letter to Walter Camp, 27 Dec. 1905, Camp Papers, Box 8, Folder 278, YUA; and *New York Daily Tribune,* 18 Dec. 1905, p. 10 and *New York Sun,* 17 Jan. 1906, in Columbia Univ. Football Scrapbook, Columbiana Collection, Columbia Univ.

50. Athletic Committee Minutes, 20 Dec. 1905, *Harvard Graduates' Magazine* XIV (March 1906), 484; W. T. Reid, Jr., telegram to Walter Camp, 19 Dec. 1905; and Reid, telegram to Camp, 21 Dec. 1905, Camp Papers, Box 20 Folder 572, Wm. Reid Folder, YUA.

51. W. T. Reid, Jr., letter to Walter Camp, 21 Dec. 1905, ibid.

52. The NCAA, until 1910, was called the Intercollegiate Athletic Association of the United States. Initially, however, it was called the National Intercollegiate Football Conference. See "National Intercollegiate Football Conference," National College Conference, letter to American colleges, ca. 1 Jan. 1906, HUA. The football committee consisted of Edward K. Hall, Dartmouth; Charles Daly, West Point; James A. Babbitt, Haverford; Charles W. Savage, Oberlin; Henry L. Williams, Minnesota; James T. Lees, Nebraska; and F. Homer Curtis, Texas. Hall, Daly, and Williams were ex-football players from Dartmouth, Harvard, and Yale. *New York Times,* 29 Dec. 1905, and *New York Sun,* 29 Dec. 1905, in

Columbia Univ. Football Scrapbook, Columbiana Collection, Columbia Univ.

53. "National Intercollegiate Football Conference," National College Conference, letter to American colleges, ca. 1 Jan. 1906, HUA, and *New York Times*, 30 Dec. 1905, in Columbia Univ. Football Scrapbook, Columbiana Collection, Columbia Univ.

54. Harvard Athletic Committee Minutes, 10 Jan. 1906, HUA, and Records of the Overseers of Harvard College, 10 Jan. 1906, HUA.

55. *Harvard Crimson*, 10 Jan. 1906, p. 1, and R. B. Meriman, "Football Reform," *Harvard Graduates' Magazine* XIV (March 1906), 426–27.

56. Theodore Roosevelt, letter to Paul Dashiell, 10 Jan. 1906, Roosevelt Collection, Vol. 152, Letterbook 30, Library of Congress, as cited in Guy M. Lewis, "Theodore Roosevelt's Role in the 1905 Football Controversy," *Research Quarterly* XI (Dec. 1969), 723. Princeton's faculty opposed the amalgamation, probably fearing that it might be left off the rules committee. See Prof. J. B. Fine, Princeton, two telegrams to Walter Camp, 9 Jan. 1906, Camp Papers, Box 8, Folder 278, YUA. Amos Alonzo Stagg of Chicago, a western token on the old rules committee, favored amalgamation, but left the decision up to Camp as he could not attend. See Stagg, letter to Camp, 11 Jan. 1906, Camp Papers, Box 23, Folder 652, YUA.

57. W. T. Reid, Jr., letter to Walter Camp, 10 Jan. 1906, Camp Papers, Box 20, Folder 272, YUA.

58. *New York Times*, 13 Jan. 1906, p. 7.

59. Hadley, letter to Camp, 2 Feb. 1906, Camp Papers, Box 49, 1906 folder, YUA.

60. *Boston Herald*, 17 Oct. 1926, Sec. E., p. 7. This account is the first that Reid gave publicly—two decades after the event.

61. Wm. T. Reid ms., sent to H. E. von Kersburg, ca. Aug. 1948, in Reid Papers, Correspondence Folder, 17–18, HUD 8010, HUA.

62. Records of Overseers, 10 Jan. 1906, HUA, and *New York Times*, 16 Jan. 1906, p. 8.

63. "American Intercollegiate Football Rules Committee Meeting, 1906," Camp Papers, Box 1, Folder 28, YUA, and Minutes of the Intercollegiate Football Rules Committee, 14 April 1906, Camp Papers, Box 1, Folder 216, YUA. The Spalding subsidy was $500.

64. Murpf, Athletic Association of Univ. of Pennsylvania, letter to James Curtis, 22 Jan. 1906, Camp Papers, Box 20, Folder 543, YUA.

65. *New York Times*, 29 Nov. 1905, p. 1.

66. Deming, "Money Power," 569–72; and Yale Faculty Records, 13 and 20 Jan. 1906, YUA; *New York Times*, 28 Oct. 1905, p. 12, and 21 Jan. 1906, p. 10; and *New York Tribune*, 16 Jan. 1906, *New York Sun*, 22 Jan. 1906, and *New York Evening Post*, 21 Dec. 1905, in Columbia Univ. Football Scrapbook, Columbiana Collection, Columbia Univ.

67. Harvard Athletic Committee Minutes, 14 Feb. 1906, HUA.

68. *New York Times*, 25 Feb. 1906, p. 11, and Parke H. Davis, *Football: The American Intercollegiate Game* (New York: Charles Scribner's Sons, 1911), 495–97.

69. Galley proofs of the "Official Foot Ball Rules, 1906," 23 April 1906, Eliot Papers, Box 276, April 1906 Folder, HUA. These rules show that the first forward pass limitation was for the untouched pass to go to the opponent where the ball touched the ground. See Bill Reid, "A Discussion of the New Football Rules," ms., p. 13, Reid Papers, General Folder, HUD 8010, HUA.

70. Carl F. Price, *Wesleyan's First Century* (Middletown, CT: Wesleyan Univ. 1932), 262, and John Rydjord, *A History of Fairmont College* (Lawrence: Regents Press of Kansas, 1977), 163. Washburn's "Bottles" Hope may have thrown the first pass in the experimental game. See Riley Ondek, "Birth of the Bomb," *Sports History* I (Mar. 1988), 39.

71. Records of the Overseers of Harvard College, 9 May 1906, HUA, and *Harvard Crimson*, 10 May 1906, p. 1.

72. "Topics from the President's Report," *Harvard Graduates' Magazine* XIV (March 1906), 406.

73. James V. Koch, "The Economics of 'Big-Time' Intercollegiate Athletics," *Social Science Quarterly* LII (Sep. 1971), 248–49.

74. Intercollegiate Athletic Association of the United States [NCAA] *Proceedings*, 29 Dec. 1906, pp. 2–4.

75. J. E. Sullivan, letter to Palmer E. Pierce, in ibid., 24.

76. "Constitution and By-Laws," ibid., 29–37.

77. James Bryce, "America Revisited: The Changes of a Quarter Century," *Outlook* LXXIX (25 March 1905), 735.

78. Intercollegiate Athletic Association of the United States [NCAA] *Proceedings*, 2 Jan. 1909, pp. 2–4, and 28 Dec. 1909, pp. 3–5.

Chapter XV.   The Swarthmore Case: An Addendum on Freedom

1. *The Last Will and Codicils of Anna T. Jeanes Deceased* (Philadelphia: J. B. Lippincott, 1907), 9, in Anna T. Jeanes, 1822–1907, File, Swarthmore College Library.

2. "Summary of the Opinions of College and University Presidents," *Swarthmore College Bulletin* V (Dec. 1907), 10–23.

3. "Statement of President Joseph Swain to the Board of Managers of Swarthmore College," *ibid.*, 8.

4. Yale Univ. Faculty Minutes, 22 Feb. 1906, and Prof. Woolsey, Chairman, "Report of the Athletic Investigation Committee, 31 January 1906," Walter Camp Papers, Yale Univ. Archives.

5. Following the 1925 decision by Harold "Red" Grange to drop out

of the Univ. of Illinois before graduation to play professional football, the National Football League agreed the following year not to sign college football players until after the class they were in graduated. This violation of an individual's freedom and constitutional rights by the National Football League has never been challenged in the courts and still exists.

Epilogue.   A Twentieth-Century Meaning of American College Athletics

1. Frederick Jackson Turner, "Alumni Speech," (1906), Turner Papers, Box 2, Univ. of Wisconsin Athletics Folder, State Historical Society of Wisconsin Archives.

2. Princeton Faculty Minutes, 29 Nov. 1886, 10 Oct. 1887, 19 Oct. and 9 Nov. 1888, Princeton Univ. Archives.

3. John R. Behee, *Fielding Yost's Legacy to the University of Michigan* (Ann Arbor, MI: privately printed, 1971), 70–72.

4. Samuel H. Ranck, "Alumni Representation in College Government," *Education* XXII (Oct. 1901), 107–10.

5. Paul Hardin, "University Presidents Must Speak Out," *New York Times*, 22 March 1987, Sec. S, p. 7, and Douglas Lederman, "Trustees' Role in Cleaning Up Sports Abuses Seen Crucial," *Chronicle of Higher Education* XXXIII (3 June 1987), 36.

6. Ernest L. Boyer, "College Athletics: The Control of the Campus," in Donald Chu et al., *Sport in Higher Education* (Champaign, IL: Human Kinetics, 1985), 409.

7. "From a Graduate's Window," *Harvard Graduates' Magazine* XIV (Dec. 1905), 222.

8. Lawrence Veysey, "Letter to the Editor," *New York Review of Books*, 4 March 1982, p. 44.

9. Henry S. Pritchett, "Progress of the State Universities," Carnegie Foundation for the Advancement of Teaching *Annual Report* VI (1911), 108.

10. Herschel Nissenson, "Fans Questioning 'Bama's Hiring of Curry," *Centre Daily Times,* 8 March 1987, p. C-6.

11. It might be argued that booster clubs are another group which has influenced the direction of big-time athletics. Most booster clubs, however, appear to be dominated by alumni or by those who wished they were graduates.

12. See Roger L. Geiger, *To Advance Knowledge: The Growth of American Research Universities, 1900–1940* (New York: Oxford Univ. Press, 1986), 48–49, 80, for figures on Harvard-endowed chairs and the Yale Alumni Fund.

INDEX

Academic eligibility. *See* Eligibility
Academics and athletes, 157, 158, 267n.54
Achieved status, 263n.28
Advertising through athletics, 43, 46, 49, 192
Agassiz, Alexander, 31
Alabama, University of, 216
Alabama claims, 39, 42, 112
All-American football teams, 88
Allegheny College, 184
Allotment of seats, 143
Alumni: on athletic committee, 132; on athletic teams, 176; control of football rules, 94; financing of athletics, 34, 40, 212; involvement in athletics, 129, 214
Amateur Athletic Union, 207
Amateur code, 65, 143
Amateurism: defined, 166; hypocrisy in, 66, 106, 167, 171, 259n.12; lack of ancient Greek concept, 166; myth of, 114, 147; and participation against professionals, 58, 59; rules of (*see also* Eligibility), 143; spirit of, 147; and upper class, 65, 162, 166–67, 172, 173, 256n.2, 263–64n.28
Amateur-professional controversies, 61, 62–66, 128, 162–64, 165–74, 263–64n.28
Amateur-professional dilemma, 165–66, 171–72, 174

America, 110
American College Base Ball Association, 59
American Council on Education, 214
American League, 65
America's Cup, 110, 114
Ames, James Barr, 130
Ames, Knowlton "Snake," 63, 185
Amherst College, 30, 43, 52–55, 59, 61, 62, 67, 104, 106, 107, 136, 160, 170
Andover preparatory school, 158, 193
Andover Theological Seminary, 101
Andrews, W. H., on athletic recruiting, 184–85
Anglo-Saxon Olympics, 110
Anglo-Saxon superiority, 96, 116
Anson, Cap, 60
Army-Navy football abolished, 93
Ascribed status, 263n.28
Association football (soccer), 70
Athletic committees: and eligibility rules, 182; need for, 137; powers of, 142; recommendation for creation of, 142
Athletic conferences: of 1883–84, 138; of 1898, 138–44; of 1905–6, 199–206; proposal of 1886, 136–38; proposal of Charles Eliot, 135–36
Athletic eligibility. *See* Eligibility
Athletic grants-in-aid. *See* Athletic scholarships; Subsidization
Athletic reserve fund, 122–23

Athletics: and academics, 185; control of, 144–45, 214, 216; evils of, 129, 193; and excesses, 124; and financial waste, 193; and governance, 144–46; and physical freedom, 212; place of, in education, 139, 192; prestige of, 33, 37, 43, 45, 214, 218; loss of, 165; regulation of, 121

Athletic scholarships, 140, 158, 171, 184–87, 188; *see also* Subsidization

Athletocracy, 132, 198

Attendance at classes by athletes, 157, 158

Authority and totalitarianism, 57, 212

Away games, 127

Babbitt, James A., 204, 272n.52

Bacon, Robert, 102

Bacon, Wilbur, 35

Baker, Ray Stannard, as a muckraker, 192

Bancroft, Frank, 60

Bancroft, William, 128

Bandy, 10, 22

Banning sports, 8, 10, 68–69, 73, 199, 205, 229n.39, 237n.24; and crisis of 1905–6, 206; threatened, 122; through financial gift, 209

Barnard, Frederick A. P., 46

Bartlett, S. C., 13

Barzun, Jacques, 52

Bascom, John, 54

Baseball, 8, 10, 22, 59, 69, 119; development of, 52–66; firsts, 219; rules of, 53. *See also* Summer baseball

Basketball, 22, 119; firsts, 220

Bates College, 160

Bathing, 10

Beebe, William, 123

Beloit College, 69

Bennett, James Gordon, Jr., 104, 108

Benton, Otis, 104–5

Betting, 5, 7, 8, 31, 32, 34, 40, 43, 44, 45, 259n.12

Bicycle racing, 109, 119; firsts, 219

Biglin, John, 149

Big Ten Conference, 94, 132, 134, 138, 192; on banning freshmen and graduates, 182; on eligibility rules, 180; and joining the NCAA, 207; remaining out of NCAA, 207

Big Three, 57, 77, 135; on banning graduate participation, 182; on eligibility rules, 180; leadership of, 81, 92, 194, 201; and power conflicts, 62, 265n.23; remaining out of NCAA, 206; and White House conference, 193

Billiards, 9, 33, 70, 121

Biomechanical analysis, 158

Black athletes, 260n.35

Blaikie, William, 36, 40, 41, 104, 246n.9

Blew, John, 149

"Block" game, 79, 87

Bloody Monday, 20–21, 68

Boat clubs, 3, 26, 30, 31, 32, 34, 47

Boat houses, 34

Boating, 5; *see also* Crew

Bona fide students, 143, 182–84

Books, burial of, 236n.4

Booster clubs, 275n.11

Boosterism, 46

Boston Athletic Association, 115, 116

Boston Brahmins, 43, 125, 163

Boston Red Stockings, 59

Bowdoin College, 30, 42, 43, 47, 55, 149, 160

Bowie, Duncan, 104–5, 108

Bowling, 10, 22

Bowling on the green, 5

Boxing, 5, 22, 35, 44, 110

Brainard, Asa, 57

Briggs, LeBaron, 85, 115, 202, 272n.48

British Amateur Rowing Association, 166

British-American competition, 38–42, 108, 110–14

British-American relations, 38–42, 112

British elitism, 63–64

British influence: on American culture, 38, 110; on American education, 3–12; on baseball, 52; on concept of amateurism, 166–67, 172, 263–65n.28; on track and field, 99–100, 106

British public schools, 100

Brooklyn Atlantics, 57
Brooks, Marshall, 109
Brown University, 9, 23, 29, 31, 32, 42, 55, 59, 60, 61, 62, 63, 64, 69, 140, 160, 179, 191, 207
Brown, Joseph, eligibility controversy, 176
Brown Conference Committee Report, 140–44
Brown Conference of 1898, 138–44, 181
Brutality. *See under* Football
Bryce, James, laissez-faire policy, 207
Bull-baiting, 5
Bumping races, 6
Burke, Thomas, 116
Burr, Francis, 196
Bush, Archie, 57
Butler, Nicholas Murray: on banning football, 199; condemnation of rules committee, 201
Byron, Lord (George), 5, 6

Caledonian Games, 103, 104, 106
California, University of, 201, 207, 210
Cambridge University Athletic Club, 101
Camp, Alice Graham Sumner, 86
Camp, Walter, 48, 136, 163, 186, 196, 203, 218; as athletic dictator, 198; biography of, 83–88; as coach, 85, 240n.2, 240n.4; development of all-American teams, 88; development of football signals, 87; on eligibility rules, 177; "Father" of American football, 63; favoring yards and down rule, 204–5; football rules development, 86–88, 204–5; investigation of football injuries, 91; investigation of summer baseball, 64–65; on opposing Charles Eliot, 95; on opposing freshman participation, 181; on opposing unilateral eligibility rules, 179; as player, 78, 79; and secret athletic fund, 170, 205; as secretary of football rules committee, 94; on student control, 118, 122, 138; on warning of throwing

contests, 187; at White House conference, 194
Canada, 39, 75
Cane rushes, 19
Captains, leadership of, 35, 45, 47, 54, 55, 57–58, 69–72, 74, 85, 91, 119, 125–26, 153, 186
Carlisle Indians, 160
Carnegie Foundation for the Advancement of Teaching, 215
Carnegie Report on American College Athletics, 214
Carroll College, 206
Cavanaugh, John, on manliness, 97
Cayuga Lake, 47
Chapel, 11, 15, 19, 23, 31
Character building, 11, 129
Cheating in classroom, 193
Cheers, organized, 79
Chess match, 33, 233–34n.13
Chicago, University of, 81, 207; and athletic scholarships, 188–89
Chicago Coliseum, 81
Chicago White Stockings, 57, 60
Cincinnati Red Stockings, 57
Civil War, 33, 34, 39, 55–56
Claflin, J. T., 54
Clark, Ellery, 115, 116
Clarkson, John, 64
Clarkson, Walter, 64
Clark University, 65
Class battles, 13, 23, 68, 69
Classical curriculum, 6, 11, 12, 14
Cleveland, President Grover, 93, 112
Cleveland Forest Cities, 57
Coaches, 55, 85; alumni, 36, 148, 149, 155; amateur, 162; amateur coaching criticized, 161; amateur-professional debate, 151, 162–64; approval of, 125; British, 162; power of, 217; pressures of, 156, 160–61; professional, 4, 35, 40, 43, 44, 47, 98, 109, 128, 135, 136, 138, 139, 140, 147–64, 162, 171, 193, 214, 256n.2; professionals banned, 126, 149; professors as, 163; salaries, 147, 152, 155, 156, 163
Cock-fighting, 5, 8
Coffin, Captain, 154

Colleges, formation of, 9
College Baseball Association, 185
College of New Jersey (Princeton University), 9
College of Philadelphia (University of Pennsylvania), 9, 10, 102, 103
College of Rhode Island (Brown University), 9
College Rowing Association, 47
College Rowing Association Regatta, 42
College Union Regatta, 32
Collegiate way, 11–12
Colors, college, 7, 29, 70, 75, 77, 80, 237n.12
Columbia University (King's College), 9, 30, 44, 46, 49, 50, 51, 62, 72, 73, 74, 80, 102, 103, 109, 115, 136, 137, 145, 149, 150, 160, 171, 179, 184, 192, 199, 201
Commercialization, 52, 98, 139, 141, 192, 213, 217, 218, 229n.41; and crew, 26–37, 44, 108; and football, 82; and the first contest, 3–4, 27–29; at Henley, 8; by railroads, 3–4, 27–29; by Albert Spalding, 204
Community, sense of, 21
Competition, against professionals, 127, 136, 169
Competitive spirit, 10
Connecticut game (baseball), 53
Connolly, Jim, 115
Convention, football, 74
Cook, Robert, 45, 51
Cooperation among colleges. *See* Inter-institutional control
Corbin, William "Pa," 85, 91, 186
Cornell, Ezra, 47
Cornell Football Association, 72
Cornell-Leander crew race, 152
Cornell University, 44, 45, 47, 48, 50, 51, 72, 73, 93, 102, 104, 106, 107, 109, 132, 140, 148, 149, 150–54, 160, 203, 207
Coubertin, Baron de, 114–15
Coulter, Henry, 149
Count de Paris, 40
Courtney, Charles, 51; as amateur rower, 150, 259n.12; biography of,

150–54; on British sportsmanship, 153; as coach, 150, 153, 258n.11, 259–60n.30; as professional rower, 150–51
Courtney-Hanlan matches, 150–51
Crew, 5, 22, 26–51, 69, 119, 125; firsts, 219; professional watermen, 6, 27
Cricket, 5, 6, 22, 52, 64, 69, 119, 125; firsts, 219; international, 250n.71
Cross country, 22, 100–102, 119; firsts, 220
Crowds. *See* Spectators
Cudgel-playing, 5
Curry, Bill, 216
Curtis, F. Homer, 272n.52
Curtis, James T., 198
Cutts, Oliver, 155

Dalrymple, Abner, 60
Daly, Charles, 272n.52
Dartmouth College, 9, 10, 13, 16, 21, 22, 30, 44, 55, 59, 61, 132, 140, 149, 160, 167, 179, 210
Dashiell, Paul, 202, 203; and officiating controversy, 197
Davis, Andrew, 118
Davis, Bill, 206
Dean, Dudley, 63
Debating clubs. *See* Literary societies
Deland, Lorin F., 90–91, 157, 272n.48
Deming, Clarence, as muckraker, 122, 205
Dennis, L. M., 203
Dickens, Charles, 40
Diet, 35, 47–48, 157
Drinking, 26–27, 121, 154
Drug testing and student freedom, 218
Dual league of Harvard and Yale, 232n.51
Duke University (Trinity), 22
Duke Athletic Association, 119
Dunham, George, 32
Dunne, Finley Peter, muckraker, 192

Edwards, Duncan, 178
Effeminacy, 97, 244n.62, 244–45n.68, 245n.70; *see also* Manliness
Egalitarianism, 23, 49–50, 51; and athletic prizes, 249n.47

Elder, Samuel, 181
Eligibility, 63, 135, 161; and academics, 158, 161, 181; of alumni, 176; and bona fide students, 182–84; of freshman, 143, 180–82; of graduate students, 140, 176–80, 265n.22; and half-year residency, 179, 183, 184; and one-year residency, 183, 184; limited to four years, 137, 143; and loss of freedom, 211; for more than four years, 139; and NCAA home rule policy, 207; and one-year rule for transfers, 143; of professional school students, 59, 139, 176; of professionals, 63, 104, 155; rule development, 175–90; rule violations, 214; rules, lack of, 71; of special students, 183; of transfer students, 139, 143, 183–84; and the undergraduate rule, 178; of undergraduates, 140
Eliot, Charles W., 129, 177, 201, 209; and athletic reform, 215–16; and athletic scholarships, 188; on competing against professionals, 125, 128, 135–36, 169; and decline of leadership role in athletics, 199; describes Walter Camp, 200; on drinking, 26; as exponent of British model of athletics, 141; on interinstitutional control, 135–36; on manliness, 97; and opposition to football, 95, 195, 206; on opposition to freshman participation, 181; as professional athlete, 31; and relations between Harvard and Yale, 198; on training, 35; on violence, 91
Elites: academic, 5, 33, 48; athletic, 64; social, 15, 30
Elkins, James, 3, 28
Elliott, boat builder, 40
Englehardt, George, 149
Enrollment, college, 17
Equipment: baseball, 66; crew, 40, 231n.34; headgear, 239n.60. *See also* Uniforms
Ernst, Harold, 59

Esprit de corps, 55, 83
Ethics in athletics, 145; *see also under* Football
Eton Public School, 6, 41, 100
Excellence in athletics, 34, 141, 148, 218; and freedom of opportunity, 172
Exeter preparatory school, 193
Extracurriculum, 13, 15, 17, 22–23, 56, 69, 121; and loss of freedom, 212

Facilities, 34, 70, 78, 132; *see also* Stadiums
Faculty athletic control, 118–33; and banning of sports, 9, 10, 14, 36, 68, 89, 94, 95, 130, 237n.24; and the Brown Conference, 138–43; and eligibility, 177; failure of, 130, 132, 134–46, 214–15; lack of, at Harvard, 255n.61; and legislation, 58, 63, 73, 76, 120–24, 127, 182, 205, 229n.39; loss of, at Dartmouth, 255n.61; NCAA support of, 208; problems of, 145–46
Faculty athletic guidelines, 142
Faculty collusion with athletes, 193
Fagging, 8, 17
Fairmont College, 187, 206
Fans. *See* Spectators
Faulkner, George, 128
Fay, Joseph, 176
Fencing, 22, 119; firsts, 220
Field days (track), 106
Field hockey, 10, 22
Financing athletics, 34, 40, 44, 46, 119, 132
Fine, John B., 194
Firsts (in all sports, 1852–1905), 219–20; American rugby football game, 76; Baseball game, 52–55; Football game, 69–72; Harvard-Yale baseball game, 35; intercollegiate crew, 3, 27–29; intercollegiate crew, cricket in England, 6; international crew meet, 38–42; international track meet, 111; rugby football game, 74–77; track meet, 105. *See also under individual sport*

Fishing, 5, 10, 22

Fives, 22; *see also* Handball

Football, 5, 8, 13, 22, 78, 119; abolishment of, 128, 130, 199; allotment of seats, 143; benefits of, 91; brutality of, 63, 67, 69, 83, 88–95, 129, 145, 159, 191–208; burial of, 67–69; development of, 67–98; downs and yards, 86, 203; ethics, 191–208; firsts, 219; flying wedge, 90–91, 157, 242n.35; forward pass, 203, 205–6, 274n.69, 274n.70; interference, 87; open style of play, 90; played indoors, 239n.73; professional, 211; quarterback development, 86–87; reform of, 145, 198–208; rule demands by Harvard, 203–4; rules, 70, 73–79, 86, 90, 129, 205–6, 238n.35; rules committee, 200, 201, 202–4, 207, 273n.56; rushes, 20–21; scrimmage and scrummage, 79, 86; secret practices, 91; signals, 87; spying on opponents, 91

Football Facts and Figures, 91, 92–94

Forbes, W. Cameron, 272n.48

Fox hunting, 5

Franklin, Ben, 103

Frantz, Orville "Home Run," and athletic scholarship, 188

Fraternities and social freedom, 16, 23, 212

Freeborn, Chick, 153

Freedom: and anarchy, 24, 56, 212; and equality, 24–25, 226n.42, 263n.26; as an ideology, 13, 23–25, 226n.42, 263n.26; institutional, 10, 208, 210; of opportunity, 55, 162, 172, 263n.36; and the professional athletic model, 172–74; to pursue profits, 3; to recruit athletes, 187; and responsibility, 120–24; student (*see* Freedom of students)

Freedom of students: to achieve athletic excellence, 172; to compete, 51, 52, 55, 58, 117, 145, 148; and drug testing, 218; to earn money professionally, 62, 275n.5;

and the elective system, 225n.17; and the extracurriculum, 23–25, 95, 118; intellectual, 23, 24–25, 212; loss of, 68, 123, 128, 132, 153, 190, 211; physical, 23, 24–25, 210–12; pursuit of, 3–4, 16, 23–25, 107; and signing professional contracts, 217; social, 23, 24–25, 212; to transfer schools, 217

French Revolution, 24

Freshman, 5, 8, 17; eligibility, 71, 180–82; initiation rites, 8; and sophomore battles, 13, 19, 21, 69; teams, importance of, 180

Friends University, 187

Fund-raising. *See* Financing athletics

Gambling. *See* Betting

Gamesmanship vs. sportsmanship, 263–64n.28, 266n.37

Garrett, Robert, 115

Gate receipts, 3–4, 75, 80, 81, 120, 123, 139, 140, 169, 193

Georgetown University, 81, 109, 189

Georgia, University of, 56, 186

Gladstone, William, 40

Glass, Edgar, 155

Glee clubs, 33

Glen Mitchell trotting park, 108

Goldie, George, 103

Golf, 119; firsts, 220

Governing boards, 10, 16, 135; attitudes toward athletics, 97; banning sports, 10, 33; business-oriented, 98; and control of athletics, 126, 130–132, 210, 215; on controlling presidents, 97; favoring reform of football, 206; favoring student management, 144; and football rules, 200; on inter-institutional control, 137; investigating football evils, 91; and reform of football, 164, 195, 204; sanctioning athletic scholarships, 171, 186; on usefulness of athletics, 46, 214, 245n.77

Graduate participation, 30, 59

Grant, Henry, 74

Grants-in-aid. *See* Athletic scholarships
Great Awakening, 9
Gregory, George "Dad," 189
"Gridiron" game, 87
Groton preparatory school, 193
Gummere, William S., 69–72
Gymnasium directors, 33
Gymnastics, 119; firsts, 220

Hadley, Arthur T., 145, 198; opposed to Harvard influence, 204
Hall, Edward K., 272n.52
Hall, G. Stanley, 65
Hamilton College, 47, 55, 170
Hampden Park, 104
Handball, 5, 10, 22
Hanlan, Ned, 150–51
Hare and hound running, 22, 100–102
Harlan, John, 125
Harper, William Rainey, 163; on manliness, 97
Harriers, 102
Harris, Harold, on amateurism, 167
Harrow Public School, 6
Hart, Albert B., 51, 113; on role of athletes in college, 185
Harvard: and athletic scholarships, 188; breaks relations with Princeton, 178; condemnation of Yale athletics, 192; and eligibility controversies, 59–61, 62–66, 136–37, 176–80, 185–86; and football rushes, 20–21, 67–68; lack of faculty control, 255n.61; lack of student control, 255n.61; leadership in academics, 130, 163; leadership in athletics, 37, 57, 74–78, 80; and the NCAA, 206–7; nonfreshmen on freshmen teams, 180–81; withdrawal from football association, 89–90, 93, 178, 183
Harvard Athletic Association, 102, 119
Harvard Athletic Committee: and athletic governance, 144–45; on eligibility, 177; and football reform, 89, 202; on inter-institutional control, 136; as a model, 127–31; and summer baseball, 62–66
Harvard Board of Overseers: opposed to professional coach, 164; vote on football, 204, 206
Harvard College Foot Ball Club, 73
Harvard Corporation, 144, 206
Harvard governing boards, and reform of football, 195
Harvard Graduate Football Association, 156
Harvard Graduates' Athletic Association, 272n.48; and reform of football, 195, 201
Harvard-Oxford boat race, 38–42, 58, 110, 112
Harvard-Princeton controversy, 177–78
Harvard and Yale: athletic domination by Yale, 163; attitude of arrogance, 232n.43; and big-time athletics, 213–14; broken relations, 42, 50, 94, 112; Burr-Quill incident, 196–97; chess match, 33; and commercialism, 4, 27–29, 31–34, 36; compared with Oxford and Cambridge, 49, 51; dual competition as elitist, 173; dual league, 232n.51; dual meets, 49, 56, 107; first contests, 3–4, 27–29, 33, 167; leadership in athletics, 8, 76–77, 107, 109, 178–79, 213; withdrawal from regatta, 48–50, 107, 148, 149
Harvard-Yale, Oxford-Cambridge track meet, 114
Haughton, Percy, 161, 164
Haverford College, 204
Hayes, President Rutherford B., 61
Hazing, 8, 17, 21, 67
Heffelfinger, Walter "Pudge," 85, 92, 93
Henley Regatta, 7, 50, 151, 152
Hennan, "Benicia Boy," 35
Heston, Willie, 189
Higginson, Major Henry L., 197
Higginson, Thomas Wentworth, 67
Hildebrand, Arthur, 194
Hitchcock, Edward, 136

Hogan, James, and athletic subsidization, 188

Hollis, Ira N., 144–145; and athletic scholarships, 188; opposed to professional coach, 163

Holy Cross University, 160

Home grounds, 126, 140, 143

Home rule and eligibility rules, 207

Honor, loss of, 124

Honor, to colleges from athletics, 33

Horse racing, 5, 8, 27

Horseback riding, 5, 22

How to Get Strong and How to Stay So, 36

Hughes, Thomas, 40, 47, 72, 100, 246n.9

Hunting, 5, 9, 10, 22

Ice hockey, 119; firsts, 220

Ice skating, 10, 22

Imperialism, 116; and sports, 96

Individual sports, 22

Initiation rites, 67

Injuries, 90, 91, 93, 94, 129, 145, 199, 243n.52, 272n.46

"In loco parentis," 10, 14, 15, 17, 34, 68, 120–24, 210

Intercollegiate Association of Amateur Athletes of America, 107–9, 137, 248n.42

Intercollegiate Athletic Association of the United States, 272n.52

Intercollegiate Conference of Faculty Representatives, 134; *see also* Big Ten

Intercollegiate Cross Country Association, 102

Intercollegiate Football Association, 77, 78, 80, 84, 89, 90, 178; crisis of 1889, 177–78, 183; decline of, 93, 179; eligibility controversy, 177; and subsidization, 185

Intercollegiate Regatta Association, 76

Intercollegiate Rowing Association, 49, 51, 107

Intercollegiate Rowing Association Regatta, 51

Inter-institutional control, 133, 162, 216; attempts at, 134–46; and

eligibility, 175–90; failure of, 181; and the NCAA, 208; and professional coaching, 164

International contests: crew, 38–42; cricket, 250n.71; lacrosse, 250n.58; track, 110–17

International Olympic Committee, 115

Ivy League, 64, 109, 140; and bigtime athletics, 213; leadership in athletics, 213

Jeanes, Anna T., and banning sports, 209

Johanson, Carl, 177

Johnson-Clarendon Convention, 39

Journalists, 41, 192

Kansas, University of, 56, 187

Kenyon College, 55

Kilpatrick, Charles, 113

King James I, 5

King's College. *See* Columbia University

Kipling, Rudyard, 116

Kirchwey, George, 145, 199

Kivlan, James, 85

Lacrosse, 110, 119, 125; international, 250n.58; firsts, 219

Lafayette College, 81, 139

Laissez-faire policy and athletics, 120–24, 128, 134, 136, 145, 146, 175–90, 191, 207, 213

Lake Chautauqua, 150

Lake George regatta, 151

Lake Quinsigamond, 31, 32, 33, 35, 36, 42, 57

Lake Saratoga, 44, 46, 48, 49, 167

Lake Winnipesaukee, 3, 28, 167

Lawrence Base Ball Club, 53

Leander Boat Club, 152

Lees, James T., 204, 272n.52

Leggett, William, 69–72

Lehigh University, 137

LeMoyne, Harry, 159

Letter of the rules, 88, 182, 194, 266n.37

Lewis, William H., black coach, 260n.35

Lind, Jenny, 40
Literary magazines, 17
Literary societies, 15–16, 23, 170, 212, 224n.13
Lodge, Henry Cabot, on imperialism and sport, 116
London Athletic Club, 113–14
Lord's Ground, 6
Loues, Spiridon, 116

McCosh, James, 103, 123, 135, 138; on role of athletes in college, 185
MacCracken, Henry, 134, 145–46; and football reform, 198–99
MacCracken Conference, 198–202
McGill University, 75, 104, 108
Machiavellian politics in athletics, 204
Mackie, H. A., 179
Manhattan Athletic Club, 111
Manliness, 41, 54, 83, 95–98, 129, 244n.62, 244n.68
Mann, J. M., 109
Marathon race, 116
Marbles, 22
Marietta College, 69
Marylebone Cricket Club, 6
Massachusetts Agricultural College, 42–43, 148, 149
Massachusetts game (baseball), 53
Mass plays, 88–95, 206
Meiklejohn, Alexander, 132–33; on benefits and evils of football, 191
Meritocracy of effort and talent, 174
Merivale, Charles, 7
Michael, J. E. "Big Mike," 70
Michigan, University of, 73; and recruitment of athletes, 189; and tramp athletes, 184
Michigan Athletic Association, 119
Middlebury College, 55
Mill, John Stuart, 40
Mind-body dualism, influence on athletics, 211
Minnesota, University of, 202, 204, 207, 210
Missouri Athletic Association, 119
Molyneux, "Professor," 33
Molyneux, Tom, 110
Momentum plays, 88–95

Montreal Cricket Club, 76
Moore, Harold, 198
Morley, Dick, 199
Morrissey, John, 44
Morse, Samuel F. B., Jr., 206
Muckrakers, 122, 192–94, 270n.10
Munro, Wilfred, 140
Murphy, Michael, 109, 204
Muscular Christianity, 31
Musical societies, 17
Myth of amateurism, 114, 147

Nassau Baseball Club, 53
National Association of Base Ball Players (NABBP), 53, 57
National Association of Professional Base Ball Players, 59, 125
National Collegiate Athletic Association, 4, 66, 132, 134, 146, 187, 214; as cartel, 206; chooses president, 202; creation of, 191–208; lacking power and prestige, 206–8; as moral force, 207; and uniform playing rules, 208
National Cross-Country Association, 102
National Football League, and signing football players, 275n.5
National Intercollegiate Football Conference, 272n.52
Nationalism, 41
National League, 59, 125
Naval Academy, 81, 203, 207
Nebraska, 187, 204
Needham, Henry Beech, as a muckraker, 192–93
New England game (baseball), 53
New York Athletic Club, 109, 113–14; influence on track and field, 247n.21
New York Herald Olympic Games, 105
New York Knickerbockers, 53
New York University, 198, 201
New York Yankees, 65
Nichols, Edward, 194, 272n.48
Nine pins, 22
Northrop, Cyrus, on institutional freedom, 210

Northwestern University, 93, 132
Norton, Charles Eliot, 127, 162
Notre Dame, 85
NYAC-LAC track meet, 113–14

Oberlin College, 204
Officiating, 197
Olney, Richard, 112
Olympic Games, 111, 114–17; internationalization of, 111; modern origins, 251n. 74; of 1896, 92, 114–17; of 1900, 116
Olympic Myth of Greek Amateur Athletics, The, 166
Oregon Athletic Association, 119
Ostrom, John N., 47; and university jobs for athletes, 185
Ottignon, Charley, 33
Owsley, John, 194
Oxford University, 36
Oxford and Cambridge universities, 26, 32, 38, 39, 49, 51, 65, 100, 103, 105, 111, 113; amateur model, 163; athletic connection, 4–8; educational monopoly in England, 172

Paine, Thomas, 24
Paper chasing, 101–2
Parental permission to participate, 125
Paris Exposition, 39
Parker, Bartol, 196
Participation against professionals, 137, 138
Paternalism, 11, 14–15, 24, 120–24, 129, 210
Patton, Francis, on manliness, 97
Payment of athletes. *See* Subsidization
Peabody, Endicott, 193, 242n.41
Pennsylvania, University of, 9, 29, 51, 63, 72, 89, 102, 106, 116, 139, 140, 150, 160, 177, 178, 179, 184, 186, 192, 206; and tramp athletes, 184; withdraws from football association, 93
Penn, William, and the holy experiment, 210
Penn State University, 160, 171, 183–

84; and sanctioned athletic scholarships, 186
Phelan, Michael, 33
Phi Beta Kappa, 16
Philadelphia Athletics, 57
Philadelphia Centennial Exposition, 150
Philadelphia Cricket Club, 72
Phillips, Edward, 104–5
Physical educators, 33, 136
Pierce, President Franklin, 3–4, 29
Pierce, Palmer, president of NCAA, 202, 207
Platteville Normal School, 56
Player size, 71, 79, 105, 158
Poe, Edgar Allan, 186
Pole, J. R., on equality of opportunity, 172
Polo, 119; firsts, 220
Polo Grounds, 78, 79, 80, 89
Pot-hunting in track, 101, 106, 108, 167
Poughkeepsie regatta, 150, 154
Power conflicts, 130, 132, 200, 201, 211; and football rules committee, 273n.56
Preparatory schools, 193; *see also individual schools*
Pre-season practice, 139
Presidents, college: attitudes toward athletics, 97; banning sports, 95; Big Ten influence, 180; caught between faculty and governing boards, 216; on eligibility rules, 180; influence on athletics, 210, 216–17; and paternalism, 14–15; position threatened by athletics, 216–17; purchasing rowing shell, 47
Presidents' Commission of the NCAA, 214
Price, George, 149
Princeton Athletic Association, 119
Princeton University, 9, 10, 15, 16, 23, 24, 55, 59, 72, 90, 109, 136, 137, 140, 160, 192, 207; and baseball, 53; competition with Yale, 61; and development of the athletic committee, 121, 123–26, 134; and development of track, 102–3, 106;

and the 1873 football convention, 74; and the eligibility controversy of 1889, 177–79; and the first football game, 69–72; and the Intercollegiate Football Association, 77; joining the regatta, 44; Olympic participants, 115–16, 251n.83; and the Thanksgiving Day game, 77–82, 87; wedge formation, 242n.35

Pritchett, Henry S., and presidential reform, 216

Prizes, 29, 31–33, 43, 44, 46, 101, 104, 107, 108, 167; money, 32, 34, 36, 104, 106, 169; professional, 150

Prize fighting. *See* Boxing

Professional athletic contract and loss of freedom, 217

Professional model of athletics, 172–74; relative to excellence and winning, 174

Professional spirit, 147–48, 165

Professionalism, defined, 167

Professionalization, 3–4, 34–37, 52, 141, 185, 192, 213, 217, 218; importance of coaches to, 171; nineteenth-century standards, 167–72

Professionals: and crew, 6, 27; and lower class, 256n.2

Progressive period, 135

Protestant Reformation, 9

Pryor, J. W., 109

Public schools, British, 6

Punishments, 14

Queen's College (Rutgers University), 9

Queen's Grounds, 111

Quoits, 22

Rail transportation, 3, 27, 32, 46, 48, 51, 54, 57, 62–66, 70, 150, 159

Randolph-Macon College, 186

Rationalization, 28, 55, 141, 213, 218; of coaching, 154–62; and development of football, 86; and professional coaching, 147–64, 261n.42; and winning, 34, 40, 47

Reade, Charles, 40

Recruitment of athletes, 4, 129, 159, 170, 175, 184–87, 193; *see also* Subsidization

Reeves, J. M., and use of headgear, 239n.60

Reform of football, 145, 198–208

Regulation of athletics, 121

Reid, William T., Jr., 154–62; on academic eligibility, 158; amateur coaching criticized, 161; amateur-professional coach debate, 162; as chairman of Harvard football rules committee, 201–2; coaching pressure, 160–61; on recruiting, 159, 189; and reform of football, 194–98; on scheduling opponents, 159–60; salary, 156; at White House conference, 194

Reid, William T., Sr., 93, 155

Religion, on campus, 11, 17

Remington, Frederic, 92

Report on Intercollegiate Sport of 1898, 140

Revolutionary War, 15, 23–24, 170

Richards, Eugene L., 122, 137

Richmond, Lee, 60–62, 65

Riflery, 119; firsts, 219

Riots. *See* Student rebellions

Rituals and athletics, 21, 69, 218

Rives, George, 103

Robinson, Brad, 206

Rockefeller, John D., 188, 192

Roosevelt, President Theodore, 192, 202; and Dashiell affair, 197–98; and football reform, 131, 193, 201, 203; and Harvard brutality, 196; on manliness, 95–98; and muckraker correspondence, 270n.10; and reform, 191

Rousseau, Jean Jacques, 24

Rowing. *See* Crew

Rowing Association of American Colleges, 42

Rowing clubs, 26–27

Rowing machines, 36

Rugby, Americanization of, 83–98

Rugby Public School, 100

Rutgers University, 69–72, 74, 89, 106

Rutgers Athletic Association, 119

Sabbath participation, 28, 124, 252n.86
Sailing, 22
St. George's Cricket Grounds, 78, 79
St. Louis University, 206
St. Mary's College, 189
Santa Clara College, 189
Santayana, George, on athletic excellence, 141–42
Saratoga Regatta, 185
Saratoga Rowing Association, 44, 46
Sargent, Dudley A., 127, 129; on amateur coaching, 162; on brutality, 90; on inter-institutional control, 136, 137; and professional coaching, 254n.38
Savage, Charles W., 272n.52
Schaff, David, 73
Scheduling contests, 57, 59, 159
Schneider, Jack, 206
Scholars as athletes, 3, 188, 267n.54
Schuylkill Navy, 29
Scientific management, 157
Scottish sports, 103
Sharpe, Captain, 153
Sheridan, Philip A., 69
Sherrill, Charles, 109, 111
Shinny, 10
Sinclair, Upton, 191
Sinzer, Fred, 149
Sloane, William Milligan, 92, 125, 138; influence on Olympic participation, 251n.82; and the Olympics, 114–17
Slosson, Edwin, on manliness, 97
Smith, Andrew, and tramp athletes, 184
Soccer, 70, 72–74; firsts, 220
Social class bias, 125, 127, 144, 256n.2, 263–64n.28
Social Darwinism, 84
Social elites, 43, 48–51, 79, 80, 162, 166
Socialization following contests, 56, 72, 76
Solter, Art, 206
Spalding, Albert, 63
Spalding sporting goods company,

157, 198; subsidizing football rules committee, 204
Spectators, 7, 11, 27, 32, 36, 40, 43, 44, 47, 51, 55, 57, 61, 66, 76, 79, 80, 111, 150, 151, 169, 189, 196; disturbances, 33, 36; and social class, 7
Spirit of the rules, 88, 89, 182, 194, 266n.37
Sport in Britain, 167
Sportsmanship, 29, 41, 153, 263–64n.28, 266n.37
Springfield regatta, 30
Springfield YMCA, 160
Stadiums, 82, 98, 160, 193, 214, 218; *see also* Facilities
Stagg, Amos Alonzo, 90, 163, 204, 273n.56; and athletic scholarships, 188; condemns Eastern rules makers, 94
Stanford Athletic Association, 119
Stanford University, 114, 207
Steeplechase, 100–101
Steffens, Lincoln, as a muckraker, 192
Stern, Daniel M., 109
Stevens, H. W., 109
Stevens, John C., 110
Stewart, Mrs. Douglas, 80
Stickney, Highland, 185
Student control of athletics, 77, 118–33, 137, 138, 210, 212, 253n.18; instability of, 61, 211; lack of, at Harvard, 255n.61; loss of, 217; and responsibility in athletics, 212; and subscriptions, 45, 120
Student freedom. *See* Freedom of students
Student government, 17
Student managers, 120
Student musical groups, 121, 124
Student publications, 121
Student rebellions, 11, 14–15, 23
Subsidization, of athletes, 139, 143, 184–87, 214
Sullivan, James E., on laissez-faire policy, 207
Summer baseball, 62–66, 139, 140, 143, 193, 208

Summer practice, 139, 143
Summer resorts, 29, 44, 62, 139, 143
Sumner, Charles, 38–39
Sumner, William Graham, 84
Swain, Joseph, on banning sports, 210
Swarthmore College: and institutional fredom, 209–12; and student freedom, 209–12
Sweeney, Michael, 113
Swimming, 5, 10, 22, 119; firsts, 220
Symbolism of sport, 41
Syracuse, 160, 184

Taft, President William H., on eligibility, 177
Tarbell, Ida, as a muckraker, 192
Taylor, Frederick W., 87, 157
Taylor, Norton, 106
Taylor, William, 107
Team sports, importance of, 22
Technological revolution, 54
Tennis, 5, 119; firsts, 219
Texas, 204
Thanksgiving Day games, 43, 67, 77, 78–82, 87, 239–40n.74, 239n.75
The Theory of the Leisure Class, 81
Thomas, Joab, 216
Thorpe, Jim, 160
Throwing of contests, 34, 187
Thwing, Charles F., on manliness, 96
Tom Brown at Oxford, 41
Tom Brown's School Days, 40, 47, 72, 100, 101, 246n.9
Totalitarianism in athletics, 212
Track and field, 99–117, 119; crouch start, 249n.53; firsts, 219
Trainers, professional, 35
Training, 28, 32, 34–37, 42, 47, 112, 214; lack of, 154
Training table, 143, 170
Tramp athletes, 139, 143, 183–84, 193
Transfer athletes, and loss of freedom, 217
Trap shooting, 119; firsts, 220
Travel expenses, 30
Treatise on American Football, 90
Trinity College, 30, 44, 55, 149, 183
Trollope, Anthony, 163

Troy Haymakers, 57
Trustees. *See* Governing boards
Tucker, William, on institutional freedom, 132
Tufts University, and first football game, 76
Tug-of-war, 109
Turner, Frederick Jackson: and athletic evils, 214; on evils of football, 191–92
Tutoring of athletes, 157, 158, 170, 205
Twain, Mark, 52
Tyng, James, 59

Uniform playing rules and the NCAA, 208
Uniforms: baseball, 54; crew, 40; football, 75, 79, 238n.48, 239n.60; track, 105
Union College, 30, 47, 107; death of player, 198
University Athletic Club of New York City, and football rules, 94
Upham, Preston, 158
U.S. Military Academy, 69, 160

Vacation practice opposed, 143
Vanderbilt, Commodore Cornelius, 48, 80
Van Tassel, Irvin, 206
Veblen, Thorstein, 81
Venezuelan boundary dispute, 112, 152
Vermont, University of, 23
Veysey, Lawrence, on presidential image making, 216
Victory. *See* Winning
Victory celebrations, 33, 46, 48, 55, 80, 233–34n.13
Violence. *See* Football, brutality of
Virginia, University of, 56, 107
Virility. *See* Manliness

Ward, Ellis, 149
Ward, Hank, 149
Ward, Josh, 43, 148–49

Warner, Glenn, "Pop," 177
Washburn College, 206
Washington Olympics, 57
Water polo, 119; firsts, 220
Webb, Creighton, 107
Wefers, Bernie, 109, 113
Weiss, Paul, on amateurism, 167
Welch, Lewis S., 198
Wesleyan University, 30, 80, 105, 107, 149, 160, 178, 199, 206; on eligibility rules, 177; threatens athletic break, 183; withdraws from football association, 93
Westchester Hare and Hounds Club, 102
Westminster Public School, 6
West Point, 69, 160
West Virginia University, 139
Wheeler, Benjamin Ide: condemnation of rules committee, 201; on institutional freedom, 210
White, Andrew D., 47, 73, 185
White, Herbert, 161
White, John W., 127
White, J. William, on manliness, 96
White House conference and football reform, 193–94
White Man's Burden, The, 116
Whitney, Caspar, 63; on amateurism, 148; on death of professionalism, 165; on gentlemanly sport, 153; opposed to professional coach, 164
Whitney, Mrs. William, 80
Whiton, James M., 3, 221n.1
Wiebe, Robert, 193
Wilder, Burt, 132
William and Mary, College of, 8, 11, 107, 186
Williams College, 43, 52–55, 56, 62, 67, 69, 106, 107, 109, 136, 160, 170

Williams, Henry L., 90, 202, 204, 272n.52
Wilson, President Woodrow, 126
Winchester Public School, 6
Winning, importance of, 28, 33, 34, 36–37, 40, 45, 59, 72, 98, 112, 139, 147, 148, 164, 214
Winslow, Bill, 60
Wisconsin, University of, 55
Wolfeboro, 29
Wood, William, 35, 45, 148
Worcester baseball team, 60
Wordsworth, Charles, 6, 7
Wordsworth, William, 6
Wray, James, 164
Wrenn, Robert, 272n.48
Wrestling, 22; firsts, 220
Wyatt, Halifax, 101

Yale: athletic dominance, 84, 113, 148; and athletic scholarships, 188; and banning of sports, 10, 69; boat clubs, 3, 26, 31–33; eligibility controversies, 45, 60–62, 64–66, 176–80, 183; Football Association, 73, 74; and football development, 72–98; and football rushes, 21, 68; and international track, 110–14, 116; leadership in athletics, 113, 122, 136, 148, 192, 198; and the NCAA, 206–7; and the need for inter-institutional rules, 181; professional coaching, 34–36, 148; and professionalized track, 106; and student control, 121–23, 140, 145, 253n.18
Yost, Fielding H.: and recruitment of athletes, 189; as a tramp athlete, 139, 184
Young, David, 166